Statelessness Determination Procedures and the Right to Nationality

This book advances the study of the right to nationality, the prevention of statelessness, and the protection of stateless persons, taking Nigeria as a case study. Much recent literature on the subject of statelessness has been written from a US/European perspective. This work addresses this imbalance with an in-depth study of statelessness and best practice in how to prevent it in an African country. The book appraises international legal regimes on statelessness, their efficacy or otherwise in practice, what can be improved under international law, and the relevance of these regimes in the Nigerian context. The regional frameworks include those of the African Union, the Council of Europe, the EU, the Organization of American States, and the Arab League. Comparisons are also drawn with specific countries that already have an enshrined Statelessness Determination Procedure including Ivory Coast, the UK, France, Moldova, and the Netherlands, which does not have a formal procedure but has alternative means of identification. The book assesses the successes and challenges faced in these countries, and evaluates the chances for legal transplantation in Nigeria. Presenting an in-depth analysis of how statelessness is approached in the global south, the work will be of interest to researchers, academics, and policy-makers working in this field as well as those concerned with nationality from an international law perspective.

Solomon Oseghale Momoh is a Protection Associate at the Office of the United Nations High Commissioner for Refugees.

Studies in Citizenship, Human Rights and the Law

The series *Studies in Citizenship, Human Rights and Law* encourages a pluralistic vision of citizenship. The aim is to promote inclusiveness and rights at the local and global levels while approaching citizenship from a socio-legal perspective. The series may include comparative approaches along with books that focus on single jurisdictions, and brings together research monographs and edited collections which allow the expression of different schools of thought. Grounded in law and legal theory, where relevant, the series also welcomes contributions that take an interdisciplinary approach to rights and citizenship.

Series Editor:
Leïla Choukroune is Professor of International Law and Director of the University of Portsmouth Research and Innovation Theme in Democratic Citizenship. Her research focuses on the interactions between international trade and investment law, human rights, development studies, jurisprudence and social theory. It is also applied to emerging countries, India, China and East Africa in particular.

Titles in this series:

The Development of Child Protection Law and Policy
Children, Risk and Modernities
Kieran Walsh

Sex Work, Labour, and Empowerment
Lessons from the Informal Entertainment Sector in Nepal
Sutirtha Sahariah

Statelessness Determination Procedures and the Right to Nationality
Nigeria in comparative perspective
Solomon Oseghale Momoh

For more information about this series, please visit:
https://www.routledge.com/Studies-in-Citizenship-Human-Rights-and-the -Law/book-series/StudiesCHRL

Statelessness Determination Procedures and the Right to Nationality

Nigeria in Comparative Perspective

Solomon Oseghale Momoh

LONDON AND NEW YORK

First published 2023
by Routledge
4 Park Square, Milton Park, Abingdon, Oxon OX14 4RN

and by Routledge
605 Third Avenue, New York, NY 10158

Routledge is an imprint of the Taylor & Francis Group, an informa business

© 2023 Solomon Oseghale Momoh

The right of Solomon Oseghale Momoh to be identified as author of
this work has been asserted in accordance with sections 77 and 78 of the
Copyright, Designs and Patents Act 1988.

All rights reserved. No part of this book may be reprinted or reproduced or
utilised in any form or by any electronic, mechanical, or other means, now
known or hereafter invented, including photocopying and recording, or in
any information storage or retrieval system, without permission in writing
from the publishers.

Trademark notice: Product or corporate names may be trademarks or
registered trademarks, and are used only for identification and explanation
without intent to infringe.

British Library Cataloguing-in-Publication Data
A catalogue record for this book is available from the British Library

Library of Congress Cataloging-in-Publication Data
A catalog record has been requested for this book

ISBN: 978-1-032-24473-0 (hbk)
ISBN: 978-1-032-24475-4 (pbk)
ISBN: 978-1-003-27873-3 (ebk)

DOI: 10.4324/9781003278733

Typeset in Galliard
by Deanta Global Publishing Services, Chennai, India

In loving memory of my dad, Late Prof. Solomon Oseremen Momoh

Contents

Acknowledgments	ix
Abbreviations	xi
Table of Cases	xiii
Table of Statutory Instruments	xv

1 Introduction   1
    1.1 Background 1
    1.2 Statement of Problem 4
    1.3 Context and Scope of the Book 7
    1.4 Methodology 9
    1.5 Structure of the Book 12

2 Principles and Concept of Statelessness and Nationality   14
    2.1 Introduction 14
    2.2 Sociological Background 14
    2.3 What is Statelessness? 16
    2.4 Main Causes of Statelessness 22
    2.5 Peculiarity of the Risk of Statelessness in Nigeria 38
    2.6 Conclusion 45

3 Legal and Policy Framework on Nationality and Statelessness   47
    3.1 Introduction 47
    3.2 International Legal Framework on the Right to Nationality
    and Prevention of Statelessness 47
    3.3 Regional Frameworks on the Right to Nationality and
    Prevention of Statelessness 64
    3.4 Identified Gaps in the International and Regional
    Frameworks 104
    3.5 Conclusion 106

viii   *Contents*

4 Procedural Framework for Determining Statelessness: Applicable Standards and Criteria   107

4.1 *Introduction 107*

4.2 *Statelessness Determination Procedures: Definition and Purpose 109*

4.3 *Standards and Criteria for Good Statelessness Determination Procedures 112*

4.4 *Nationality Verification Procedures 124*

4.5 *Conclusion 124*

5 Analysis of Institutional and Procedural Frameworks for Determining Statelessness in Five States   126

5.1 *Introduction 126*

5.2 *Some SDP Development and Practice Examples 126*

5.3 *Comparative Table of Procedures in the Selected States 164*

5.4 *Conclusion 166*

6 Adapting (Legal Transplantation) Some of the Existing Best Practices on Statelessness Determination Procedure in the Nigeria Context   167

6.1 *Introduction 167*

6.2 *The Legal Transplant Option 167*

6.3 *Bespoke Statelessness Determination Procedure for Nigeria 184*

6.4 *Proposed Flowchart for a Determination Procedure for Nigeria 197*

6.5 *Conclusion 198*

7 Conclusion: Statelessness and the Right to Nationality – Summary of Key Discussions and Findings   199

7.1 *Introduction 199*

7.2 *Summary of Approach 200*

7.3 *Conclusion 206*

Bibliography   207

Index   227

Acknowledgments

First and foremost, I thank the Almighty God for seeing me through a journey that appeared to not have a definite date of completion. I am grateful that this beautiful journey has now successfully come to an end.

It is often said that 'the journey of a thousand miles begins with a footstep,' so also it was with writing this book. In taking these research steps, I was not alone; I was with two of the best supervisors a researcher could possibly pray to be blessed with. My special appreciation goes to my supervisors, Prof. Cedric Ryngaert and Dr. Hanneke van Eijken. I commend them for successfully converting a practitioner into a researcher. They ensured that I was sufficiently motivated to take every step required to research and complete my PhD. Without their unflinching support, advice, motivation, and professionalism, this journey would not have come to a successful end. Words cannot express how much I appreciate them.

I sincerely appreciate Dr. Salvatore Nicolosi for his encouragement and efforts towards exposing me to academic activities at Utrecht University. I cannot forget the opportunity you gave me in teaching and research at the Department of European and International Law. My special thanks also go to Prof. Gerard-René de Groot for the books he generously donated to me and his valuable advice on how to complete my thesis. I would also like to thank members of my reading committee Prof. Mr. Frans Pennings, Prof. B.M. Oomen, Prof. P.E. Minderhoud, Prof. T. Akpoghome, Prof. S.A. De Vries, including Prof. Gerard-René de Groot for their constructive approach to thesis assessment and defence. Ms. Eva Simkens, your translation of my research summary to Dutch is very much appreciated.

For my colleagues at the United Nations High Commissioner for Refugees (UNHCR) Office in Nigeria, words are not enough to thank Ms. Brigitte Mukanga-Eno who graciously signed my request for approval to undertake an external study without hesitation, thank you for believing in my capacity to undertake a PhD. I cannot forget to thank Mr. Roger Hollo for ensuring that I was able to have my articles published at the time I was facing internal challenges. Mr. John McKissick, thank you for recommending me to help draft Nigeria's first standard operating procedures (SOPs) for statelessness determination procedure (SDP); this helped me put my research on Nigeria to practical use. My special

x *Acknowledgments*

thanks also go to UNHCR Nigeria Country Representative, Ms. Chansa Kapaya, for her giving nod for me to publish the outcome of this research. In no special order, my thanks go to other UNHCR colleagues who supported me one way or the other during my research: Ms. Simbo Vincent, Mr. Austin Itua, Ms. Pamella Nyaidho, Mr. Clement Nwosu, and including colleagues at the UNHCR PAS and Ethics Office in Geneva and UNHCR colleagues at the Regional Bureau in Dakar.

Completing research usually requires fieldwork or speaking with practitioners. In my case I had the opportunity of speaking with two gentlemen for the Nigerian context, Mr. Titus Murdakai and Mr. D.A. Tukur of the National Commission for Refugees, Migrants and Internally Displaced Persons (NCFRMI) and the Nigeria Immigration Service (NIS), respectively, who kindly obliged me with interviews on asylum procedures and statelessness cases that underscored the effect of the absence of a statelessness determination procedure in Nigeria. And for the Moldovan context, I had the opportunity of receiving very useful resources from Mr. Iulian Popov, Head of Asylum and Integration Directorate in Moldova. These gentlemen were always ready to oblige me with an interview anytime I approached them.

I sincerely appreciate my LL.M supervisor, Prof. Sunday Edeko, who did not hesitate to write a reference note for me to begin this PhD programme. Thanks for trusting that I will not fail you. To Mr. Savior Ogbomon and Prof. Sunday Ighalo, thank you for the constant calls and encouraging words which helped me to put in more effort to complete my research in due course and for all the other assistance you rendered me. Mr. Trust Aigbogun, Mr. Austin Erameh, Mr. Fred Itua, and Giwa Abiola – thank you for all the encouragement.

Special thanks also go to Mr. and Mrs. Amos Egwakide Akhere and family and my Aunt Dorriety who always ensured that I had a place to stay in Europe. Because of you, I had the confidence to come to Europe for my research visits without having to worry about where to stay or how to eat.

And for my family members, I want to say that you are simply the best. I appreciate all your prayers and support through the difficult but amazing journey. While he is no longer here with us, I must say a big thank you to my late father, Prof. Solomon Oseremen Momoh. Without your counsel I would not have embarked on this very special journey. You will always be my mentor and inspiration. To my mom, Mrs. Grace Momoh, you are the best. I will always appreciate your fervent support, prayers, and advice. To my wife, Janet Momoh, thank you for the deprivations you endured during our honeymoon, I love you so much. My appreciation also goes to my siblings Eric, Erica, Ernest, and Belinda.

For the many others too numerous to mention, please know that I truly appreciate your support and assistance.

Abbreviations

ACHPR	African Charter on Human and Peoples' Right
ACNC	Advisory Committee on Nigerian Citizenship
ACRWC	African Charter on the Rights and Welfare of the Child
ArCHR	Arab Charter on Human Rights
AU	African Union
AUCIL	African Union Commission on International Law
CEDAW	Convention on the Elimination of All Forms of Discrimination against Women
CERD	Convention on the Elimination of All Forms of Racial Discrimination
CESEDA	Code of Entry and Stay of Foreigners and the Right of Asylum
CJEU	Court of Justice of the European Union
CNMW	Convention on the Nationality of Married Women
COE	Council of Europe
ECCJ	ECOWAS Community Court of Justice
ECOSOC	Economic and Social Council
ECOWAS	Economic Community of West African States
ECtHR	European Court of Human Rights
EMN	European Migration Network
ENS	European Network on Statelessness
EU	European Union
FEC	Federal Executive Council
GTA	Greentree Agreement
IACtHR	Inter-American Court of Human Rights
ICCPR	International Covenant on Civil and Political Rights
ICGLR	International Conference of the Great Lakes Region
ICJ	International Court of Justice
IDPs	Internally displaced persons
ILC	International Law Commission
MOI	Ministry of Interior
NAP	National Action Plan

xii *Abbreviations*

NCFRMI	National Commission for Refugees, Migrants and Internally Displaced Persons
NCWD	National Council for the Welfare of Destitute
NHRC	National Human Rights Commission
NIMC	National Identity Management Commission
NIN	National Identity Number
NPC	National Population Commission
OAS	Organization of American States
OFPRA	French Office for the Protection of Refugees and Stateless Persons
OSCE	Organization for Security and Co-operation in Europe
RECs	Regional Economic Communities
RSD	Refugee Status Determination Procedure
SADC	Southern African Development Community
SDP	Statelessness Determination Procedure
TEC or EEC	Treaty Establishing the European Community
TEU	Treaty on European Union
TFEU	Treaty on the Functioning of the European Union
UDHR	Universal Declaration of Human Rights
UN	United Nations
UNHCR	United Nations High Commissioner for Refugees
UNICEF	United Nations International Children's Fund

Table of Cases

Amnesty International v. Zambia African Commission Communication
   No. 212/98.. 92
Application of the Minister for Justice for interpretation of Article
   E (2) & Article XIV (4) of the Fundamental Law. Hungarian
   Constitutional Court decision. Case III / 01664/2014 115
AS (Guinea) v. Secretary of State for the Home Department 119

Biao v. Denmark Application No. 38590/10 Strasbourg 24 May 2016............. 77

Cameroon v. Nigeria: Equatorial Guinea Intervening Nigeria,
   ICJ Judgment of 10 October 2002 29

Dilcia Yean and Violeta Bosico v. Dominican Republic IACtHR,
   8 September 2005 .... 85, 86

Foulon and Bouvet v. France Application Nos. 9063/14 and
   10410/14 78

Genovese v. Malta Application No. 53124/09.. 77

Ibidapo v. Lufthansa Airlines (SC 238/1994) [1997] 5
   (4 April 1997)... 176
IHRDA & OSJI (on behalf of children of Nubian descent in Kenya)
   v. Kenya No.002/Com/002/2009 98

Janko Rottman v. Freistaat Bayern Case C-135/08 71

Karassev v. Finland Application No. 31414/96.. 76

xiv   *Table of Cases*

Mario Vicente Micheletti and others v. Delegación del Gobiernoen
   Cantabria Case C-369/90 European Court Reports 1992
   I-04239 70
Modise v. Botswana African Commission Communication
   No. 97/93 (2000) 91

Nottebohm case (Liechtenstein v. Guatemala) [1955] ICJ 1 .... 18, 19, 122
Nubian Children v. Kenya (2011) 21, 31
Nyali Ltd. v. Attorney-General [1956] 1 QB 16 182

The Queen v. Secretary of State for the Home Department, ex parte:
   Manjit Kaur. Case C-192/99 75

R Haines QC (Chairperson) Auckland Refugee Status Appeals Authority,
   Decision No. 72635/012002 .... 28, 64
Rottmann v. Freistaat Bayern, C-135/08 .... 36, 37

Shugaba v. Minister of Internal Affairs [1981] 2 Nigerian Constitutional
   Law Reports (NCLR) 459 22

Trop v. Dulles, 356 U.S. 86 (1958) 102 .... 1, 45
Tunis and Morocco Case in 1923 2

Table of Statutory Instruments

African

Abidjan Declaration 2015 .... 103, 104

    Arts. 1–13.. 101, 102

    Art. 21 102

    Art. 3 103

    Art. 4 .... 101, 102

    Art. 5 .... 102, 103

    Arts. 14–17... 101, 102

    Arts. 18–20... 102

    Arts. 21–25... 102

    Arts. 24... 103

    Arts. 25... 103

African Charter on the Rights and Welfare of the Child (ACRWC)............... 89, 97

    Art. 3 99

    Art. 6 .... 89, 99

    Art. 6(1) 97

    Art. 6(2) 97

    Art. 6(3) 97

    Art. 6(4) 97, 98

    Art. 6(h) 100

    Art. 11(3) 99

    Art. 14(2)(b) 99

    Art. 14(2)(c)... 99

    Art. 14(2)(g) 99

    Arts 32–46... 98

    Art. 42 98

    Art. 43(1) 98

African Charter on Human and People's Rights (ACHPR)................. 4, 49, 88, 89, 90, 91

    Art. 2 .... 88, 91, 95

xvi *Table of Statutory Instruments*

Art. 3 .... 88, 91
Art. 3(2) 91
Art. 4 .... 88, 91
Art. 5 .... 88, 91
Art. 6(g) 92
Art. 6(h) 92
Art. 12(1) 91
Art. 12(2) 91
Art. 13(1) 91
Art. 13(2) 91
Art. 18(1) 91, 92
Art. 18(2) 92
Art. 30 91
Art. 14 .... 9, 1
African Union Convention for the Protection and Assistance of Internally
   Displaced Persons (Kampala Convention) 180
(Draft) Protocol to the African Charter on Human and Peoples' Right on
   the Specific Aspects of the Right to a Nationality and the Eradication of
   Statelessness in Africa 10, 89, 93, 94, 102, 103, 108
Art. 1 95
Art. 2 .... 35, 94
Art. 3(2) 95
Art. 3(2)(c) 95
Art. 4(1) 95
Art. 4(2) 95
Art. 5(1)(a)–(c) 96
Art. 5(2)(a)–(c) 96
Art. 6 .... 35, 96
Art. 6(3) 96
Art. 7(1) 96
Art. 8(a) 96
Art. 10(2) 96
Art. 11 96
Art. 18(1) 97
Art. 19 96
Art. 20 96
Protocol to the African Charter on Human and Peoples' Rights on the Rights of
   Women in Africa (Maputo Protocol) 26, 35, 89, 92, 99, 103
Art. 2 .... 35, 100
Art. 6 35
Art. 6(g) 88, 89

Table of Statutory Instruments   xvii

Art. 6(h) 100
Art. 7 .... 88, 89
Art. 66 99
Refugee Convention 1969
Art. 1(2) 20

Americas

American Convention on Human Rights 10, 49, 84
Art. 1(1) 85
Art. 1 84
Art. 20 84
Art. 20(1) 84
Art. 20(2) 85
Art. 20(3) 52, 85
Art. 22(8) 52, 86

Arab States

Arab Charter on Human Rights (ArCHR)
Art. 3(3) 88
Art. 26(2) 88
Art. 29 .... 86, 87
Art. 29(1) 52
Art. 29(2) 87
Art. 29(3) 87
Art. 43 88

Asian

ASEAN Declaration of Human Rights 2012
Art. 18 52

Austria

Federal Law Concerning Austrian Nationality (1985)
Art. 27(1) 71

Brazil

Brazilian Decreto nº 9.199, de 20 de novembro de 2017
Art. 99 122
Brazil's Migration Act Law No. 13,445 of 24 May 2017
Art. 26 194

xviii *Table of Statutory Instruments*

Burma

Burma Citizenship Law 1982
Art. 3 .... 30, 31

Commonwealth

Commonwealth of Independent States Convention on Human Rights and
Fundamental Freedoms 1995
Art. 24 52

European

European Convention on Human Rights 1950 (ECHR) 66, 75
Art. 3(2) 74
Art. 5(1)(f) 139
Art. 5(4) 139
Art. 8 .... 76, 78
Art. 8(2) 78
Art. 14 76
European Convention on Nationality (ECN) 10, 19, 49, 49, 67, 75,
78, 82, 94, 129
Art. 2(a) 79
Art. 3 .... 79, 82
Art. 4 79
Art. 4(a)–(d) 79
Art. 4(c) 52
Art. 5 79
Art. 5(2) 77
Art. 6 79
Art. 6(2) 80
Art. 7 .... 79, 161
Art. 7(2) 81
Art. 7(3) 81
Art. 8 .... 77, 79, 81
Art. 9 79
Art. 12 81
Art. 14 77
Art. 16 80
Art. 18(3) 80
European Convention on the Avoidance of Statelessness in Relation
to State Succession 75
Art. 2 82

Table of Statutory Instruments xix

Art. 3 82
Art. 4 82
Art. 5(1) 83
Art. 5(2) 83
Art. 6 83
Art. 7 83
Treaty Establishing the European Community (TEC or EEC) 68
    Art. 3(c) 70
    Art. 7 70
    Art. 52 .... 70, 71
    Art. 53 70
    Art. 56 70
Treaty on European Union (TEU or the Maastricht Treaty) 68, 71
    Art. 6 78
    Art. 9 69
Treaty on the Functioning of the European Union (TFEU)
    Art. 20 ....69–70, 72
    Art. 20(1) 67
    Art. 67 69
    Art. 67(2) 68, 69, 84
    Art. 78 69
    Art. 78(1) 68, 69, 84
    Art. 79 69
    Art. 79(1) 69
Treaty of Lisbon 2007 67–68
    Art. 61(2) 66, 84

France

Code for Entry and Residence of Foreign Persons and the Right of Asylum
    (CESEDA)
    Art. L. 313-1 195
    Art. L. 313-26 195
    Art. L. 314-11 9 149
    Art. L. 380-1 195
    Art. L. 812-1 148
    Art. L. 812-2 148
    Art. L. 812-3 150
    Art. L. 812-4 148
    Art. L. 812-7 195
    Art. R. 812-2 192

xx   *Table of Statutory Instruments*

French Civil Code
    Art. 19-1 150
    Art. 21-17 .... 150, 194, 195
    Art. 21-18 .... 150, 194
    Art. 58 150

Germany

Land of Bavaria
    Art. 48(1) 72

Ivory Coast

Commission Nationale d'Eligibilite (CNESA)
    Art. 1 152
    Art. 2 153
    Art. 3 153
    Art. 7 153
    Art. 8 153
    Art. 12 .... 153, 196

Liberia

Constitution of 1847
    Art. V, s. 13 22
Constitution of 1986
    Art. 27(b) 22, 30, 32

Malta

Maltese Citizenship Act
    Art. 5(2)(b) 77

Moldova

Administrative Litigation of Law of the Republic of Moldova 145
    Art. 17(1) 195
Citizenship of the Republic of Moldova. LAW No. 1024-XIV
    Art. 1 141
    Art. 1(c) 145
    Art. 11 142
    Art. 17(c) 144
    Art. 17(c)–(f) 145
    Art. I(c) 145

Law No. 200 on the Regime of Foreigners in the Republic of Moldova
- Art. 3 141
- Art. 4 195
- Art. 85 144
- Art. 87 .... 191, 192
- Art. 87(1) 142, 143, 190, 192
- Art. 87(3) 195
- Art. 87(1)–(2) 144
- Art. 87(1)–(3) 143, 144
- Art. 87(2) 143, 145, 193, 196
- Art. 87(2)–(6) 142
- Art. 87(3) 143, 145, 195, 196
- Art. 87(4) 144
- Art. 87(5) 143, 144

The Netherlands (Dutch)

Manual on Dutch Nationality Act 2003 .... 157, 158
Nationality Act 161
- Art. 3(2) 157
- Art. 6(1) 157
- Art. 6(1)(b) 157, 160
- Art. 8(4) 157, 160

Nigeria

Child Rights Act 7, 20, 26, 43, 56
Citizenship Acts 1960 and 1961 2
Constitution 1960 .... 24, 25
Constitution 1979 .... 176, 77
Constitution 1999 .... 9, 10, 56, 129, 200
- Ch. III 2, 43, 187
- s. 14 3
- s. 25 .... 3, 7, 32
- s. 25(1) 32
- s. 25 (1b) 32
- s. 25 (c) 32
- s. 26 .... 3, 7, 32
- s. 26(1)(a) 194
- s. 26(2) 3, 191
- s. 26(2)(a) 26, 191
- s. 27 .... 3, 32, 191

xxii   *Table of Statutory Instruments*

s. 27(1)(b) 194
s. 27(1)(e) 194
s. 27(2) 26
s. 27(2)(i)–(ii) 194
s. 30 38
s. 30(1) 38
s. 36(1) 38
s. 72(2)(d) 194
s. 245(1)(i) 3
s. 251(1) 3, 196
s. 318 3
s. 318(1) 32

Immigration Act 56

National Commission for Refugees, Migrants and Internally Displaced Persons
Act 180, 186, 187, 188, 189, 192, 193
Art. 8(7) 195
Part V 190, 191
s. 8 190, 195
s. 17 194

National Human Rights Commission (Amendment) Act 2010 177

National Identity Management Agency Act 2007
s. 5(c) 6
s. 5(d) 6

Paraguay

Law on Protection and Facilities for the Naturalization of Stateless
Persons 2018
Arts. 23–28 190
Art. 31 189
Art. 32 189
Art. 38 192
Art. 44 193

Spain

Spanish Civil Code
Art. 9 70

United Kingdom

Borders Citizenship and Immigration Act 2009
s. 55 133

Table of Statutory Instruments xxiii

(BNA) 73, 137
    Schedule 1 137
Children's Act 2004
    s. 11 133
Housing Act 1996
    Part 6 195
    Part 7 195
Immigration Act 1971 .... 73, 74, 75
    s. 3(1)(c) 195
Immigration Act 2009 133
Immigration and Asylum Act 1999 138
    s. 31(1) 138
Immigration and Asylum Act 2002 135
Immigration Rules 140, 196
    Part 9 139
    Part 14 .... 105, 129–137, 165, 195

United Nations (UN)

Convention on the Elimination of All Forms of Discrimination against
    Women (CEDAW) 26, 33, 35, 49, 53, 88
    Art. 1 .... 35, 64
    Art. 2 .... 53, 64
    Art. 3(1) 64
    Art. 9 .... 34, 35, 36, 48, 53–54
    Art. 18 64
Convention on the Elimination of all Forms of Racial Discrimination (CERD)
    Art. 5(d)(iii) 52, 64
Convention on the Reduction of Statelessness 1961 .... 10, 15,
    20, 28, 35, 49, 55, 59, 61–62, 79, 85, 100, 101, 129, 130, 135, 140, 147,
                   155, 186, 188, 200, 203, 206
    Art. 1 .... 43, 56, 80, 98, 137
    Art. 2 .... 81–82, 137
    Art. 3 82
    Art. 4 43
    Art. 7 36
    Art. 8 .... 36, 38, 62, 81, 130
    Art. 8(1) 61
    Art. 8(3) 61
    Art. 10(1) 45
    Art. 12 43
    Art. 20 85

xxiv *Table of Statutory Instruments*

Convention Relating to the Status of Refugees 1951 .... 10, 21, 22, 49, 57–60, 86, 113, 115, 187, 188

    Art. 1(2) 22

    Art. 1(a)(2) 17, 20, 57

    Art. 31(2) 195

    Art. 18(2) 97

Convention Relating to the Status of Stateless Persons 1954 .... 10, 20, 21, 28, 46, 49, 56–59, 67, 69, 100, 101, 104, 110, 111, 113, 129, 130, 135, 139, 147, 155, 157, 161, 185, 186, 187, 189, 195, 200, 201, 203, 206

    Art. 1 .... 17, 60, 109, 136, 204

    Art. 1(1) 16, 17, 136

    Arts. 1–4 61

    Arts. 3 59

    Arts. 3–32 110

    Arts. 5–7 61

    Arts. 6 59

    Art. 7 .... 161, 162

    Art. 7(1) 69

    Art. 8 .... 130, 161

    Art. 9 130

    Art. 15 .... 122, 194

    Art. 17 .... 122, 194

    Art. 19 .... 122, 194

    Art. 20 139

    Art. 21 .... 122, 139, 194

    Art. 22 .... 122, 139, 194

    Art. 23 .... 122, 139, 194

    Art. 24 .... 122, 130, 139, 194

    Art. 26 161

    Art. 28 .... 122, 194

    Art. 32 .... 60, 105, 111, 115, 122, 137, 140, 162

Convention on the Rights of the Child (CRC) 10, 43, 49, 54–56, 97, 113, 142, 161

    Art. 1 54

    Art. 3 133

    Art. 7 .... 43, 110, 162

    Art. 7(1) 56

    Art. 7(2) 56

    Art. 8 43

    Art. 8(1) 52, 54

Table of Statutory Instruments   xxv

Convention on the Nationality of Married Women (CNMW) 10, 63, 64, 113
    Art. 1 36
Convention on the Rights of Persons with Disabilities (CRPD)
    Art. 19(1)(a) 52
    Art. 19(1)(b) 52
Declaration on the Nationality of Natural Persons in Relation to the Succession
    of States 10, 49
Geneva Convention 69
Hague Convention on Certain Questions Relating to the Conflict of
    Nationality Laws 10, 49, 122
Hague Protocol Relating to a Certain Case of Statelessness 10, 49, 113
International Covenant on Civil and Political Rights (ICCPR) 26, 35, 62
    Art. 2(2) 158
    Art. 2(3) 158, 159
    Art. 3 35
    Art. 5(4) 159
    Art. 7 147
    Art. 24 158
    Art. 24(3) 43, 110, 159
    Art. 24f 63
International Covenant on Economic, Social and
    Cultural Rights (ICESCR) 62, 87
Universal Declaration of Human Rights (UDHR) 87, 89, 113
    Art. 14 52
    Art. 15 ....20, 37, 43, 48, 49, 50–54, 63, 79, 84, 95, 110, 201
    Art. 15(2) 62
    Art. 20(2) 85
    Art. 20(3) 85

1 Introduction

1.1 Background

At least ten million people are stateless worldwide[1] and are therefore without any form of legal recognition by any State. Statelessness results in denial of socio-economic rights, political rights, equality, and the right to be part of the community.[2] The phenomenon occurs for several reasons, including discrimination against a particular group of people, gaps in nationality legislations and administrative procedures, State succession or dissolution, and boundary adjustments, amongst others.[3] Every State has its law to determine how its nationality can be acquired or withdrawn. 'If these laws are not carefully written and correctly applied, some people can be excluded and left stateless.'[4] The right to a nationality has been described as a 'fundamental human right,'[5] which is necessary for the enjoyment of other human rights.[6] This right avails the bearer with the diplomatic protection of the State.[7] Consequently, in the United States case of *Trop v. Dulles*, the Supreme Court described the right to nationality as the 'right to have rights.'[8] Statelessness puts a person in a situation where s/he cannot access some basic

---

1 United Nations '"12 million" stateless people globally, warns UNHCR chief in call to States for decisive action' https://news.un.org/en/story/2018/11/1025561 (accessed 11 January 2020).
2 UNHCR 'Ending statelessness' https://www.unhcr.org/en-lk/stateless-people.html (accessed 23 April 2019). This often leads to denial of access to basic and essential services such as healthcare, education, housing, bank account, ability to get married. It also leads to disenfranchisement: the inability to hold a political office or vote in elections.
3 UNHCR 'Protection of stateless people and prevention of statelessness: Legal information and documents' 1 August 2007.
4 UNHCR 'Ending statelessness' *Ibid.*
5 OHCHR 'Right to a nationality and statelessness' https://www.ohchr.org/EN/Issues/Pages/Nationality.aspx (accessed 12 January 2021).
6 UNHCR *50th Anniversary of the 1954 Convention relating to the Status of Stateless Persons Panel Discussion Wednesday, 6 October 2004 (1500-1630) Conference Room XIX, Palais des Nations, Geneva* (2004) 1.
7 International Justice Resources Centre 'Citizenship & nationality' https://ijrcenter.org/thematic-research-guides/nationality-citizenship/ (accessed 23 April 2019).
8 See *Trop v. Dulles*, 356 U.S. 86 (1958) 102.

DOI: 10.4324/9781003278733-1

2 Introduction

rights such as education, healthcare, employment, and freedom of movement, due to their lack of legal documentation; all of which will be explained in the course of this book. Being a citizen of a country solidifies the individual's stake or right to belong to that country by law. Chapter III of the 1999 Constitution of the Federal Republic of Nigeria provides for three methods of acquisition of Nigerian citizenship; they are by birth, registration, or naturalization. The chapter however excludes people who do not meet the specific criteria contained therein from becoming Nigerian citizens. This book escalates information and creates awareness of the gaps in the 1999 Constitution of Nigeria, especially Chapter III which focuses on the right to citizenship and other relevant legislation in Nigeria. It discussed the risk of statelessness of certain categories of persons in the country while highlighting some key notions peculiar to Nigeria, for instance, the need for clarity on how to acquire Nigerian nationality, elimination of ethnic affiliation in the acquisition of nationality, gender discrimination, and the need to protect children born in Nigeria to foreign parents. This book appraised the right to nationality under the Nigerian Constitution and measures to protect, identify, and prevent statelessness, comparing them with what is obtainable in other jurisdictions in Africa, Europe, and the Americas. It moreover tried to proffer solutions to the problems associated with the acquisition of Nigerian citizenship and measures to be taken to prevent statelessness.

It has been noted that, in international law, the issue of nationality 'falls within the domestic jurisdiction of each state,'[9] or within the 'reserved domain' of States as declared by the Permanent Court of International Justice in *Tunis and Morocco Case* in 1923.[10] Issues of nationality and statelessness confront many nations the world over, especially in West Africa with an estimated one million[11] stateless population. Nigeria, being the most populous nation not just in West Africa, but the entire Africa region, is worth examining.

Chapter III of the 1999 Constitution of the Federal Republic of Nigeria regulates access to citizenship. Apart from the Constitution, since the repeal of the 1960 and 1961 Nigerian Citizenship Acts through the Constitution (Amendment) Decree of 1974, Nigeria has not had citizenship implementing legislation.[12] While it is of note that the law does not discriminate against women in terms of their ability to transmit their citizenship to their children,

---

9 'Report on nationality, including statelessness by M Hudson, Special Rapporteur' https:// legal.un.org/ilc/documentation/english/a_cn4_50.pdf (accessed 12 January 2021) 7.

10 Nationality Decrees Issued in Tunis and Morocco on 18 November 1921, Advisory Opinion, 1923 PCIJ (ser. B) No. 4 (Feb. 7) para. 40; B Manby *Citizenship law in Africa: A comparative study* (2010) 21.

11 UNHCR 'Statelessness in West Africa: Turning your world upside down' 1 https://data2 .unhcr.org/ar/documents/download/53820 (accessed March 2018); R Atuguba, F Tuokuu and V Gbang 'Statelessness in West Africa: An assessment of stateless populations and legal, policy, and administrative Frameworks in Ghana' (2020) 8 (1) *Journal on Migration and Human Security* 15.

12 E Nwogugu 'Recent changes in Nigerian nationality and citizenship law' (1976) 25 (2) *International and Comparative Law Quarterly* 427. See also Citizenship Rights in Africa

Introduction 3

it does however restrict their ability to transmit nationality to their non-citizen spouses.[13] Other notable gaps in the Constitution relate to the use of ambiguous terminologies[14] which exposes a lot of the *in situ*[15] population to the risk of statelessness in Nigeria. These ambiguities relate to the lack of clarity on how to acquire Nigerian nationality; the legal requirement of ethnic affiliation in the acquisition of nationality; gender discrimination in the transmission of nationality; and the lack of provisions to ensure the acquisition of nationality for foundlings and children born in Nigeria to foreign parents.

The question of belonging to an 'indigenous' community or being a 'settler' creates a situation in Nigeria where a huge part of the population, usually considered 'non-indigenes' who live in parts of the country other than with their indigenous communities are left without any of the benefits enjoyed by the 'citizens' of their host communities. They often pay more for education, are unable to get jobs within the civil services of the component states, are not able to run for political office or hold certain positions, and experience other forms of subtle discrimination.[16]

The sections relating to 'assimilation,' 'useful contribution,' 'good character,' belonging to an 'indigenous community' to Nigeria, 'federal character,' 'indigene,' and 'indigenous'[17] are ambiguous and difficult to interpret, and no definition is provided for them in the Constitution either. With the foregoing gaps affecting many *in situ* populations in Nigeria with no soft landing (see Chapter 2, especially Part 2.4), stateless persons in the migratory context[18] are even more vulnerable as there is no system in place to determine their statelessness status in Nigeria.[19]

(CRA) Blog 'Nigeria' http://citizenshiprightsafrica.org/region/nigeria/ (accessed on 6 August 2020).

13 Citizenship Rights in Africa (CRA) Blog, *Ibid*. See 1999 Constitution of the Federal Republic of Nigeria, ss. 25 & 26(2).

14 These include 'assimilation'; 'useful contribution'; 'good behaviour'; and belonging to an 'indigenous community' to Nigeria, all relating to naturalization. And 'federal character'; 'indigene'; and 'indigenous,' relating to both Nigerian citizens by birth and others who acquire or are seeking to acquire Nigeria citizenship by registration or naturalization.

15 *In situ* population refers to the population whose habitual residence is the country they currently live in and which they consider to be their own country.

16 B Manby, *Struggles for citizenship in Africa* (2009) 110. See also Citizenship Rights in Africa (CRA) Blog, *Ibid,* and S Edeko 'Statelessness: The implication of the deprivation of nationality in Africa' Public Lecture in Baze University, Abuja to Mark UNHCR Nigeria 3rd Anniversary of the #ibelong campaign, November 2017. It is important to note that Nigeria is a Federation with 36 component states. The world 'non-indene' is not used in the Constitution, but is often used by Nigerians and in certain official documents because of the presence of words such as 'indigene' and 'indigenous' in the Constitution, both of which are not defined in the Constitution.

17 See Constitution of the Federal Republic of Nigeria 1999, ss. 14, 25, 26, 27, and 318.

18 Stateless persons in the migratory context generally refers to stateless persons whose place of habitual residence is not the country in which they currently live.

19 *In situ* populations claiming Nigerian nationality may have access to court subject to s. 245(1)(i) of the 1999 Constitution of Nigeria for the court to verify/confirm their nationality, including through an administrative procedure of the Ministry of Interior.

4   *Introduction*

1.2 Statement of Problem

Statelessness has been described as 'a profound violation of an individual's human rights.'[20] It exposes individuals to insecurity in terms of access to rights and services,[21] leading to the affected individuals' inability to access healthcare, education, travel documents, open a bank account, or even buy and sell goods and services.

Stateless people are often without legal status and excluded from society throughout their lives, and denied basic human rights.[22] They are usually not able to obtain identity and travel documents, which not only impedes their ability to travel but can also cause many problems in their day-to-day life and may in some cases lead to prolonged detention of the individual.[23] Denial of rights and inability to access services can cause ripple effects not only on the affected individuals and their families but also the wider society and the international community of States because exclusion can lead to social tensions with a significant impact on socio-economic development.[24]

In 2015, the African Commission on Human and People's Rights (ACHPR) published a study on the right to nationality in Africa, which confirmed that the continent is faced with many cases and risks of statelessness.[25] The report highlighted the causes of statelessness in Africa to include the colonial history of African States, arbitrary denial or deprivation of the nationality of persons on grounds of race, ethnicity, language, religion, gender discrimination, gaps in legislation, transfers of territory, and boundary delimitation, population movements, the issue of cross-border nomadic population, and the failure of many States to ensure that all children born on the territory are systematically registered at birth, among others.[26]

At least ten million stateless people in the world face different difficulties due to their status; out of the estimated stateless people worldwide, one million of them

---

20 Quote attributed to A Guterres, former United Nations High Commissioner for Refugees and current (at the time of writing) Secretary General of the United Nations. See UNHCR, *Global Action Plan to End 2014–24 Statelessness* (2014) 1 (cover).

21 D Owen 'On the right to have nationality rights: Statelessness, citizenship and human rights' (2018) 65 *Netherlands International Law Review* 301.

22 OSCE and UNHCR *Handbook on statelessness in the OSCE area: International standards and good practices* (28 February 2017) 5 https://www.refworld.org/docid/58b81c404 .html (accessed 10 June 2022).

23 UNHCR *Protecting the rights of stateless persons: The 1954 Convention relating to the Status of Stateless Persons* (January 2014) 2 https://www.refworld.org/pdfid/4cad88292.pdf (accessed 2 February 2021). See also Institute on Statelessness and Inclusion (ISI) 'The world's stateless' (December 2014) 42 https://files.institutesi.org/worldsstateless.pdf (accessed 2 February 2021).

24 Institute on Statelessness and Inclusion (ISI) *Ibid* 31; UNHCR 'What is statelessness? #IBELONG the campaign to end statelessness by 2024' 1 https://www.unhcr.org/ibelong/wp -content/uploads/UNHCR-Statelessness-2pager-ENG.pdf (accessed 6 August 2020).

25 African Union, African Commission on Human and Peoples' Rights *The Right to Nationality in Africa* (2015).

26 *Ibid*, 3, 5, 40.

Introduction 5

are estimated to live in West Africa alone,[27] which is a serious problem for the region. Although the Economic Community of West African States (ECOWAS) has put several initiatives in place to end statelessness in the region in line with the United Nations High Commissioner for Refugees (UNHCR) global action to end statelessness by 2024, including some initiatives by the African Union (hereinafter referred to as the AU). These initiatives, however laudable, may not yield the desired result if member States do not integrate the initiatives in their respective States.

In Europe, over 600,000 people continue to be stateless or at risk of statelessness due mainly to the dissolution of the former Yugoslavia and the Soviet Union, leading to statelessness in the Baltic States and Eastern Europe.[28] According to the European Network on Statelessness (ENS), today, more than 370,000 people lack nationality in Estonia and Latvia,[29] former Soviet republics. The UNHCR reports that 'Montenegro, which was formerly part of the Yugoslav federation, has more than 3,300 registered stateless people, while Estonia and Latvia, ex-Soviet republics, have some 91,000 and 267,000 stateless people respectively.' It further highlighted that economic migration or migration due to war also significantly result in the statelessness of persons, emphasizing that other large stateless populations are the result of policies that exclude people considered to be foreigners, despite their deep roots in the countries concerned. Based on the current citizenship legislation in Myanmar, more than one million people in Myanmar's Rakhine State are stateless.[30]

In Nigeria, in addition to the millions of people who are at risk of statelessness due to different factors, including lack of legal documentation to establish their Nigerian nationality, about 300,000 Bakassi returnees[31] and about seven million Almajiris[32] specifically are at risk of statelessness. These two groups will

27 UNHCR 'Statelessness in West Africa: Turning your world upside down' *Op Cit* 1.
28 UNHCR 'Ending statelessness in South Eastern Europe: #IBelong campaign' May 2018 2 https://reliefweb.int/report/world/ending-statelessness-south-eastern-europe-ibelong (accessed 7 August 2020). See also European Network on Statelessness (ENS) 'Issues: What is statelessness' https://www.statelessness.eu/issues#:~:text=The%20dissolution%20of %20the%20Soviet,undetermined%20nationality%20in%20Eastern%20Europe (accessed 7 August 2020).
29 European Network on Statelessness (ENS) *Ibid*.
30 UNHCR *Statelessness around the world* https://www.unhcr.org/statelessness-around-the -world.html (accessed 7 August 2020).
31 Bakassi returnees or indigenes are a population of those affected by the ICJ judgment in 2002, in the boundary dispute between Nigeria and Cameroon, wherein the ICJ ceded the territory known as the 'Bakassi peninsula' to Cameroon. The Bakassi peninsula is an island between Nigeria and Cameroon which, before the judgment, was a territory in the Cross River State of Nigeria.
32 See I AbdulQadir 'The Almajiri system of education in Nigeria today' http://www.gamji .com/article5000/NEWS5956.htm (accessed 27 March 2018).
   Note that the term Almajiri(s) could be used to describe a young Islamic scholar(s) who at a tender age is sent by his parents to go and live with an Islamic mentor/scholar who will teach the child the Koran and ways of Islam; it could also refer to a system of Islamic educa-

6 Introduction

be comprehensively explained in Chapter 2 of this work. Stateless persons are denied access to documentation which is usually a prerequisite for access to basic services. For Nigeria, every legal resident, including non-Nigerians, is obliged to register with the National Identity Management Commission (NIMC) and be issued with a National Identity Number (NIN) and identity card;[33] a person who is stateless or at risk of statelessness who cannot prove his nationality will be denied access to such identity document, because, for foreigners, they may be required to provide their national identity document (which will be used for the registration and reflected in the identity card), including proof that they are legally in Nigeria.

Unlike in some countries where birth certificates are not issued to children whose parents cannot establish their nationality, the authorities in Nigeria register every birth in the country[34] in compliance with international law, this does not however translate into citizenship rights.

Stateless persons are also denied the right to vote or even contest as candidates for election, which is necessary for a people to feel they are part of a government. As part of the many implications of the risk in Nigeria, the Bakassi returnees in the country were particularly hit by the denial of their right to vote in the 2012 Governorship election in Cross River State of Nigeria[35] because Bakassi LGA, which used to be one of the Local Government Areas in Nigeria, had been handed over to Cameroon, and consequently delisted from the list of LGAs. The implication of the decision to delist the Bakassi LGA meant that the location had to be removed from all Government platforms, including the database of the Independent National Electoral Commission (INEC), resulting in the absence of a voters' register for Bakassi indigenes during the election. The Bakassi indigenes were thus disenfranchised.[36]

To keep up with the need to belong, stateless persons are sometimes forced to falsify identity documents, especially as they are often unable to acquire properties of their own, sometimes unable to get married, access housing schemes, education, healthcare, open bank accounts, even access the labour market. By their inability to access or provide services, 'poverty becomes an integral part of

---

tion (though no longer considered a formal system) practised mainly in Northern Nigeria. The scholars of this system are so removed from the rest of society, that the majority of them do not have birth certificates or any legal documentation.

33 See s. 5(c) and (d) of the National Identity Management Agency Act 2007.

34 Those born in hospitals are immediately registered by the authorities. However, those born at home, especially in hard-to-reach areas, do not usually get registered due to a number of factors ranging from lack of access to authorities, distance to government facilities, poverty, illiteracy, and lack of knowledge on usefulness of birth certificates.

35 C Odinkalu 'Stateless in Bakassi: How a changed border left inhabitants adrift' (April 2012) *Open Society Initiative.*

36 See Business Day Newspaper, '15 years after relocation poverty, neglect claw deeper on Bakassi people' (23 April 2017); Vanguard Newspaper, 'We're now stateless, Bakassi Indigenes cry out' (10 June 2017).

Introduction 7

stateless life,'[37] which in turn hurts the society at large. Statelessness could result in serious socio-economic and political problems,[38] as well as global instability. Carol Batchelor highlighted,

> if one state fails to grant nationality to a person or group, this becomes a potential problem for all states. Unless the state which fails to grant nationality decides, nonetheless, to allow the stateless persons to remain resident with full legal entitlements equivalent to that of nationals.[39]

The 1999 Constitution of Nigeria has lots of gaps with regards to access to nationality, as it did not make provisions for prevention and reduction of statelessness as prescribed in the two Statelessness Conventions and the Convention of the Rights of the Child. Children born in Nigeria do not automatically get Nigerian nationality; even the Nigerian Child Rights Act is silent on the issue of the right to nationality for a child, thereby exposing foundlings, children of unknown nationalities, children born to foreign parents or adopted from a foreign country to the risk of statelessness. The gaps in the Constitution are a result of lack of clarity in the three methods of acquisition of nationality in Nigeria, which are by birth, registration, and naturalization. Some other aspects of the problem are (1) Gender discrimination; whereby Nigerian women cannot transmit their nationality to their foreign spouses in the same way men can transmit nationality to their foreign wives;[40] and (2) Ethnic discrimination, for instance, if a person is from an ethnic group considered not to be indigenous to Nigeria, that individual will find it difficult to prove their Nigerian nationality.[41]

1.3 Context and Scope of the Book

The purpose of this book is to appraise existing statelessness determination procedures and the right to nationality in different States in Africa, Europe, and the Americas with fairly good State practice, with Nigeria in a comparative perspective. In Nigeria, like most African States, there are no measures to protect, identify, and prevent (the risk) of statelessness. Therefore, drawing on the analysis of existing challenges across a variety of national contexts, this book tries to proffer solutions for States in the process of developing their statelessness determination procedures (SDP).

---

37 UNHCR and Asylum Aid 'Mapping statelessness in the United Kingdom' (2011) 25 https://www.unhcr.org/protection/basic/578dffae7/unhcr-mapping-statelessness-in-the -united-kingdom.html (accessed 7 August 2020).
38 See, A Pazzynski 'How statelessness affects global poverty' (24 July 2016) *The Borgen Project Blog* https://borgenproject.org/statelessness-global-poverty/ (accessed 14 January 2021).
39 C Batchelor 'Transforming international legal principles into national law: The right to a nationality and the avoidance of statelessness' (2006) 25 (93) *Refugee Survey Quarterly* 10.
40 See s. 26 of the 1999 Constitution of Nigeria.
41 See s. 25 *Supra.*

8 *Introduction*

Uncertainties surround the mode of acquisition of Nigerian citizenship, especially as there is no interpretation section in the Constitution for what is meant by 'useful contribution,' 'good character,' amongst others, interpretation of which, at the moment is subject to the wills and caprices of those in authority, and worse, the need for a person to prove he/she is from a community 'indigenous to Nigeria' in cases of citizenship by birth. Specifically, for Nigeria, this book tries to proffer solutions to the problems associated with the acquisition and transmission of nationality in Nigeria, and propose measures for the determination and verification of nationality.

Under international law, each State through the operation of its laws determines who it considers its citizen.[42] Often, the laws adopted by the States leave some persons without a nationality.[43] This situation leaves a huge population helpless and in '*limbo*'. According to Lucy Gregg, Chris Nash, and Nick Oakeshott:

> within this complex international maze of citizenship laws, many people find that they fall through the cracks between them. An individual can, for example, become the victim of a conflict of laws, in which two States each claim that the other is responsible for the bestowal of nationality. This is especially likely to happen when a person's State of birth grants nationality by descent (jus sanguinis), while his or her parents were born in a State that attributes nationality by birth on its territory (jus soli). In addition, some States employ a mechanism whereby automatic loss of nationality occurs, for instance after a prolonged absence from the country (in some States as few as three or five years is considered a 'prolonged absence').[44]

The challenges associated with statelessness cannot be overemphasized in today's society which requires the presentation of identity documents.[45] With the complexities in the legislation of many States, many people are unable to acquire the vital documents to prove their nationality or establish their legal status.[46] However, many States around the world, including in Africa,[47] have begun to make revisions to their nationality laws to remove the complexities and barriers to the acquisition of their nationality. It is about time Nigeria reviewed the

---

42 C Batchelor 'Statelessness and the problem of resolving nationality status' (1998) 10 (1) *International Journal of Refugee Law* 156, 183.

43 D Owen 'On the right to have nationality rights: Statelessness, citizenship and human rights' (2018) 65 Netherlands International Law Review 303.

44 UNHCR and Asylum Aid *Mapping statelessness in the United Kingdom, Ibid* 23.

45 UNHCR *Regional representation in West Africa: Partnership proposal for universities 2016 for a training of law professors on stateless in Accra 2016* (unpublished).

46 These complexities sometimes could prevent people from acquiring nationality easily. For instance, a person would have to live in Nigeria for at least 15 years before being eligible to apply for naturalization.

47 'Among the countries that have adopted revisions to their nationality laws in Africa of greater or lesser significance since 2009/10 are Côte d'Ivoire, Kenya, Libya, Mali, Mauritania, Namibia, Niger, Senegal, Seychelles, South Africa, Sudan, Tunisia and Zimbabwe.'
    B Manby *Citizenship Law in Africa: A Comparative Study, Ibid* v.

Introduction 9

current process or enacted dedicated citizenship legislation to give clarity to the citizenship provisions in the 1999 Constitution.

The primary focus of this book is on the gaps in nationality law in Nigeria, the nature and scope of the risk[48] of statelessness in Nigeria, and the need for a stateless determination procedure, as well as a procedure to verify the nationality of the many who are at risk of statelessness in Nigeria. The book makes reference to good practice procedures in some selected States, such as Brazil, France, Ivory Coast, Moldova, Paraguay, and the United Kingdom, all known to have statelessness determination procedures, and including the Netherlands for its alternative procedure which will be very useful for Nigeria.

This book sought to identify and examine the peculiarity of the risk of statelessness in Nigeria, with a particular focus on the need for a mechanism for identification, reduction, prevention, and protection of statelessness using a comparative lens. Those mainly exposed to the risk of statelessness in Nigeria include children born to foreign parents within the territory of Nigeria, children adopted by Nigerian citizens, foreign men married to Nigerian women, persons in the territory of Nigeria who hold no nationality or citizenship of another country, displaced persons (especially border populations), including the people of Bakassi affected by the 2002 ICJ judgment ceding Bakassi to Cameroon, *Almajiris* and nomads with no form of identity documents, etc.[49] Before answering the question, key definitions and explanations will be provided, such as the meaning of statelessness; risk of statelessness; nationality and citizenship; and effect of deprivation of citizenship.

The book, moreover, sought to examine existing international and regional legal instruments relevant to the topic and make recommendations based on international and regional standards, including good State practices for the protection, identification, reduction, and prevention of statelessness which will be relevant for Nigeria. This is intending to inspire changes in relevant laws and policies in Nigeria using good State practice, and the implication of adopting such good practices. The approach for this part of the research question is the human rights-based approach.

1.4 Methodology

The descriptive and evaluative approach was used in this book, examining the phenomenon and nature of the risk of statelessness and nationality challenges in Nigeria. The study analyzed and compared nationality and statelessness protection, identification, prevention, and reduction measures in jurisdictions in Europe, the Americas, and Africa. Reliance was placed heavily on primary and

---

48 In reference to Nigeria particularly, 'risk of statelessness' is used because there is no official record of statelessness, which may be as a result of Nigeria not having a statelessness determination procedure (SDP) and the fact that no mapping has been officially conducted. However, those at risk of statelessness sometimes face the same problems, as will be explained in the course of the work.
49 These groups will be explained thoroughly in Chapter 2.

10 Introduction

secondary sources of law. For primary sources, the study particularly relied on statutes, treaties, and conventions such as the 1999 Constitution of the Federal Republic of Nigeria; the 1954 and 1961 Statelessness Conventions; and case law, among others. For secondary sources, it relied on reported and unreported cases, journals, textbooks, and publications in national dailies; interviews of government and NGO officials, UNHCR reports and publications, the Economic Community of West African States (ECOWAS), and other relevant bodies.

The primary discipline of this book is law, with primary legal sources from international legal norms on the right to nationality and prevention of statelessness;[50] regional frameworks from the African Union (AU), the Economic Community of West African States (ECOWAS), the Council of Europe (CoE), the European Union (EU), the Organization of American States (OAS), and from the Arab League,[51] including national legal frameworks in the selected States.

Though the primary discipline of this book is law, literature from other disciplines such as sociology[52] (sociological effect of statelessness and absence of nationality) and anthropology, particularly socio-cultural anthropology which studies the 'processes of cultural change and social transformation,'[53] relevant for the discussion on the need for legal transplant and borrowing of legal ideas and norms explored in this book. These were explored to achieve the aim of this book. This is in consideration of the fact that the topic of the study, statelessness, and the right to nationality has a basis in law and social science, and in consideration of the fact that the movement of legal norms, 'cultural change and social transformation' has a basis in anthropology.

1.4.1 Evaluative Case Study Approach

This book is approached from an evaluative case study, which is 'a method of learning about a complex instance, based on a comprehensive understanding of

---

50 International instruments such as the 1930 Hague Convention on Certain Questions Relating to the Conflict of Nationality Laws; the 1930 Hague Protocol Relating to a Certain Case of Statelessness; the 1951 Convention Relating to the Status of Refugees; the 1954 Convention Relating to the Status of Stateless Persons; the 1958 Convention on the Nationality of Married Women; the 1961 Convention on the Reduction of Statelessness; the 1967 Protocol Relating to the Status of Refugees; the 1979 Convention on the Elimination of All Forms of Discrimination Against Women; the 1989 Convention on the Rights of the Child; and the 1999 UN Declaration on the Nationality of Natural Persons in Relation to the Succession of States, amongst others.

51 Regional instruments such as the 1969 American Convention on Human Rights; the 1997 European Convention on Nationality; the Arab Charter on Human Rights; and the evolving (Draft) Protocol to the African Charter on Human and Peoples' Right on the Specific Aspects of the Right to a Nationality and the Eradication of Statelessness in Africa, among others.

52 'Sociology is the study of human social relationships and institutions' University of North Carolina 'What is sociology?' https://sociology.unc.edu/undergraduate-program/sociology-major/what-is-sociology/ (accessed 25 February 2021).

53 UC Davis 'What is anthropology?' https://anthropology.ucdavis.edu/undergraduate/what-is-anthropology (accessed 25 February 2021).

Introduction 11

that instance obtained through extensive description and analysis of that instance taken as a whole and in its context.'[54] To this end, the current legal and policy framework in Nigeria was evaluated through desk review and interviews of relevant government officials to gain a comprehensive understanding and describe the existing practice in Nigeria in order to make useful recommendations for change based on existing good State practices. The desk review involved evaluation of relevant laws and policies in force in Nigeria against the evaluative yardstick or standards with regard to access to nationality and protection against statelessness, such as the presence of a legal framework (i.e., a statelessness determination procedure (SDP) back by legislation); the binding nature of the SDP; the structure and location of the SDP; access to procedure; procedural guarantees; method of assessments of facts; management of combined refugee and statelessness claims; prospect for naturalization; and review and appeal of decision. While the interviews focused mainly on practical examples that caseworkers have encountered.

Furthermore, to achieve the aim of the evaluative approach, States with a so-called good practice were identified, their legal and institutional frameworks described, and their shortfalls analyzed for possible areas of commonalities to consolidate on with regard to borrowing and transferring legal and institutional norms for Nigeria.

With regard to the selection of States, the procedure in a few States with SDP formalized in law, such as Ivory Coast,[55] the UK,[56] France,[57] and Moldova,[58] was analyzed, including the practice in the Netherlands[59] which does not have

---

54 L Morra and A Friedlander 'Case study evaluations' *World Bank Operations Evaluation Department* 3 https://ieg.worldbankgroup.org/sites/default/files/Data/reports/oed _wp1.pdf (accessed 25 February 2021).

55 Ivory Coast is relevant for this research as it currently hosts the highest number of stateless persons in West Africa. Before achieving the status of being the first and currently the only African State with a statelessness determination procedure adopted in September 2020, it had alternative routes to regularization of status, which are also lacking in Nigeria at the moment.

56 The UK adopted an SDP in 2013. Nigeria is a former colony of the UK; therefore they share a legal culture. Nigeria and the UK both have a common law system, and their governance systems share some administrative similarities which may be relevant for developing an SDP for Nigeria.

57 France is selected because it has the oldest mechanism for SDP, formalized in law since the 1950s; apart from that, it has many good examples relevant for Nigeria.

58 Moldova is a developing country like Nigeria. Therefore, in the absence of a country with an SDP in Africa, it is necessary to examine the achievement of a developing State like Moldova to see what Nigeria as a developing nation can also learn from it. Apart from being a developing State like Nigeria, the SDP in Moldova has been described by the UNHCR as one of the most advanced in Europe.

59 The Netherlands, although without an SDP, has a formal method of identifying (not protection) statelessness which is relevant for Nigeria with no mechanizing of collecting statistics at all. It is selected due to recent progress made towards achieving an SDP, especially the 2014 State Secretary of Security and Justice's directive for examination on how to establish an SDP for the Netherlands and also considering that statelessness matters in the Netherlands

12 *Introduction*

a formal procedure at the moment, but has alternative means of identification, all of which could be relevant for Nigeria with some contextual changes. The other States considered in the comparative part for Nigeria (Part 6.2) are Brazil and Paraguay, specifically for their laudable good practice. They were analyzed together with the first above mentioned States as part of the analysis of good practices for a bespoke procedure for Nigeria.

1.5 Structure of the Book

The first part of the book examines the conceptual ideas of statelessness with particular reference to Nigeria, reviewing some of the relevant conventions, treaties, and protocols while examining the nature of the phenomenon in Nigeria. The study draws good practice examples from some selected jurisdictions in Africa, Europe, and the Americas, all considered because of the legal and procedural frameworks put in place in these countries.

The second part of the book explores the need for a more flexible approach to the issue of statelessness in Nigeria, drawing from relevant international law standards,[60] practices recommended by the United Nations High Commissioner for Refugees (UNHCR), and the practice of States with the aim of proposing legal transplant or the borrowing of ideas for Nigeria. The book, moreover, examines the guidance proffered in the UNHCR Global Action Plan to End Statelessness 2014–2024,[61] the resultant UNHCR Good Practice Papers on protection, identification, and prevention of statelessness,[62] and the UNHCR Handbook on the Protection of Stateless Persons.[63]

---

are handled at an *ad hoc* level by a competent court, which countries like Nigeria without any procedure whatsoever could adopt in the interim.

60 These standards could roughly be divided into the following categories: protection, avoidance, and identification. See K Swider and M den Heijer 'Why union law can and should protect stateless persons' (2017) 19 (2) *European Journal of Migration and Law* 106.

61   UNHCR *Global action plan to end statelessness 2014–2024* (November 2014) https:// www.unhcr.org/protection/statelessness/54621bf49/global-action-plan-end-statelessness -2014-2024.html (accessed 7 August 2020).
    The ten Global Action Points agreed with State parties are: Action 1: Resolve existing major situations of statelessness. Action 2: Ensure that no child is born stateless. Action 3: Remove gender discrimination from nationality laws. Action 4: Prevent denial, loss or deprivation of nationality on discriminatory grounds. Action 5: Prevent statelessness in cases of State succession. Action 6: Grant protection status to stateless migrants and facilitate their naturalization. Action 7: Ensure birth registration for the prevention of statelessness. Action 8: Issue nationality documentation to those with entitlement to it. Action 9: Accede to the UN statelessness conventions. Action 10: Improve quantitative and qualitative data on stateless populations.

62 'In 2015 UNHCR launched a series of good practice papers, each of which corresponds to one of the 10 Actions in the Global Action Plan to end statelessness by 2024. Each paper highlights examples of how States, UNHCR and other stakeholders have addressed statelessness in a number of countries.' See web link to the already published UNHCR Statelessness Good Practice Papers https://www.refworld.org/statelessness.html (accessed 5 December 2020).

63 UNHCR *Handbook on protection of stateless persons under the 1954 Convention on Relating to the Status of Stateless Persons* (2014) https://www.unhcr.org/dach/wp-content/uploads

Introduction 13

The book is comprised of seven chapters. Following this introductory chapter is Chapter 2, which examines the key definitions of the notion of citizenship, nationality, and statelessness, its nature, scope, and phenomenon, the responsibility of the government to protect and ensure the reduction of statelessness within its territory as provided in the two Statelessness Conventions that Nigeria has ratified and the Abidjan Declaration on the eradication of statelessness in West Africa. The book provides insight into persons who are at risk of statelessness in Nigeria, the causes of the risk, and problems associated with statelessness. Chapter 3 offers insight into existing international, including regional (ECOWAS, AU, and EU) standards to prevent and reduce statelessness of relevance for Nigeria.

Chapters 4 and 5 discuss statelessness determination procedures, standards and criteria for a good statelessness determination procedure, and some development and good practice examples relevant for Nigeria. Chapter 6 discusses how to adapt (legal transplant) some of the existing best practice statelessness determination procedures in the Nigerian context, the types of legal transplants, and how to develop a bespoke statelessness determination for Nigeria. These were done taking into account the legal, administrative, and cultural similarities and differences. While Chapter 7, the concluding chapter, discusses the summary of findings and contribution to knowledge.

/sites/27/2017/04/CH-UNHCR_Handbook-on-Protection-of-Stateless-Persons.pdf (accessed 7 August 2020).

2 Principles and Concept of Statelessness and Nationality

2.1 Introduction

In a bid to provide direction and some answers to the research question that this book aims to answer, this chapter examines the general phenomenon, scale, and nature of statelessness or risk of statelessness, with specific emphasis on Nigeria. The chapter begins by introducing the sociological effect of statelessness and how it affects society. It examines concepts, such as the notion of *de jure* and *de facto* statelessness against the backdrop of the question, what is statelessness? The relationship between statelessness and refugees will also be examined. This chapter also examines the correlation between citizenship and nationality, and the use thereof in civil and common law traditions, explaining why and how both words will be used as synonyms in this work. The chapter moreover examines the cause of statelessness, especially the cause of the risk in Nigeria, and concludes with an overview of the peculiarity of the risk of statelessness in Nigeria.

2.2 Sociological Background

Citizenship has been said to be a 'fundamental element of human security. As well as providing people with a sense of belonging and identity, it entitles the individual to the protection of the state and provides a legal basis for the exercise of many civil and political rights.'[1] Nationality provides people with a sense of identity, State protection,[2] a sense of belonging, and involvement in a community.[3] The

---

1 UNHCR *The state of the world's refugees: A humanitarian agenda* (January 1997) 1. The 'human security' used in this research refers to not just physical safety of the human person, but 'job security, income security, health security, environmental security, security from crime-these are the emerging concerns of human security all over the world.' See UNDP *Human development report* (1994) particularly at 4. Human security has moreover been defined as 'the vital core of all human lives in ways that enhance human freedoms and human fulfillment. Human security means protecting fundamental freedoms—freedoms that are the essence of life.' Commission on Human Security *Human security now: Protecting and empowering people* (2003) 4.
2 UNHCR *Nationality and statelessness: A handbook for parliamentarians no 11* (2005) 3.
3 See F Eid 'Citizenship, community and national identity: Young people perceptions in a Bahraini context' (2015) 7 *Journal of Case Studies in Education* 13, 14.

DOI: 10.4324/9781003278733-2

Principles and Concept of Statelessness and Nationality 15

absence of it portends serious humanitarian implications, resulting in the absence of State protection, social exclusion, poverty, and unemployment, lack of access to birth registration, health, education, and inability to procure travel documents, including exposure to physical and sexual violence.[4]

The deprivation resulting from denial or absence of citizenship leads to a situation of human insecurity.[5] As people are unable to access services due to their status, they are often at loggerheads with not just their communities, but also with the State, causing a threat to peace and security due to manifest intolerance and prejudice.[6] On the impact of statelessness on society, the UNHCR notes thus:

> From a short-term perspective, it may appear that the surrounding community can benefit from the disenfranchisement and economic marginalization of the stateless population, who due to their status are unable to participate in economic activities by their inability to get access to jobs or access land and housing, which the community perceived to be overstretched. However, in the longer run, the exclusion of a certain population group is unlikely to be in anyone's interests.[7]

According to the UNHCR, stateless persons may end up without any residence status or, and sometimes, in prolonged detention. It may also lead to severe negative effects for social cohesion and stability.[8] On the other hand, access to nationality ensures social cohesion within the society where everyone feels a sense of belonging. 'This creates inclusive societies that foster the prosperity of people and nations. Statelessness is therefore also an important development problem.'[9] Therefore, preventing and reducing statelessness is necessary to tackle the socio-economic effect of exclusion.[10]

The next part examines the definition of statelessness, nationality, and the correlation between statelessness status and refugee status, the main causes of statelessness, and the *peculiarity*[11] of the risk of statelessness in Nigeria.

---

4 M Lynch 'Lives on hold: The human cost of statelessness' (2005) *Refugees International* 1.
5 C Sokoloff and R Lewis 'Denial of citizenship: A challenge to human security' (2005) 28 *European Policy Centre (EPC)* Issue Paper 4.
6 UNHCR *The state of the world's refugees: A humanitarian agenda* (1997) 19.
7 See UNHCR *Self-study module on statelessness* (2012) 35.
8 UNHCR *Preventing and reducing statelessness: The 1961 Convention on the Reduction of Statelessness* (2014) 2.
9 A Speech by UNHCR Assistant Representative for Protection, V Türk at the opening of the Regional Ministerial Meeting on statelessness in West Africa, 9 May 2017 in Banjul.
10 UNHCR *Preventing and reducing statelessness: The 1961 Convention on the Reduction of Statelessness, Op Cit* 2.
11 The peculiarity of the risk of statelessness as used in this book means the specific situation in Nigeria that exposes *in situ* populations in Nigeria to the risk of statelessness. A few of the peculiarities later described in this chapter may also be peculiar to other jurisdictions. But the focus is on the specific situation in Nigeria that exposes its population to statelessness.

16 *Principles and Concept of Statelessness and Nationality*

2.3 What is Statelessness?[12]

Statelessness is a situation whereby a person cannot lay claim to the nationality of any country. It could be described as a state of legal *limbo*[13] or 'non-existence' in the eyes of the law, whereby an individual faces a lot of hardship or is unable to exercise his basic right to services, such as healthcare, education, national identity, and travel documents, amongst others. According to the Convention Relating to the Status of Stateless Persons 1954 (hereinafter referred to as the 1954 Convention), '"stateless person" means a person who is not considered as a national by any State under the operation of its law.'[14]

There are two categories of statelessness under international law, i.e., *de facto* (by fact) and *de jure* (by law).[15] The *de facto*[16] category is often criticized by scholars, as the Convention is designed to protect only *de jure* stateless persons. It does not consider whether a person has a nationality that is not effective, but rather that a person is not legally recognized by any State.[17] The definition in the Convention can therefore be said to cover only a few portions of persons who are actually not receiving the protection of a State.[18] Though the final Act has a non-binding recommendation that calls on States to consider sympathetically the possibility of according to *de facto* stateless persons the treatment which the

---

12 The Conventions only give definition for *de jure* statelessness; this book will try to expand the definition to cover *de facto* stateless persons not defined by the Conventions, emphasizing that *de facto* stateless persons suffer the same problems as *de jure* stateless persons. Authors with a similar opinion will be referenced.

   This section will give an insight into the ideal and definition of statelessness under international law. It tries to expand the definition beyond what is given in the Statelessness Conventions. The ensuing subsections will examine the notion of nationality and citizenship, and the correlation between statelessness and refugees.

13 See M Rürup 'Lives in limbo: Statelessness after two world wars' (2011) 49 *Bulletin of German Historic Institute (GHI)* 114.

14 1954 Convention Art. 1(1).

15 A de Chickera 'Chapter 2: Critiquing the categorisation of the stateless' (2010) *The Equal Rights Trust* 52 https://www.equalrightstrust.org/ertdocumentbank/chapter%202.pdf (accessed 20 November 2020).

16 'de facto (by fact) statelessness, (is) often conceptualised as ineffective citizenship.'

   In order words, those so classified may have citizenship but may have barriers or obstacles preventing them from enjoying their citizenship rights. These obstacles could sometimes be deliberate or inadvertent government policies or law in force.

   J Tucker 'Questioning de facto statelessness by looking at de facto citizenship' (2014) 19 *Tilburg Law Review* 276. See also A Harvey 'Statelessness: The "de facto" statelessness debate' (2010) 24 (3) *Tottels Journal of Immigration Asylum and Nationality Law* 257–264.

17 C Batchelor 'The 1954 Convention Relating to the Status of Stateless Persons: Implementation within the European Union Member States and recommendations for harmonization' (2005) 22 (2) *Refuge: Canada's Journal on Refugees* 36; see also (Non)Citizens of the World 'Statelessness versus legal invisibility under international law' (May 2011) http://non citizensoftheworld.blogspot.com.ng/2011/05/statelessness-versus-legal-invisibility.html (accessed 22 March 2018).

18 (Non)Citizens of the World *Ibid.*

Principles and Concept of Statelessness and Nationality 17

Convention offers to *de jure* stateless people.[19] Experts in the field of statelessness have stated that 'the issue under Article 1(1) is not whether or not the individual has a nationality that is effective, but whether or not the individual has a nationality at all' (*de jure* statelessness).[20] This means that there are instances where a person has a nationality but is not being treated as a national, that is, the nationality is ineffective or better still the person is *de facto* stateless.

De facto statelessness is difficult to define mainly due to the absence of a legal framework for it and the different understanding of the concept.[21] A '*de facto* stateless person is normally regarded as a person who does possess a "nationality", but does not possess the protection of his country of nationality and who resides outside the territory of that state, *i.e.* a person whose nationality is ineffective,'[22] or 'persons outside the country of their nationality who are unable or, for valid reasons, are unwilling to avail themselves of the protection of that country.'[23] These valid reasons could be connected to the same reasons why people become refugees, i.e., 'well-founded fear of being persecuted for reasons of race, religion, nationality, membership of a particular social group or political opinion,' amongst others.[24]

On the use and expanded meaning of *de facto* statelessness, Hugh Massey notes that:

> Traditionally reserved for persons who are outside the State of their nationality and lacking in that State's protection, the protection in question being diplomatic and consular protection and assistance (as opposed to protection on the territory of the State of nationality itself) [...] The expanded concept tends to suggest that *de facto* stateless persons may include certain persons who are inside the State of their nationality, not just those who are outside it.[25]

Based on the forgoing, one can say that *de facto* statelessness includes *in situ* populations residing in their countries of habitual residence or nationality who are mostly not treated as nationals. Therefore, considering the similarities of deprivations of both categories of statelessness, this book will toe the same line as scholars who 'believe that the 1954 Convention's definition of statelessness is too

---

19 See the Final Act of the Convention relating to the Status of Stateless Persons 1954 Art. 1; B Blitz and M Lynch *Statelessness and the benefit of citizenship: A comparative study* (2011) 6.
20 UNHCR *The Concept of Stateless Persons under International Law* Expert Meeting Prato, Italy 27–28 May 2010 para. 3 at 14.
21 J Tucker 'Questioning de facto statelessness by looking at de facto citizenship' (2014) 19 *Tilburg Law Review* 276–277.
22 P Weis 'The United Nations Convention on the Reduction of Statelessness, 1961' (1962) 11 (4) *The International and Comparative Law Quarterly* 1073–1096, 1086.
23 H Massey *UNHCR and de facto statelessness* Legal and Protection Policy Research Series para. 10 at 61.
24 See Convention Relating to the Status of Refugees 1951 Art. 1(a)(2).
25 H Massey *UNHCR and de facto statelessness, Op Cit* ii–iii.

18 Principles and Concept of Statelessness and Nationality

narrow and limiting because it excludes those persons whose citizenship is practically useless or who cannot prove or verify their nationality.'[26]

Data on statelessness today are mostly a reflection of *de jure* statelessness; this is however changing as awareness of *de facto* statelessness is increasing with more realization that both categories of stateless people suffer basically the same deprivations.[27] It is therefore incumbent on States to put mechanisms in place not just to identify, protect, and prevent *de jure* statelessness, but also the same mechanisms for *de facto* stateless persons, particularly mechanisms for nationality verification and confirmation.

2.3.1 Nationality and Citizenship[28]

In the *Nottebohm Case*, the International Court of Justice held that nationality is 'a legal bond having as its basis a social fact of attachment, a genuine connection of existence, interests and sentiments, together with the existence of reciprocal rights and duties.'[29] Before the 19th century, there were no clear rules governing issues on nationality, Bronwen Manby notes that

> the rules on nationality first developed during the nineteenth century, as European empires expanded, and also as European states and the United States disputed questions of jurisdiction over people and companies. At this time, nationality [...] was completely a matter of state sovereignty, and the main concerns were that it should be clear which state had that sovereignty.[30]

At that time, for the sake of clarity as to jurisdiction over a person, dual nationality was discouraged.

Apart from law and legal studies, other disciplines have their understanding and application of the term nationality. Even the understanding of the term varies within different legal traditions.

> Other disciplines, such as political science or sociology, have different ways of using the terms in other contexts. And even in law, different languages have different nuances, and different legal traditions have different usages at national level. In national law, "citizenship" is the term used by lawyers in the Commonwealth tradition to describe this legal bond, and the rules adopted at

---

26 D Weissbrodt and C Collins 'The human rights of stateless persons' (2006) 28 *Hum. Rts. Q.* 251. See also A de Chickera 'Critiquing the categorisation of the stateless' *Op Cit* 53 & 54.

27 B Blitz and M Lynch *Statelessness and the benefit of citizenship, Op Cit* 6.

28 Nationality and citizenship will be used interchangeably in this research to connote the legal bond between a person and a State.

29 International Court of Justice *Nottebohm Case (Liechtenstein v. Guatemala)*, 6 April 1955 p. 23.

30 B Manby 'People without a country: The state of statelessness' (2017) 17 (3) *Insights on Law & Society* 17

country level by which it is decided whether a person does or does not have the right to legal membership of that state and the status of a person who is a member. Nationality can be used in the same sense, but tends to be more restricted to international law contexts. In the French civil law tradition, meanwhile, *nationalité* is the term used at both international and national levels to describe the legal bond between a person and a political entity, and the rules for membership of the community. Where a Commonwealth state has a national citizenship act, a member of the Francophonie has a *code de la nationalité*.[31]

Tanel Kerikmäe further clarifies thus:

> There has been confusion historically with the terms of 'citizenship' and 'nationality'. In some cases, the terms are used as synonyms. However, even when the terms are used in the same legal system, they can designate different phenomena. 'Citizenship' has been used to denote the status of persons who enjoy full political rights and privileges, while 'nationals' are persons who are subjects of the state but who do not have full rights and privileges within the state that they are permanently residing in.[32]

Considering that both terms are now used interchangeably or as synonyms by international law scholars, and considering that this book will reference scholars from both common law and civil law traditions, the definition of nationality in the European Convention on Nationality[33] is adopted in this book to mean the 'legal bond between a person and a State and does not indicate the person's ethnic origin.'[34] The terms nationality and citizenship will be used interchangeably or as synonyms in this book to connote the legal bond between a person and a State, with 'no indication to race or ethnicity.'

The forgoing definition, similar to that of the ICJ in the *Nottebohm Case*, affirms that 'nationality connects an individual to a State and is the fundamental basis for acquiring and exercising the rights, protection, and obligation inherent in full membership in a society.'[35] As has been noted, every State regulates under its laws who its nationals are, which has been observed to have some consequences in international law.[36] The right to nationality is enshrined in the

---

31 B Manby *Nationality, migration and statelessness in West Africa: A study for UNHCR and IOM* (2015) iv.
32 T Kerikmäe 'European Convention on Nationality and states' competence: The issue of human rights' (1997) *Juridica international Law Review*. See also F Horn *Conception and principles of citizenship in modern Western democracies* (1998) 3.
33 European Convention on Nationality, Strasbourg, 6.XI.1997.
34 *Ibid* Art. 2(a).
35 UNHCR *Citizens of nowhere: Solutions for the stateless in the U.S.* (2012) 10.
36 I Shearer and B Opeskin 'Nationality and statelessness' in B Opeskin, R Perruchoud, and J Redpath-Cross (Eds.) *Foundations of International Migration Law* (2012) 2.

20 *Principles and Concept of Statelessness and Nationality*

Universal Declaration of Human Rights (hereinafter referred to as the UDHR),[37] and the 1954 and 1961 Conventions, amongst other applicable international law instruments.

Nationality is usually granted either through descent known as *jus sanguinis*,[38] whereby children acquire the nationality of their parents or through birth in a country's territory, known as *jus soli*[39] or a combination of both the *jus sanguinis* and *jus soli*. The application of both is recommended under international law. Neither the Constitution of the Federal Republic of Nigeria nor the Child Rights Act[40] grants nationality or citizenship by birth to children born to foreign parents on Nigerian territory.

2.3.2 Correlation between Statelessness and Refugees Status

The Convention Relating to the Status of Refugees 1951 defines a refugee as follows:

> someone who owing to well-founded fear of being persecuted for reasons of race, religion, nationality, membership of a particular social group or political opinion, is outside the country of his nationality and is unable or, owing to such fear, is unwilling to avail himself of the protection of that country; or who, not having a nationality and being outside the country of his former habitual residence as a result of such events, is unable or, owing to such fear, is unwilling to return to it.[41]

The OAU Convention Governing the Specific Aspects of Refugee Problems in Africa[42] defines refugee as follows:

> The term 'refugee' shall also apply to every person who, owing to external aggression, occupation, foreign domination or events seriously disturbing public order in either part or the whole of his country of origin or national-ity, is compelled to leave his place of habitual residence in order to seek ref-uge in another place outside his country of origin or nationality.[43]

---

37 UDHR Art. 15.

38 *Jus sanguinis* is the Latin term meaning 'right of blood.'

39 *Jus soli* is a Latin term that means 'law of the soil.' See also I Shearer and B Opeskin 'Nation-ality and statelessness' *Op Cit* 6. 'A well-known example of *jus soli* is the Fourteenth Amend-ment of the United States Constitution, which has provided, since 1868, that all persons born in the United States are citizens of the United States. There has been ongoing debate about whether birthright citizenship should be granted to the children of undocumented migrants.'

40 2013 Cap A452 Laws of the Federation of Nigeria.

41 Convention Relating to the Status of Refugees 1951 Art. 1(A)(2).

42 1001 U.N.T.S. 45.

43 OAU Refugee Convention 1969 Art. 1(2).

Principles and Concept of Statelessness and Nationality 21

Why is it necessary to examine the relationship between statelessness and refugees? Jason Tucker notes that 'exploring the relationship between statelessness and refugee-ness is of importance as the current framing of this nexus in the discourse of international law is based on an assumption of the primacy of protection under international refugee law as compared to international statelessness law.'[44] It is important to note that not all refugees are stateless, and not all stateless persons are refugees, though statelessness affects at least 1.5 million refugees globally.[45] Generally, most refugees retain their nationalities throughout their refuge abroad, just like most stateless persons have never left their places of habitual residence.[46]

Considering the overlap between its statelessness mandate and its refugee mandate,[47] the UNHCR recommends that, 'although an individual can be both stateless as per the 1954 Convention and a refugee as per the 1951 Convention, at a minimum, a stateless refugee must benefit from the protection of the 1951 Convention and international refugee law.'[48] This means that a stateless refugee should be protected both under the 1951 Refugee Convention and the 1954 Statelessness Convention. This is especially in consideration of the fact that most of the rights conferred on stateless persons in the 1954 Convention are the same as those in the 1951 Convention, save for the non-penalization for unlawful presence or entry and the *non-refoulement* principles in the 1951 Convention.[49]

It has been observed that 'statelessness does not generally constitute persecution under the refugee definition but may well be an element of persecution taken cumulatively with other factors.' One of such factors includes arbitrary deprivation of nationality, which is often based on one of the Convention grounds[50] of persecution on grounds of race,[51] religion, nationality, membership

---

44 J Tucker 'The indefinite statelessness of refugees in Denmark and Sweden: Comparing the impacts of the temporary asylum laws' (2017) 17 (8) *MIM working paper series* 3.

45 See Syrianationality.org 'The link between refugees and statelessness' 1 http://www.syrianationality.org/pdf/link-between-refugees-statelessness.pdf (accessed 10 August 2020). See also M MacGregor 'Living in limbo: Europe's stateless refugees' *Info Migrants* (12 September 2018) https://www.infomigrants.net/en/post/11941/living-in-limbo-europe-s-stateless-refugees (accessed 10 August 2020).

46 UNHCR *Self-study module on statelessness* (2012) 14.

47 UNHCR *Action to address statelessness – A strategy note* (2010) 5.

48 UNHCR *Handbook on protection of stateless persons* (2014) 7 at para. 12.

49 IPU & UNHCR *Nationality and statelessness: Handbook for parliamentarians no 22* (2014) 11.

50 UNHCR *Self-study module on statelessness, Op Cit* 14.

51 See *Nubian Children v. Kenya* (2011), concerning the status of Kenyan Nubians, where the African Committee of Experts on the Rights and Welfare of the Child held that the Nubians, despite having been brought to Kenya more than one hundred years ago to serve in the British colonial army, still could not establish their citizenship status in Kenya. Those mainly affected by the discrimination were Nubian children, as many were not registered as Kenyan citizens at birth. As a result, they lived in poverty with little or no access to education, health care, and public services. It further held that the decision not to recognize the Nubian children as Kenyan citizens violated provisions of the African Charter on the Rights and Welfare

22 Principles and Concept of Statelessness and Nationality

of a particular social group, or political opinion.[52] Although many stateless persons face persecution, not all of them face persecution in sense of the 1951 Refugee Convention; this does not take away from the fact that they are also vulnerable and in need of protection considering the absence of State protection for them.[53]

As stated above, sometimes refugees could be stateless and *vice versa*. A stateless refugee would have to meet the criteria set out in the Refugee Conventions to be considered under the refugee protection regime. These criteria relate to the definition of refugee in the 1951 Convention, such as well-founded fear, persecution (either from State or non-State actors), the Convention grounds (race, religion, nationality, political opinion, and membership of a particular social group), outside their country of nationality or habitual residence, and unable or, owing to such fear, unwilling to return to it.[54]

Stateless persons who are not refugees do not necessarily need to be outside of their places of habitual residence; they may not have a well-founded fear of persecution by State or non-State actors, as most stateless persons are actually willing to avail themselves of the protection of their countries of habitual residence, except where they are not recognized by their host countries or any other country as nationals under their laws. A stateless refugee will remain stateless even when the situation which led to their refugee status no longer exists and they cease to be a refugee.

2.4 Main Causes of Statelessness

Statelessness is caused by several factors, including gaps in the nationality legislation of States; conflict of laws; discrimination against a certain group, which may sometimes be on account of *race*,[55] ethnicity, religion, gender, membership

---

of the Child, particularly Art. 3 on non-discrimination and Art. 6 on the right to a name and nationality, and protection against statelessness.

52 See also the case of *Shugaba v. Minister of Internal Affairs* [1981] 2 Nigerian Constitutional Law Reports (NCLR) 459, wherein Alhaji Shugaba Abdurrahaman Darman, a member of the Borno State House of Assembly and majority leader as he then was of the opposition party to the Federal Government, was deported to the Republic of Chad by the Nigeria Government on an allegation that he was not a Nigerian. The deportation is believed to have been largely motivated due to the political opinion of Alhaji Shugaba, as he was a vocal member of the opposition party. The decision to deport him, although after the fact, was upturned by the Nigerian Supreme Court.

53 M Fullerton 'The intersection of statelessness and refugee protection in US asylum policy' (2014) 2 (3) *Journal on Migration and Human Security (JMHS)* 144.

54 Convention Relating to the Status of Refugees 1951, Art. 1(2).

55 'The great object of forming these Colonies, being to provide a home for the dispersed and oppressed children of Africa, and to regenerate and enlighten this benighted continent, none but persons of colour shall be eligible to citizenship in this Republic." And Article 27(b) of the 1986 Liberia Constitution states that "In order to preserve, foster and maintain the positive Liberian culture, values and character, only persons who are Negroes or of Negro descent shall qualify by birth or by naturalization to be citizens of Liberia.'Art. V, s 13 of the 1847 Constitution of Liberia.

Principles and Concept of Statelessness and Nationality   23

of a particular social group; administrate procedures; loss or deprivation of nationality; State secession, inheritance; legacy of colonization, etc.

Loss or deprivation of nationality by States could be a cause of statelessness. These losses or deprivations often occur as a result of legislation, sometimes targeted at a particular group, making it difficult for them to (re)acquire or access nationality. Such legislation, legitimate or otherwise, which leads to statelessness may be a

> disproportionate means of achieving public policy goal and would generally be arbitrary and in violation of international human rights law manifest itself in an obvious, aggressive and even persecutory manner, such as when entire groups are deprived of their nationality based on ethnicity or religion; or it can be more subtle and latent, such as the failure of states to prioritise legal reform that would plug gaps in the law which could cause statelessness.[56]

Therefore, the General Assembly of the United Nations in 2013 reaffirmed that 'loss or deprivation of nationality must meet certain conditions in order to comply with international law, in particular the prohibition of arbitrary deprivation of nationality.'[57]

A few of the causes of statelessness, such as effect of colonization, gaps in national legislation and administrative procedures, conflict of laws, transfer of territory, discrimination against a certain group, and loss or deprivation of nationality are elucidated below.

2.4.1 Colonial History

Many of the statelessness situations today in Africa are a result of colonialization and the resultant apathy, and lack of cohesion. During the colonial era, several different peoples, tribes, and ethnic groups were forced into being single states by colonial administrations for mainly economic and administrative convenience.[58] According to Aghemelo *et al.*, 'Africa was largely controlled by its indigenous peoples in 1878 but had, by 1914 become almost totally subjugated and divided

---

56 Institute on Statelessness and Inclusion (ISI) 'Cause of statelessness' http://www.institutesi.org/world/causes.php (accessed 22 March 2018).

57 Such other conditions include voluntary acquisition of another nationality, fraud, acts seriously prejudicial to the vital interests of the State, services to a foreign government or military, extended period of absence, etc. However, there are restrictions on the use of these grounds where they lead to statelessness.

> UN General Assembly '*Annual report of the United Nations High Commissioner for Human Rights and reports of the Office of the High Commissioner and the Secretary-General*' A/HRC/25/28. 19 December 2013 4.

58 See E Utuk 'Britain's colonial administrations and developments, 1861–1960: An analysis of Britain's colonial administrations and developments in Nigeria' (1975) *Dissertations and Theses* Paper 2525.

24 *Principles and Concept of Statelessness and Nationality*

into colonies by the European powers.'[59] Francis Menjo Baye further observed that:

> The colonial boundaries in these configurations were not established according to the various indigenous groupings. Grouping nations together in some cases and dividing them in others was a common feature as long as it was consistent with the security and economic interests of the colonial powers. After independence, most of Africa became and is still troubled by the legacy of trying to get originally different indigenous groupings to live peacefully in a single country or to get the same ethnic group to live peacefully in different neighbouring countries.[60]

These acts of 'forced nationhood,' where borders were drawn up by the colonial administration without consultation with the locals, led to resentments, conflicts, and widespread loss and deprivation of nationality in many African States after independence. As part of the divide and rule policy of colonial administration, 'It is not surprising that many newly independent states thus struggled with nation building, national identity and the treatment of minorities. While colonial history does not justify in any way discrimination, arbitrariness and disenfranchisement, this historical context must be understood and addressed in order to reduce statelessness.'[61] Those mostly affected by statelessness in Africa include populations affected by colonial drawn borders, descendants of colonial-era migrants,[62] and nomadic tribes.[63] Many of these statelessness situations are underreported or unnoticed due to the absence of mechanisms in place to protect, identify, and prevent statelessness.

2.4.1.1 *How it Applies to Nigeria*

In Nigeria, although there is no clear colonial legacy of ethnic discrimination in the acquisition of Nigerian citizenship in the 1960 Independence Constitution, the present Constitution of Nigeria does have a provision, which, apart from being discriminatory against women, encourages ethnic discrimination in the acquisition of Nigeria citizenship by birth. For instance, to establish citizenship

---

59 A Aghemelo and S Ibhasebhor 'Colonialism as a source of boundary dispute and conflict among African States: The World Court judgement on the Bakassi Peninsula and its implications for Nigeria' (2006) *Journal of Social Science, Kamla-Raj* 178.

60 F Menjo Baye 'Implications of the Bakassi conflict resolution for Cameroon' (2010) 10 (1) *African Journal on Conflict Resolution* 10.

61 Institute on Statelessness and Inclusion (ISI) 'The world's stateless' *Ibid* 25.

62 B Manby 'Who belongs? Statelessness and nationality in West Africa' *The online Journal of Migration Policy Institute* https://www.migrationpolicy.org/article/who-belongs-statelessness-and-nationality-west-africa (accessed 12 April 2018). An example is the colonial-era migrants affected, the Nubians in Kenya, who despite been brought to Kenya to serve in the British Army many years ago are still not considered true Kenyans.

63 *Ibid.*

Principles and Concept of Statelessness and Nationality 25

by birth for a person born in Nigeria before independence on 1 October 1960 as provided in section 25 of the Constitution, the person will have to establish that their parents or any of their grandparents belongs or belonged to a '*community indigenous*' to Nigeria despite being born in Nigeria.

2.4.2 Gaps in National Legislation and Administrative Procedures

Gaps in legislation and administrative procedures relating to methods of acquisition, restoration, loss, or deprivation of nationality are some of the major causes of statelessness across the world. The absence of or lack of clarity in legislation and administrative procedures often exposes people to actual or risks associated with statelessness. Therefore, an applicant may be qualified for the grant of nationality but may be denied access due to administrative bottlenecks, such as excessive administrative fees, inability to produce documents, unrealistic deadlines, etc.[64]

2.4.2.1 How it Applies to Nigeria

In Nigeria specifically, the process is cumbersome, to acquire Nigerian nationality other than by birth, as provided in sections 26 and 27 of the Constitution which make provision for the acquisition of citizenship of Nigeria by registration and naturalization respectively; apart from the requirements of 'good character,' 'being of full age,' and intention to be domiciled in Nigeria, the President of the Federal Republic of Nigeria must be satisfied that these requirements have been met before a person can become Nigerian citizen. In addition to satisfaction of the President, for citizenship by naturalization, there is the requirement of the Governor of the *state*[65] in Nigeria where the applicant proposes to be resident, to certify that the applicant is acceptable to the local community where the applicant intends to reside permanently and has assimilated into the way of life of Nigerians in that community.

There is a need to simplify the process of acquiring Nigerian nationality, by requiring a designated authority within the Nigeria Immigration Service (NIS) or any other designated agency to act on behalf of the President without recourse to the person of the President, the same process is recommended for states to designate a focal person or focal agency to be specified in Chapter III of the

---

64 See Decision of R Haines QC (Chairperson) Auckland Refugee Status Appeals Authority, *Decision No. 72635/01*2002 para. 80(d). An example, s. 26(1) of the Constitution of Nigeria, provides that 'a person to whom the provisions of this section apply may be registered as a citizen of Nigeria, if the President is satisfied.' There is no clear indication on how this is supposed to happen. Other ambiguous terminologies and administrative bottlenecks include, 'opinion of the Governor of State,' 'assimilation into local community,' 'meaningful contribution,' etc.

65 Nigeria is a Federal Republic with 36 states; state used in this context refers to component states within the Federal Republic of Nigeria.

26 Principles and Concept of Statelessness and Nationality

Constitution. The barrier of age and requirement of the applicant to be a person capable of making a useful contribution to the advancement, progress, and well-being of Nigeria tend to exclude people who may be vulnerable and not capable of making any form of contribution, it tends also to exclude young persons and foundlings within the territory of Nigeria whose nationality cannot be confirmed.

There are obvious gaps in the legislation regarding women and children; the Constitution and the Child Rights Act did not make any provision on the protection of children born in the territory of Nigeria who will otherwise be stateless, or children found in the territory of Nigeria whose nationality cannot be confirmed. Section 26(2)(a) of the Constitution further made provision on the acquisition of Nigerian citizenship by registration for women married to Nigerian men, but it is silent on the possibility of women passing their nationality to their foreign spouse, which makes it impossible for Nigerian women to smoothly pass their nationality to their foreign spouses, contrary to the provisions in CEDAW, the Protocol to the African Charter on Human and Peoples' Rights on the Rights of Women in Africa, (hereinafter referred to as the Maputo Protocol),[66] and the International Covenant on Civil and Political Rights (hereinafter referred to as the ICCPR).[67]

For non-Nigerians who wish to acquire Nigerian Citizenship through naturalization, such a person needs to show clear intention to be domiciled in Nigeria, such desire is expressed in the fulfilment of the requirement that the applicant has domiciled in Nigeria for not less than 15 consecutive years or 'aggregate of 15 years.'[68] The aggregation of 15 years would only begin to count after the applicant has resided in Nigeria for an uninterrupted 12 months, during 20 years immediately preceding that period of 12 months; otherwise, any application for Nigerian citizenship through naturalization will not be successful.[69] The implication of this provision for a person in Nigeria who is stateless and wishes to naturalize is that they may be unable to acquire Nigerian citizenship and be unable to access basic services for 15 to 20 years until they meet the complex requirements for naturalization.

2.4.3 Conflict of Laws

As noted earlier, each State has its nationality rules, and these rules differ from one State to the other. The absence of uniform rules on nationality often results in a conflict of laws, exposing people to various degrees of risk of statelessness or

---

66 Nigeria needs to take steps to domesticate the CEDAW and the Protocol Rights of Women.
67 International Covenant on Civil and Political Rights, New York, 16 December 1966, came to force in 23 March 1976.
68 1999 Constitution of the Federal Republic of Nigeria s. 27(2); G Okeke and C Okeke 'The acquisition of Nigerian citizenship by naturalization: An analytical approach' (2013) 8 (2) *IOSR Journal of Humanities and Social Science* (IOSR-JHSS) 58.
69 *Ibid* 58–59; 1999 Constitution of the Federal Republic of Nigeria s. 27(2).

Principles and Concept of Statelessness and Nationality   27

actual statelessness.[70] Some of these conflicting rules include application of *jus solis* rules in some States as opposed to the application of *jus sanguinis* rules in others, including rules such as automatic loss of nationality after a prolonged period of stay abroad, a woman losing her nationality for marrying a foreigner, the inability of a woman to pass nationality to her child or spouse, etc. The application of these conflicting rules has some implications in the struggle against statelessness. A good example of statelessness resulting from a mixture of application of the *jus soli* and *jus sanguinis* rules in the 1920s was cited by Martin Stiller when he noted thus:

> Problems leading to statelessness arose, however, when these modes [*jus soli* and *jus sanguinis*] were mixed: in the 1920s, for example, statelessness could result from the birth of a child to U.S.-American parents in Germany. Children in such cases would be left stateless, since *ius soli* was decisive for U.S.-American nationality, whereas Germany followed ius sanguinis. That is, neither the U.S.-American nor the German nationality was granted to these children, as they were neither born in U.S. territories nor by German parents, and neither state considered itself responsible for granting nationality.[71] (Brackets mine.)

A person, therefore, becomes stateless because two or more States to which s/he is associated claim that another is responsible for granting nationality to the individual.[72] Conflict of nationality laws of States in most cases results in statelessness, not because of the bad intention of the States involved, but due to the absence of legal leeway.

2.4.3.1 How it Applies to Nigeria

In Nigeria, for instance, citizenship by birth is only through descent, i.e., a person 'either of whose parents or any of whose grandparents belongs or belonged to a community indigenous to Nigeria' that in itself is a problem, because if a child is born on Nigerian territory to foreign parents who come from a country where citizenship is granted solely based on birth in the territory, it means that the parents will not be able to pass their nationality to such a child and the child will be unable to acquire Nigerian nationality on account of its birth in Nigeria. The same fate applies to children born in Nigeria to parents who are from countries

---

70 N Ahmad 'The right to nationality and the reduction of statelessness – The responses of the international migration law framework' 5 (1) *Groningen Journal of International Law, Migration and International Law* 8.

71 M Stiller 'Statelessness in international law: A historic overview' (2012) 3 *DAJV Newsletter* 96. See also Samore, *AJIL*, 1951, 476.

72 UNHCR and Asylum Aid *Mapping statelessness in the United Kingdom* (2011) 23.

28 Principles and Concept of Statelessness and Nationality

where prolonged absence from territory results in loss of nationality as this will result in a conflict of Nigerian law with that of the other country.

2.4.4 Transfer of Territory

Transfer of State territory or sovereignty to another, including State succession, dissolution, boundary adjustment, and independence are also major causes of statelessness across the world. Statelessness would result from these occurrences especially where the new States or receiving States, as the case may be, enact new nationality laws, policies, and administrative procedures or interpret existing legislation in such a way that they prevent those impacted by such events from acquiring nationality either automatically or through simplified procedures.[73] Despite the grave danger posed by it, the transfer of territory or sovereignty is only partially addressed in international instruments and principles.[74]

It has been observed that 'since the end of the Second World War and the establishment of over 100 new, independent countries,'[75] statelessness has become a very much prominent issue. But the issue of statelessness did not receive much attention at the time until a few decades ago. The UNHCR and Open Society in a joint publication noted that in the first few decades of the adoption of the 1954 and 1961 Conventions, statelessness did not receive much attention on the global stage. The problem of statelessness began to receive the needed attention after the dissolution of the former Soviet Union and the break-up of the former Yugoslavia in the 1990s.[76] A good example of statelessness resulting from the transfer of sovereignty or re-establishment of independence is the case of Estonians of Russian origin; Maureen Lynch and Thatcher Cook captured it thus:

> In June 1940, Soviet troops occupied Estonia, abolishing its independence and establishing a new Soviet order. From 1944 to 1991, Estonia belonged to the Soviet Union. During this time, thousands of Estonians were killed or deported, while Russians were forced to migrate to Estonia. The Russian-speaking population in Estonia jumped from eight to approximately 40 percent. On August 20, 1991, Estonia re-established independence. At that time, the government restricted automatic citizenship to those who held it before the Soviet occupation and their descendants, leaving hundreds of thousands of individuals stateless. When Estonia joined the European Union

---

73 Decision of R Haines QC (Chairperson) Auckland Refugee Status Appeals Authority, *Decision No. 72635/01* 2002 para. 80(b), *Op cit.*

74 UNHCR and IPU *Nationality and statelessness: Handbook for parliamentarians no 11, Op Cit* 34.

75 M Shaw *International Law* 5th ed. (2003) 861.

76 Since the dissolution of USSR and break up of former Yugoslavia, 'new States continue to be formed, most recently with the creation of the Republic of South Sudan in 2011.'

   UNHCR and Open Society Justice Initiative Report, *Citizens of nowhere: Solution for the stateless in the U.S. Ibid.* 13.

Principles and Concept of Statelessness and Nationality   29

on May 1, 2004, over 160,000 Russian-speaking non-citizens remained in limbo. These individuals are being forced to choose between learning a new language and passing an exam to acquire Estonian citizenship; applying for Russian citizenship and thus surrendering the benefits of EU membership; or remaining stateless with limited political access and foreign travel restrictions.[77]

2.4.4.1 How it Applies to Nigeria

A Nigerian example is the *Cameroon v. Nigeria: Equatorial Guinea Intervening*[78] case on the boundaries dispute between Nigeria and Cameroon, especially on the Bakassi Peninsula, a peninsula in the Gulf of Guinea, between Nigeria and Cameroon, which was occupied by over 300,000 people historically and culturally tied to Cross River states of Nigeria and was part of the 774 Local Government Areas (LGAs) in Nigeria. In 2002, the International Court of Justice (ICJ) passed judgment ceding Bakassi Peninsula to Cameroon, ruling *inter alia*:

> The Court notes that Nigeria is under an obligation in the present case expeditiously and without condition to withdraw its administration and its military and police forces from that area of Lake Chad which falls within Cameroon's sovereignty and from the Bakassi Peninsula.[79]

The implication of the judgment was that the Bakassi people, who were originally Nigerians with historic and cultural ties to the Cross River and Akwa Ibom States of Nigeria, needed to decide between applying for residence permits or naturalizing as Cameroonians or resettling in Nigeria outside of the peninsula. The majority of them turned down the possibility of naturalization or residence permit in Cameroon; this posed many challenges for both countries. Although the judgment was followed by a 2006 Greentree Agreement (GTA)[80] signed by both countries, wherein Cameroon committed not to force Nigerian nationals living in the Bakassi Peninsula to leave the zone or to change their nationality and pledged to respect their culture, language, and beliefs, and respect their right to continue their agricultural and fishing activities. The GTA only resolved the citizenship rights question of Bakassi inhabitants who chose to remain within Bakassi but was silent about the majority who chose to be resettled in Nigeria.

---

77 M Lynch and T Cook 'Left behind: Stateless Russians search for equality in Estonia' (2004) *Refugee International RI Bulletin* 1.

78 *Case Concerning the Land and Maritime Boundary between Cameroon and Nigeria*, ICJ Judgment of 10 October 2002.

79 *Ibid.*

80 A formal treaty signed between the Republic of Cameroon and the Federal Republic of Nigeria on 12 June 2016, which resolved the Cameroon–Nigeria border dispute over the oil and gas rich Bakassi peninsula.

30 *Principles and Concept of Statelessness and Nationality*

Cameroon has since reneged on the GTA by forcefully evicting Bakassi people back to Nigeria where they are not fully integrated. Bakassi peninsula being a remote island, many of the inhabitants did not have any form of identification, whether Nigerian or Cameroonian national identity documents. This situation has put this group of persons at risk of statelessness in Nigeria where they lack access to land and basic services, including voting rights. According to the Open Society Report (OSF) in April 2012, the Bakassi returnees now displaced in the Cross River state of Nigeria were unable to vote in the February 2012 Governorship elections in the state because their records were no longer on the voters' register, their settlements no longer existed in Nigeria, and they had no means of proving their entitlement to vote. On voting day, they took to the streets to protest over their apparent statelessness.

2.4.5 Ethnic and Racial Discrimination

Brad K. Blitz asserts that what is 'common to all forms of statelessness is the notion of discrimination and inequality.'[81] Laura Van Waas further asserts that 'discriminatory deprivation of nationality fundamentally describes the situation where a state withholds or withdraws the nationality of an individual on the basis of a distinction that is deemed unreasonable and untenable, such as on the grounds of some immutable characteristic like skin colour,' etc.[82] Statelessness could result from discriminatory laws and procedures, either deliberately or inadvertently put in place to prevent a particular group of people or section of the population to (re)acquiring or retaining their nationality. These discriminatory practices or laws as earlier noted could be on grounds of gender, race, and the same grounds that lead people to become refugees, i.e., religion, nationality, ethnicity, political opinion, or membership of a particular social group.[83]

Discrimination based on ethnicity, race, and membership of a particular social group is witnessed in many States across the world. In Estonia, the Russian speaking population is bound to learn the Estonian language and pass the language proficiency test before they can acquire Estonian citizenship, the implication of which is that those who do not pass the exam may either become stateless or at risk of statelessness.[84] In a similar vein, Myanmar's 1982 Citizenship Law excluded the Rohingya as one of the ethnic groups in Myanmar that qualify for nationality.[85] As a matter of law, Burmese citizenship is based on being a member

---

81 See B Blitz *Statelessness, protection and equality* (2009) 1.
82 L Van Waas 'Nationality matters: Statelessness under international law' (2008) 29 *School of Human Rights Research Series* 95.
83 See the Liberia Constitution, particularly in Art. 27(b), which limits citizenship acquisition to a particular race/colour. See Z Albarazi 'Stateless: A global issue' Amnesty International workshop on Arbitrary Deprivation of Citizenship, October 2016 10.
84 See M Lynch and T Cook *Ibid* 1.
85 See Burma Citizenship Law 1982 Art. 3.

Principles and Concept of Statelessness and Nationality 31

of one of the ethnic groups that settled in Myanmar before 1823.[86] This put a legal barrier on the Rohingyans from acquiring the nationality of the country they have lived in all their lives and see as home.[87] They are often denied access to work, the right to marry, freedom of movement, and are subjected to violence.[88]

Other examples include the situation of Kenyan Nubians, who despite having lived in Kenya for more than one hundred years are still not able to establish their Kenyan citizenship status due to discrimination. As a result, Nubian children were not registered as Kenyan citizens at birth, thereby exposed to the risk of statelessness, lack of access to education, healthcare, and public services until a 2011 decision of the African Committee of Experts on the Rights and Welfare of the Child held, *inter alia*, that the practice of not recognizing the Nubian children as Kenyan citizens violated provisions of the African Charter on the Rights and Welfare of the Child.[89]

The Kurdish population in Syria is not left out. In 1962 the Syrian government conducted a census in the Hassakeh governorate through Decree No. 93; Hassakeh is occupied predominantly by the Kurdish population.[90] It is reported that, apart from the fact that the population was given insufficient time to prepare for the census, they were asked to prove residence in Syria since 1945 or lose their citizenship. This resulted in an estimated 120,000 Kurds, i.e., 20 per cent of Syria's Kurdish population, losing their citizenship at the time, a number which has since doubled to an estimated 300,000 today.[91] 'The Kurds are among the largest stateless ethnic groups in the world, with some 30 million concentrated in an area straddling Turkey, Iraq, Iran, and Syria.'[92] Racial discrimination in the acquisition of nationality is very eloquent in the Liberian Constitution which states that:

---

86 'Nationals such as the Kachin, Kayah, Karen, Chin, Burman, Mon, Rakhine or Shan and ethnic groups as have settled in any of the territories included within the State as their permanent home from a period anterior to 1185 B.E., 1823 A.D. are Burma citizens.'
 Ibid Art. 3. See also Burmese Rohingya Organisation UK (BROUK) *Myanmar's 1982 citizenship law and Rohingya. A briefing* (December 2014) https://burmacampaign .org.uk/media/Myanmar%E2%80%99s-1982-Citizenship-Law-and-Rohingya.pdf (accessed 15 August 2020).
87 See, A-S Gonzalez '"We have a state": Confronting the statelessness of the Rohingya people' https://www.refugeesinternational.org/reports/2019/6/3/wenbsphave-anbspstate-confronting-the-statelessness-of-the-rohingya-peoplenbsp#:~:text=The%20Myanmar%20government's%20refusal%20to,in%20Myanmar%20to%20this%20day (accessed 20 February 2021).
88 See L Yoshikawa and M Teff 'Bangladesh: The silent crisis' (2011) *Refugee International Field Report.*
89 See *Nubian Children v. Kenya* (2011).
90 M Lynch and P Ali 'Buried alive: Stateless Kurds in Syria' (2006) *Refugee International* 1.
91 International Justice Resources Centre *Citizenship & nationality, Op Cit*; Human Rights Watch (HRW) *Syria: The silenced Kurds* (October 1996) 8 (4)(E) 12.
92 Associated Press (AP) 'A look at the Kurds, a stateless nation in a restive region' (25 September 2017) https://apnews.com/a5f111ce84bd4e41a27f0ff2289efa1c/A-look-at-the -Kurds,-a-stateless-nation-in-a-restive-region#:~:text=The%20Kurds%20are%20among %20the,Most%20are%20Sunni%20Muslims (accessed 15 August 2020).

32   Principles and Concept of Statelessness and Nationality

In order to preserve, foster and maintain the positive Liberian culture, values and character, only persons who are Negroes or of Negro descent shall qualify by birth or by naturalization to be citizens of Liberia.[93]

2.4.5.1 How it Applies to Nigeria

Nigeria is a federation, with 36 component states. Even though there is no citizenship at the component state level, by section 25 of the 1999 Constitution, 'belonging' to any of the communities indigenous to a state in Nigeria is a basis for Nigerian citizenship by birth,[94] i.e., being or affiliated to aboriginals who have occupied a local Nigeria community for centuries. The effect of the above provision is that, to establish Nigerian citizenship, one has to first establish that s/he 'belongs' to a community or his parents or grandparents were 'members' of a community indigenous to a component state in Nigeria. Apart from its implication for Nigerians who cannot trace their ancestry to any indigenous community in Nigeria, it is particularly bad for persons at risk of statelessness or stateless persons with no claim to any other nationality, including foreigners who acquire Nigerian citizenship through any other means than by birth.

On ethnicity and the question of being from a community indigenous to Nigeria, as provided in Chapter III of the Constitution, the book draws attention to the very complex question of where do naturalized Nigerians and their offspring belong, against the backdrop of the definition of Nigerian citizen in section 25 of the Constitution. Should stateless persons wait to be 'assimilated', 'accepted' by a local community, make 'useful contributions' as envisaged in sections 26 and 27 of the Constitution on registration and naturalisation respectively, before their immediate protection needs, i.e., the need for nationality, be granted? How long would offspring of naturalized Nigerians[95] and stateless persons have to

---

93 Liberia Constitution 1986, Art. 27(b).

94 E Babatunde, 'Rethinking the 1999 Constitution within recent dynamics of Nigeria's national security: Indigene-settler crisis in Jos, Plateau' (2017) 62 *Journal of Law, Policy and Globalization* 47; see Constitution of the Federal Republic of Nigeria 1999, ss. 25(1) and 318(1).

95 In Nigeria, naturalized Nigerians are not able to automatically transmit nationality to their offspring. Though the website of the Ministry of Interior Citizenship and Business Department https://ecitibiz.interior.gov.ng/citizenship/overview (accessed 12 March 2020) provides that 'issuing of Citizenship by Confirmation (Under the Section 25 (1b and c) of the Constitution of the Federal Republic of Nigeria 1999 as Amended) [...] applies to individuals of Nigerian descent who wish to gain the Nigerian citizenship. The descendants could also have acquired their citizenship through naturalization.' (It is important to note that citizenship by confirmation is not provided for in the Constitution of Nigeria, 1999.) I had in the course of writing this book a discussion with a senior official of the Ministry of Interior's Citizenship and business in May 2009 who revealed that since 2016, the Ministry of Interior has suspended the procedure of issuing Nigerian 'citizenship by confirmation' (option procedure) to descendants of naturalized Nigerians; all that is available to them at the moment is naturalization, which takes at least 15 years of legal residence for an applicant to qualify to apply for, including other requirements for naturalization. The official

Principles and Concept of Statelessness and Nationality   33

live in Nigeria before they are considered persons belonging to a community 'indigenous to Nigeria'?[96]

2.4.6 Gender Discrimination

Gender discrimination in nationality law has been an age-long practice in many States across the world. However, there is a growing number of States showing strong commitments to reverse the trend and grant women equal rights to access, and change, retain, and transmit their nationality on equal terms as men.[97] Despite the growing number of States that have reviewed or committed to reviewing their nationality laws, there are still 25 countries today where women cannot pass nationality to their children on the same conditions as men.[98] Out of these 25 countries, 24 of them are State parties to the CEDAW. '21 of them received recommendations addressing this subject in the most recent review, making the CEDAW the mechanism which has most consistently and comprehensively addressed gender discrimination in nationality law.'[99] It is reported that 'over 50 countries maintain other forms of gender discrimination such as denying women equal rights to confer nationality to spouses, stripping women of citizenship upon marriage to a foreigner, or maintaining higher barriers for single fathers to confer nationality to children.'[100]

---

further stated that the Ministry has set up a committee to identify the appropriate method to grant Nigerian nationality to such Nigeria descendants. The committee is yet to submit its recommendation, which possibly means that the procedure of acquiring citizenship by confirmation by descendants of naturalized Nigerians remains suspended. See B Manby and S Oseghale Momoh, 'Report on citizenship law: Nigeria' Global Governance Programme (Global Citizenship Observatory (GLOBALCIT)) Country Reports, 2020/12, [Global Citizenship] 19.

96 See B Manby and S Oseghale Momoh *Ibid* 23.

97 European Network on Statelessness 'Ensuring gender equal nationality laws is key to ending statelessness' https://www.statelessness.eu/blog/ensuring-gender-equal-nationality-laws-key-ending-statelessness (accessed 24 August 2018).

98 UNHCR *Background note on gender equality, nationality laws and statelessness 2018* (8 March 2018) 1 & 6. See also Global Campaign for Equal Nationality Rights https://equalnationalityrights.org/the-issue/the-problem (accessed 24 August 2020). The following are 25 countries where women cannot pass their nationality to their children on the same terms as men: 'The Bahamas, Bahrain, Barbados, Brunei, Burundi, Eswatini, Iran, Iraq, Jordan, Kiribati, Kuwait, Lebanon, Liberia, Libya, Malaysia, Mauritania, Nepal, Oman, Qatar, Saudi Arabia, Somalia, Sudan, Syria, Togo, United Arab Emirates.' Out of these 25, eight of them, including Burundi, Liberia, Libya, Mauritania, Somali, Sudan, Swaziland, and Togo are in Africa, while two of them, Liberia and Togo, are in the ECOWAS sub-region.

99 Institute of Statelessness and Inclusion (ISI) 'Every mother's right' 4 http://www.institutesi.org/gender_factsheet.pdf (accessed 24 August 2018).

100 European Network on Statelessness, *Ensuring gender equal nationality laws is key to ending statelessness, Op cit.* See also the Global Campaign for Equal Nationality Rights, UNHCR and UNICEF *Gender discrimination and childhood statelessness* (2019) 9. Nigeria is one of the countries where women cannot pass nationality on an equal basis as men. Specifically, women in Nigeria cannot transmit their nationality to foreign spouses.

34 *Principles and Concept of Statelessness and Nationality*

CEDAW, which is frequently described as an *international bill of rights for women*[101] makes provisions regarding the right of women to acquire, change, or retain their nationality, and equality of rights between men and women concerning the nationality of their children.[102] Gender equality in nationality law is necessary not just for the sake of achieving gender equality generally, but also because of the role it would play in the prevention and reduction of statelessness.[103] Gender discrimination, especially in combination with *jus sanguinis* principles can increase the incidence of statelessness. 'To give an example, some states confer citizenship at birth according to paternal descent. A woman from such a country married to a stateless man would not be able to pass her citizenship to her child, who would be stateless.'[104] Often, it does not matter that the woman herself is not stateless; she still would not be able to pass her nationality to her children.[105] Where a father is unable to confer nationality on a child because he is stateless, or the child was born out of wedlock (as in countries where it is practised), and other legal and administrative barriers, equality in nationality law will ensure that a child can acquire nationality from the mother in such situation/and or at birth.[106]

With eight out of the 25 countries where women cannot confer nationality to their children on the same footing as men in Africa, the implication[107] of these

---

101 See UN Women web page https://www.un.org/womenwatch/daw/cedaw// (accessed 24 August 2020).

102 See CEDAW Art. 9.

103 Institute of Statelessness and Inclusion (ISI) 'Gender equality, nationality and statelessness' http://www.institutesi.org/ourwork/genderequality.php (accessed 24 August 2018).

   However, some scholars have noted that 'The broad definition given to equality by the CEDAW Committee does not necessarily require comparisons to be made between men and women, but rather it focuses on ending patriarchal domination, oppression and the exclusion of women wherever it occurs. Equality is therefore less about making or justifying distinctions between men and women and more about equal access to and enjoyment of human rights.'

   Asylum Aid 'Gender equality, displacement and statelessness: Putting CEDAW to work' (2010) 89 *Women and Asylum News (WAN)* 2 https://www.asylumaid.org.uk/wp-content/uploads/2013/02/WAN_JanFeb_2010_issue_89.pdf (accessed 24 August 2018).

104 M Fullerton 'The intersection of statelessness and refugee protection in US asylum policy' (2014) 2 (3) *Journal on Migration and Human Security (JMHS)* 149.

105 Often in such circumstance does not matter that:

   '(i) where the father is stateless; (ii) where the laws of the father's country do not permit him to confer nationality in certain circumstances, such as when the child is born abroad; (iii) where a father is unknown or not married to the mother at the time of birth; (iv) where a father has been unable to fulfill administrative steps to confer his nationality or acquire proof of nationality for his children because, for example, he has died, has been forcibly separated from his family, or cannot fulfill onerous documentation or other requirements; or (v) where a father has been unwilling to fulfill administrative steps to confer his nationality or acquire proof of nationality for his children, for example if he has abandoned the family.'

   UNHCR *Background note on gender equality, nationality and statelessness* (2018) 2.

106 *Ibid.*

107 The implication includes a growing generation of persons who cannot establish their nationality, and persons who are excluded from being part of the national system amongst others.

Principles and Concept of Statelessness and Nationality 35

discriminatory legislations restricting women to pass their nationality to their children could be a huge problem for Africa in the long run.

2.4.6.1 How it Applies to Nigeria

Though Nigerian women can transmit their nationality to their children, there is however some form of discrimination against women with regard to the absence of a provision that allows for Nigerian women to transmit their nationality to their foreign husbands. This is a clear violation of the principles of equality laid down in the relevant articles of the ICCPR,[108] the Maputo Protocol,[109] and the relevant provisions of the CEDAW.[110] The CEDAW will be succinctly reviewed in Chapter 3 of this research.

2.4.7 Loss or Deprivation of Nationality

It is universally agreed that states have different laws which provide for conditions under which a person would cease to be their national. Therefore, different terminologies are used to describe such situations. According to the United Nations High Commissioner for Human Rights, 'A common approach, which is applied in the 1961 Convention on the Reduction of Statelessness, is to refer to "loss" with regard to the automatic lapse of nationality, *ex lege* and without State interference, and "deprivation" for administrative and judicial acts of competent national authorities invoking a stipulation of the nationality law to withdraw nationality. While "loss" and "deprivation" cover two distinct processes',[111] the result of both is that the person involved is no longer considered a national by the State, and if he or she does not hold another nationality, they become stateless automatically.

International law does not specifically prohibit deprivation of nationality, as long as such deprivation is not arbitrary[112] and does not result in statelessness. There are different grounds or conditions upon which States may deprive a person of nationality automatically by operation of law or in the exercise of executive discretion. These include loss as a result of voluntary acquisition of another nationality or serving in a foreign government or military.[113] The 1961 Convention

---

108 International Covenant on Civil and Political Rights Art. 3.
109 Protocol to the African Charter on Human and Peoples' Rights on the Rights of Women in Africa Arts. 2, 6.
110 CEDAW Arts. 1, 9.
111 Annual report of the United Nations High Commissioner for Human Rights and reports of the Office of the High Commissioner and the Secretary-General *Human rights and arbitrary deprivation of nationality*, A/HRC/25/28, 19 December 2013 4. Also see, A Edwards 'The meaning of nationality in international law in an era of human rights' in A Edwards & L Van Waas (Eds.) *Nationality and statelessness under international law* (2014) 21.
112 J Brandvoll 'Deprivation of nationality' in A Edwards and L van Waas (Eds.) *Nationality and statelessness under international law, Ibid* 199.
113 I Shearer and B Opeskin, *Nationality and statelessness, Op Cit* 7.

36 *Principles and Concept of Statelessness and Nationality*

on the Reduction of Statelessness specifically provides that States may retain the right to deprive a person of nationality 'if at the time of signature, ratification or accession it specifies its retention of such right on one or more of the following grounds, being grounds existing in its national law at that time.' Some of these rights or discretion apply to loss due to acts considered seriously prejudicial to the vital interests of the State; an oath or formal declaration of allegiance to another State, or repudiation of allegiance to the State; and for a naturalized person, misrepresentation or fraud and long residence abroad.[114]

A few States, however, apply automatic loss of nationality for women married to foreign nationals; this is contrary to the provisions of the 1957 Convention on the Nationality of Married Women[115] and the 1979 Convention on the Elimination of All Forms of Discrimination Against Women, both of which calls on States to grant equal rights with men to acquire, change, or retain their nationalities.[116]

As noted above, although international law does not specifically prohibit deprivation of nationality, this discretion must be exercised with regard to the proportionality of the offence and the consequence for the offender.[117] An example in this regard is the case of *Rottmann v. Freistaat Bayern*,[118] which concerned the discretion of States to revoke the nationality. In February 1998, Mr. Rottmann, an Austrian by birth, applied to the German authorities to naturalize as a German. When he acquired German nationality in 1999, he automatically lost his Austrian nationality.[119] However, when the German authorities discovered that Mr. Rottmann had failed to inform during his application for naturalization that he had a criminal case pending at the Criminal Court in Graz, Austria (*Landesgericht für Strafsachen Graz*), on 4 July 2000 the German authorities withdrew his naturalization retroactively. This decision was reaffirmed in a 25 October 2005 second instance decision of the *Bayerischer Verwaltungsgerichtshof* (administrative court of the Land of Bavaria) which ruled that 'even though the effect of that withdrawal, once definitive, would be to render the person concerned stateless,' that the decision to withdraw the applicant's status obtained by deception was in accordance with German law. The *Bundesverwaltungsgericht* (federal administrative court) also affirmed the earlier decisions on appeal to it.

---

114 Convention on the reduction of statelessness 1961 Arts. 7 and 8.

115 Art. 1.

116 Art. 9.

117 H van Eijken and P Phoa 'Exploring obstacles in exercising core EU citizenship rights' (2016) *BEUCITIZEN* 7–8.

118 *Rottmann v. Freistaat Bayern*, C-135/08, European Union: Court of Justice of the European Union, 2 March 2010.

119 According to Austrian Law nationality law:

'Any person who acquires foreign nationality at his own request, or by reason of a declaration made by him or with his express consent, shall lose his Austrian nationality unless he has expressly been given the right to retain [it].'

Law on nationality (*Staatsbürgerschaftsgesetz*, 'the StbG', BGBl. 311/1985), para. 27(1).

The Federal Administrative Court referred the case to the Court of Justice of the European Union (CJEU) to determine, *inter alia*, 'whether it is contrary to European Union law, in particular to Article 17 EC, for a Member State to withdraw from a citizen of the Union the nationality of that State acquired by naturalization and obtained by deception' especially where it would lead to statelessness. The CJEU ruled that

> It is not contrary to European Union law, in particular to Article 17 EC, for a Member State to withdraw from a citizen of the Union the nationality of that State acquired by naturalization when that nationality was obtained by deception, on condition that the decision to withdraw observes the principle of proportionality.[120]

On the distinction between loss and deprivation of nationality, the Human Rights Council stated thus:

> The distinction between loss and deprivation is not always clear, as where one State provides for the automatic loss of nationality on a particular ground, while another may adopt the same ground as a basis for attributing to the authorities the power to deprive an individual of his or her nationality. In some instances, the withdrawal of nationality – for example, on the ground of fraud – may be deemed under domestic law to be an act of nullification rather than loss or deprivation of nationality. Regardless of the terminology or legal construction in domestic law, measures that result in the loss or deprivation of nationality should be qualified as such and are subject to relevant international norms and standards.[121]

Charlotte-Anne Malischewsk opined that the discretion to deny nationality on the ground of fraud result in 'a form of double punishment whereby those whose actions are already deemed illegal under law are not only subject to the sanctions of the law such as imprisonment, but are doubly punished by having their citizenship revoked.'[122] Municipal laws which allow a country to deprive a person of its nationality, especially where those laws do not take into consideration whether or not a person would become stateless as a result of such action could be said to violate international law and, as such, an obstacle to the struggle to prevent and reduce statelessness as provided for in the UDHR[123] and the Statelessness Conventions.

---

120 *Rottmann v. Freistaat Bayern, Ibid* para. 65.
121 UN General Assembly *Annual report of the United Nations High Commissioner for Human Rights and reports of the Office of the High Commissioner and the Secretary-General* A/ HRC/25/28 19 December 2013 3–4 at para. 3.
122 C-A Malischewsk 'Where the exception is the norm: The production of statelessness in India' (2014) 2 (8) *International Human Rights Internship Working Paper Series* 23.
123 See UDHR Art. 15.

38 *Principles and Concept of Statelessness and Nationality*

2.4.7.1 How it Applies to Nigeria

Section 30, especially sub-section 30(1) of the 1999 Constitution of Nigeria empowers the President to deprive a person, other than a person who is a citizen of Nigeria by birth or by registration, of his citizenship if he is satisfied that such a person has within seven years after becoming naturalized, been sentenced to imprisonment for a term of not less than three years. The above provision appears arbitrary and contrary to the principle against 'double jeopardy' in section 36(1) of the Constitution which makes provision against double punishment, it is also contrary to the obligations in Article 8 of the 1961 Convention that obliges States not to deprive a person of his nationality if such deprivation would render him stateless.

2.5 Peculiarity of the Risk of Statelessness in Nigeria

In Nigeria there are no official records of stateless persons; this may be because there is no statelessness determination procedure (SDP) in place. However, there is a huge population of Nigerians who are at risk of statelessness as will be described below. The government is becoming increasingly aware of the risk in Nigeria due to constant advocacy by the UNHCR and Civil Society Organizations (CSOs), especially through the UNHCR and Economic Community of West African States (hereinafter referred to as ECOWAS)[124] jointly organized Ministerial conference on statelessness in February 2015, which led to the Abidjan Declaration of Ministers of ECOWAS States on the Eradication of Statelessness and the ECOWAS Plan of Action on the Eradication of Statelessness 2017–2024, known as the Banjul Plan of Action,[125] respectively. The advocacy also led to the 2016 UNHCR and the Ministry of Interior of Nigeria jointly organizing a workshop for stakeholders on the risk of statelessness in Nigeria, where a National Action Plan (NAP) to End Statelessness in Nigeria was drafted.[126]

An eye-opener for the government and stakeholders on the risk of statelessness in Nigeria is the ongoing insurgency in the Northeast of Nigeria, which has created a huge number of internally displaced persons (IDPs) in the region, many of whom are without documentation. Reports from humanitarian organizations show that more than 90 per cent[127] of the population did not have any means of identification. To prevent the risk of statelessness of the displaced population in the Northeast, the UNHCR entered into an agreement with the National Identity Management Commission (NIMC) in 2017 to mobilize resources and

---

124 A community of West African nations coming together for economic and political integration, modelled after the EU.

125 With adoption of the Banjul Plan of Action on 9 May 2017, ECOWAS became the first region in the world to adopt a plan of action to end statelessness.

126 The NAP was adopted in November 2020 after several advocacies by UNHCR and key stakeholders.

127 UNHCR Nigeria *Vulnerability screening report* November 2017.

equipment to IDP sites to ensure registration and production of national identity cards for the displaced population in the Northeast of Nigeria.[128]

Apart from the gaps in legislation and administrative processes which have been identified earlier, including poor documentation and record-keeping culture as a possible trigger of the risk of statelessness in Nigeria, certain persons in the country are effectively at risk of statelessness. These categories of persons do not have any means of documentation to be identified as Nigerians. A lot of children in remote parts of Nigeria are born in private houses or traditional clinics where no birth certificate is issued to new births by the mostly uneducated traditional birth attendant (TBA).[129] A child born in such a condition grows up without ever getting a birth certificate, which is sometimes issued jointly by the hospitals and the National Population Commission (NPC), in the case of births in government hospitals or in private hospitals.

Other populations at risk in Nigeria that his study will examine are the Almajiris[130] in the Northern part of Nigeria; nomads and herdsmen who move about the country, sometimes outside Nigeria in search of pasture for their cattle to graze; Bakassi returnees; and internally displaced persons due to the insurgency in the Northeast, many of whom are without any form of national identity documents.

2.5.1 Almajiri System of Education

According to M Yusha'u *et al.*,

> the word 'Almajiri' is derived from the Arabic word 'Almuhajirun' migrants. It refers to a traditional method of acquiring and memorizing the Glorious Qur'an in Hausa/Fulani land where boys at their tender ages are sent out by their parents or guardians to other villages, towns or cities for Qur'an education under a knowledgeable Islamic scholar called Malam.[131]

---

128 The Guardian *NIMC, UNHCR to enrol 100,000 displaced persons in e-identity card* (13 December 2017) https://guardian.ng/news/nimc-unhcr-to-enroll-100000-displaced -persons-in-e-identity-card/ (accessed 9 July 2018).

129 Efforts are being made to address this with the following steps. For instance, if the child is going to be immunized, there will be a record of the birth. When the child is to resume school, birth registration will be required. Birth for now can be registered at any time before age 18, although an illiterate parent may not remember the actual date of birth. However, parents who may never think about school enrolment or immunization for their children may never get their children registered for birth certificates.

130 Young persons who embrace a Quranic system of education in the Northern part of Nigeria where pupils leave the parents or communities to be under the tutelage of an Islam scholar. Many of the pupils start as early as the age of three, and often not with any form of national identity documentation/birth certificates.

131 'In Hausa land (Northern part of Nigeria) the term Almajiri could take any of the following forms; any person irrespective of gender, who begs for assistance on the street or from house to house as a result of some deformity or disability; children between the age of

40 *Principles and Concept of Statelessness and Nationality*

An author described the Almajiri system of education in pre-colonial time, *inter alia*, as follows:

> During the pre-colonial era, the Almajiri education system, originally called the Tsangaya was established under the Kanem-Borno Empire of Nigeria, one of the oldest ruling empires in the world extending from the frontiers of Northern Nigeria across the Chadian region up to the borders of Libya. It was established as an organized and comprehensive system of education for learning Islamic principles, values, jurisprudence and theology. It was a replica of Islamic learning centres in many Muslim countries such as the madrasah in Pakistan, Malaysia, Egypt and Indonesia etc. The system was funded by the state treasury and the state zakka funds, and was under the control of the emirs of the traditional government system that existed before the coming of the British. Since Islam encourages charity to a welfarer and to a student of learning, the community as well readily supported these Almajiri most of whom came from faraway places to enrol in the Tsangaya schools. In return, the Almajiris offered services such as laundry, cobbling, gardening, weaving, sewing e.t.c as charity to the community that contributed to their wellbeing; hence they gave the society what the society gave to them.[132]

The Almajiri system of education in the Northern part of Nigeria has been of great concern to authorities, especially as the system which used to be a source of pride has, since post-colonial administration, become an embarrassment.[133] According to a study by Gabriel Terwase Ngbea and Hilary Chukwuka Achunike, which draws from the data of Nigeria's National Council for the Welfare of Destitute (NCWD), there are currently about seven million Almajiris in Nigeria,[134] UNICEF puts the estimate at about ten million.[135] The Almajiris lack formal education, hence are

---

    seven and fifteen who attend informal religious school who equally roam about with the purpose of getting assistance or alms; or even a child who engages in some form of labour to earn a living.'

    M Yusha'u *et al.* 'Problems and prospects of Integrated Almajiri education in Northern Nigeria' (2013) 2 (3) *Scientific Journal of Pure and Applied Sciences* 126.

132 Naijainfoman 'History of Almajiri education in Nigeria' https://naijainfoman.wordpress .com/2012/06/07/history-of-almajiri-educational-system/ (accessed 02 April 2018).

133 M Yusha'u *et al. Op Cit* 125. The embarrassment is as a result of the fact that graduates of the Almajiri system are not considered to have acquired formal education and many of the products of the system are not considered employable in the formal sectors. Hence, they result to begging and engaging in menial jobs for survival.

134 G Terwase Ngbea and H Chukwuka Achunike 'Poverty in Northern Nigeria' (2014) 2 (2) *Asian Journal of Humanities and Social Studies* 296. See also I AbdulQadir 'The Almajiri system of education in Nigeria today' http://www.gamji.com/article5000/NEWS5956 .htm (accessed 27 March 2018).

135 UNICEF 'Children adjust to life outside Nigeria's Almajiri system' (17 September 2020) https://www.unicef.org/nigeria/stories/children-adjust-life-outside-nigerias-almajiri-sys- tem (accessed 19 January 2021).

Principles and Concept of Statelessness and Nationality 41

unable to compete for the limited job opportunities available.[136] Very many of them are without any form of identity documents, putting them at risk of statelessness. The system has also become a tool for exploitation, as most of the children end up getting little or no education and are not integrated into the national identity and documentation system. Rather the Almajiris spend most of their time working and begging to fend for themselves and on behalf of their teachers.[137]

2.5.2 Nomads and Pastoralists

It has been reported that there is an estimated 30 million pastoralists in Africa, Nigeria alone accounts for about ten million of that number.[138] Out of the pastoralist ethnic groups in Nigeria, such as 'Kenembu, Buduma, Bodawi, Shuwa-Arab, Koyo, Manga, Fulbe, and Borobro' among others, 95 per cent of them are of the Fulani (as known as Fulbe) ethnic group.[139] This ethnic group, bearing at least 13 names across West Africa, is spread across several States within the region, and with a population of about 25 million people.[140] According to E Fabusoro and A Oyegbami, on the migration of the Fulanis:

> Their immigration spanned several centuries; they traversed the West African savanna in small groups; their unit of migration is the compound family, reflecting the Patrilineal system. The deteriorating environmental conditions, land degradation and the recurrent drought that hit the Sahel region during the 1960–70s largely account for the exodus of Fulani herdsmen from their homelands into the Northern Guinea savanna of West Africa. The last three decades have been characterised by a further change in the pastoral

---

136 F Taiwo 'Transforming the Almajiri education for the benefit of the Nigerian society' (2013) 3 (9) *Journal of Educational and Social Research* 86.

137 See W Iliyasu 'A critical assessment on the exploitation of Almajirai (beggars) labour in Northern Nigeria' 2 https://www.researchgate.net/publication/330135447_A_Critical_Assessment_on_the_Exploitation_of_Almajirai_beggars_Labour_in_Northern_Nigeria (accessed 1 February 2021).

138 E Fabusoro and A Oyegbami 'Key issues in livelihoods security of migrant Fulani pastoralists: Empirical evidence from Southwest Nigeria' (2009) *Journal of Humanities, Social Sciences and Creative Arts* 1. Also see I Islam *From nomadism to sedentarism: An analysis of development constraints and public policy issues in the socioeconomic transformation of the pastoral Fulani of Nigeria* (2001).

139 C Alarima and F Obikwelu 'Assessment of utilization of primary health care services among settled Fulani agropastoralists in Ogun State, Nigeria' (2018) 17 (1) *Agro-Science Journal of Tropical Agriculture, Food, Environment and Extension* 27.

140 DW 'West Africa: Fulani conflict getting worse' (7 August 2018) https://www.dw.com/en/west-africa-fulani-conflict-getting-worse/a-43679371 (accessed 20 August 2020).
'The Fulanis in Nigeria are mixed among Hausas in the Northern part of the country and are the custodian of the nation's herd. Hausa is a major ethnic tribe spread across the Northern part of Nigeria. The Hausa are a Sahelian people chiefly located in the West African regions of Northern Nigeria and Southeastern Niger.'
E Fabusoro and A Oyegbami *Op Cit* 1.

42 Principles and Concept of Statelessness and Nationality

migratory pattern. Fulani pastoralists have moved even further Southwards to the fringes of the humid tropical forest.[141]

Today the Fulani pastoralist or herders can be found in almost all the West African countries, with many of them not able to lay claim to a particular country of origin or establish an effective nationality of the countries they traverse in search of pastures for their herds of cattle. Arguably, some of the herders are unwilling to be identified with a particular country for fear that they may be restricted from cross-border grazing if they do.

In Nigeria, the Fulani ethnic group is found in the Northern parts of the country. Although no one can clearly say where the ethnic group migrated from, some scholars have noted that the Fulanis arrived in Nigeria from the Futa Jallon and Futa Toro in about the 12th century. Since then, they have lived mainly amongst the Hausa ethnic group.[142] The ethnic group, traditionally nomad moving from one community or region to the other owns arguably more than 90 per cent of Nigeria's livestock.[143]

By their way of life, being nomadic pastoralists, they do not like to be restricted to a particular region or country; this often creates a problem of identity and issue of 'belonging' in the territories they traverse. Based on their nomadic nature, many of them are denied *indigene certificates*[144] by local government authorities who assert that the pastoralists are not from their communities. This may be due to fear that the pastoralists will take over the community lands, especially considering the incessant clashes between farms (landowners) and herders in the North Central area of Nigeria. As a result many of the pastoralists, mainly of Fulani origin, do not have access to a means of identification to prove their nationality, thereby putting a vast majority of them at risk of statelessness.

2.5.3 Foundlings and Children Born in Nigeria to Foreign Parents

According to a UNHCR and Plan International study, 'there are an estimated six million stateless children around the world.'[145] More than 70,000 children are born stateless each year;[146] these children grow up without a nationality. They are there-

---

141 *Ibid* 2.
142 A Adebayo 'Contemporary dimensions of migration among historically migrant Nigerians' (1997) 32 (1–2) *Journal of Asian and African Studies* 1–2; See also E Fabusoro and A Oyegbami *Op Cit* 1.
143 I Mohammed Abbass 'No retreat no surrender: Conflict for survival between Fulani pastoralists and farmers in Northern Nigeria' (2012) 8 (1) *European Scientific Journal* 332.
144 It is a certificate issued by states and local governments in Nigeria, certifying that a person is an indigene of a particular community with the state. It is one of the major documents use for proving Nigerian nationality.
145 UNHCR and Plan *Under the radar and under protected: The urgent need to address stateless children's rights* (2012) 5.
146 Institute on Statelessness and Inclusion *The world's stateless: children*, L van Waas and A de Chickera (Eds.) (2017) 125; UNHCR *I am here, I belong: The urgent need to end childhood statelessness* (2015) 1.

Principles and Concept of Statelessness and Nationality   43

fore denied access to birth certificates or any evidence of birth, denied access to education and healthcare, and from realizing their full potential. They face discrimination, harassment by authorities, and in many cases exploitation and abuse.[147]

In furtherance of the general right to nationality in the Universal Declaration of Human Rights,[148] the Convention on the Right of the Child[149] and the International Covenant on Civil and Political Rights[150] both provide for the right of the child to acquire a nationality.[151] Even though 'all Contracting States to the 1961 Convention are also party to the Convention on the Rights of the Child,'[152] States are still caught between municipal law on the acquisition of nationality and their international law obligation to grant nationality to children born in or found in their territories who would otherwise be stateless.[153] This is particularly so, as none of the international law instruments gives a clue as to which State is obliged to grant nationality to the child.[154]

For Nigeria, Chapter III of the Constitution and the Child Rights Act with regard to children do not comply with international law. The best interest of the child is not taken into account in the Constitution or the Child Rights Act of Nigeria, as they did not make provisions to ensure access to nationality for children born or found in the territory of Nigeria who would otherwise be stateless. It is important to note that children born to foreign parents in Nigeria do not get access to Nigerian nationality even if one or both parents are stateless.

2.5.4 *Internally Displaced Persons*

More than two million people are currently displaced in the Northeast of Nigeria[155] due to armed conflict between the Government of Nigeria and the *Jama'atu Ahlu s-Sunnati lil-Da'wa wal-Jihad/Islamic State of West Africa Province group* otherwise known as *Boko Haram* insurgents.[156] According to UNHCR Nigeria's *Vulnerability Screening Report* issued in November 2017, 96 per cent of vulner-

---

147 UNHCR *Ibid* 2 & 4.
148 UDHR Art. 15.
149 CRC Arts. 7 & 8.
150 ICCPR Art. 24(3).
151 Section 24(1) of the ICCPR provides that 'Every child has the right to acquire a nationality.'
152 UNHCR *Commemorating the Refugee and Statelessness Conventions, Op Cit* 78.
153 See 1961 Convention Arts. 1, 4, & 12. In addition to the forgoing provisions on the right to nationality for a child who would otherwise be stateless, the CRC further provides in Art. 3(1) that 'In all actions concerning children, [...] the best interests of the child shall be a primary consideration.' Arguably, the best interest of the child would start by giving the child 'the right to have rights' i.e., acquisition of a nationality.
154 G-R de Groot 'Children, their right to a nationality and children statelessness' in A Edward and L Van Waas (Eds.) *Nationality and statelessness under international law* (2014) 145.
155 NEMA & IOM *Northeast Nigeria: Displacement Report* 32 (June 2020) p. 6.
156 ICRC *Internal displacement in Northeast of Nigeria: Operationalising the Kampala Convention in Borno, Adamawa and Yobe States* (2016) 7.

44 *Principles and Concept of Statelessness and Nationality*

able displaced households in the assessment reported not having any legal identification document. The absence of documentation is reported to impede access to services such as healthcare and education, and inability to enforce property rights, restricted movements, and even cases of unlawful arrest and detention.[157]

As a result of the cross-border movement of the *Boko Haram* insurgents, with some of its fighters alleged by the Nigerian Government to be foreigners or from outside of Nigeria, there is often a suspicion of the young displaced population, the majority of whom lack any form of identity documents. Consequently, many of the young displaced persons are put through rigorous screenings, and some have been arrested and arbitrarily detained on many occasions. Apart from the fear of recruitment of the young population by the insurgents, the population in the Northeast is mainly Hausa, Fulani, and Kanuri people who are also found in some, especially border, areas of Cameroon, Niger, and Chad that border the North-eastern parts of Nigeria. Before the beginning of the insurgency in the North-eastern part of Nigeria, partly due to the rugged and porous nature of borders along the North-eastern part of the country, these populations enjoyed almost unhindered cross-border movements into Nigeria for the purpose of trade. The population also shares some similarities in language, culture, religion, and looks, making it difficult to ascertain the nationality of the displaced persons without legal identities, except with the test of accent, and knowledge of the individual of the local community s/he claims to come from in Nigeria.

To stem the tides, ensure legal protection for the displaced population, and prevent the risk of statelessness for many of the displaced population, the UNHCR in June 2017 entered an agreement with the National Identity Management Commission (NIMC) of Nigeria, an agency with the statutory responsibility of issuing free national identity cards to Nigerians, and non-Nigerians legally resident in Nigeria, to mobilize resources and equipment to the hard to reach areas of the Northeast where many of the displaced persons lack national identity cards or any legal identity documents.[158]

2.5.5 *Bakassi Returnees*

As discussed in the previous section on State secession, over 300,000 Bakassi returnees in Nigeria are persons who are at risk of statelessness, considering that many of the returnees do not have legal documents to establish their Cameroonian or Nigerian nationality. In the aftermath of the ICJ judgment[159] ceding the former Nigerian territory Bakassi Peninsula to Cameroon in 2002, both countries

---

157 UNHCR *Vulnerability screening on-going operational screening in Borno, Yobe and Adamawa States* (2017) 1 & 3.

158 The Guardian 'NIMC, UNHCR to enroll 100,000 displaced persons in e-identity card' (13 December 2017) https://guardian.ng/news/nimc-unhcr-to-enroll-100000-displaced -persons-in-e-identity-card/ (accessed 19 January 2021).

159 *Cameroon v. Nigeria: Equatorial Guinea Intervening. Case Concerning the Land and Maritime Boundary between Cameroon and Nigeria*, ICJ Judgment of 10 October 2002.

signed a Greentree Agreement (GTA) in 2006. Under the GTA, Nigeria committed to withdrawing its troops and administrative structures from the territory and Cameroon also committed not to force Nigerian nationals living in the Peninsula to leave the zone or to change their nationality. It further committed to respecting their culture, language, and beliefs, respecting their right to continue their agricultural and fishing activities. The agreement only made provisions to resolve the citizenship rights of Bakassi inhabitants who chose to remain within Bakassi but were manifestly silent about the majority who chose to be resettled in Nigeria.[160]

Though Cameroon has reneged on its obligation in the GTA, the Nigeria Government on its part has not done anything to ensure the integration of the Bakassi indigenes back into Nigerian society. The majority of the returnees have lived in some makeshift camps in Nigeria since 2005 in a protracted situation that has drawn the attention of spirited Nigerians and humanitarian agencies to come to the aid of the returnees, now displaced in Nigeria. Many of them have neither Cameroon nor Nigeria legal identity documents. Children are born in such a condition where they are not registered at birth, thereby being excluded from basic and essential services, breeding new generations of possible stateless persons. The risk is particularly bad considering the similarities of the peoples of Nigeria and Cameroon who live in the border areas. With much cross-border trading, ceremonies, and inter-marriage in the border areas, it is difficult to establish the nationality of a person without identity documents who comes from the border communities of Nigeria or Cameroon, more so for the Bakassi people who for more than 19 years after the ICJ judgment ceding their ancestral lands to Cameroon are yet to be integrated into Nigerian society.

Going by the facts on the ground concerning the status of the Bakassi returnees, whether or not Nigeria and/or Cameroon (although Cameroon is not a party to any of the Statelessness Conventions) have fulfilled their international law obligation under Article 10(1)[161] of the 1961 Convention which birthed the GTA is not in any way clear at all.

2.6 Conclusion

The right to nationality has been described as the 'right to have rights,'[162] and a fundamental human right. Without the possession of nationality, a person could

---

160 Agreement Between the Republic of Cameroon and the Federal Republic of Nigeria Concerning the Modalities of Withdrawal and Transfer of Authority in the Bakassi Peninsula (Otherwise known as the Greentree Agreement).

161 Provides that, every treaty between Contracting States providing for the transfer of territory shall include provisions designed to secure that no person shall become stateless as a result of the transfer. A Contracting State shall use its best endeavours to secure that any such treaty made by it with a State which is not a party to this Convention includes such provisions.

162 See *Trop v. Dulles*, 356 U.S. 86 (1958) 102.

46 *Principles and Concept of Statelessness and Nationality*

be said to be in a situation of legal nonexistence. This chapter examined the general phenomenon, scale, and nature of statelessness or the risk of statelessness. It moreover explained the sociological effect of statelessness and how it affects society, emphasizing the peculiarity of the risk in Nigeria. The chapter examined the notions of *de jure* and *de facto* statelessness against the backdrop of the question, what is statelessness? The arguments in the chapter aligned with the sentiments of scholars who 'believe that the 1954 Convention's definition of statelessness is too narrow and limiting because it excludes those persons whose citizenship is practically useless or who cannot prove or verify their nationality,'[163] considering the similarities of deprivations of both categories of statelessness.

It is of note that there is neither an official record nor an estimated number of stateless persons in Nigeria, due mainly to the absence of a mechanism to determine or record statelessness. In the coming chapters, this research examines the factors that expose a large part of the Nigerian population to the risk of statelessness. The need for a statelessness determination procedure, as well as a procedure to verify the nationality of the very many *in situ* populations without any means of identification will be discussed.

---

163 D Weissbrodt and C Collins *Ibid* 251. See also A de Chickera 'Critiquing the categorisation of the stateless' *Op Cit* 53 & 54.

3 Legal and Policy Framework on Nationality and Statelessness

3.1 Introduction

This chapter discusses the international legal and policy frameworks on the right to nationality and the prevention of statelessness. The international legal framework is broken into sub-headings to discuss the regional frameworks. The regional frameworks such as the African Union (AU), the Council of Europe (CoE), the European Union (EU), the Organization of American States (OAS), and the Arab League frameworks will be discussed. Under the AU, the Economic Community of West African States (ECOWAS) sub-regional framework on the right to nationality and prevention of statelessness will be examined. Out of the eight regional economic communities (RECs) in Africa, ECOWAS is considered as it is the most advanced REC within the African region, especially with regard to its advancement on the topic of statelessness and the right to nationality. The Federal Republic of Nigeria, which is the focus of this research, is also located in the ECOWAS sub-region.

The CoE is specifically considered because it is the regional body with the most advanced human rights framework, more specifically with regard to the right to nationality and reduction of statelessness. The EU is considered not just for its advanced human rights framework, but also because of the concept of community citizenship shared by both regions.

3.2 International Legal Framework on the Right to Nationality and Prevention of Statelessness

This section is divided into two parts, one on international law rules on nationality and the other on rules to prevent statelessness.

Since the early years of the United Nations, statelessness was regarded as an important global problem.[1] According to Laura Van Waas:

---

1 N Ahmad 'The right to nationality and the reduction of statelessness – the responses of the International Migration Law Framework' (2017) 5 (1) *Groningen Journal of International Law* 2.

DOI: 10.4324/9781003278733-3

48 *Legal and Policy Framework on Nationality and Statelessness*

In the early years of the United Nations, statelessness featured prominently on its agenda. In March 1948, the Economic and Social Council (ECOSOC) requested the Secretary-General to undertake a study of 'the existing situation in regard to the protection of stateless persons', to explore the need for further standard setting at the international level to address their vulnerable position. Just a few months later, on 10 December 1948, the UDHR proclaimed that 'everyone has the right to a nationality' and 'no one shall be arbitrarily deprived of his nationality' – an expression of the international community's parallel interest in preventing new cases of statelessness from arising.[2]

As discussed in the previous chapter, the right to nationality is a fundamental human right that everyone should enjoy.[3] Though States are at liberty to decide the conditions under which an individual can acquire, change, and retain their nationality, this power should not be absolute.[4] States must however comply with their international law obligations concerning the grant and loss of nationality,[5] especially where such discretion would lead to statelessness. In furtherance of the discussions as to why the topic of statelessness remains an important issue today and the relevance of the international framework for the protection of stateless persons, Nafees Ahmad noted that:

> The desire of states to exercise control over stateless persons in their jurisdictions has prevented effective action [...] However, the entire gamut of statelessness has to be addressed within the framework of International Law. The problem of statelessness has posed new challenges to the international community that is mired in a responsibility shifting game.[6]

Based on the foregoing background, this part discusses the important international legal frameworks put in place over the years to ensure the right to nationality and prevention of statelessness globally.

The 20th century witnessed a lot of development in the advancement and adoption of numerous international and regional instruments on statelessness.[7]

---

2 L Van Waas 'The UN statelessness conventions' in A Edwards and L Van Waas (Eds.) *Nationality and statelessness under international law* (2014) 64. See also Resolution 116 (VI) D, Resolutions adopted by the Economic and Social Council during its sixth session (2 February to 11 March 1948), 18. And Universal Declaration of Human Rights, Paris, 10 December 1948, GA Res. 217A (III), UN Doc. A/810 at 71 Art. 15.

3 See UDHR Art. 15

4 See CEDAW Art. 9.

5 OHCHR 'Right to nationality and statelessness' https://www.ohchr.org/EN/Issues/Pages/Nationality.aspx (accessed 17 July 2018).

6 N Ahmad *Op Cit.*

7 TL Lee *Statelessness, human rights and gender: Irregular migrant workers from Burma in Thailand* (2005) 19–20.

Legal and Policy Framework on Nationality and Statelessness 49

These international instruments include the 1930 Hague Convention on Certain Questions Relating to the Conflict of Nationality Laws,[8] the 1930 Hague Protocol Relating to a Certain Case of Statelessness,[9] the 1951 Convention Relating to the Status of Refugees,[10] the 1954 Convention Relating to the Status of Stateless Persons,[11] the 1958 Convention on the Nationality of Married Women,[12] the 1961 Convention on the Reduction of Statelessness,[13] the 1967 Protocol Relating to the Status of Refugees,[14] the 1979 Convention on the Elimination of All Forms of Discrimination Against Women,[15] the 1989 Convention on the Rights of the Child,[16] and the 1999 UN Declaration on the Nationality of Natural Persons in Relation to the Succession of States.[17]

Regional instruments on the right to nationality, which also impact the status of stateless persons, are the 1969 American Convention on Human Rights,[18] the 1997 European Convention on Nationality,[19] the Arab Charter on Human Rights, and the evolving (Draft) Protocol to the African Charter on Human and Peoples' Right on the Specific Aspects of the Right to a Nationality and the Eradication of Statelessness in Africa,[20] among others.

Some of the Conventions mentioned above will be discussed extensively in the following sections. The Universal Declaration of Human Rights is examined as the instrument that influenced the adoption of the 1954 Convention and other human rights instruments, particularly on the right to nationality. The 1979 Convention on the Elimination of all Forms of Discrimination against Women and the 1990 Convention on the Rights of the Child are examined because women and children are the most at risk of statelessness and because women often find themselves in a position where they are unable to retain or transmit their nationality to their spouses or children. The 1954 and 1961 Conventions are the principal instruments for the protection, prevention, and eradication of statelessness. These two instruments are therefore very relevant to the topic of

---

8 Entered into force on 1 July 1937. League of Nations *Treaty Series* vol. 179, 89.
9 Entered into force on 1 July 1937 in accordance with Arts. 9 and 10. League of Nations *Treaty Series* vol. 179, 115.
10 Entered into force on 22 April 1954. United Nations *Treaty Series* vol. 189, 137.
11 Entered into force 6 June 1960. United Nations *Treaty Series* vol. 360, 117.
12 Entered into force 11 August 1958. United Nations *Treaty Series* vol. 309, 65.
13 Entered into force 13 December 1975. United Nations *Treaty Series* vol. 989, 175.
14 Entered into force 4 October 1967. United Nations *Treaty Series* vol. 606, 267.
15 Entered into force 3 September 1981. United Nations *Treaty Series* vol. 1249, 13.
16 Entered into force 2 September 1990. United Nations *Treaty Series* vol. 1577, 3.
17 Adopted by the International Law Commission at its 51st session in 1999, later annexed to General Assembly resolution 55/153 of 12 December 2000. See Introductory Note by V Mikulka 'Articles on nationality of natural persons in relation to the succession of States 1999' https://legal.un.org/avl/ha/annprss/annprss.html (accessed 20 January 2020).
18 1144 UNTS 123, OASTS No 36 (entered into force 18 July 1978).
19 ETS 166 – Convention on Nationality, 6.XI.1997.
20 As at the time of writing, the Protocol to the African Charter on Human and Peoples' Right (ACHPR) was only a draft waiting to be adopted at the AU level, though conferences have been held at the sub-regional level (including ECOWAS level) to review the draft.

50 *Legal and Policy Framework on Nationality and Statelessness*

this book. Others are considered due to their relevance to the discussion on the rights and dignity of human persons, especially with regard to non-discrimination in the application of the right to nationality.

3.2.1 *International Law on the Right to Nationality*

3.2.1.1 *Article 15 of the 1948 Universal Declaration of Human Rights*

The Universal Declaration of Human Rights (hereinafter UDHR or the Declaration) was adopted by the United Nations General Assembly on 10 December 1948.[21] The Declaration was adopted as a non-binding document.[22] On the history of the UDHR, the United Nations notes *inter alia*:

> With the end of that war, and the creation of the United Nations, the international community vowed never again to allow atrocities like those of that conflict happen again. World leaders decided to complement the UN Charter with a road map to guarantee the rights of every individual everywhere. The document they considered, and which would later become the Universal Declaration of Human Rights, was taken up at the first session of the General Assembly in 1946.[23]

In support of the above assertion, the general belief of scholars is that the UDHR was adopted to prevent horrible events that occurred during the second world war from happening in the future.[24] However, some scholars believe that the history of the UDHR is obscure and not well known.[25] Nevertheless, 'the main

---

21 UN 'Universal declaration of human rights' https://www.un.org/en/universal-declaration -human-rights/ (accessed 5 December 2020).

22 T Li-ann 'Reading rights rightly: The "UDHR" and its creeping influence on the development of Singapore Public Law' (2008) December *Singapore Journal of Legal Studies* 271.

23 UN 'History of the document: Universal Declaration of Human Rights' http://www.un .org/en/sections/universal-declaration/history-document/index.html (accessed 24 April 2018).

24 A Eckert 'Universality by consensus: The evolution of universality in the drafting of the UDHR' (2001) 1 (2) *Human Rights & Human Welfare* 22; OHCR 'The United Nations Human Rights Treaty System Fact Sheet No. 30/Rev.1' 3 https://www.ohchr.org/ Documents/Publications/FactSheet30Rev1.pdf (accessed 27 August 2020); I Goris, J Harrington and S Köhn 'Statelessness: What it is and why it matters' (2009) 32 *Forced Migration Review* 4; See also P Sun 'Drafting process of the UDHR with non-Western influence' in *Historic Achievement of a Common Standard* (2018).

25 See S Waltz, 'Reclaiming and rebuilding the history of the Universal Declaration of Human Rights' (2002) 23 (3) *Third World Quarterly* 437. Some scholars think that the document is Eurocentric, for instance:
    'American Anthropological Association (AAA) was worried about the problem of ethnocentrism (holding the values of one's own culture as superior to those of other cultures).'
    J Morsink *The Universal Declaration of Human Rights: Origins, drafting, and intent* (2000) ix.

purpose of the Declaration was to ensure basic and natural rights to every human being, rights which people cannot buy, sell or inherit, because they belong to everyone without any distinctions based on race, sex, language or religion.'[26] The UDHR, generally agreed to be the foundation of international human rights law, has inspired more than 80 legally binding international human rights treaties and declarations,[27] with its principles incorporated into the Constitutions of most of the 195 nations of the world.[28] According to the United Nations, in 1999, the UDHR set a world record of 'being the most translated document in the world,' translated into hundreds of languages. Today, there are 523 different translations available online.[29]

From the adoption of the UDHR, which at that time was adopted as a non-binding Declaration,[30] up until now, there have been lots of controversies and debates amongst scholars as to whether or not the Declaration is legally binding on States.[31] The debate on the nature of the UDHR commenced even before the Declaration was drafted and adopted.[32] Although the Declaration is not a legally binding document, considering that it is meant to guide States 'as a common standard,'[33] over the years most parts of the UDHR acquired the status of customary international law and are binding on States.[34] In this regard, since the over 70 years of the adoption of the UDHR, 'international and regional human

---

There is also the opinion that:
'many of the principles that underpin the modern law of human rights can be traced back centuries, and even further.'
W A Schabas 'Introductory essay: The drafting and significance of the Universal Declaration of Human Rights' in *The Universal Declaration of Human Rights: The Travaux Préparatoires* (2013) ixxi.

26 Đ B Kekez 'The relevance of the Universal Declaration of Human Rights' (2013) *Scientific Cooperations International Journal of Law and Politics* 71 http:// http://ase-scoop.org/papers/IWLP-2015/6.Kekez.pdf (accessed 14 June 2022).

27 H Hannum 'The status of the Universal Declaration of Human Rights in national and international law' (1995) 25 (287) *Georgia Journal of International and Comparative Law* 312; UN 'The foundation of international human rights law' http://www.un.org/en/sections/universal-declaration/foundation-international-human-rights-law/index.html (accessed 24 April 2018).

28 N Flowers 'Human rights here and now: Celebrating the Universal Declaration of Human Rights' http://hrlibrary.umn.edu/edumat/hreduseries/hereandnow/Part-1/short-history.htm (accessed 24 April 2018).

29 See OHCHR 'About the Universal Declaration of Human Rights translation project' https://www.ohchr.org/en/udhr/pages/introduction.aspx (accessed 20 June 2018).

30 T Li-ann *Op Cit* 271; H J Steiner, P Alston and R Goodman *International human rights in context: Law, politics, morals, text and materials* (2008) 107.

31 See also Đ B Kekez *Op Cit* 71.

32 See S Waltz *Op Cit* 445–446.

33 See preamble of the UDHR.

34 R B Lillich 'The growing importance of customary international human rights law' (1995) 25 (1) *Georgia Journal of International and Comparative Law* 1; Human Rights Resource Center, University of Minnesota '*Section 1: Foundation of Human Rights Education*' 3 http://hrusa.org/thisismyhome/resources/MN_HR_Ed_Fundamentals.pdf (accessed 24 April 2018).

52 *Legal and Policy Framework on Nationality and Statelessness*

rights instruments and principles have emerged to protect the rights enshrined in Article 15'[35] as shall further be discussed in this part.

The UDHR is comprised of 30 principles, notably its famous Article 15 which emphasizes the right of everyone to nationality and the right not to be arbitrarily deprived of it.[36] This provision ensures the right to nationality for every person without regard to age, race, sex, or religion. Article 15 could be said to have influenced the principles of the right to nationality and the prohibition of arbitrary denial of nationality in several binding international treaties.[37] Closely related to Article 15, are the provisions in Article 14 which state that 'everyone has the right to seek and to enjoy in other countries asylum from persecution.' On the motivation for the inclusion of the right to nationality and prevention of arbitrary denial of nationality in the UDHR, Indira Goris, Julia Harrington, and Sebastian Köhn assert that:

> The inclusion of the right to nationality in Article 15 of the Universal Declaration of Human Rights, like the UDHR as a whole, was motivated by the impulse to respond to the atrocities committed during the Second World War, among them mass denationalisations and huge population movements. Hundreds of thousands of Jews who survived the Nazi-perpetrated genocide fled their home countries, while millions of ethnic Germans were expelled from eastern European states, and millions of Poles, Ukrainians, Byelorussians and other minority populations of the Soviet Union either were forcibly expelled or fled for their safety.[38]

In the same vein, David C. Baluarte asserts that the inclusion of the right to nationality in the UDHR, 'marked a shift away from sovereign control of nationality.'[39] Article 15 of the UDHR, which over the years has been treated as

---

35 M Adjami and J Harrington 'The scope and content of Article 15 of the Universal Declaration of Human Rights' (2008) 27 (3) *Refugee Survey Quarterly* 94 https://doi.org/10.1093/rsq/hdn047 (accessed 24 April 2018).

36 Article 15 provides thus, 'everyone has the right to a nationality' and that 'no one shall be arbitrarily deprived of his nationality nor denied the right to change his nationality.'

37 'The principle that arbitrary deprivation of nationality is forbidden also follows from Article 5(d)(iii) of the 1965 International Convention on the Elimination of all Forms of Racial Discrimination, Article 8(1) of the 1989 Convention on the Rights of the Child (no "unlawful interference"), Article 19(1)(a) and (b) the 2006 Convention on the Rights of Persons with Disabilities, as well as in regional treaties such as in Article 20(3) of the 1969 American Convention on Human Rights, Article 24 of the 1995 Commonwealth of Independent States Convention on Human Rights and Fundamental Freedoms, Article 4(c) of the European Convention on Nationality, Article 29(1) of the 2004 Arab Charter on Human Rights, and Article 18 of the 2012 ASEAN Declaration of Human Rights.'

   G-R de Groot 'Survey on rules on loss of nationality in international treaties and case law' (2013) 57 *CEPS Paper in Liberty and Security in Europe* 4.

38 I Goris, J Harrington, and S Köhn *Op Cit* 4; M Adjami and J Harrington *Op Cit* 96.

39 'Indeed, such limitations imposed by human rights law are often viewed as antithetical to state sovereignty to the extent that they compromise on the principle of non-intervention in internal affairs.'

Legal and Policy Framework on Nationality and Statelessness 53

customary international law, limits States' discretion with regard to deprivation of nationality.

3.2.1.2 1979 Convention on the Elimination of all Forms of Discrimination against Women

Before the adoption of the Convention on the Elimination of All Forms of Discrimination against Women in 1979,[40] the laws of many States did not provide for equal rights of women, especially with regard to the issue of nationality.[41] The Convention was opened for signature on 1 March 1980 'at the mid-decade conference of the United Nations Decade for Women.'[42] It however entered into force on 3 September 1981. As of the time of writing, there are 189 State parties to the CEDAW, including Nigeria with ratification made on 13 June 1985.[43]

The CEDAW is a 'key international human rights instrument and the only one exclusively addressed to women,' and also the primary instrument on women's rights.[44] Rebecca Cook describes the CEDAW as 'the definitive international legal instrument requiring respect for and observance of the human rights of women.'[45] The Optional Protocol to the Convention was adopted on 6 October 1999 at the 54th Session of the General Assembly and entered into force on 22 December 2000.[46]

The Optional Protocol introduced a mechanism through which individuals could bring complaints of violation of rights under the CEDAW before the Committee on the Elimination of Discrimination against Women (hereinafter, CEDAW Committee),[47] including a procedure through which the Committee

---

D C Baluarte 'The risk of statelessness: Reasserting a rule for the protection of the right to nationality' (2017) 19 (1) *Yale Human Rights and Development Journal* 54. See also L Henkin 'Human rights and state "sovereignty"' (1996) 25 *Georgia Journal of International and Comparative Law* 34.

40 United Nations *Treaty Series* vol. 1249, 13.

41 UNHCR *Background Note on Gender Equality, Nationality Laws and Statelessness* (2018) 2.

42 A Byrnes and M Freeman 'The impact of the CEDAW Convention: Paths to equality' (2012) A study for the World Bank. World Development Report 6.

43 United Nations *Treaty Series* vol. 1249, 13.

44 B Rudolf, MA Freeman and CM Chinkin *The UN convention on the elimination of all forms of discrimination against women: A commentary* (2012); O Nwankwo 'Briefing on the domestication of the Convention on the Elimination of all forms of Discrimination against Women (CEDAW)' (2010) at Civil Resource Development and Documentation Centre (CIRDDOC), Nigeria.

45 RJ Cook 'Enforcing women's rights through law' (1995) 3 (2) *Gender and Development* 8. The essential articles of the CEDAW that address non-discrimination and equality in nationality matters are the following: Article 2, which obliges states to repeal all discriminatory provisions in their national laws against women, and Article 9, which makes provisions on equal nationality rights between women and men, including with regard to the nationality of their children.

46 United Nations *Treaty Series* vol. 2131, 83.

47 Optional Protocol to the CEDAW Art. 2; L Hodson 'Women's rights and the periphery: CEDAW's Optional Protocol' (2014) 25 (2) *The European Journal of International Law* 562.

54 *Legal and Policy Framework on Nationality and Statelessness*

may investigate grave or systematic violations of rights (allegedly) committed by a State party.[48] Nigeria ratified the Optional Protocol to the CEDAW on 22 November 2004,[49] thereby reaffirming its commitment to the obligations of the Treaty.[50]

Despite having a significant number of State parties,[51] the CEDAW is one of the Conventions with a huge number of reservations,[52] including reservations against Article 9 which obliges States to 'grant women equal rights with men to acquire, change or retain their nationality.' Despite the reservations to this all-important Article 9 in the struggle against statelessness, Radha Govil and Edwards Alice assert thus:

> It is arguable that the combined effect of the rights to nationality and non-discrimination contained in many other international instruments form part of a body of international norms that reinforce the equal right of women in relation to nationality matters and that strengthen the content of Article 9 of CEDAW, notwithstanding the many reservations to this Article.[53]

As discussed in the previous chapter, although Nigeria is compliant with the CRC in terms of women's ability to pass their nationality to children, Nigerian women are however unable to pass their nationality to their foreign spouses. This is a violation of the CEDAW.[54]

3.2.1.3 1990 Convention on the Rights of the Child

The Convention on the Rights of the Child[55] (hereinafter CRC) was adopted by resolution 44/25 of 20 November 1989 at the 44th session of the General

---

48 *Ibid* Art. 8.
49 UN Treaty Collection *Optional Protocol to CEDAW* https://treaties.un.org/pages/ViewDetails.aspx?src=TREATY&mtdsg_no=IV-8-b&chapter=4&lang=en (accessed 10 Decemeber 2018).
50 'Even though Nigeria has shown a sustained compliance with the provisions of Article 18 of the CEDAW Convention in submitting the statutory periodic reports, its failure to domesticate the Convention has remained a source of concern on the extent of its commitment to women's rights protection.'
    Women's UN Report Network (WUNRN) 'Nigeria – Consideration of Bill to Domesticate CEDAW' http://wunrn.com/2006/08/nigeria-consideration-of-bill-to-domesticate-cedaw/ (accessed 26 April 2018).
51 As of September 2020, there are 189 State parties to the Convention.
52 RJ Cook 'Reservations to the Convention on the Elimination of All Forms of Discrimination against Women' (1990) 30 (3) *Virginia Journal of International Law* 664.
53 R Govil and A Edwards 'Women, nationality and statelessness: The problem of unequal rights' in A Edwards & L Van Waas (Eds.) *Nationality and statelessness under international law* 169–193.
54 It is important to note that Nigeria is one of the few States that did not make any reservations to the Articles of the CEDAW.
55 United Nations *Treaty Series* vol. 1577, 3; depositary notifications C.N.147.1993. Article 1 of the CRC defines a child thus: 'For the purposes of the present Convention, a child means

Legal and Policy Framework on Nationality and Statelessness 55

Assembly of the United Nations[56] and entered into force on 2 September 1990, 'thirty days after the date of deposit of the twentieth instrument of ratification, as provided for in its article 49.'[57] In 1978, Poland initiated the process for a legally binding child right's instrument that would be binding on States when its representative submitted a draft Convention to the United Nations Commission on Human Rights.[58] 'It is also worth mentioning that, following the initiative of a Pole – Ludwik Rajchman – in 1946, the United Nations General Assembly created UNICEF.'[59] Today, the CRC is the most ratified human rights treaty in the world with 140 signatories and a total of 196 parties as of September 2020. Nigeria ratified the CRC on 19 April 1991.[60]

The CRC defines a child as 'every human being below the age of eighteen years unless under the law applicable to the child, majority is attained earlier.'[61] Through the Convention, States commit to 'ensure that the child is protected against all forms of discrimination or punishment on the basis of the status' of the parents,[62] and ensure respect for the economic, social, and cultural rights of children through the establishment of standards for achieving health, education, legal, civil, and social services for children.[63]

More importantly, the CRC provides for the right of a child to be registered and acquire nationality immediately after birth.[64] However, the Convention did not specify the nationality to which a child should have a right.[65] The obligation imposed under the Convention on the Reduction of Statelessness 1961 specifically calls on States to grant nationality automatically at birth (by operation of law) or

---

every human being below the age of eighteen years unless under the law applicable to the child, majority is attained earlier.'

56 UN Treaty Collection *Op cit.* See also, *Official Records of the General Assembly, Forty-fourth Session, Supplement No. 49 (A/44/49)*, 166.

57 UN Audio Visual Library of International Law, *Convention on the Rights of the Child New York, 20 November 1989* http://legal.un.org/avl/ha/crc/crc.html (accessed 25 April 2018).

58 L Krappmann 'The weight of the child's view (Article 12 of the Convention on the Rights of the Child)' (2020) 18 *International Journal of Children's Rights* 503; Humanium 'The beginnings of the Convention on the Rights of the Child' https://www.humanium.org/en/convention/beginnings/ (accessed 10 December 2018).

59 Poland was always in the forefront of the protection of the rights of the child, 'the delegates of Poland actively participated in the process of drafting the Declaration of the Rights of the Child, which was adopted by the United Nations in 1959.'

   Office of the United Nations High Commissioner for Human Rights, *Legislative History of the Convention on the Rights of the Child* (2007) 1 HR/PUB/07/1/ xxxvii.

60 UN Treaty Collection *Op Cit.*

61 Convention on the Rights of the Child 1990 Art. 1.

62 *Ibid* Art. 2.

63 *Ibid* Arts. 4, 19, 26 and 37; UN Audio Visual Library of International Law *Convention on the Rights of the Child, Op Cit.*

64 *Ibid* Art. 7.

65 See G-R de Groot 'Children, their right to a nationality and child statelessness' in A Edwards and L Van Waas (Eds.) *Nationality and statelessness under international law* (2014) 114–168.

56 *Legal and Policy Framework on Nationality and Statelessness*

by lodging an application on behalf of the child per their municipal laws for children born in their territory who would otherwise be stateless.[66] However, 'the obligation imposed by Article 7(2) of the CRC is not exclusively directed to the country of birth of a child, but to all countries with which the child has a link by way of parentage, residence or place of birth.'[67] The implication is, a State that does not apply *jus soli* may not grant nationality at birth to a child born in its territory if there is a remote possibility of the child acquiring another nationality, particularly of any of the parents.

It is important to ensure that children are immediately able to acquire the nationality of the State wherein they were born, especially where there is no possibility of the child to acquire the nationality of any other State, including the nationality of the parents. The forgoing safeguard is necessary for municipal laws, considering that the absence of nationality seriously affects a child's ability to enjoy basic rights, including rights to healthcare, education and social protection, and prevention of childhood statelessness.[68]

A joint study conducted by UNHCR and UNICEF in 2017 reveals that about '29% of all States have no provision in their nationality laws to grant nationality to stateless children born on their territory or of unknown origin found on their territory.'[69] This statistic includes Nigeria as it currently has no law in place to grant nationality to stateless children born in its territory. Nigeria is a party to the CRC,[70] and compliant with most of the provisions of the CRC, especially on universal birth registration.[71] It is however not compliant with the very essential obligation in the Convention which obliges States to 'ensure the implementation of the rights set out in the Convention, in particular where the child would *otherwise be stateless.*'[72] As earlier discussed in Chapter 1 of this book, there is no protection safeguard in any legislation[73] in Nigeria to prevent statelessness of a foundling or of a child born to foreign parents on Nigerian territory who would otherwise be stateless.

3.2.2 *International Law on Prevention of Statelessness*

3.2.2.1 *The 1954 Convention Relating to the Status of Stateless Persons*

In August 1949, an *ad hoc* committee of representatives of 13 governments to consider among others the 'means of eliminating the problem of statelessness'

---

66 *Convention on the Reduction of Statelessness* 1961, Art. 1.
67 See G-R de Groot 'Children, their right to a nationality and child statelessness' *Op Cit.*
68 UNHCR & UNICEF, *Convention on the Rights of the Child: Quick reference guide statelessness and human rights treaties* (2017) 1.
69 *Ibid.*
70 Nigeria signed the CRC on 26 January 1990, and ratified the Convention on 19 April 1991.
71 Convention of the Rights of the Child 1990, Art. 7(1).
72 *Ibid* Art. 7(2).
73 Neither the Child Rights Act, the Immigration Act, nor the 1999 Constitution of Nigeria makes any provision to guarantee the right to nationality of foundlings in Nigeria.

Legal and Policy Framework on Nationality and Statelessness   57

was appointed by the Economic and Social Council (Hereinafter ECOSOC).[74] With the recommendations of the committee which include, amongst others, that States 're-examine their nationality laws with a view to reducing so far as possible cases of statelessness which arise from the operation of such laws,' and that the International Law Commission (hereinafter ILC) put together an agreement or convention for the elimination of Statelessness, the ILC decided to initiate the task with the topic 'Nationality, including statelessness' by appointing Manley O. Hudson, as Special Rapporteur for the study.[75]

By the end of 1950, the Office of United Nations High Commissioner for Refugees (UNHCR) had been established,[76] The UNHCR offered assistance in the study. The process was also supported by 'Dr. Paul Weis who joined the Special Rapporteur (Manley O. Hudson, a United States lawyer and former judge of the Permanent Court of International Justice) at Harvard for some seven weeks in October–November 1951.'[77] At the July 1951 conference of plenipotentiaries to consider both refugee and statelessness matters, the 1951 Convention relating to the Status of Refugees was adopted, while the draft Protocol relating to the Status of Stateless Persons was postponed.[78] Rather States were asked to share comments on those aspects of the 1951 Convention they considered appropriate to extend to non-refugee stateless persons.[79]

In 1952, with the resignation of Mr. Manley O. Hudson due to health reasons, the ILC appointed Mr. Roberto Córdova as the new Special Rapporteur on the topic of nationality, including statelessness. Mr. Roberto Córdova submitted the two draft Conventions (one on elimination of future statelessness and the

---

74 UN Codification Division Publications 'United Nations conference on the elimination or reduction of future statelessness (Geneva, 24 March to 18 April 1959 and New York, 15–28 August 1961)' https://legal.un.org/diplomaticconferences/1959_statelessness/ (accessed 25 August 2020); T Bloom *Problematizing the conventions on statelessness, UNU-GCM Policy Report 02/01, United Nations University Institute on Globalization, Culture and Mobility (UNU-GCM)* (2013) 8.

75 UN Codification Division Publications, *Op Cit.*

76 The mandate of the Office of the UNHCR at that time was only for protection of stateless persons who were refugees. See Refugee Convention 1951, Art. 1(a)(2). See also Statute of UNHCR, para. 6(a)(II).

77 G Goodwin-Gill *Convention on the reduction of statelessness* (2011) United Nations Audiovisual Library of International Law 1 http://legal.un.org/avl/pdf/ha/crs/crs_e.pdf (accessed 17 April 2018).

78 UNHCR, *Information and Accession Package: The 1954 Convention Relating to the Status of Stateless Persons and the 1961 Convention on the Reduction of Statelessness* (rev. ed. 1999) 7; UN Treaty Collections, 'Convention relating to the status of refugees Geneva, 28 July 1950' https://treaties.un.org/pages/ViewDetailsII.aspx?src=TREATY&mtdsg_no=V-2&chapter=5&Temp=mtdsg2&clang=_en#:~:text=The%20Convention%20was%20adopted%20by,Nations%20on%2014%20December%201950 (accessed 25 August 2020).

79 C Batchelor 'The 1954 Convention Relating to the Status of Stateless Persons: Implementation within the European Union Member States and recommendations for harmonization' (2005) 22 (2) *Refugee: Refugees and Stateless Persons in Limbo* 34 https://refuge.journals.yorku.ca/index.php/refuge/article/view/21330 (accessed 18 April 2018). See also Convention relating to the Status of Refugees, 28 July 1951, 189 U.N.T.S. 2545, 137.

58   Legal and Policy Framework on Nationality and Statelessness

other on the reduction of future statelessness) to the ILC in 1953. The ILC thereafter invited governments to submit their comments on the documents.[80] In 1954, the Convention Relating to the Status of Stateless Persons (hereinafter 1954 Convention) was finally adopted at the Conference on the Status of Stateless Persons of the United Nations, held at the Headquarters of the United Nations in New York from 13 to 23 September 1954.[81] On the historic link between the 1951 Refugee Convention and the 1954 Statelessness Convention, the UNHCR and IPU note that:

> Historically, refugees and stateless persons both received protection and assistance from the international refugee organizations that preceded UNHCR. The draft Protocol on Statelessness was intended to reflect this link between refugees and stateless persons. But the urgent needs of refugees and the impending dissolution of the International Refugee Organization meant that there was not sufficient time for a detailed analysis of the situation of stateless persons at the 1951 Conference of Plenipotentiaries that had been convened to consider both issues.[82]

While there was much focus and attention on the situation of refugees even before the adoption of the refugee convention, the statelessness situation did not receive much attention, partly because of its invisible nature.[83] 'Since the 1950s and 1960s when the two main UN statelessness conventions were adopted the issue of statelessness [was] practically forgotten for long decades, having been largely absent from the global human rights agenda.'[84] Nevertheless, since the dissolution of the former Soviet Union in the 1990s, which resulted in large scale statelessness in Europe, the issue of statelessness began to receive the needed attention.[85]

---

80 Yearbook of The International Law Commission 1953 Volume II. *Nationality, Including Statelessness. Document A/CN.4/64 Report on the elimination or reduction of statelessness* (1953) 167–195 and at 221; T Bloom *Op Cit* 8.

81 UN Treaty Collection *United Nations Treaty Series* vol. 360, 117; See also, Official Records of the Economic and Social Council, 17th Session, Supplement, No. 1 (E/2596) 12.
    As of September 2020, there are 94 State parties to the 1954 Convention.
    See UN Treaty Collection https://treaties.un.org/Pages/ViewDetailsII.aspx?src =TREATY&mtdsg_no=V-3&chapter=5&Temp=mtdsg2&clang=_en (accessed 5 September 2020).

82 UNHCR and Inter Parliamentary Union (IPU) *Nationality and statelessness: A handbook for parliamentarians no 11* (2005) 10.

83 T Bloom *Problematizing the conventions on statelessness, Op Cit* 7:
    'Indeed, one commentator describes the situation for stateless persons as a continuing blind spot on the international community's agenda.'

84 See T Molnár 'Remembering the forgotten: International legal regime protecting the stateless persons—stocktaking and new tendencies' (2014) 11 *US-China Law Review* 825. See also M Fullerton 'Without protection: Refugees and statelessness, a commentary and challenge' (2013) *Brooklyn Law School Legal Studies Research Papers, Working Paper Series, Research Paper No. 351* 2.

85 UNHCR and Open Society Justice Initiative Report *Citizen of nowhere: Solution for the stateless in the U.S.* (2012) 13.

The 1954 Stateless Convention is very similar to the 1951 Refugee Convention in terms of rights.[86] Despite the similarities and historic relationship between the two Conventions, the protection regime in the 1951 Convention is stronger than that of the 1954 Convention.[87] The 1954 Convention aims to ensure that stateless persons enjoy minimum standards of treatment with respect to their human rights, including establishing a definition for statelessness.[88] The 1954 Convention offers the most extensive rights for stateless persons at the international level,[89] regulating the status of stateless persons who are not refugees.[90] The 1954 Convention and the Convention on the Reduction of Statelessness 1961 (hereinafter 1961 Convention)[91] are the principal international instruments for the protection of statelessness.[92] Moreover, the 1954 Convention provides for a range of rights to which stateless persons are entitled, including standards of treatment of stateless persons.[93] These rights range from non-discrimination,[94] the right to property,[95] the right to employment,[96] and the right to access to documentation, such as birth certificates and travel documents, amongst others.[97]

The foregoing rights enable stateless persons to be useful not just to themselves, but also to the society in which they live, ensuring solidarity and national stability.[98] However, for stateless refugees, they are protected under the Convention

---

'In 1995 UNHCR's Executive Committee adopted a conclusion on the Prevention and Reduction of Statelessness and the Protection of Stateless Persons. The United Nations General Assembly then took up the issue in its "omnibus" resolution on UNHCR of the same year. This resolution established a truly global mandate for UNHCR on statelessness.'

    M Manly 'UNHCR's mandate and activities to address statelessness' in A Edwards & L Van Waas (Eds.) *Nationality and statelessness under international law* (88–115).

86 A de Chickera 'The protection of stateless persons in detention under international law' (2009) *The Equal Rights Trust (ERT) Legal Working Paper* 5.

87 T Molnár *Op Cit* 830.

88 L Van Waas 'The UN statelessness conventions' *Op Cit* 71; UNHCR 'UN Conventions on Statelessness' https://www.unhcr.org/un-conventions-on-statelessness.html (accessed 5 February 2019).

89 UNHCR *Introductory Note by the Office of the United Nations High Commissioner for Refugees (UNHCR) on the 1954 Convention Relating to the Status of Stateless Persons* (1954) 3 https://www.unhcr.org/ibelong/wp-content/uploads/1954-Convention-relating-to-the -Status-of-Stateless-Persons_ENG.pdf (accessed 14 June 2022).

90 UNHCR *Protecting the rights of stateless persons: The 1954 Convention relating to the Status of Stateless Persons* (2014) 3; C Batchelor *Op Cit* 9.

91 United Nations *Treaty Series* vol. 989, 175.

92 M Manly *Op Cit* 93.

93 M Foster and H Lambert 'Statelessness as a human rights issue: A concept whose time has come' (2016) 28 (4) *International Journal of Refugee Law* 566; UNHCR *Protecting the Rights of Stateless Persons, Op Cit* 3.

94 See Convention Relating to the Status of Stateless Persons 1954 Arts. 3 & 6.

95 *Ibid* Arts. 13 & 14.

96 *Ibid* Arts. 17 & 18.

97 *Ibid* Arts. 27 & 28.

98 UNHCR *Objectives and key provisions of the 1954 Convention relating to the Status of Stateless Persons* (2001) http://www.unhcr.org/protection/statelessness/3bd7d3394/objectives

60 *Legal and Policy Framework on Nationality and Statelessness*

Relating to the Status of Refugees 1951.[99] The UNHCR advises that 'when an applicant raises both a refugee and a statelessness claim, it is important that each claim is assessed and that both types of status are explicitly recognised' considering that protection under the refugee convention guarantees better protection.[100]

One of the key elements of the 1954 Convention is the definition of a stateless person. According to it, 'the term stateless person means a person who is not considered as a national by any State under the operation of its law.'[101] This definition of statelessness has been adopted in several treaties, international and national human rights instruments, and has now obtained the status of customary international law.[102] With regard to the absence of the principle of *non-refoulement*[103] in the text of the Convention, the UNHCR stated that 'the Final Act of the Convention indicates that *non-refoulement* in relation to danger of persecution is a generally accepted principle. The drafters, therefore, did not feel it necessary to enshrine this in the articles of a Convention geared toward regulating the status of *de jure* stateless persons.'[104] However, the Convention obliges States to facilitate the assimilation and naturalization of stateless persons, ensure an expedited naturalization process, and reduce the charges and costs of such proceedings as much as possible.[105]

Concerning the subsequent Convention on the Reduction of Statelessness, Guy S. Goodwin-Gill asserts that 'the reduction and elimination of statelessness, however, were to require further international cooperation and the coordination

---

-key-provisions-1954-convention-relating-status-stateless-persons.html (accessed 19 April 2018).

99 C Batchelor *Op Cit* 9.

100 UNHCR *Handbook on protection of stateless persons* (2014) 31 at para. 78.

101 Convention Relating to the Status of Stateless Persons 1954, Art. 1.

102 K Bianchini 'Protecting stateless persons: The implementation of the Convention Relating to the Status of Stateless Persons across EU States' (2018) 11 *International Refugee Law Series* 74; M Foster and H Lambert *Op Cit* 566. As noted earlier, scholars have criticized the definition for been too restrictive, limiting the definition of who a stateless person is to just *de jure* statelessness.

103 *Refoulement* is a French word meaning to 'push back' or 'send back.' *Non-refoulement* is a fundamental principle of international law which forbids a country receiving asylum seekers from returning them to the country where they would likely be in danger of persecution based on their race, religion, nationality, membership of a particular social group, or political opinion.

104 With regards to *de facto* statelessness:

'The Final Act of the Convention recommends that each Contracting State, when it recognises as valid the reasons for which a person has renounced the protection of the State of which he is a national, consider sympathetically the possibility of according to the person the treatment which the convention accords to stateless persons. This recommendation was included on behalf of de facto stateless persons who, technically, still held a nationality but did not receive any of the benefits generally associated with nationality, such as national protection.'

UNHCR *Objectives and key provisions of the 1954 Convention relating to the Status of Stateless Persons* (2001).

105 1954 Convention Art. 32.

Legal and Policy Framework on Nationality and Statelessness 61

and harmonisation of national laws. This was to be the goal set for the International Law Commission and its work towards the 1961 Convention on the Reduction of Statelessness.'[106] The work of the ILC also resulted in setting the stage for the 1961 Convention on the Reduction of Statelessness.[107]

3.2.2.2 *The 1961 Convention on the Reduction of Statelessness*

Pursuant to General Assembly resolution 896 (IX) of 4 December 1954, the 1961 Convention on the Reduction of Statelessness (hereinafter 1961 Convention) was adopted and opened for signature by the United Nations Conference on the Elimination or Reduction of Future Statelessness. The 1961 Convention, which was adopted on 30 August 1961, was preceded by the Conference meetings of 24 March to 18 April 1959 at the European Office of the United Nations at Geneva and at the Headquarters of the United Nations at New York from 15 to 28 August 1961. The 1961 Convention entered into force on 13 December 1975.[108] The 1961 Convention was enacted as a complement to the 1954 Convention, but with a specific focus on reduction and avoidance of statelessness.[109]

The main aim of the 1961 Convention is the provision of safeguards for the reduction, prevention, and avoidance of statelessness.[110] While the 1961 Convention does not interfere with how a State decides who its nationals are, nor how nationality is deprived or lost, it however has some legal guarantees on avoidance of statelessness or against creating a statelessness situation with such discretion.[111] The discretion of States to deprive nationality must meet certain criteria or international standards. For instance, arbitrary deprivation of nationality

---

106 G Goodwin-Gill *Op Cit* 5.
107 See the UN *Yearbook of the International Law Commission 1961. Summary records of the 13th session 1 May–7 July 1961* (1961) 293 at para. 68.
108 United Nations *Treaty Series* vol. 989, 175.
109 UNHCR's *Introductory note in Text of the 1961 Convention on the Reduction of Statelessness* (1961) 3.
110 L van Waas 'The UN statelessness conventions' *Op Cit* 71; UNHCR 'UN Conventions on Statelessness' *Op Cit*. The following is a summary of the major Articles which focus on the obligation of States to prevent statelessness: Articles 1–4 of the Convention focus on the granting of nationality at birth to avoid cases of statelessness, Articles 5–7 of the Convention focus on the regulation of loss or renunciation of nationality, Articles 8–9 on the regulation of deprivation of nationality, while Article 10 regulates the issue of transfer of territory. See UNHCR *Objectives and key provisions of the 1961 Convention on the Reduction of Statelessness* (2001) https://www.unhcr.org/protection/statelessness/3bd7d3914 /objectives-key-provisions-1961-convention-reduction-statelessness.html (accessed 21 January 2021).
111 See Convention on the Reduction of Statelessness 1961, Art. 8(1) provides 'A Contracting State shall not deprive a person of its nationality if such deprivation would render him stateless'; L Bucken and G-R de Groot 'Deprivation of nationality under article 8 (3) of the 1961 Convention on the reduction of statelessness' (2018) 25 (1) *Maastricht Journal of European and Comparative Law* 40.

62 Legal and Policy Framework on Nationality and Statelessness

by States is restricted by customary international law and general principles of law, and other relevant international treaties,[112] apart from the 1961 Convention.[113]

As of September 2020, there are five signatories and a total of 75 parties to the 1961 Convention,[114] despite the very relevance of this Convention for the reduction of statelessness which is a big issue today. Nigeria acceded to both the 1954 Convention Relating to Status of Stateless Persons and the 1961 Convention on the Prevention and Reduction of Statelessness in 2011.[115]

3.2.2.3 Other Relevant International Law Instruments

As mentioned earlier, although the 1954 Convention Relating to the Status of Stateless Persons and the 1961 Convention on the Reduction of Statelessness are the principal conventions on the issue of statelessness, there are other complementary international human rights instruments on the issue of statelessness.[116] Another international human rights instrument that addresses the right to a nationality is the 1966 International Covenant on Civil and Political Rights (hereinafter ICCPR),[117] which is one of 'the two treaties that give legal force to the Universal Declaration of Human Rights (the other being the International Covenant on Economic, Social and Cultural Rights, (hereinafter ICESCR).'[118] On the relevance of the ICCPR for the protection of stateless persons, the Institute of Statelessness and Inclusion (ISI) notes thus:

It is important to note that 'the 1930 Hague Convention on Certain Questions relating to the Conflict of Nationality Laws was the first international treaty to enshrine general rules on the avoidance and reduction of statelessness.'

G-R de Groot 'Survey on rules on loss of nationality in international treaties and case law' *Op Cit* 3.

112 Organization for Security and Co-Operation in Europe (OSCE) and UNHCR *Handbook on statelessness in the OSCE area: International standards and good practices* (2017) 29. Article 1 of the 1930 Hague Convention on Certain Questions Relating to the Conflict of Nationality Laws provides that 'it is for each State to determine under its own law who are its nationals. This law shall be recognised by other States in so far as it is consistent with international conventions, international custom, and the principles of law generally recognised with regard to nationality.' On the limitation on deprivation of nationality, an example is Universal Declaration of Human Rights, Art. 15(2) which provides 'No one shall be arbitrarily deprived of his nationality nor denied the right to change his nationality.'

113 See 1961 Convention Art. 8.

114 UN Treaties Collection *Op Cit.*

115 *Ibid*; Submission by the United Nations High Commissioner for Refugees (UNHCR) Nigeria For the Office of the High Commissioner for Human Rights' Compilation Report – Universal Periodic Review 2012 1.

116 UNHCR 'UN Conventions on Statelessness' *Op Cit.*

117 United Nations *Treaty Series* vol. 999, 171 and vol. 1057, 407. As of September 2020, the ICCPR currently has 173 State parties; Nigeria acceded to it 29 July 1993.

118 Seton Hall Law 'International law: International human rights' https://shlawlibrary.libguides.com/IntLaw/HumanRights (accessed 10 September 2020).

'The ICCPR is "one of the three instruments which constitutes what is sometimes known as the 'International Bill of Rights.'"'

The ICCPR is relevant to statelessness in two fundamental ways: first, it provides certain protections with respect to the right to a nationality and the non-discriminatory enjoyment of this right; second, it provides for the protection of fundamental civil and political rights by all persons – regardless of nationality or statelessness – including the right to life, freedom of religion, freedom of speech, freedom of assembly, and rights to due process and a fair trial. Implementation is monitored by the Human Rights Committee, a body of independent experts that meets three times annually in Geneva.[119]

Article 24 of the ICCPR provides for the right of every child to be registered immediately after birth, including the right to a name and acquisition of nationality. However, this provision is not to be interpreted as an obligation of States to grant nationality to every child born on its territory. In clarifying this provision of the ICCPR, at the 35th session of the Human Rights Committee, on 7 April 1989,[120] it was noted thus:

> Special attention should also be paid, in the context of the protection to be granted to children, to the right of every child to acquire a nationality, as provided for in article 24, paragraph 3. While the purpose of this provision is to prevent a child from being afforded less protection by society and the State because he is stateless, it does not necessarily make it an obligation for States to give their nationality to every child born in their territory. However, States are required to adopt every appropriate measure, both internally and in cooperation with other States, to ensure that every child has a nationality when he is born. In this connection, no discrimination with regard to the acquisition of nationality should be admissible under internal law as between legitimate children and children born out of wedlock or of stateless parents or based on the nationality status of one or both of the parents. The measures adopted to ensure that children have a nationality should always be referred to in reports by States parties.[121]

Another relevant international human rights instrument is the 1957 Convention on the Nationality of Married Women (hereinafter CNMW)[122] which reemphasizes the provisions in Article 15 of the Universal Declaration of Human

---

A Conte and R Burchill *Defining civil and political rights: The jurisprudence of the United Nations Human Rights Committee* (2009) 1 http://ebookcentral.proquest.com/lib/uunl/detail.action?docID=438372 (accessed 27 April 2018).

119 Institute of Statelessness and Inclusion (ISI) 'Statelessness and human rights' http://www.statelessnessandhumanrights.org/other-human-rights-frameworks/the-international-covenant-on-civil-and-political-rights-iccpr (accessed 27 April 2018).

120 OHCHR *CCPR General Comment No. 17: Article 24 (Rights of the child)* Adopted at the 35th session of the Human Rights Committee, on 7 April 1989.

121 *Ibid* Art. 8.

122 Convention on the Nationality of Married Women, 309 U.N.T.S. 65, entered into force 11 August 1958.

64 Legal and Policy Framework on Nationality and Statelessness

Rights, by recognizing that 'everyone has the right to a nationality' and that 'no one shall be arbitrarily deprived of his nationality nor denied the right to change his nationality.'[123] In the CNMW, States commit to promote 'universal respect for, and observance of, human rights and fundamental freedoms for all without distinction as to sex.'[124] Relevant Articles of the CNMW makes provisions to ensure that neither marriage, dissolution of marriage, nor acquisition, renunciation or change of nationality of a husband should affect the nationality of a wife.[125] The 1965 Convention on the Elimination of All Forms of Racial Discrimination (hereinafter CERD)[126] is another relevant instrument on the right to nationality. Articles 2, 3, 4, and 5 particularly prohibit discrimination of all forms without distinction as to race, colour, or national or ethnic origin. In addition, Article 5 specifically prohibits discrimination with regard to access to nationality. Additionally, the 1996 Convention on the Rights of Persons with Disabilities (CRPD) in its Article 18 stresses the need for States to ensure that persons with disabilities 'have the right to acquire and change a nationality and are not deprived of their nationality arbitrarily or on the basis of disability.'

3.3 Regional Frameworks on the Right to Nationality and Prevention of Statelessness

Drawing inspiration from the international frameworks on nationality and protection of stateless persons, the advocacy for States and regions to 'adopt nationality legislation with a view to reducing statelessness, consistent with fundamental principles of international law,'[127] several regional frameworks have been put in place to protect, identify, reduce, and prevent statelessness globally.

---

123 *Ibid*, Preamble.

124 *Ibid*.

125 Article 1: Each Contracting State agrees that neither the celebration nor the dissolution of a marriage between one of its nationals and an alien, and the change of nationality by the husband during marriage, shall automatically affect the nationality of the wife.

    Article 2: Each Contracting State agrees that neither the voluntary acquisition of the nationality of another State nor the renunciation of its nationality by one of its nationals shall prevent the retention of its nationality by the wife of such national.

    Article 3(1): Each Contracting State agrees that the alien wife of one of its nationals may, at her request, acquire the nationality of her husband through specially privileged naturalization procedures; the grant of such nationality may be subject to such limitations as may be imposed in the interests of national security or public policy. (2): Each Contracting State agrees that the present Convention shall not be construed as affecting any legislation or judicial practice by which the alien wife of one of its nationals may, at her request, acquire her husband's nationality as a matter of right.

126 United Nations *Treaty Series* vol. 660, 195. The Convention was adopted by the General Assembly of the United Nations in resolution 2106 (XX) of 21 December 1965. As at the time of writing, it has 179 State parties. Nigeria acceded to it on 16 October 1967

127 Executive Committee of the High Commissioner's Programme 46th session. Contained in United Nations General Assembly Document A/AC.96/860 and document no. 12A (A/50/12/Add.1). *Prevention and Reduction of Statelessness and the Protection of Stateless*

Legal and Policy Framework on Nationality and Statelessness   65

This section, therefore, examines some of the regional frameworks across the world, it is broken into rules on nationality and prevention of statelessness in the EU and the Council of Europe (CoE) for the European States, the Organization of American States (OAS) for the Americas, the Arab League for the Arabs and the African Union (AU) rules for the African States. As mentioned earlier in the introduction to this chapter, apart from the AU rules, ECOWAS rules are also be examined for reasons first above mentioned.

3.3.1 Europe

3.3.1.1 The European Union and the Council of Europe Legal Framework on Right to Nationality and Prevention of Statelessness

This section is divided into two parts, one part on EU Law and the other on the Council of Europe (hereinafter CoE) on nationality and prevention of statelessness. Before going further, it is important to distinguish the CoE from the EU.

The CoE is a regional organization with its headquarters in Strasbourg. It was founded on 5 May 1949 to promote democracy, human rights, and the rule of law in Europe. As Europe's leading international human rights organization, the CoE is comprised of 47 member States, with 27 of them also members of the European Union.[128] On the other hand, the European Union (EU) was founded in 1951 by six European States, namely Belgium, Germany, France, Italy, Luxembourg, and the Netherlands. Today, it comprises of 27 member States[129] who have 'delegated some of their *competence on certain matters* so that decisions on specific matters of joint interest can be made democratically at European level. No country has ever joined the EU without first belonging to the Council of Europe.'[130] On the difference between EU law and Council law, Florence Benoît-Rohmer and Heinrich Klebes note:

> Unlike EU law, the Council law is not a full-scale legal system, since it cannot be regarded as independent of international law – but it forms a coherent whole, based on the Council's founding charter, or Statute.[131]

    Persons No. 78 (XLVI) – 1995 http://www.unhcr.org/excom/exconc/3ae68c443f/prevention-reduction-statelessness-protection-stateless-persons.html (accessed 20 April 2018).

128 Council of Europe 'Do not get confused' https://www.coe.int/en/web/about-us/do-not-get-confused?desktop=true (accessed 5 July 2018); See CoE website https://www.coe.int/en/web/about-us/who-we-are; and International Democracy Watch (IDW) website via http://www.internationaldemocracywatch.org/index.php/council-of-europe (accessed 10 September 2020).

129 See European Union website https://europa.eu/european-union/about-eu/countries_en and https://ec.europa.eu/neighbourhood-enlargement/policy/from-6-to-27-members_en (accessed 10 September 2020).

130 Council of Europe 'Do not get confused' *Op Cit.*

131 F Benoît-Rohmer and H Klebes 'Council of Europe law: Towards a pan-European legal area' (2005) *Council of Europe* 11 http://www.supremecourt.ge/files/upload-file/pdf/coelaweng.pdf (accessed 5 July 2018).

66 *Legal and Policy Framework on Nationality and Statelessness*

On the similarities between the CoE and the EU, it is important to note:

> The Council of Europe and the European Union share the same fundamental values – human rights, democracy and the rule of law – but are separate entities which perform different, yet complementary, roles [...] The European Union refers to those same European values as a key element of its deeper political and economic integration processes. It often builds upon Council of Europe standards when drawing up legal instruments and agreements which apply to its 28 member states. Furthermore, the European Union regularly refers to Council of Europe standards and monitoring work in its dealings with neighbouring countries, many of which are Council of Europe member states.[132]

3.3.1.2 EU Law

The 2007 Lisbon Treaty states that 'stateless persons shall be treated as third-country nationals'[133] in the EU. This provision is seen as an important indication of the readiness of the EU to tackle the issue of statelessness and create a framework for the protection of stateless persons within the Union.[134] While some scholars are of the view that the EU does not have the competence to regulate the issue of nationality which is within the domain of member States, others by virtue of the statelessness provision of the Lisbon Treaty, believe that the EU has some competence on the matter[135] and should even do more in that regard.[136] Katja Swider notes that:

> The existing literature on statelessness in EU law assumes the lack of EU competence to pass legally binding legislation on statelessness (and nationality in general), and therefore concludes that the potential for EU involvement with statelessness is limited to soft-law measures. This assumption is, however, not entirely correct. It is true that Member States still retain nearly

---

132 Council of Europe 'The Council of Europe and the European Union: Different roles, shared values' https://www.coe.int/en/web/portal/european-union (accessed 5 July 2018).

'The Lisbon Treaty increased the scope for European Union action in many areas where the Council of Europe already has significant experience and expertise. This has led to increased cooperation on issues [...]. It has also opened the way for the European Union itself to sign up to the European Convention on Human Rights, and to other Council of Europe agreements.'

133 Treaty of Lisbon 2007 Art. 61(2).

134 G Gyulai 'Statelessness in the EU framework for international protection' (2012) 14 *European Journal of Migration and Law* 284.

135 K Konstantina 'Addressing statelessness in Greece under EU law' 3 http://wwww.lse.ac.uk/Hellenic-Observatory/Assets/Documents/HO-PhD-Symposia/The-9th-HO-PhD-Symposium/Symposium-Papers/Session-1/Migration-I-Security.pdf (accessed 17 September 2020).

136 See K Swider and M den Heijer 'Why union law can and should protect stateless persons' (2017) 19 (2) *European Journal of Migration and Law.*

complete sovereignty on granting and withdrawing nationality, and therefore the harmonization of EU rules on the reduction and prevention of statelessness through nationality laws would not be acceptable under the current treaty regime.[137]

It has been observed that there is no clear obligation to determine statelessness under the EU.[138] Therefore, the primacy of EU law in this regard is determined by each member State,[139] and member States are often very protective of their sovereignty in matters of nationality, particular from the inception of community citizenship.[140] Even the TFEU supports this position by stating that 'citizenship of the Union shall be additional to and not replace national citizenship.'[141] However, with the evolvement of EU legislation, stateless persons, including refugees are sometimes treated as third-country nationals.[142] It is important to note that the European Convention on Nationality which refers to the 1954 Convention's definition of statelessness[143] excludes *de facto* statelessness[144] which is equally deserving of protection.

3.3.1.3 The Treaty of Lisbon

There is no specific EU law on statelessness, save for some provisions in the Treaty on the Functioning of the European Union, providing some protection

---

137 K Swider 'Protection and identification of stateless persons through EU law' (2014) *SSRN Electronic Journal* 10. See also, G Gyulai *Op Cit* 284. See, T Molnár 'Stateless persons under international law and EU law: A comparative analysis concerning their legal status, with particular attention to the added value of the EU legal order' (2010) 51 *Acta Juridica Hungarica* 304 http://real.mtak.hu/44538/1/ajur.51.2010.4.4.pdf (accessed 21 June 2018).

138 See, C Vlieks 'Strategic litigation: An obligation for statelessness determination under the European Convention on Human Rights?' (2014) *Discussion Paper 09/14 on Strategic Litigation. A commissioned research by the European Network on Statelessness* (ENS) *with Support from Oak Foundation*; See also N Radnai 'Statelessness determination in Europe: Towards the implementation of regionally harmonised national SDPs' (2017) *Statelessness Working Paper Series No. 2017/08 Institute on Statelessness and Inclusion* 8 http://www.institutesi .org/WP2017_08.pdf (accessed 3 May 2018).

139 N Radnai *Ibid.* See also G Gaja 'European community and union law and domestic (municipal) law' in R Wolfrum (Ed.) *The Max Planck Encyclopedia of Public International Law* (2014).

140 K Swider and M den Heijer *Op Cit* 124.

141 TFEU Art. 20(1).

142 T Molnár 'Stateless persons under international law and EU law: A comparative analysis concerning their legal status, with particular attention to the added value of the EU legal order' *Op Cit* 300.

143 UNHCR and IPU *Nationality and statelessness: A handbook for parliamentarians* (2005).

144 'A de facto stateless person is normally regarded as a person who does possess a nationality, but does not possess the protection of his State of nationality and who resides outside the territory of that State, i.e., a person whose nationality is ineffective.'

P Weis 'The United Nations Convention on the Reduction of Statelessness, 1961' (1962) 11 (4) *The International and Comparative Law Quarterly* 1086.

68   *Legal and Policy Framework on Nationality and Statelessness*

measures for third-country nationals, particularly Articles 67(2) and 78(1), which make provision concerning the protection of third-country nationals, including stateless persons, which could be invoked with regard to prevention of statelessness within the EU.

Initially known as the Reform Treaty,[145] the Treaty of Lisbon which entered into force on 1 December 2009, amends the Treaty on European Union (hereinafter TEU or the Maastricht Treaty) and the Treaty Establishing the European Community (hereinafter TEC or EEC Treaty).[146] While the TEU retains its title, the EEC Treaty became the Treaty on the Functioning of the European Union (hereinafter TFEU or the Rome Treaty).[147] The TFEU provides for the organizational, institutional, functional, and procedural details of the EU.[148]

The main focus of this part is to assess the TFEU (or the Rome Treaty as it is sometimes called) as part of the Treaty of Lisbon, bearing in mind that the TFEU birthed the European Economic Community (hereinafter EEC) which is seen as a stepping stone or an essential part of politically united Europe and the creation of the EU.[149] The TFEU (then known as the EEC Treaty), which remains the legal basis for the EU and its institutions, was signed on 25 March 1957 in Rome by the following six founding members: Belgium, Germany, France, Italy, Luxembourg, and the Netherlands with the main aim of achieving an economic, social, and politically integrated Europe. The Treaty entered into force on 1 January 1958.[150] Unlike the TEU and EEC Treaties, the Lisbon Treaty 'specifically addresses the legal position of stateless persons,'[151] particularly Article 67(2) which obliges the Union to:

> frame a common policy on asylum, immigration and external border control, based on solidarity between Member States, which is fair towards third-country nationals. For the purpose of this Title, stateless persons shall be treated as third-country nationals.

---

145 European Commission 'Lisbon Treaty' https://ec.europa.eu/home-affairs/what-we-do/networks/european_migration_network/glossary_search/lisbon-treaty_en (accessed 30 September 2020).

146 *Ibid.*

147 See House of Commons Library 'The Treaty of Lisbon: amendments to the Treaty establishing the European community' (2007) *Research Paper 07/86 6 December 2007* Introductory page researchbriefings.files.parliament.uk/documents/RP07-86/RP07-86.pdf (accessed 14 May 2018).

148 See EUR-Lex 'Treaty on the Function of the European Union' https://eur-lex.europa.eu/legal-content/EN/TXT/?uri=LEGISSUM%3A4301854 (accessed 30 September 2020).

149 European Economic Community *A Handbook on the European Economic Community* (1965) viii & 1; E Allen 'What is the Treaty of Rome?' https://www.telegraph.co.uk/news/0/treaty-rome/ (accessed 14 May 2018).

150 EUR-Lex 'Treaty of Rome (EEC)' https://eur-lex.europa.eu/legal-content/EN/TXT/HTML/?uri=LEGISSUM:xy0023&from=EN (accessed 2 October 2020); E Allen *Op Cit.*

151 K Swider and M den Heijer *Op Cit* 127. See TFEU Art. 67(2).

Furthermore, Article 78(1) of TFEU provides that:

> The Union shall develop a common policy on asylum, subsidiary protection and temporary protection with a view to offering appropriate status to any third-country national requiring international protection and ensuring compliance with the principle of non-refoulement. This policy must be in accordance with the Geneva Convention of 28 July 1951 and the Protocol of 31 January 1967 relating to the status of refugees, and other relevant treaties.

The TFEU moreover in Article 79(1) obliges the Union to develop a common immigration policy aimed amongst other things at ensuring third-country nationals residing legally within the Union are treated fairly.[152] The foregoing provisions are consonant with the provisions of the 1954 Convention[153] and to a large extent offer protection guarantees to stateless persons within the EU. However, save for Article 67(2), which specifies that stateless persons shall be treated as third-country nationals, none of the provisions of the TFEU is specifically targeted at stateless persons (especially as not all stateless persons would meet the requirement of legal residence required of third-country nationals who may as well already enjoy protection through other EU legislation).[154] The principle of *non-refoulement* in Article 79 of the TFEU would only apply to stateless refugees, i.e., stateless persons with a well-founded fear of being persecuted in their countries of origin. This category of stateless person, although without legal residence, on the basis of such fears cannot be reasonably expected to return to their 'countries of origin' or habitual residence.

The combined effect of the above-mentioned provisions, especially Article 67 (which mentioned stateless persons) and Article 78 (which stipulates compliance with the refugee convention (principle of *non-refoulement*)) and other relevant provisions is that stateless persons in the EU should be accorded the same treatment as third-country nationals.

The TEU first introduced the European citizenship,[155] re-enacted or established in Article 20 of the TFEU. It was however clarified that nationality of a member State is the basis of being an EU citizen; the provision further states that citizenship of the EU shall only be an addition and not a replacement of national citizenship. Meaning EU citizenship is meant to complement that of member States, and the competence to regulate and determine nationality rests with member States, provided that this discretion is exercised with due regard

---

152 TFEU Art. 79(1).
153 1954 Convention Art. 7(1), which provides: 'Except where this Convention contains more favourable provisions, a Contracting State shall accord to stateless persons the same treatment as is accorded to aliens generally.'
154 K Swider and M den Heijer *Op Cit* 127–128.
155 See TEU (Maastricht Treaty), Art. 9.

70 Legal and Policy Framework on Nationality and Statelessness

to international law. Although Article 20 does not refer to stateless persons, the provision has however been applied in some EU Court of Justice (hereinafter ECJ) cases with regard to cases of deprivation or loss of nationality, which ultimately helps to prevent statelessness.

The principle of 'nationality of a member State' as a basis of EU citizenship was emphasized in the ECJ case of *Mario Vicente Micheletti and others v. Delegación del Gobiernoen Cantabria.*[156] In this case, the applicant, Mr. Micheletti, had dual Argentine and Italian nationality, having acquired the latter in accordance with Italian Law,[157] which provides that the child of an Italian mother or father is an Italian citizen. In 1989, the applicant, considering the idea of settling in Spain, applied to the Spanish authorities for a temporary Community residence card, submitting for that purpose a valid Italian passport issued by the Italian Consulate in Rosario, Argentina. The Spanish authorities issued him with a residence card for a validity period of six months. Before the expiration of the six months' validity, as a Community citizen, the applicant applied to the Spanish authorities for a permanent residence card in order to establish a dentistry office in Spain. That application and successive administrative appeal were dismissed pursuant to Article 9 of the Spanish Civil Code, which provides that 'in cases of dual nationality where neither nationality is Spanish, the nationality corresponding to the habitual residence of the person concerned before his arrival in Spain is to take precedence'; for the applicant, Argentina was considered as his country of habitual residence.

In his appeal for annulment of the decision of the Spanish authorities before the national court, 'the national court, considering that the solution of the dispute called for an interpretation of Community law, stayed the proceedings and referred the case to the court (ECJ) for a preliminary ruling' on the issue of EU law.[158] In its ruling, the ECJ noted *inter alia*:

> It must be borne in mind that Article 52 of the Treaty grants freedom of establishment to persons who are 'nationals of a Member State'. Under international law, it is for each Member State, having due regard to Community law, to lay down the conditions for the acquisition and loss of

---

156 Case C-369/90 European Court Reports 1992 I-04239.

157 Article 1 of Law No 555 of 13 June 1912 (*Gazzetta Ufficiale della Repubblica Italiana of 30 June 1912*), which, as amended by Article 5 of Law No 123 of 21 April 1983 (Gazzetta Ufficiale della Repubblica Italiana of 26 April 1983).

158 *Mario Vicente Micheletti and others v. Delegación del Gobiernoen Cantabria, Op Cit* para. 6, on the matter referred, the ECJ ruled thus:

> 'May Articles 3(c), 7, 52, 53 and 56 of the EEC Treaty, and Directive 73/148 and the relevant provisions of secondary law on the free movement of persons and freedom of establishment be interpreted as being compatible and thus as allowing the application of domestic legislation which does not recognize the 'Community rights' inherent in a person's status as a national of another Member State of the EEC merely because that person simultaneously possesses the nationality of a non-member country and that country was the place of his habitual residence, his last residence or his actual residence?'

Legal and Policy Framework on Nationality and Statelessness 71

nationality. However, it is not permissible for the legislation of a Member State to restrict the effects of the grant of the nationality of another Member State by imposing an additional condition for recognition of that nationality with a view to the exercise of the fundamental freedoms provided for in the Treaty. Consequently, it is not permissible to interpret Article 52 of the Treaty to the effect that, where a national of a Member State is also a national of a non-member country, the other Member States may make recognition of the status of Community national subject to a condition such as the habitual residence of the person concerned in the territory of the first Member State. That conclusion is reinforced by the fact that the consequence of allowing such a possibility would be that the class of persons to whom the Community rules on freedom of establishment were applied might vary from one Member State to another.

It is important to note that *Micheletti* is a 1992 pre-Union citizenship case. European citizenship was introduced the following year with the enactment of the TEU.[159] Similarly, in *Janko Rottman v. Freistaat Bayern*,[160] the applicant, Dr. Rottmann, was an Austrian by birth, born in Graz in the Republic of Austria. In 1995, there was an investigation concerning him on suspicion of fraud; after being heard in the *Landesgericht für Strafsachen Graz* (hereinafter the Criminal Court of Graz) where he denied the allegations, he transferred his residence to Munich, Germany. On account of the criminal case, in February 1997, the Criminal Court of Graz issued a warrant for the arrest of the applicant. In February 1998, the applicant applied for naturalization as a German national but failed to mention his criminal case back in Austria. In February 1999, the applicant was issued with a naturalization document dated 25 January 1999. By Austrian nationality law, acquiring a foreign nationality means that the applicant has lost his Austrian nationality.[161]

However, in August 1999, the Austrian authorities informed the city of Munich of the warrant for the arrest of Dr. Rottmann issued in Graz. In September 1999, the Austrian public prosecutor's office further informed the city of Munich, that 'the applicant in his criminal proceedings in Graz had already been questioned as an accused person before the *Landesgericht für Strafsachen* Graz in July 1995.' In July 2000, after allowing the applicant to be heard, 'the *Freistaat Bayern* withdrew the naturalisation with retroactive effect, on the

---

159 H van Eijken 'European citizenship and the competence of Member States to grant and to withdraw the nationality of their nationals' (2011) 27 (72) *Utrecht Journal of International and European Law* 66.

160 Case C-135/08.

161 'A person who acquires a foreign nationality upon his application, his declaration or his express consent loses the nationality if he was not granted the right to retain the nationality before.'

   Staatsbürgerschaftsgesetz, 'the StbG', BGBl. 311/1985 (Federal Law concerning Austrian Nationality) (1985) Art. 27(1).

72 *Legal and Policy Framework on Nationality and Statelessness*

grounds that the applicant had not disclosed the fact that he was the subject of judicial investigation in Austria and that he had, in consequence, obtained German nationality by deception. The withdrawal of his naturalisation obtained in Germany has not yet become definitive, by reason of the action for annulment of that decision brought by the applicant in the main proceedings.' On appeal by the applicant, the *Bayerischer Verwaltungsgerichtshof* (administrative court of the Land of Bavaria) in its judgment on 25 October 2005 held that:

> the withdrawal of the applicant's naturalisation on the basis of the first sentence of Article 48(1) of the Code of administrative procedure of the Land of Bavaria was compatible with German law, even though the effect of that withdrawal, once definitive, would be to render the person concerned stateless.

The applicant further appealed the decision of the administrative court of the Land of Bavaria, and the decision of the administrative court of Bavaria was upheld at appeal. According to the national court:

> It is not sufficiently clear whether the status of being stateless and the loss of citizenship of the Union validly acquired previously, linked to the withdrawal of naturalisation, is compatible with European Union law, in particular, with Article 17(1) EC.[162]

To be properly guided, the administrative court stayed the proceedings and referred the case to the ECJ for a preliminary ruling on two issues of law.[163] On

---

162 Now Article 20 TFEU:

> '(1) Citizenship of the Union is hereby established. Every person holding the nationality of a Member State shall be a citizen of the Union. Citizenship of the Union shall be additional to and not replace national citizenship.
>
> (2) Citizens of the Union shall enjoy the rights and be subject to the duties provided for in the Treaties. They shall have, *inter alia*:
>> (a) the right to move and reside freely within the territory of the Member States;
>> (b) the right to vote and to stand as candidates in elections to the European Parliament and in municipal elections in their Member State of residence, under the same conditions as nationals of that State;
>> (c) the right to enjoy, in the territory of a third country in which the Member State of which they are nationals is not represented, the protection of the diplomatic and consular authorities of any Member State on the same conditions as the nationals of that State;
>> (d) the right to petition the European Parliament, to apply to the European Ombudsman, and to address the institutions and advisory bodies of the Union in any of the Treaty languages and to obtain a reply in the same language.
>
> These rights shall be exercised in accordance with the conditions and limits defined by the Treaties and by the measures adopted thereunder.'

163 The issues referred to the EU Human Rights Court included:

> '(1) Is it contrary to Community law for Union citizenship (and the rights and fundamental freedoms attaching thereto) to be lost as the legal consequence of the fact that the withdrawal in one Member State (the Federal Republic of Germany), lawful as such

Legal and Policy Framework on Nationality and Statelessness 73

the issues brought before it, the court in its ruling held that 'It is not contrary to European Union law, in particular to Article 17 EC, for a Member State to withdraw from a citizen of the Union the nationality of that State acquired by naturalisation when that nationality was obtained by deception, on condition that the decision to withdraw observes the principle of proportionality.'[164]

Further on the competence of a State to determine its citizens, in the case of *the Queen v. Secretary of State for the Home Department, ex parte: Manjit Kaur*,[165] Ms. Kaur born in Kenya in 1949 to a family of Asian origin and became a citizen of the United Kingdom and Colonies by virtue of the British Nationality Act 1948. However, she did not fall within any of the 'categories of Citizens of the United Kingdom and Colonies recognised under the Immigration Act 1971 as having a right of residence in the United Kingdom. The British Nationality Act 1981 conferred on her the status of a British Overseas Citizen. As such, she has, in the absence of special authorisation, no right under national law to enter or remain in the United Kingdom.' As she had always done when she first entered the UK in 1990, having severally resided temporarily in British territory, in 1996 Ms. Kaur re-applied for leave to remain in the UK. By a decision of 22 January 1997, the application was refused by the Home Department. On 20 March 1997, Ms. Kaur decided to appeal to the High Court of Justice of England and Wales for judicial review of the decision. But this time, seeking to remain and obtain gainful employment in the UK, and move freely to other member States to purchase goods and services and, if necessary, seek work in the other member States.

Recognizing 'that the outcome of the proceedings before it depended on the interpretation of Community law, the High Court of Justice of England and Wales, Queen's Bench Division (Crown Office), decided to stay the proceedings

---

under national (German) law, of a naturalisation acquired by intentional deception, has the effect of causing the person concerned to become stateless because, as in the case of the applicant [in the main proceedings], he does not recover the nationality of another Member State (the Republic of Austria) which he originally possessed, by reason of the applicable provisions of the law of that other Member State?

(2) [If so,] must the Member State [...] which has naturalised a citizen of the Union and now intends to withdraw the naturalisation obtained by deception, having due regard to Community law, refrain altogether or temporarily from withdrawing the naturalisation if or so long as that withdrawal would have the legal consequence of loss of citizenship of the Union (and of the associated rights and fundamental freedoms) [...], or is the Member State [...] of the former nationality obliged, having due regard to Community law, to interpret and apply, or even adjust, its national law so as to avoid that legal consequence?'

164 Specifically, the court in answering the first question and the first part of the second question stated thus:

'that it is not contrary to European Union law, in particular to Article 17 EC, for a Member State to withdraw from a citizen of the Union the nationality of that State acquired by naturalisation when that nationality has been obtained by deception, on condition that the decision to withdraw observes the principle of proportionality.'

The court refrained from ruling on the second question which required it to rule on 'whether a decision not yet adopted is contrary to European Union law.'

165 Case C-192/99 European Court reports 2001.

74 Legal and Policy Framework on Nationality and Statelessness

and to refer the questions'[166] on Community law to the ECJ for a preliminary ruling. The ECJ in its ruling held *inter alia*:

> it is for each Member State, having due regard to Community law, to lay down the conditions for the acquisition and loss of nationality. On the basis of that principle of customary international law, the United Kingdom has, in the light of its imperial and colonial past, defined several categories of British citizens whom it has recognised as having rights which differ according to the nature of the ties connecting them to the United Kingdom. The United Kingdom has defined those rights in its domestic legislation, in particular in the Immigration Act 1971, which became applicable from 1 January 1973 the same date as that on which the Treaty on the Accession of the United Kingdom entered into force. That national legislation reserved the

166 The questions for determination include:

(1) When determining whether the Applicant, as a British Overseas Citizen not entitled (under United Kingdom law) to enter or remain in the United Kingdom, is a 'person holding the nationality of a Member State' and therefore is 'a citizen of the Union' for the purpose of Article 8 of the EC Treaty:

  1. What is the effect (if any) as a matter of Community law of
    a. the United Kingdom's 1972 Declaration 'on the definition of the term nationals' which was made at the time of Accession to the European Communities and annexed to the Final Act of the Accession Conference, and
    b. the United Kingdom's 1982 Declaration 'on the meaning of a UK national', and
    c. Declaration No 2 to the Treaty on European Union signed on 7 February 1992 that nationality is to be decided solely by reference to the national law of the Member State concerned and Member States may declare, for information, who are to be considered to be their nationals for Community purposes?

  2. If and to the extent that the United Kingdom is not entitled, as a matter of Community law, to rely on the Declarations referred to in (1) above, what are the relevant criteria for identifying whether a person has nationality of a Member State for the purposes of Article 8 where domestic law identifies various categories of nationality only some of which confer a right to enter and remain in that Member State?

  3. In this context, what is the effect of the principle of respect for fundamental human rights under Community law claimed by the Applicant, in particular where the Applicant relies on Article 3(2) of the Fourth Protocol to the European Convention on Human Rights that no one shall be deprived of the right to enter the territory of the State of which he is a national, which has not been ratified by the United Kingdom?

(2) In the circumstances of the present case, does Article 8a(1) of the EC Treaty:

  (a) Confer rights on a citizen of the Union to enter and remain in the Member State of which he is a national even where those rights are otherwise denied by national law.
  (b) Confer rights additional to those which existed under the EC Treaty prior to its amendment by the Treaty on European Union.
  (c) Give rise to directly effective rights which citizens of the Union may invoke before national courts and tribunals.
  (d) Apply to situations which are wholly internal to a single Member State?

Legal and Policy Framework on Nationality and Statelessness 75

right of abode within the territory of the United Kingdom to those citizens who had the closest connections to that State.

The ECJ went on to rule that the 'adoption of the (1972) declaration[167] did not have the effect of depriving any person who did not satisfy the definition of a national of the United Kingdom of rights to which that person might be entitled under Community law. The consequence was rather that such rights never arose in the first place for such a person.'

3.3.1.4 Council of Europe Law

After the dissolution of the Soviet Union and the resultant nationality crisis in Yugoslavia and former Czechoslovakia in the 1990s, the Council of Europe adopted the European Convention on Nationality in 1997 to resolve the nationality crisis that was brewing in Europe at the time.[168] This Convention was followed in 2006 by the European Convention on the Avoidance of Statelessness in Relation to State Succession.[169] However, the effectiveness of these Conventions has been undermined by poor ratifications which may be due to a lack of political will amongst member States.[170]

On the development of laws regulating issues of human rights and prevention of statelessness, the CoE appears to be ahead of other regional organizations the world over. The CoE's European Convention on the Avoidance of Statelessness in Relation to State Succession is one of those outstanding efforts to prevent statelessness. As mentioned earlier, the CoE laws are not legally binding, except when ratified by member States, as the Council is not a full-scale legal system like the EU.

3.3.1.4.1 RULES ON NATIONALITY

3.3.1.4.1.1 The 1950 European Convention on Human Rights The 1950 European Convention on Human Rights (hereinafter referred to as the ECHR) was adopted on 4 November 1950 and entered into force on 3 September 1953.[171] The Convention is binding on all 47 Council of Europe member

---

167 '1972 Declaration, of the categories of citizens to be regarded as its nationals for the purposes of Community law by designating, in substance, those entitled to the right of residence in the territory of the United Kingdom within the meaning of the Immigration Act 1971 and citizens having a specified connection with Gibraltar.'

The Queen v. Secretary of State for the Home Department, ex parte: Manjit Kaur. Case C-192/99 para. 22.

168 M Adjami and J Harrington *Op Cit* 99–100. See ETS No. 166.

169 CETS No. 200.

170 A de Chickera *Op Cit* 25 at para. 53.

171 Council of Europe. ETS 5 – Human Rights (Convention), 4.XI.1950.

76 *Legal and Policy Framework on Nationality and Statelessness*

States.[172] Although the ECHR does not guarantee the right to a nationality *per se*,[173] Caia Vlieks notes that the European Court of Human Rights (hereinafter referred to as the ECtHR), 'the supervisory body of the ECHR, has dealt with questions regarding nationality and statelessness. Moreover, the ECtHR has also ruled on numerous causes in which stateless persons were the complainant and therefore plays a crucial role in protecting the fundamental rights of stateless persons in Europe.'[174] In view of the absence of a specific mention of the right to nationality in the ECHR, the ECtHR has on many occasions relied on ECHR, Articles 8[175] and 14[176] in determining cases of breach of the right to nationality. In some instances, it has made a connection between the right to respect for private and family life in Article 8 either alone or in conjunction with Article 14 on the prohibition of discrimination with the right to nationality, especially with regard to arbitrary denial of nationality.[177]

The ECtHR's Factsheet of January 2018 reports that 'most of the cases concerning citizenship rights brought before the ECHR have concerned applicants claiming the right to acquire citizenship and the denial of recognition of such citizenship'[178] on discriminatory grounds, including lack of respect for the private and family life of the parties. The Report further noted that in these cases, especially the case of *Karassev v. Finland*,[179] the ECtHR observed that, 'although right to a citizenship is not as such guaranteed by the Convention or its Protocols, the Court does not exclude that an arbitrary denial of a citizenship might in certain circumstances raise an issue under Article 8 of the Convention because of the impact of such a denial on the private life of the individual.'[180]

---

172 See M Adjami and J Harrington *Op Cit* 99.

173 M Foster and H Lambert *Op Cit* 579.

174 C Vlieks *Op Cit* 1.

175 '1. Everyone has the right to respect for his private and family life, his home and his correspondence.
　　2.　There shall be no interference by a public authority with the exercise of this right except such as is in accordance with the law and is necessary in a democratic society in the interests of national security, public safety or the economic well-being of the country, for the prevention of disorder or crime, for the protection of health or morals, or for the protection of the rights and freedoms of others.'

176 'The enjoyment of the rights and freedoms set forth in this Convention shall be secured without discrimination on any ground such as sex, race, colour, language, religion, political or other opinion, national or social origin, association with a national minority, property, birth or other status.'

177 See U Kilkelly 'The right to respect for private and family life: A guide to the implementation of Article 8 of the European Convention on Human Rights' *Council of Europe human rights handbooks, No. 1*; see also K de Vries 'Right to respect for private and family life' in P Van Dijk, F Van Hoof, A Van Rijn, and L Zwaak (Eds.) *Theory and practice of the European Convention on Human Rights* (5th ed. 2018) 667–733.

178 Council of Europe 'European Court of Human Rights, deprivation of citizenship' (2018) 1 http://www.refworld.org/docid/5a5f7ce94.html (accessed 21 May 2018).

179 Application No. 31414/96.

180 Council of Europe 'European Court of Human Rights, deprivation of citizenship' *Op Cit* 1.

In *Genovese v. Malta*,[181] concerning the acquisition of nationality by descent, the applicant, a British citizen was denied Maltese citizenship on the ground that he was born out of wedlock. In his submission to the ECtHR, the applicant noted that he 'had suffered discrimination in the enjoyment of his rights under Article 8 on the ground of his illegitimate status and/or the sex of his Maltese parent.' Due to his 'illegitimacy' as someone born out of wedlock, the applicant could not benefit from the provision of Article 5(2)(b) of the Maltese Citizenship Act which would have enabled him to acquire the citizenship of his Maltese father. Furthermore, the applicant could have acquired Maltese citizenship under the same provision, if the applicant's mother was Maltese. The Maltese Government submitted that since citizenship was not a right covered by the Convention, differential treatment based on illegitimate status could not violate Article 14 of the Convention, emphasizing that protection in the Convention is with regard to discrimination when compared with other persons of different sex. However, the ECtHR, ruling in favour of the applicant, observed that 'no reasonable or objective grounds have been adduced to justify such difference of treatment of the applicant as a person born out of wedlock,' noting that the Maltese authorities violated Article 14, in conjunction with Article 8 of the Convention.

Furthermore, in *Biao v. Denmark*,[182] about discrimination in Danish nationality law with regard to family reunification matters, the Danish authorities refused to grant family reunification to enable the wife (the second applicant) of the applicant who was born Ghanaian to come to join the first applicant (a Danish of Togolese origin) in Denmark. The applicants complained that the refusal by the Danish Ministry of Refugee, Immigration and Integration Affairs to grant the second applicant a residence permit in Denmark based on family reunion breached their rights under Article 14 of the Convention in conjunction with Article 8, as well as Article 5(2) of the Convention. The applicants submitted, amongst other things, that being subjected to the *28-year rule*,[183] whereby, those who were born Danish citizens are exempt from the requirement of attachment with regard to family reunification without having to wait for 28 years to be so exempted, amounted to indirect discrimination.

In its ruling, the ECtHR held that 'in the present case, the purportedly neutral 28-year rule actually singles out a group of citizens, naturalised foreigners, and gives privileged treatment to Danish citizens by birth,' and concluded 'that Article 14 of the Convention, taken in conjunction with Article 8, has been

---

181 Application No. 53124/09.
182 Application No. 38590/10 Strasbourg 24 May 2016.
183 The attachment rule under s 9(7) of the Danish Aliens Act, provides, *inter alia* 'unless exceptional reasons make it inappropriate, including regard for family unity, a residence permit under subsection (1)(i)(a), when the person living in Denmark has not been a Danish national for 28 years, and under subsection (1)(i)(b) to (d) can only be issued if the spouses' or the cohabitants' aggregate ties with Denmark are stronger than the spouses' or the cohabitants' aggregate ties with another country.'

78   Legal and Policy Framework on Nationality and Statelessness

violated with respect to the first applicant and, by extension, with respect to the second applicant.'

Similarly, in *Foulon and Bouvet v. France*,[184] the French authorities, considering the illegality of the surrogate mother arrangement in France, refused to register the births of children born to French citizens in India. The ECtHR held that the refusal to register the births of the children was a violation of the right to respect for the private life of the children provided for in Article 8 of the ECHR.

The right to respect for private and family life as envisaged in the ECHR cannot be interfered with by a public authority 'except such as is in accordance with the law and is necessary in a democratic society in the interests of national security, public safety or the economic well-being of the country, for the prevention of disorder or crime, for the protection of health or morals, or for the protection of the rights and freedoms of others.'[185] Katalin Berényi notes that, 'the ECHR appeared to be the most powerful tool for strategic litigation (in Europe), not only based on its essence but also due to the fact that the other CoE instruments directly touching upon statelessness have been ratified by a marginal number of States which considerably undermines their enforcement.'[186] It is important to note that the EU member States are bound by the ECHR by virtue of Article 6 of the TEU.

3.3.1.4.1.2 The European Convention on Nationality   On 7 November 1997, the European Convention on Nationality[187] (hereinafter referred to as the ECN) was adopted by the Committee of Ministers of the Council of Europe.[188] Considered the most advanced and detailed regional instrument in the field of nationality,[189] the Council of Europe notes that, 'the ECN was drafted following the democratic changes that had taken place in Central and Eastern Europe since 1989 in order to guide the new democracies in drafting new nationality and aliens' laws.'[190] As of the time of writing, 21 States have ratified the ECN.[191]

The ECN's definition of nationality is widely accepted by international law scholars. Accordingly, it defines nationality to mean 'the legal bond between

---

184 Application Nos. 9063/14 and 10410/14.
185 See Art. 8(2) of the ECHR.
186 K Berényi 'Addressing the anomaly of statelessness in Europe: An EU law and human rights perspective' *A Doctoral (PhD) thesis submitted to the National Public Service University, Budapest* (2018) 137 https://akk.uni-nke.hu/document/akk-uni-nke-hu/Statelessness _PhD%20dissertation_Katalin%20Berenyi_20180312.pdf (accessed 22 May 2018).
187 ETS 166 – Convention on Nationality, 6.XI.1997.
188 A Zimmermann 'Council of Europe: European Convention on Nationality' (1998) 37 (1) *International Legal Materials* 44.
189 L Pilgram 'International law and European nationality laws' (2011) Research for the EUDO Citizenship Observatory Comparative Reports jointly supported by the European Commission grant agreement and the British Academy Research Project CITMODES 6.
190 Council of Europe: Parliamentary Assembly, *Access to nationality and the effective implementation of the European Convention on Nationality* (23 January 2014) Doc. 13392 p. 10.
191 For a full list see https://www.coe.int/en/web/conventions/full-list/-/conventions/ treaty/166/signatures (accessed 1 May 2018).

Legal and Policy Framework on Nationality and Statelessness 79

a person and a State and does not indicate the person's ethnic origin.'[192] The ECN identifies the competence of States to determine who its nationals are,[193] emphasizes the general principles relating to nationality,[194] and the rules relating to acquisition,[195] loss,[196] and recovery[197] of nationality. It, more importantly, adopts many of the safeguards geared towards the reduction of statelessness in the 1961 Convention.[198]

The beauty of the ECN is that it reiterates the principles in Article 15 of the UDHR as follows:

> The rules on nationality of each State Party shall be based on the following principles: a; everyone has the right to a nationality; b statelessness shall be avoided; c no one shall be arbitrarily deprived of his or her nationality.' It further added in sub-Article d: 'neither marriage nor the dissolution of a marriage between a national of a State Party and an alien, nor the change of nationality by one of the spouses during marriage, shall automatically affect the nationality of the other spouse.[199]

Mirna Adjami and Julia Harrington note that the ECN acknowledges the principles of Article 15 of the UDHR as rights, not necessarily under the European legal context.[200]

Article 5 of the ECN obliges States to be guided by the principle of non-discrimination, emphasizing the reason not to make 'distinctions or include any practice which amounts to discrimination on the grounds of sex, religion, race, colour or national or ethnic origin' in their nationality laws. Article 6 makes provision for the acquisition of nationality *ex lege* for children one of whose parents possesses, at the time of the birth, the nationality of that State party, foundlings found in its territory who would otherwise be stateless, children born on the territory of a State party who do not acquire at birth another nationality, amongst others.

To further give strength to the principles in Articles 4 and 5 of the ECN within the context of State succession, Article 18 provides thus, 'in matters of nationality in cases of State succession, each State Party concerned shall respect the principles of the rule of law, the rules concerning human rights and the principles contained

---

192 ECN Art. 2(a). However, the part of the definition excluding ethnicity may not go down well with many African States like Nigeria where one's nationality is often tied to ethnicity.
193 ECN Art. 3.
194 ECN Art. 4.
195 *Ibid* Art. 6.
196 *Ibid* Arts. 7 & 8.
197 *Ibid* Art. 9.
198 See Organization for Security and Co-Operation in Europe (OSCE) and UNHCR *Handbook on statelessness in the OSCE area, Op Cit* 34.
199 ECN Art. 4(a)–(d).
200 See M Adjami and J Harrington *Op Cit* 100.

80 *Legal and Policy Framework on Nationality and Statelessness*

in Articles 4 and 5 of this Convention.' Sub-article 2 of the same Article went further to give the necessary guidance on the steps States should take when deciding on the granting or the retention of nationality in cases of State succession, 'that each State Party concerned shall take account in particular of: a the genuine and effective link of the person concerned with the State; b the habitual residence of the person concerned at the time of State succession; c the will of the person concerned; d the territorial origin of the person concerned.'

It further obliges State parties with regard to the acquisition and retention of nationality in cases of State succession, where the acquisition of nationality is subject to the loss of foreign nationality,[201] not to make the renunciation or loss of another nationality a condition for the acquisition or retention of its nationality where such renunciation or loss is not possible or cannot reasonably be required.[202]

Similar to the provisions of the 1961 Statelessness Convention,[203] the ECN provides for the acquisition of nationality at birth for children born on a territory of a State who do not acquire the nationality of another country at birth.[204] Gerard-René de Groot *et al.*[205] asserts thus:

> ECN in fact has many similarities with the regime of the 1961 Convention, but there are some important differences. The 1961 Convention allows a State to postpone the real access to its nationality to the moment the stateless person involved reaches the age of 18 years, whereas according to the ECN, the access has to be given after five years of lawful and habitual residence while a child is still a minor. The 1961 Convention also allows States to reject an application because of a sentence for a crime which constitutes a threat for the national security or because of a sentence to more than five years imprisonment. The ECN does not allow this ground for a rejection of the application. As such, the obligations of the ECN are stricter than those under the 1961 Convention, reflecting developments in the prohibition of statelessness under international law.

---

201 ECN Art. 18(3).
202 ECN Art. 16.
203 See 1961 Convention Art. 1.
204 Art. 6(2) Each State Party shall provide in its internal law for its nationality to be acquired by children born on its territory who do not acquire at birth another nationality. Such nationality shall be granted:

(a) at birth *ex lege*; or
(b) subsequently, to children who remained stateless, upon an application being lodged with the appropriate authority, by or on behalf of the child concerned, in the manner prescribed by the internal law of the State Party. Such an application may be made subject to the lawful and habitual residence on its territory for a period not exceeding five years immediately preceding the lodging of the application.

205 G-R de Groot *et al. Practice and approaches in EU Member States to end statelessness* commissioned by the European Parliament's Policy Department for Citizens' Rights and Constitutional Affairs at the request of the LIBE Committee 22.

The ECN provides for loss of nationality by children whose parents lose that nationality except in cases, where a parent voluntarily serves in a foreign military or conduct seriously prejudicial to the vital interests of the State Party. The ECN however clarified that if one of the parents retains nationality, the children will not lose such nationality.[206] The ECN prohibits loss of nationality that could result in statelessness, save for very exceptional situations,[207] similar to those in Article 8 of the 1961 Statelessness Convention. The ECN encourages States to recognise the right to renunciation of nationality in their internal laws, provided a person would not become stateless by virtue of such right. It further provides that such renunciation may only be affected by nationals whose habitual residence is abroad.[208]

Despite being the most advanced regional instrument on nationality, the ECN suffers some setbacks. On the factors undermining the success of the ECN, Lisa Pilgram lists the following issues: 'the ECN has attracted more reservations than any of the other specialised or general human rights treaties, the absence of any form of independent reviewing and enforcement mechanism makes it difficult to monitor compliance and promote progress concerning the standards set by the Convention, although common obstacles to ratification are state objections to only a few of the ECN's provisions, these obstacles are very significant.'[209] These objections or reservations may be due to the requirement for 'each State Party to ensure that decisions relating to the acquisition, retention, loss, recovery or certification of its nationality be open to an administrative or judicial review in conformity with its internal law.'[210] Although it is not clear whether the administrative or judicial review of conformity would be done by an international, regional, or national body, the requirement is perceived as subjecting too much of the States' sovereignty and powers to administrative or judicial review, contrary to Article 3 of the ECN which provides that 'each State shall determine under its own law who are its nationals.'

3.3.1.4.2 RULES ON STATELESSNESS

3.3.1.4.2.1 *Articles 2 and 3 of the European Convention on the Avoidance of Statelessness in Relation to State Succession*

State succession was mentioned earlier in Chapter 2 of this research as one of the causes of statelessness; it is one of the major causes of statelessness the world over,

---

206 ECN Art. 7(2).
207 *Ibid* Art. 7(3).
208 *Ibid* Art. 8.
209 L Pilgram 'European Convention on Nationality (ECN) 1997 and European nationality laws' Research for the European Union Democracy Observatory (EUDO) Citizenship Observatory Policy Briefs (EUDO Policy Brief No. 4) 1 http://cadmus.eui.eu/bitstream /handle/1814/51626/RSCAS_EUDO_CIT__PB_2011_03.pdf?sequence=1 (accessed 1 May 2018).
210 See Art. 12 of the ECN.

82 *Legal and Policy Framework on Nationality and Statelessness*

particularly in Africa. It is commendable that the Council of Europe developed a specific framework to avoid statelessness due to state succession.

The European Convention on the Avoidance of Statelessness in Relation to State Succession[211] opened for signature on 19 May 2006 and entered into force on 1 May 2009 with ratification at that time by three member States.[212] As of the time of writing, the Convention has nine State parties (seven ratifications) signatories.[213] According to a CoE and Organization for Security and Co-operation in Europe (OSCE) report of 2006, the provision regarding State succession in Chapter VI of the ECN 'contains only principles but no specific rules on nationality in the case of State succession.' Therefore, building upon Chapter VI of the ECN, the European Convention on the Avoidance of Statelessness in Relation to State Succession was enacted to provide for 'more detailed rules to be applied by States in the context of State succession with a view to preventing, or at least reducing as far as possible, cases of statelessness arising from such situations.'[214]

The objectives of the Convention are based mainly on the principles in Articles 2 and 3, which are on the right to nationality and prevention of statelessness, respectively. Article 2 of the Convention provides that, 'everyone who, at the time of the State succession, had the nationality of the predecessor State and who has or would become stateless as a result of the State succession has the right to the nationality of a State concerned.' In furtherance of the above rights, the State concerned, in its responsibility to prevent statelessness according to Article 3, 'shall take all appropriate measures to prevent persons who, at the time of the State succession, had the nationality of the predecessor State, from becoming stateless as a result of the succession.' While Article 4[215] of the Convention makes provision on non-discrimination in the application of the Convention.

The Convention obliges States parties (successor States) to

> grant its nationality to persons who, at the time of the State succession, had the nationality of the predecessor State, and who have or would become

---

211 CETS No. 200.

212 See Council of Europe 'Chart of signatures and ratifications of Treaty 200, Council of Europe Convention on the avoidance of statelessness in relation to State succession' https://www.coe.int/en/web/conventions/full-list/-/conventions/treaty/200/signatures (accessed 23 May 2018). As at the time of writing only Austria, Hungary, Luxemburg, Montenegro, the Netherlands, Norway, and the Republic of Moldova have ratified the Convention, while Germany and Ukraine have signed the Convention.

213 Council of Europe 'Chart of signatures and ratifications of Treaty 200' *Op Cit.*

214 Council of Europe 'Council of Europe activities in the field of nationality/citizenship' OSCE Human Dimension Implementation Meeting Warsaw, 2–13 October 2006 Working Session 10 'Democratic Institutions' Citizenship and Political Rights Contribution of the Council of Europe 2. https://www.osce.org/odihr/21396?download=true (accessed 22 may 2018).

215 'States concerned shall not discriminate against any person concerned on any ground such as sex, race, colour, language, religion, political or other opinion, national or social origin, association with a national minority, property, birth or other status.'

Legal and Policy Framework on Nationality and Statelessness   83

stateless as a result of the State succession if at that time, they were habitually resident in the territory which has become territory of the successor State, or they were not habitually resident in any State concerned but had an appropriate connection with the successor State.[216]

Even where an applicant affected by State succession (a person concerned) can acquire the nationality of another State concerned on the basis of an appropriate connection with that State, the Convention still precludes a successor State from refusing to grant its nationality to such a person who has expressed his/her will to acquire its nationality.[217]

With regard to withdrawal of nationality in the event of State succession, the Convention places a responsibility on the predecessor State not to withdraw its nationality from its nationals who have not acquired the nationality of a successor State and who *would otherwise become stateless* as a result of the State succession.[218] For a person who has or would become stateless as a result of State succession, Article 8 obliges States parties not to insist on its standard requirements of proof necessary for the granting of its nationality where it is not reasonable for such persons to meet the standard requirements. The Convention further made provision on the prevention of statelessness at birth in Article 10, by obliging State parties to grant its nationality at birth to a child born following State succession on its territory to a parent who, at the time of State succession, had the nationality of the predecessor State if that child would otherwise be stateless.

On application of the Convention, Article 15(1) provides that it shall only apply in respect of a State succession that has occurred after it entered into force. This arguably excludes many other cases of statelessness due to State succession occurring before 2009, though Article 15(2) encourages State parties concerned to declare by notification addressed to the Secretary-General of the Council of Europe at the time of expressing its consent to be bound by the Convention, or at any other time, that it will also apply the provisions of the Convention to any State succession which occurred before the entry into force of the Convention. While this book is not encouraging retroactive laws to be made, it would arguably be in the best interest of persons affected by State succession, if Article 15(1) of the Convention had been more definite by recommending the application of the Convention in all cases of statelessness resulting from State succession.

---

216 Article 5(1) of the European Convention on the Avoidance of Statelessness in Relation to State Succession. Article 5(2) further provides that, 'For the purpose of paragraph 1, subparagraph b, an appropriate connection includes *inter alia*:

   a legal bond to a territorial unit of a predecessor State which has become territory of the successor State;

      birth on the territory which has become territory of the successor State;

      last habitual residence on the territory of the predecessor State which has become territory of the successor State.'

217 *Ibid* Art. 7.

218 *Ibid* Art. 6.

84 *Legal and Policy Framework on Nationality and Statelessness*

Arguably, there is no specific EU law on statelessness, save for some provisions in the Treaty on the Functioning of the European Union, which offers some protection measures for third-country nationals[219] including stateless persons. The 2007 Lisbon Treaty states that 'stateless persons shall be treated as third-country nationals'[220] in the EU. The EU legal frameworks are germane for their advancement on the issue of access to nationality, which is relevant to the discussion on the prevention of statelessness, considering the close relationship between access to nationality and the risk of statelessness. For the Council of Europe, in addition to its frameworks on prevention of statelessness, the ECtHR, 'has dealt with questions regarding nationality and statelessness [...] also ruled on numerous causes in which stateless persons were the complainant and therefore plays a crucial role in protecting the fundamental rights of stateless persons in Europe.'[221] All of these frameworks (including case law) contribute to the discussion on the prevention of statelessness and would be relevant for further discussion in comparison with other regional frameworks, particularly those of the African Union.

3.3.2 *The Americas*

3.3.2.1 *The Organization of American States (OAS)*

The relevant human rights instrument in the OAS for the protection of the right to nationality and prevention of statelessness is the American Convention on Human Rights.[222] In particular, Articles 1 and 20 of the Convention are the relevant sections with regard to the right to nationality and prevention of statelessness in the region.

The American Convention on Human Rights (hereinafter the Pact of San José, Costa Rica or American Convention) was adopted in San Jose, Costa Rica on 22 November 1969, and entered into force on 18 July 1978.[223] The Convention is not only 'one of the two main instruments within the Organization of American States (hereinafter OAS) that outline states' human rights obligations,'[224] it is, moreover, the 'first regional instrument to reaffirm Article 15 of the UDHR's universal promise of the right to nationality.'[225]

In line with the UDHR, the American Convention provides that, 'every person has the right to a nationality.'[226] On reduction of statelessness, in line with

---

219 See TFEU Arts. 67(2) and 78(1).

220 Treaty of Lisbon 2007 Art. 61(2).

221 C Vlieks *Op Cit* 1.

222 UN Treaty Collection Vol. 1144, I-17955.

223 *Ibid.*

224 Center for Women, Peace and Security 'American Convention on Human Rights' http:// blogs.lse.ac.uk/vaw/regional/the-americas/american-convention/ (accessed 19 June 2018).

225 G-R de Groot 'Survey on rules on loss of nationality in international treaties and case law' *Op Cit* 16.

226 The American Convention Art. 20(1).

Legal and Policy Framework on Nationality and Statelessness 85

the 1961 Convention, the American Convention further provides that 'every person has the right to the nationality of the State in whose territory he was born if he does not have the right to any other nationality.'[227] This expands the right to nationality guaranteed in the UDHR by specifying the country who has the responsibility or to whose nationality a person is entitled, i.e., the country of birth (*iure soli*) of a person who would otherwise be stateless.[228] And Article 20(3) provides that, 'no one shall be arbitrarily deprived of his nationality or of the right to change it.' The foregoing principles on the right to nationality and the right not to be arbitrarily deprived of that right were acknowledged by the Inter-American Court of Human Rights' Advisory Opinion[229] on proposed amendments to the naturalization provision of the Constitution of Costa Rica Requested by the Government of Costa Rica, where concerning issue III relating to the right to nationality, the Court affirmed thus:

> The right of every human being to a nationality has been recognized as such by international law. Two aspects of this right are reflected in Article 20 of the Convention: first, the right to a nationality established therein provides the individual with a minimal measure of legal protection in international relations through the link his nationality establishes between him and the state in question; and, second, the protection therein accorded the individual against the arbitrary deprivation of his nationality, without which he would be deprived for all practical purposes of all of his political rights as well as of those civil rights that are tied to the nationality of the individual.[230]

With regard to the prohibition of discrimination in the acquisition of nationality, the Inter-American Court of Human Rights in *Dilcia Yean and Violeta Bosico v. Dominican Republic*,[231] where the Dominican Republic authorities arbitrarily deprived children of the right to nationality on grounds of race, thereby leaving them stateless, held that the Dominicans were in breach of the non-discrimination obligation in Article 1(1).[232] In the same case, on the discretionary powers of the State with regard to deprivation of nationality, the Court held thus:

---

227 *Ibid* Art. 20(2).
228 G-R de Groot 'Survey on rules on loss of nationality in international treaties and case law' *Op Cit* 16
229 OC-4/84 of 19 January 1984.
　　'The Inter-American Court of Human Rights has supervisory authority over the American Convention and has issued several opinions in cases concerning the scope and content of the protections enshrined in that Convention's article 20.'
　　M Adjami and J Harrington *Op Cit* 99.
230 *Ibid* 10 para. 34.
231 IACtHR, 8 September 2005.
232 'The States Parties to this Convention undertake to respect the rights and freedoms recognized herein and to ensure to all persons subject to their jurisdiction the free and full exercise of those rights and freedoms, without any discrimination for reasons of race, color,

86 Legal and Policy Framework on Nationality and Statelessness

The determination of who has a right to be a national continues to fall within a State's domestic jurisdiction. However, its discretional authority in this regard is gradually being restricted with the evolution of international law, in order to ensure a better protection of the individual in the face of arbitrary acts of States. Thus, at the current stage of the development of international human rights law, this authority of the States is limited, on the one hand, by their obligation to provide individuals with the equal and effective protection of the law and, on the other hand, by their obligation to prevent, avoid and reduce statelessness.[233]

Considering that some stateless persons could also be refugees, Article 22(8) of the American Convention on Freedom of Movement and Residence is worthy of note. The Article provides for similar guarantees as in the 1951 Refugee Convention's principle of *non-refoulement*; it states thus: 'in no case may an alien be deported or returned to a country, regardless of whether or not it is his country of origin, if in that country his right to life or personal freedom is in danger of being violated because of his race, nationality, religion, social status, or political opinions.'

3.3.3 Arab World

3.3.3.1 The Arab League

For the Arab League, the relevant instrument on the right to nationality and prevention of statelessness is the Arab Charter on Human Rights (Article 29). 'While the Arab League started to deal with selected human rights issues in the late 1960s, an Arab Charter on Humans Rights as the cornerstone of a regional human rights regime only entered into force in 2008 – much later than its American, European, and African counterparts.'[234] Though originally, the Arab Charter on Human Rights (hereinafter ArCHR or the Charter) was adopted in 1994, it was not ratified by any Arab League State members until 2004 due to widespread criticism of the original draft by human rights pundits across the world for not meeting minimum international human rights standards.[235]

After ten years of deliberations and consultations, the League of Arab States on 22 May 2004 finally adopted the Charter. The Charter entered into force on

---

sex, language, religion, political or other opinion, national or social origin, economic status, birth, or any other social condition.'

233 *Dilcia's case*. IACtHR, 8 September 2005 para. 140.

234 V van Hüllen 'Just leave us alone: The Arab League and human rights' 135 http://aei.pitt .edu/79693/1/van_Hullen.pdf (accessed 22 June 2018).

235 D Vitkauskaite-Meurice 'The Arab Charter on Human Rights: The naissance of new regional human rights system or a challenge to the universality of human rights?' (2010) 119 (1) *Jurisprudence* 171.

Legal and Policy Framework on Nationality and Statelessness 87

15 March 2008,[236] with ratifications by seven Arab League State members.[237] The Charter, according to Dalia Vitkauskaite-Meurice 'attempt[s] to create a new formula to address the historic and fundamental question of whether Islamic principles can be compatible with the universality of human rights.'[238] Article 29 of the Charter provides that 'everyone has the right to nationality. No one shall be arbitrarily or unlawfully deprived of his nationality.' It went further in sub-article (2) of the same Article to encourage State parties to take appropriate measures, 'in accordance with their domestic laws on nationality, to allow a child to acquire the mother's nationality, having due regard, in all cases, to the best interests of the child.'

The Charter emphasizes the equality of men and women in its Article 3(3), which provides 'men and women are equal in human dignity, in rights and in duties, within the framework of the positive discrimination established in favor of women by Islamic Shari'a and other divine laws, legislation and international instruments. Consequently, each State Party to the present Charter shall undertake all necessary measures to guarantee the effective equality between men and women.' The above provision can be interpreted separately or jointly with Article 29(2) and (3)[239] to include equality in transmission, retention, and acquisition of nationality by both males and females. On the emphasis on women's rights in the Charter, Mohamed Y. Mattar notes *inter alia*:

> the emphasis on women's rights in the Charter reflects the concern of its drafters that women in Arab countries face disadvantages that their counterparts in other regions of the world do not experience to the same extent. Such disadvantages are evident in the concluding observations of the United

---

236 See, O Willem Vonk *et al*. 'Protection against statelessness trends and regulations in Europe' (2013) *Research for the EUDO Citizenship Observatory Country Reports* 32. http://cadmus.eui.eu/bitstream/handle/1814/30201/eudocit_vink_degroot_statelessness_final.pdf;sequence=1 (accessed 20 June 2018).

237 The seven States are:
'Algeria, Bahrain, Emirates Arab Units, Jordan, Libya, Palestine, and Syria who were later followed by Yemen and Qatar.'
M Amin Al-Midani 'The enforcement mechanisms of the Arab Charter on Human Rights and the need for an Arab Court of Human Rights' https://acihl.org/articles.htm ?article_id=22 (accessed 23 August 2018).

238 D Vitkauskaite-Meurice *Op Cit* 171.
The preamble of the Charter states *inter alia*:
'acknowledging the close interrelationship between human rights and world peace, reaffirming the principles of the Charter of the United Nations and the Universal Declaration of Human Rights, as well as the provisions of the United Nations International Covenant on Civil and Political Rights and International Covenant on Economic, Social and Cultural Rights and the Cairo Declaration of Human Rights in Islam.'

239 (2). States parties shall take such measures as they deem appropriate, in accordance with their domestic laws on nationality, to allow a child to acquire the mother's nationality, having due regard, in all cases, to the best interests of the child.
(3). Non one shall be denied the right to acquire another nationality, having due regard for the domestic legal procedures in his country.

88   *Legal and Policy Framework on Nationality and Statelessness*

Nations Committee on the Elimination of Discrimination against Women ('CEDAW') on the various reports submitted by the Arab countries.[240]

The Charter precludes State parties from expelling a foreigner lawfully in the territory, except within the ambits of law and after that person has been given a fair hearing, and except for compelling national security reasons. It moreover prohibits collective expulsion in all circumstances.[241]

3.3.4 Africa

3.3.4.1 Frameworks on the Right to Nationality and Prevention of Statelessness in Africa

This section will examine the frameworks on the right to nationality and prevention of statelessness put in place by the African Union (AU) which is the umbrella body of the entire African States, as well as measures put in place by the Economic Community of West African States (ECOWAS). As mentioned in section 3.1 of this book, out of the eight RECs in Africa, ECOWAS is examined in this section for being the most advanced REC within the AU, especially with regard to the issue of statelessness and the right to nationality. The Federal Republic of Nigeria, which is the focus of this book, is also located in the ECOWAS sub-region.

To make proper recommendations for Nigeria, it is important to examine the relevant legal and policy frameworks within the AU and ECOWAS that Nigeria can draw from, considering its membership of both organizations.

3.3.4.1.1 AFRICAN UNION

The African Charter on Human and Peoples' Right (hereinafter ACHPR) does not specifically provide for the right to nationality. However, such right can be inferred from some specific Articles of the ACHPR, and from the position of the African Commission when it makes decisions with regard to the right to nationality. The right to nationality can be inferred from the following principles of the ACHPR:[242] the principle on prohibition of discrimination,[243] the principle of equal rights and protection,[244] the principle against arbitrary deprivation of rights,[245] and respect for human dignity,[246] among others.

---

240 M Mattar 'Article 43 of the Arab Charter on Human Rights: Reconciling national, regional, and international standards' 102–103 http://harvardhrj.com/wp-content/uploads/2013/05/V26-Mattar.pdf (accessed 20 June 2018).

241 ArCHR Art. 26(2).

242 L Muller *Legal identity for all – Ending statelessness in SADC. Goal 16 of the Sustainable Development Goals* (2016) 141. See also, Art. 6 of the African Charter on the Rights and Welfare of the Child. Arts. 6(g) and 7 of the Protocol on the Rights of Women in Africa.

243 ACHPR Art. 2.

244 ACHPR Art. 3.

245 ACHPR Art. 4.

246 ACHPR Art. 5.

Legal and Policy Framework on Nationality and Statelessness 89

Furthermore, to address the gap with regard to the right to nationality, African States have often 'sought to address the lack of a specific provision on nationality through the African Charter on the Rights and Welfare of the Child (ACRWC) and the Protocol to the African Charter on the Rights of Women in Africa (the Protocol on the Rights of Women).'[247] Despite the lack of a specific instrument that adequately tackles the issue of nationality in the continent, in addition to the forgoing alternative instruments, African States can rely on several other instruments when confronted with the issue of statelessness and the nationality right. Some of the specific legislation on nationality is elucidated below.

3.3.4.1.1.1 African Charter on Human and Peoples' Right and the (Draft)[248] Protocol on the Specific Aspects of the Right to a Nationality and the Eradication of Statelessness in Africa

The discussion on the (Draft) Protocol on Specific Aspects of the Right to a Nationality and the Eradication of Statelessness in Africa (hereinafter in this section referred to as the Protocol) will not be complete without also assessing the African Charter on Human and Peoples' Right (hereinafter ACHPR or Banjul Charter) which is the substantive instrument and basis for the Protocol, and the African Commission on Human and Peoples' Rights (hereinafter the African Commission), especially with regard to their contribution to access to nationality.[249]

3.3.4.1.1.1.1 The African Charter on Human and Peoples' Rights (ACHPR)

The ACHPR as a human rights instrument was an initiative of the International Commission of Jurists, an international non-government organization. From 3 to 7 January 1961, the International Commission of Jurists organized an African Conference on the Rule of Law in Lagos, Nigeria. During the Conference, '194 judges, practicing lawyers and teachers of law from 23 African nations and 9 countries from other continents explored the prospects of an African convention on human rights.'[250] Further to the adoption of an African regional human rights instruments:

---

247 L Muller *Op Cit* 141. See Art. 6 of the African Charter on the Rights and Welfare of the Child. Arts. 6(g) and 7 of the Protocol on the Rights of Women in Africa.
248 As mentioned earlier, at the time of writing, the Protocol to the ACHPR is (was) still only a draft waiting to be adopted at the AU level, although conferences have been held at the sub-regional level (including ECOWAS level) to review the draft. It is also important to note that words used in the Articles of the draft Protocol as reproduced in this research may become different from the words in the final text. This may be so, because the various AU States, as well as experts on nationality and statelessness, are still reviewing the draft at the time of writing.
249 See, Resolution 234 on Right to Nationality of the African Commission on Human and Peoples' Rights.
250 The conference adopted a resolution known as the Law of Lagos which states, *inter alia*:
    'That in order to give full effect to the Universal Declaration of Human Rights of 1948, this Conference invites the African Government to study the possibility of adopting an African Convention of Human Rights in such a manner that the Conclusions of the Confer-

90   *Legal and Policy Framework on Nationality and Statelessness*

In March 1967, the UN Commission of Human Rights decided to study the possibility of a Regional Commission on Human Rights in areas where they did not already exist. A number of other international conferences followed, which all contributed to the impetus for the conclusion of an African Charter. One such meeting was a Seminar held in Cairo in September 1969 under the auspices of the UN and the United Arab Republic, with participation from 20 African countries, the Council of Europe and the Arab League. There was general agreement by the participants that an African Commission on Human Rights should be created.[251]

Finally, on 1 June 1981, in a historic move, the 18th Assembly of Heads of State and Government of the then Organization of African Unity (now African Union, and hereinafter referred to as the AU) adopted the ACHPR in Nairobi, Kenya. But the ACHPR eventually entered into force on 21 October 1986. Today, the Charter has been ratified by all 54 African States.[252] On 9 June 1998, member States of the AU adopted a Protocol to the African Charter on Human and Peoples' Rights on the Establishment of an African Court on Human and Peoples' Rights (the African Court).[253] The Protocol which established an African Court was 'signed by 30 of the 52 Member States on the same day.'[254] However, the Protocol entered into force on 25 January 2004.[255]

---

ence will be safeguarded by the creation of a court of appropriate jurisdiction and recourse thereto made available for all persons under the jurisdiction of the signatory States.'

D Turack 'The African Charter on Human and Peoples' Rights: Some preliminary thoughts' (1983) 17 (3) *Akron Law Review* 366.

251 R D'Sa 'The African Charter on Human and Peoples' Rights: Problems and prospects for regional action' 104 www.austlii.edu.au/au/journals/AUYrBkIntLaw/1983/3.pdf (accessed 24 May 2018). See UN Doc STITAOIHRI38, 1969. See also R Gittleman 'The African Charter on Human and Peoples' Rights: A legal analysis' (1982) 22 *Virginia Journal of International Law*, 669 at 671, fn 22.

252 R Gittleman *Op Cit* 667. See also AU website on countries that have signed, ratified the ACHPR https://au.int/sites/default/files/treaties/36390-sl-african_charter_on_human _and_peoples_rights_2.pdf (accessed 21 October 2020).

253 Open Society Justice Initiative 'African Court on Human and Peoples' Rights' (June 2013) *Fact Sheet* 1.

254 N Udombana 'Toward the African Court on Human and Peoples' Rights: Better late than never' *The Yale Law Journal*, 3(45), 345–46 https://law.yale.edu/system/files/docu-ments/pdf/LawJournals/UDOMBANA.PDF (accessed 28 May 2018).

'The thirty States are Benin, Botswana, Burkina Faso, Burundi, Federal Islamic Republic of Comoros, Republic of Congo, Côte d'Ivoire, Federal Democratic Republic of Ethiopia, Equatorial Guinea, Gabon, Gambia, Ghana, Guinea-Bissau, Liberia and Great Socialist People's Libyan Arab Jamahiriya. Others are Malawi, Mali, Mauritius, Namibia, Rwanda, Senegal, Seychelles, Sierra Leone, South Africa, Sudan, United Republic of Tanzania, Togo, Tunisia, Zambia, and Zimbabwe.'

255 As of the time of writing, all 52 member States have signed the Protocol out of which 30 have ratified it. See the list of countries that signed/ratified the Protocol https://au.int /sites/default/files/treaties/36393-sl-protocol_to_the_african_charter_on_human_and _peoplesrights_on_the_estab.pdf (accessed 25 January 2021).

Legal and Policy Framework on Nationality and Statelessness 91

As earlier mentioned, although the right to a nationality is not expressly provided for under the ACHPR, African States alluded to the idea of the fundamental right to nationality through the principle on the prohibition of discrimination, the principle of equal rights and protection, the principle against arbitrary deprivation of rights,[256] and respect for human dignity, among others.[257]

3.3.4.1.1.1.2 The African Commission Article 30 of the ACHPR established the African Commission on Human and Peoples' Rights (hereinafter called the Commission) and charged it with three major functions: to ensure protection, promotion of human and peoples' rights in Africa, and interpretation of the Charter. The Commission was inaugurated on 2 November 1987 in Addis Ababa, Ethiopia and subsequently relocated to Banjul, the Gambia.[258] Over the years, when handling cases involving the right to nationality, the Commission has creatively interpreted provisions of the African Charter in such a way that the right to nationality is reasonably inferred.[259]

For instance, the Commission relied on the provisions of the ACHPR in the case of *Modise v. Botswana*[260] wherein the complainant claimed citizenship of Botswana under the circumstance that his father was a citizen of Botswana who migrated to South Africa for work. While in South Africa, his father got married, and the complainant was a product of the marriage. The complainant's mother died shortly after his birth and he was brought to Botswana, where he grew up. By virtue of his Motswana ancestry, the complainant claimed Botswana nationality by descent. 'He alleged that in 1978, he was one of the founders and leaders of an opposition party called Botswana National Front. He was of the view that it is because of his political activities that he was declared an "undesirable immigrant" in Botswana by the government.'

Even while he had a judicial action pending challenging his designation as an undesirable immigrant, the claimant was arrested, not allowed to attend the hearing of his case, jailed, and deported to South Africa four times within seven years. While in South Africa he was deported to 'no man's land' between Bophutatswana and Botswana where he remained until he was readmitted to Botswana on a humanitarian basis. The Commission found the Republic of Botswana to be in violation of Articles 3(2), 5, 12(1) and (2), 13(1) and (2), 14, and 18(1) of the ACHPR, and urged the government of Botswana to take appropriate measures to recognize Mr. Modise as its citizen by descent and also to compensate him adequately for the violations of his rights.

256 ACHPR Art. 4.
257 ACHPR *African Commission on Human and Peoples' Rights – The Right to Nationality in Africa* (May 2014) 5–6; L Muller *Op Cit* 141; See also ACHPR Arts. 2, 3, 4, and 5.
258 See the website of the Commission https://www.achpr.org/ (accessed 23 October 2020).
259 AU African Commission on Human and Peoples' Rights *Op Cit* 6.
260 African Commission *Communication No. 97/93 (2000)*.

92 *Legal and Policy Framework on Nationality and Statelessness*

Similarly, in *Amnesty International v. Zambia*,[261] a communication was submitted by Amnesty International on behalf of the complainants, William Steven Banda and John Lyson Chinula, both of whom were prominent political figures in Zambia. The complainants were foremost members of UNIP, a party that had been in power since the Zambian independence in 1964. When UNIP was defeated by MMD in the first multi-party elections in November 1991, the MMD now the ruling party was allegedly not comfortable with the profile of Banda and Chinula. It thus ensured their separate deportations on the ground that they were not Zambia citizens. The Commission holding the deportations illegal, held

> by forcing Banda and Chinula to live as stateless persons under degrading conditions, the government of Zambia has deprived them of their family and is depriving their families of the men's support, and this constitutes a violation of the dignity of a human being. Thereby violating Article 5 of the Charter, which guarantees the right to: the respect of the dignity inherent in a human being and to the recognition of his legal status. The forcible expulsion of Banda and Chinula by the Zambian government has forcibly broken up the family unit which is the core of society thereby failing in its duties to protect and assist the family as stipulated in Articles 18(1) and 18(2) of the Charter.

The African Commission at its 53rd Ordinary Session which was held from 9 to 23 April 2013 in Banjul, the Gambia adopted resolution 234 on right to nationality.[262] The resolution states *inter alia* that the 'provisions of Article 2 of the ACHPR and Article 6(g) and (h) of the Protocol to the African Charter on Human and Peoples' Rights on the Rights of Women in Africa establish the equal right of men and women to acquire their partner's nationality.' It further reiterated that 'it is in the general interest of the people of Africa for all African States to recognise, guarantee and facilitate the right to nationality of every person on the continent and to ensure that no one is exposed to statelessness.'

It was further affirmed in the resolution, 'that the right to nationality of every human person is a fundamental human right implied within the provisions of Article 5 of the African Charter on Human and Peoples' Rights and essential to the enjoyment of other fundamental rights and freedoms under the Charter.' It moreover calls on African States to 'undertake to ensure that their Constitutional legislation recognize the principles according to which a child shall acquire the nationality of the State in the territory of which he has been born if, at the time of the child's birth, he is not granted nationality by any other State in accordance with its laws'.

At that same meeting (53rd Ordinary Session of the African Commission) a focal point on statelessness was appointed from among the existing

---

261 African Commission *Communication No. 212/98.*
262 ACHPR/Res.234(LIII)2013.

Legal and Policy Framework on Nationality and Statelessness 93

Commissioners (the Special Rapporteur on Refugees, Asylum Seekers, Displaced Persons and Migrants in Africa), and through a resolution, the Resolution on the Right to Nationality, assigned the task of conducting a comprehensive study on Nationality and Statelessness in Africa to the Special Rapporteur on Refugees, Asylum Seekers, Migrants and Internally Displaced Persons in Africa.[263]

3.3.4.1.1.1.3 The Draft Protocol on Nationality   Since 2013, the AU organized a series of consultations involving States and non-State actors, regional bodies such as ECOWAS, Southern African Development Community (SADC), and the International Conference of the Great Lakes Region (ICGLR) on the draft Protocol to the African Charter on Human and Peoples' Rights on the Right to Nationality in Africa.[264] In May 2014, at its 55th Ordinary Session held in Luanda, Angola, the African Commission adopted Resolution 277 on the drafting of a Protocol to the African Charter on Human and Peoples' Rights on the Right to Nationality in Africa (hereinafter Draft Protocol on Nationality). Again, the Special Rapporteur was tasked with the assignment to coordinate the draft of a Protocol to the African Charter on the right to a Nationality and the eradication of Statelessness, drawing inspiration from the final version of the study on the Right to Nationality in Africa presented at the Session.[265]

The draft Protocol on nationality was presented at the 56th Ordinary Session of the African Commission which was held in May 2015 in Banjul, the Gambia. The draft was subsequently adopted at its 18th Extraordinary Session in Nairobi, Kenya in August 2015.[266] Further to the validation of the draft, at the 11th Ordinary Session of the Commission held in Cairo, Egypt in October 2015, the draft Protocol on nationality was presented to the African Union Commission on International Law (hereinafter AUCIL) for review to ensure conformity with international law.[267] Apart from the AU Consultation on a draft Protocol,

---

263 ECOWAS *Strategy on the adoption of the Draft Protocol to the African Charter on Human and Peoples' Rights on the Right to Nationality and the Eradication of Statelessness in Africa* (2017) 1 http://citizenshiprightsafrica.org/wp-content/uploads/2017/11/ENG-Protocol-Strategy.pdf (accessed 14 June 2022).

264 UNHCR *Draft Protocol to the African Charter on Human and Peoples' Rights on the Specific Aspects of the Right to a Nationality and the Eradication of Statelessness in Africa UNHCR's Observations* (2018) (unpublished).

265 African Commission Department of Political Affairs *Concept Note on Member States Experts Meeting on the Draft Protocol to the African Charter on Human and Peoples Rights on the Specific Aspects on the Right to a Nationality and the Eradication of Statelessness in Africa, which was held 7–11 May 2018 in Abidjan, Côte d'Ivoire* 6.

266 ECOWAS *Strategy on the adoption of the Draft Protocol to the African Charter on Human and Peoples' Rights on the Right to Nationality and the Eradication of Statelessness in Africa, Op Cit* 1.

267 'Acknowledging the Draft Protocol's relevance and its innovative aspects, the Commissioners stressed the usefulness of the legal instrument in helping to eradicate statelessness on the continent. During its 29th Ordinary Session in Kigali, Rwanda in July 2016, the Executive Council of the African Union (AU) agreed to submit the Draft Protocol for review to the Special Technical Committees (STCs) of the AU.'

94 Legal and Policy Framework on Nationality and Statelessness

ECOWAS was instrumental in inspiring action on the draft Protocol through the February 2015 Abidjan Declaration of Ministers of ECOWAS States in which they undertook 'to prevent and reduce statelessness by reforming constitutional, legislative and institutional regimes related to nationality' and 'called on the African Union to prepare and adopt a Protocol to the African Charter on Human and Peoples' Rights on the Right to Nationality.'[268]

In May 2017, the draft Protocol was formally submitted to the AU and on 7 to 11 May 2018, AU member States met to discuss the text of the draft Protocol.[269] Although in principle, the Protocol has been adopted, there were however some reservations on Article 2[270] on the definition of statelessness. Therefore, the document has been referred to the legal committee for clarification of the definition. Moreover, the definition of *nationality*[271] in the Protocol is similar to the definition of nationality in the ECN. Considering the nature of many African States, like Nigeria, where ethnicity is still the major basis for claiming nationality, arguably, the definition of nationality in the draft Protocol may pose a problem for the many African States.

The Protocol 'recalls that the history of the African continent, especially the initial establishment of borders by colonial powers, has given questions of nationality and statelessness particular characteristics in African States that are not sufficiently taken into account by the existing African and international instruments.' It also 'recalls the commitment in the 50th Anniversary Solemn Declaration of the Assembly of Heads of State and Government of the African Union to facilitate African citizenship in order to allow free movement of people, and the aspiration of the Agenda 2063 Framework Document for an African citizenship and passport and for the availability of dual citizenship for the African diaspora.'[272]

ECOWAS *Strategy on the adoption of the Draft Protocol to the African Charter on Human and Peoples' Rights on the Right to Nationality and the Eradication of Statelessness in Africa, Op Cit* 1.

268 AU 'Explanatory memo: Draft Protocol to the African Charter on Human and Peoples' Rights on the Specific Aspects of the Right to a Nationality and the Eradication of Statelessness in Africa' para. 5 https://au.int/sites/default/files/newsevents/workingdocuments /34175-wd-draft_protocol_explanatory_memo_en_may2017-jobourg.pdf (accessed 31 May 2018).

269 *Meeting of AU Member States on the draft Protocol on the Right to a Nationality in Africa.* A press release on 7 May 2018, by the Kenya Human Rights Commission https://www .khrc.or.ke/images/docs/AbidjanMeetingonNationalityStatelessnessProtocolMay72018 .pdf (accessed 28 May 2018).

270 'For the purpose of this Protocol: [...] "Stateless persons" means a person who is not considered as a national by any State under the operation of its law, including a person who is unable to establish a nationality.'

271 Draft Protocol on Nationality, Art. 2 '"Nationality" means a legal bond between a person and a State and shall not be understood as a reference to ethnic or racial origin.'

272 See the Preamble of the ACHPR (Draft) Protocol on Specific Aspects of the Right to a Nationality and the Eradication of Statelessness in Africa.

Legal and Policy Framework on Nationality and Statelessness   95

The whole essence of the Protocol is fully encapsulated in Article 1,[273] which gives the overall objectives of the Protocol. Article 3(2) of the Protocol reemphasizes the principle in Article 15 of the UDHR, where it provides that 'everyone has the right to a nationality', it further obliges African States not to arbitrarily deprive or deny anyone the right to nationality or the right to change nationality. Article 3(2)(c) provides that 'States have the obligation to act, both alone and in cooperation with each other, to eradicate statelessness and to ensure that every person has the right to the nationality of at least one State where he or she has an appropriate connection.' Appropriate connection was defined in Article 2 of the Protocol to mean,

> connection by personal or family life to a State and shall, among others, include a connection by one or more of the following attributes: birth in the relevant State, descent from or adoption by a national of the State, habitual residence in the State, marriage to a national of the State, birth of a person's parent, child or spouse in the State's territory, the State's being the location of the person's family life, or, in the context of succession of States, a legal bond to a territorial unit of a predecessor State which has become territory of the successor State.

The Protocol provided for other very important protection safeguards such as the prohibition of discrimination on the ground of race, ethnic group, colour, sex, language, religion, political or any other opinion, national or social origin, fortune, disability, or birth in the grant or refusal of nationality,[274] equal rights to women and men in the acquisition, change or retention, the transmission of their nationality to their children,[275] attribution of nationality at birth to a child whose parents had the nationality of that State at the time of the child's birth, subject to any exceptions which may be provided for by its domestic law as regards children born abroad. It, however, encourage States to always provide for the attribution of nationality to a child born abroad if either of the child's parents has its nationality and was born in its territory if the child *would otherwise be stateless*; a child

---

273 Article 1 'The object and purpose of this Protocol is to establish the obligations and responsibilities of States relative to the specific aspects of the right to a nationality in Africa and to ensure that statelessness is eradicated. (2) The provisions of this Protocol shall be interpreted in light of this object and purpose.'

274 See the Draft Protocol Art. 4(1).

275 See *Ibid* Art. 4(2).
Article 9 of the Draft Protocol provides that a State party shall provide in law that:
'Marriage or the dissolution of a marriage between a national and a non-national shall not automatically change the nationality of either spouse nor affect the capacity of the national to transmit his or her nationality to his or her children.
The change of nationality of one spouse during marriage shall not automatically affect the nationality of the other spouse or of the children. '
This protection safeguard is particularly important for women from countries where women will have to lose their nationality when they marry a foreigner.

96 *Legal and Policy Framework on Nationality and Statelessness*

born in the territory of the State of one parent also born there; a child born in the territory of the State of parents who are stateless or of unknown nationality or in other circumstances in which the child would otherwise be stateless.[276]

The Protocol also places an obligation on State parties to retroactively attribute nationality from the date of birth to a child found in its territory of unknown parents, who shall be considered to have been born within that territory of parents possessing the nationality of that State; recognition of nationality at a majority age of a person born in the territory of the State who has remained habitually resident there during a period of his or her childhood; by the declaration of the child or one of his or her parents; and a child adopted by a national.[277]

Article 6 further simplified acquisition of nationality for persons who are habitual residents in a territory, encouraging that in establishing the condition for such acquisition, States should not impose a period of residency beyond ten years, among others. Further to the provision on habitual residence, Article 7(1) provides that 'in the case where entitlement to nationality or other right under this Protocol depends on habitual residence, a State party may require that residence to be lawful, unless the person would otherwise be stateless.' Article 10(2) provides for nationality for children born out of wedlock, where it says that 'in determining the nationality of a child, the law shall not distinguish between those born in and out of wedlock.' The Protocol also allows cases of multiple nationalities,[278] contrary to the laws of some African States, including measures to prevent statelessness in cases of State succession.[279]

The Protocol tries to bridge a gap that no other African instrument before it had filled, which is access to nationality for nomadic and cross-border populations. In this regard the Protocol provides that in the case of persons whose habitual residence is in doubt, including persons who follow a pastoralist or nomadic lifestyle and whose migratory routes cross borders, or who live in border regions, that State parties should take all necessary measures to ensure that such persons have the right to nationality of at least one of the States to which they have an appropriate connection.[280] Specific provisions for the facilitation of nationality for persons who are already stateless was also made in the Protocol.[281]

---

276 See the Draft Protocol Art. 5(1)(a)–(c).
277 See *Ibid* Art. 5(2)(a)–(c).
278 *Ibid* Art. 11.
279 *Ibid* Art. 20.
280 See *Ibid* Art. 8(a).
281 Article 19 provides:

> (1) A State Party shall provide in law for a process to facilitate the recognition or acquisition of its nationality by persons having an appropriate connection to that State whose nationality is in doubt, for the attribution of the status of stateless person if it is determined that the person does not possess the nationality of the State concerned or any other State, and for the facilitation of the acquisition of its nationality by stateless persons as provided in Article 6(3) of this Protocol.

Apart from the non-expulsion principle in Article 18(1) of the Protocol, it also preserves the principle of *non-refoulement* in the 1951 Refugee Convention, in its Article 18(2) where it provides that 'a State Party shall not expel any person in violation of the principles of international human rights or refugee law, including peremptory norms with respect to the protection of persons from exposure to severe violations of their fundamental human rights, such as the prohibition of torture, and inhuman or degrading treatment or punishment, the application of the death penalty or risk of statelessness.'

3.3.4.1.1.2 African Charter on the Rights and Welfare of the Child The African Charter on the Rights and Welfare of the Child (hereinafter ACRWC) was adopted by the 26th Ordinary Session of the Assembly of Heads of State and Government of the OAU (now AU) in Addis Abba, Ethiopia in July 1990. The Charter entered into force on 29 November 1999.[282] As of the time of writing, the ACRWC has been ratified by 49 African States.[283]

The ACRWC imposes an obligation on States parties to grant the following rights which are necessary for the prevention of statelessness for the child; the right from birth to a name,[284] the right to be registered immediately after birth,[285] and ultimately, the right to acquire a nationality.[286] The ACRWC in harmony with the 1961 Convention obliges State parties to ensure that their national law complies with the principle that a 'child shall acquire the nationality of the State in the territory of which he has been born if, at the time of the child's birth he is not granted nationality by any other State in accordance with its laws.'[287] Despite the foregoing provision, not many African States have provisions guaranteeing the right to nationality for children who would otherwise be stateless. According to Bronwen Manby:

---

   (2) A State Party shall accord stateless persons in its territory treatment as favourable as possible and, in any event, shall ensure the protection of stateless persons in its territory in accordance with the obligations of the African Charter on Human and Peoples' Rights.

   (3) A State Party shall provide consular and other appropriate assistance, including the issuance of identity and travel documents, to stateless persons in their territory.

282 See AU website on Treaties and Protocol https://au.int/en/treaties/african-charter -rights-and-welfare-child (accessed 30 October 2020).

    'The charter was adopted within a year of the adoption of the United Nations Convention on the Rights of the Child (CRC).' See Health and Human Rights (H&HR) 'African Charter on the Rights and Welfare of the Child' 1 http://www.who.int/hhr/African %20Child%20Charter.pdf (accessed 31 May 2018).

283 See Ratification table of the African Commission on Human and Peoples' Rights 'African Charter on the Rights and Welfare of the Child' https://au.int/sites/default/files/trea-ties/36804-sl-AFRICAN %20CHARTER%20ON%20THE%20RIGHTS%20AND%20W ELFARE%20OF%20THE%20CHILD.pdf (accessed 30 October 2020).

284 ACRWC Art. 6(1).

285 *Ibid* Art. 6(2).

286 *Ibid* Art. 6(3).

287 *Ibid* Art. 6(4).

98 Legal and Policy Framework on Nationality and Statelessness

Only 13 African countries specifically provide in their nationality laws (in accordance with Article 1 of the 1961 Convention on the Reduction of Statelessness and Article 6(4) of the African Charter on the Rights and Welfare of the Child) that children born on their territory who would otherwise be stateless have the right to nationality; an additional 6 have provisions granting nationality to the children of stateless parents (but by itself this is not sufficient protection for those whose parents themselves have a nationality but cannot transmit it to their children).[288]

3.3.4.1.1.2.1 The African Committee of Experts on the Rights and Welfare of the Child The African Committee of Experts on the Rights and Welfare of the Child (hereinafter in this section, the Committee) which draws its mandate from Articles 32–46 of the ACRWC was established in 2001.[289] The mission statement of the Committee describes its role *inter alia*, as 'playing a leading role in the promotion and protection of the rights and welfare of the child in Africa through informing and influencing child friendly laws, policies and practices, empowering children and their parents to understand and exercise their rights, keeping governments accountable, and securing the African Children's Charter'.[290] In addition to the foregoing mission statement, the Committee is expected to formulate and lay down principles and rules aimed at protecting the rights and welfare of children in Africa and cooperate with international and regional organizations concerned with the promotion and protection of the rights and welfare of the child.[291]

State parties to the Charter are obliged to submit to the Committee through the Secretary-General of the AU, 'reports on the measures they have adopted which give effect to the provisions of the Charter and on the progress made in the enjoyment of these rights.'[292] In addition to other rights that children should ordinarily be entitled to at birth, the Committee has often raised concerns about the lack of full implementation of birth registration and the low rate of birth registration amongst member States,[293] which exposes many children to the risk of statelessness.

The Committee in its first decision in *IHRDA & OSJI (on behalf of children of Nubian descent in Kenya) v. Kenya*[294] (better known as the *Nubian Children's*

---

288 B Manby 'Citizenship Law in Africa, a comparative study' (2016) *African Minds & Open Society Foundations* 4.

289 See AU website on the work of the Committee https://au.int/en/sa/acerwc (accessed 30 October 2020).

290 AU *The African Committee of Experts on the Rights and Welfare of the Child: Strategic plan (2015–2019)* 3.

291 ACRWC Art. 42. See also AU *General Comment on Article 6 of the African Charter on the Rights and Welfare of the Child* (2014) 3 https://www.refworld.org/docid/54db21734 .html (accessed 16 June 2022).

292 See Art. 43(1) of the ACRWC.

293 AU *General Comment on Article 6 of the African Charter on the Rights and Welfare of the Child, Op Cit* 3.

294 No. 002/Com/002/2009.

Legal and Policy Framework on Nationality and Statelessness 99

case), took a clear stand with regard to stateless children. Wherein, *inter alia*, the Committee found the Government of Kenya to violate the right to birth registration and nationality,[295] non-discrimination,[296] education,[297] and health services.[298] The Committee: 'Recommends that the Government of Kenya should take all necessary legislative, administrative, and other measures in order to ensure that children of Nubian decent in Kenya, that are otherwise stateless, can acquire a Kenyan nationality and the proof of such a nationality at birth,' and that the Government of Kenya implement a birth registration system in a non-discriminatory manner, taking all necessary legislative, administrative, and other measures to ensure that children of Nubian descent are registered immediately after birth.

The Committee did not just stop at the above decision; in accordance with its Rules of Procedure, it appointed one of its members to follow up on the implementation of its decision, while advising that the Government of Kenya report on the implementation of the recommendations within six months from the date of notification of the Committee's decision.

3.3.4.1.1.3 The Protocol to the African Charter on Human and Peoples' Rights on the Rights of Women in Africa The Protocol to the African Charter on Human and Peoples' Rights on the Rights of Women in Africa (hereinafter the Maputo Protocol) was adopted by the 2nd Ordinary Session of the Assembly of the AU in Maputo, Mozambique on 11 July 2003.[299] After ratification by 15 African States, the Maputo Protocol entered into force on 25 November 2005.[300] The Maputo Protocol has been signed and ratified by 36 State parties, with 15 signing without ratifying it and three yet to sign or ratify it.[301] The Protocol, like every other Protocol to the ACHPR, is made pursuant to Article 66, which provides for special protocols or agreements, if necessary, to supplement the provisions of the African Charter, and in 'furtherance of Resolution AHG/Res.240 (XXXI) made at the 31st Ordinary Session in Addis Ababa in June 1995 by the Assembly of Heads of State and Government of the OAU recommending the African Commission on Human and Peoples' Rights to elaborate a Protocol on the Rights of Women in Africa.'[302]

---

295 ACRWC Art. 6.
296 ACRWC Art. 3.
297 ACRWC Art. 11(3).
298 ACRWC Art. 14(2)(b), (c), and (g).
299 See AU website on the Maputo Protocol https://au.int/en/treaties/protocol-african -charter-human-and-peoples-rights-rights-women-africa (accessed 31 October 2020).
300 Centre for Reproductive Health *The Protocol on the Rights of Women in Africa: An instrument for advancing reproductive and sexual rights* (February 2006) Briefing Paper 1.
301 See 'Ratification Table: Protocol to the African Charter on Human and Peoples' Rights on the Rights of Women in Africa' 14 http://www.achpr.org/instruments/women-protocol /ratification/ (accessed 2 June 2018).
302 Preamble of the Protocol to the African Charter on Human and People's Rights on the Rights of Women in Africa.

100 *Legal and Policy Framework on Nationality and Statelessness*

The Maputo Protocol obliges States parties to include the principle of equality between women and men in their national Constitutions, to enact appropriate legislation or put regulatory measures in place to prohibit and curb all forms of discrimination against women, and to ensure their effective application.[303] The Protocol also allows a woman to 'retain her nationality or to acquire the nationality of her husband';[304] this provision is very significant, in the sense that it protects women from countries where they are made to lose their nationality on account of marriage to a foreign man. Despite the safeguards in the Maputo Protocol, it has been criticized for giving leeway for abuse of the rights provided in the Protocol especially with regard to the ability of women to transmit their nationality to their children, and the silence with regard to the ability of women to transmit same to their foreign spouses. For instance, the Institute of Statelessness and Inclusion (ISI) observed thus:

> The Maputo Protocol is more limited in its promotion of women's equal right to acquire, retain and transmit nationality than the international standards, providing only that 'a woman shall have the right to retain her nationality or to acquire the nationality of her husband' and 'a woman and a man shall have equal rights with respect to the nationality of their children except where this is contrary to a provision in national legislation or is contrary to national security interests.'[305]

Article 6(h) of the Protocol, which allows a national law of member States to override the principle of equality and non-discrimination, is arguably contrary to its all-important Article 2, which seeks to ensure that States adopts the principle of equality and non-discrimination in their national laws.

3.3.4.2 *Economic Community of West African States (ECOWAS)*

The Economic Community of West African States (ECOWAS) was formed on 28 May 1975, when a Treaty establishing it was signed in Lagos. ECOWAS was established with the main aim of promoting the cooperation and regional integration of West African States. The Treaty of ECOWAS was revised in 1993.[306] Out of the 15 ECOWAS States, nine are party to the 1954 Convention on the status of stateless persons, and eight are party to the 1961 Convention on the reduction of statelessness.[307]

---

303 Maputo Protocol Art. 2.

304 *Ibid* Art. 6(g).

305 Institute of Statelessness and Inclusion 'Statelessness and human rights' http://www.sta telessnessandhumanrights.org/other-human-rights-frameworks/regional-human-rights -frameworks (accessed 4 June 2018).

306 See Revised Treaty of ECOWAS 1993 https://www.ecowas.int/wp-content/uploads /2015/01/Revised-treaty.pdf (accessed 10 May 2020).

307 UNHCR *First anniversary of the Abidjan Declaration on the eradication of statelessness* (25 February 2016) http://www.unhcr.org/news/press/2016/2/56ceda796/first-anniversary-abidjan-declaration-eradication-statelessness.html# (accessed 14 July 2018).

Legal and Policy Framework on Nationality and Statelessness 101

3.3.4.2.1 ECOWAS SUB-REGIONAL LEGAL AND POLICY FRAMEWORK ON THE PREVENTION OF STATELESSNESS

ECOWAS has been described by the AU as the most advanced regional organization in the area of combating statelessness amongst the eight Regional Economic Communities (REC) which form the pillars of the AU. In addition to its potential advantages for resolving the issue of statelessness, the AU further notes that the ECOWAS is 'the REC which has made the most progress in the area of regional integration and free movement, residence, work, and the right of establishment. Furthermore, it has a protocol that deals with the notion of ECOWAS citizenship.'[308]

Despite the absence of a binding framework[309] to address the issue of statelessness, ECOWAS is reputed for galvanizing member States to respond to the issue of statelessness through several advocacies which encouraged members States to accede to the 1954 Convention relating to the Status of Stateless Persons and/or the 1961 Convention on the Reduction of Statelessness.[310] An example of such advocacies and initiatives by ECOWAS is the February 2015 Abidjan Declaration of Ministers of ECOWAS Member States on Eradication of Statelessness in West Africa,[311] which was made after two days of high-level consultations held in Abidjan, Côte d'Ivoire between 23 and 24 February 2015 at a joint UNHCR/ ECOWAS Ministerial Conference hosted by the Government of Côte d'Ivoire.[312] The Declaration, which is the first of its kind in Africa, covers issues on prevention of statelessness,[313] on identification, and on protection of stateless persons.[314]

Below are the main measures put in place by the ECOWAS to protect against, prevent, and reduce statelessness in the sub-region succinctly examined.

3.3.4.2.1.1 Abidjan Declaration of Ministers of ECOWAS on the Eradication of Statelessness, February 2015

The Abidjan Declaration of Ministers of ECOWAS on the Eradication of Statelessness otherwise known as Abidjan Declaration, described as a 'historical instrument and a milestone in the fight against statelessness in

---

308 Department of Political Affairs African Union Commission 'Statelessness impact on Africa's development and the need for its eradication, the African Union approach to the right to nationality in Africa' para. 18 http://www.achpr.org/files/news/2016/07/d249/presentation_approach_on_statelessness_in_africa_dpa_auc.pdf (accessed 4 June 2018).

309 The lack of legal framework is not due to lack of competence within the region, but due to the unwillingness of member States over the years to identify statelessness as an issue.

310 See *Banjul Plan of Action of The Economic Community of West African States (ECOWAS) on the Eradication of Statelessness 2017–2024* 1.

311 See Abidjan Declaration 2015 Art. 4.

312 ECOWAS Commission 'ECOWAS members adopt a Declaration on eradication of statelessness in West Africa. Joint UNHCR/ECOWAS Press Release' http://www.ecowas.int /ecowas-members-adopt-a-declaration-on-eradication-of-statelessness-in-west-africa/ (accessed 4 June 2018).

313 Abidjan Declaration 2015 Arts. 1–13.

314 *Ibid* Arts. 14–17.

102 *Legal and Policy Framework on Nationality and Statelessness*

West Africa,'[315] was adopted on 25 February 2015 at the first Ministerial Conference on Statelessness in Abidjan, Côte d'Ivoire, jointly organized by the UNHCR and ECOWAS.[316] The Declaration, which is the first of its kind, includes 25 specific commitments to addressing and putting an end to statelessness in West Africa by 2024,[317] covering broad issues on prevention of statelessness,[318] and on identification and protection of stateless persons.[319] Through the Declaration, States commit to resolving existing statelessness situations[320] and develop strategies and partnerships for fighting statelessness.[321] The Declaration moreover 'called upon the African Union to prepare and adopt a Protocol to the African Charter on Human and Peoples' Rights on the right to a nationality.'[322]

The Declaration encouraged ECOWAS member States who are yet to accede to the Statelessness Conventions to do so as soon as possible and to collaborate with the UNHCR to review their nationality laws to comply with international standards.[323] To this effect, member States undertook to 'prevent and reduce statelessness by reforming constitutional, legislative and institutional regimes related to nationality in order to include appropriate safeguards against statelessness, in particular, to ensure that every child acquires a nationality at birth and that all foundlings are considered nationals of the State in which they are found.'[324] In this regard, the Institute of Statelessness and Inclusion observed that:

> Four States (Guinea, Burkina Faso, Liberia and Togo) have announced revisions of their nationality laws while Senegal is preparing a Children's Act which would protect against statelessness at birth. In terms of accessions to the UN Statelessness Conventions, Guinea-Bissau, Mali and Sierra Leone have ratified both Conventions, Burkina Faso has acceded to the 1961 Convention, and Ghana and Togo are taking steps towards accession.[325]

---

315 *Banjul Plan of Action of The Economic Community of West African States (ECOWAS) on the Eradication of Statelessness 2017–2024* 1.
316 Preamble of the Abidjan Declaration 2015.
317 Institute of Statelessness and Inclusion (ISI) 'World's stateless children' 27 https://emnbelgium.be/sites/default/files/publications/worldsstateless17.pdf (accessed 4 June 2018).
    'The conference also resulted in the adoption of 62 recommendations on how to implement the commitments made. The Abidjan Declaration was endorsed by all Heads of States in May 2015 in Accra, Ghana, during the ECOWAS Summit.'
    Banjul Plan of Action of The Economic Community of West African States (ECOWAS) on the Eradication of Statelessness 2017–2024 1.
318 Abidjan Declaration 2015 Declarations 1–13.
319 *Ibid* Declarations 14–17.
320 *Ibid* Declarations 18–20.
321 *Ibid* Declarations 21–25.
322 *Ibid* Declaration 5.
323 *Ibid* Declaration 4.
324 *Ibid* Declaration 2.
325 Institute of Statelessness and Inclusion (ISI) 'World's stateless children' *Op Cit* 28.

Furthermore, in line with State parties' commitment to the implementation of the Convention on the Elimination of All Forms of Discrimination against Women and the Protocol to the African Charter on Human and Peoples' Rights on the Rights of Women in Africa, the Declaration emphasizes the need for ECOWAS member States to ensure that men and women have equal rights to acquire, change and retain their nationality and confer nationality to their children.[326] Members also undertook to develop and implement national action plans to end statelessness in accordance with UNHCR's global campaign to end statelessness within ten years, which led to the preparation and adoption of the ECOWAS Plan of Action on Eradication of Statelessness 2017–2024[327] (otherwise known as the Banjul Plan of Action). The shortfall of the Abidjan Declaration is that it is only a declaration of intention of ECOWAS member States and not a binding instrument.

One of the very remarkable parts of the Abidjan Declaration is its Declaration 5, which calls upon the African Union to prepare and adopt a protocol to the African Charter on Human and Peoples' Rights on the Right to Nationality. The AU Draft Protocol on nationality could therefore be said to have been inspired by the February Abidjan 2015 Declaration of Ministers of ECOWAS States.

3.3.4.2.1.2 The ECOWAS Plan of Action on Eradication of Statelessness 2017–2024 (Banjul Plan of Action)

In furtherance of the commitments in the Abidjan Declaration of Ministers of ECOWAS wherein member States committed to develop national action plans to end statelessness as per UNHCR's global campaign to end statelessness by 2024, and to work with the UNHCR and other stakeholders to better understand the issue of statelessness,[328] a draft Regional Plan of Action on eradication of statelessness in ECOWAS was drafted in April 2016. This signifies the interest of member States to adopt legally binding plans and begin the implementation phase of the Abidjan Declaration.[329] On 9 May 2017, two years after the Abidjan Declaration, the draft Regional Plan of Action on Eradication of Statelessness 2017–2024 (otherwise known as Banjul Plan of Action) was validated and adopted at a Regional Ministerial Meeting held under the Chairmanship of the Republic of Benin in Banjul, the Gambia.[330]

According to UNHCR, 'the Banjul Plan of Action sets out concrete measures to end statelessness by 2024 and is legally binding on all the Member States.'[331] With the adoption of the Banjul Plan, West Africa became the first

---

326 Abidjan Declaration 2015 Declaration 3.
327 The *ECOWAS Plan of Action on Eradication of Statelessness 2017–2024.*
328 See Declarations 24 and 25 of the Abidjan Declaration 2015.
329 Institute of Statelessness and Inclusion (ISI) 'World's stateless children' *Op Cit* 26–27.
330 Economic Community of West African States (ECOWAS) *Joint Statement of the ECOWAS Ministers responsible for nationality matters on the Ministerial Meeting for the Validation and Adoption of the Banjul Plan of Action to Eradicate Statelessness in the ECOWAS Region* (9 May 2017); UNHCR, 'Mobilizing governments and civil society #ibelong campaign' 2 http://www.refworld.org/pdfid/59661b4e4.pdf (accessed 6 June 2018).
331 UNHCR 'Mobilizing governments and civil society #ibelong campaign' *Op Cit* 2.

104   *Legal and Policy Framework on Nationality and Statelessness*

region in the world to develop a plan of action to end statelessness. The Plan of Action also contains mechanisms for monitoring the implementation of the Abidjan Declaration.[332] 'By the time the Banjul Plan came into effect, 12 of the 15 ECOWAS States had acceded to the 1954 Convention and 11 had acceded to the 1961 Convention, with 2 more States in the accession process.'[333]

At the first anniversary of the Abidjan Declaration in February 2016, even before the adoption and validation of the Banjul Plan of Action, '9 of the 15 ECOWAS States had begun developing action plans for the eradication of statelessness with 2 (Benin and Gambia) having been approved at the Ministerial level.'[334] By the end of 2016, Nigeria had also joined Benin and the Gambia with the hosting of a workshop specifically to draft a National Plan of Action to end statelessness by 2014. The draft plan was later revised in December 2018 and adopted by the country's Federal Executive Council in November 2020.

Specifically, the Banjul Plan comprises six strategic objectives or targets to assist ECOWAS member States in their efforts to eradicate statelessness by 2024, which is the same time frame set by the UNHCR for the Global Campaign to end statelessness.[335] The objectives include the following, that member States put in measures to ensure compliance with relevant legal, policy, and institutional frameworks for eradicating statelessness;[336] strengthen data management systems for effective response to the challenges of statelessness;[337] allow free movement of stateless persons, integration, and protection;[338] promote advocacy and sensitization of populations and stakeholders;[339] guarantee access to proof of nationality;[340] and establish strategic and operational monitoring and follow-up mechanisms.[341]

3.4 Identified Gaps in the International and Regional Frameworks

Despite all the laudable instruments to tackle the issue of statelessness and nationality challenges at the international and regional levels, there continue to be some very identifiable gaps in these instruments. In this chapter, several international legal and policy frameworks on the right to nationality and prevention of statelessness were discussed, with a focus on regional frameworks in the AU, the CoE, the EU, the OAS, and the Arab League. Some of the very significant ones are elucidated below.

---

332 Banjul Plan of Action *Op Cit* 1, 14, and 15 at paras. 5.1.8 and 6.
333 G Edwards 'How effective is the United Nations in dealing with statelessness?' https:// garaviewnyu.com/2018/03/13/how-effective-is-the-united-nations-in-dealing-with -statelessness/ (accessed 10 November 2020).
334 Institute on Statelessness and Inclusion (ISI) 'World's stateless children' *Op Cit* 26–27.
335 See G Edwards *Op Cit.*
336 Banjul Plan of Action Objective 1.
337 *Ibid* Objective 2.
338 *Ibid* Objective 3.
339 *Ibid* Objective 4.
340 *Ibid* Objective 5.
341 *Ibid* Objective 6.

Legal and Policy Framework on Nationality and Statelessness 105

3.4.1 Access to Territory to Apply for Recognition as a Stateless Person

The most pertinent question amongst scholars on the international and regional legal frameworks is, how sufficient or otherwise are these frameworks? The two Statelessness Conventions, as well as other international and regional frameworks, are silent on the issue of access to the territory to apply for recognition as a stateless person. Municipal laws of most countries require foreigners, including stateless persons, to legally enter and reside in their territory before going through the statelessness determination procedure[342] which may or may not cumulate into naturalization. For example, in the UK, as shall be discussed in Chapter 5, in addition to the requirement to be in the UK as at the time of application,[343] the UK Home Office's Nationality: Good Character Requirement[344] prevents the naturalization of persons, including stateless persons, who irregularly enter the UK within the ten years preceding a citizenship application. This should not be the case; instead, the exceptions given to refugees in this context should also apply to stateless persons.

3.4.2 Lack of Specific Approaches to the Issue of Naturalization

Although the 1954 Convention Relating to the Status of Stateless Persons obliges States to expedite the naturalization process for stateless persons and 'reduce as far as possible the charges and costs of such proceedings,'[345] it leaves this to the discretion of States. Therefore, there are different approaches to the issue of naturalization. Most states do not allow expedited naturalization for stateless persons. Apart from Brazil's Decree No. 9, 199 of 2017, whose Article 99 allows stateless persons to access naturalization within 30 days of recognition of their statelessness, other states do not grant immediate access to naturalization. For instance, in Moldova, stateless persons have to wait for eight years before they can be eligible to apply for naturalization, while they have to wait for 15 years in Nigeria before being eligible for naturalization. No regional or international instrument is specific on how stateless persons should naturalize in the member States.

3.4.3 Absence of Provisions Against Refoulemenet

Unlike in the asylum regime, where there is a clear obligation on states not to deport or *refoule* persons seeking asylum back to the territory where their lives

---

342 However, Art. 97 of Decree 9199/17 | Decree No. 9,199 of 20 November 2017 provides that 'irregular entry into the national territory does not constitute an impediment to the request for recognition of the stateless condition and to the application of the mechanisms for the protection of the stateless person and the reduction of statelessness.'
343 See Art. 401(b) of Part 14 of the UK's Immigration Rules.
344 *Ibid.*
345 1954 Convention Art. 32.

would be in danger, the Statelessness Conventions, as well as other international and regional instruments on statelessness and the right to nationality, are silent on the issue of deportation. Unlike in asylum procedures, most States do not provide as many protective safeguards for statelessness status applicants whose application is still pending with the authorities, especially protection against deportation. This means that, in some situations, applicants for statelessness status could be deported from these States even when their application is still pending. One example is France (See Chapter 5), where although an applicant whose stateless application is rejected has a right of appeal to the Administrative Court, such appeal cannot suspend the deportation order. It is therefore recommended that pending the decision of an appeal challenging the decision rejecting an application, an applicant should be allowed to remain in the territory of the host State and enjoy some protection.

3.5 Conclusion

In this chapter, the international legal and policy framework on the right to nationality and prevention of statelessness was discussed with a focus on regional frameworks in the AU, the CoE, the EU, the OAS and the Arab League. It was observed that none of these regions is free of the problem of statelessness. This chapter concluded with an analysis of the gaps in the international and regional frameworks and possible remedies for such gaps.

4 Procedural Framework for Determining Statelessness
Applicable Standards and Criteria[1]

4.1 Introduction

Statelessness affects every region of the world. After many decades of lack of attention to the issue of statelessness, a couple of States have begun to introduce legal regimes to protect, identify, prevent, and eradicate statelessness in their domain. 'Since 2010, an accelerating proliferation of so-called statelessness-specific protection regimes can be witnessed, in particular in Europe and the Americas.'[2] These two regions are leading the way with respect to the protection, identification, prevention, and eradication of statelessness. Other States and regions may want to learn from them. Indeed, in many other States across the world, especially in Africa, there are virtually no statelessness determination

---

1 This chapter is drawn mainly from my joint article published by the *Statelessness and Citizenship Review* (SCR) in June 2020 – S Oseghale Momoh, H van Eijken, and C Ryngaert 'Statelessness Determination Procedures: Towards a Bespoke Procedure for Nigeria' (2020) 2 (1) *The Statelessness and Citizenship Review* 86–111 https://statelessnessandcitizenshipreview .com/index.php/journal/article/view/137 (accessed 20 August 2020).
2 ENS, Amicus Curiae by G Gyulai, submitted by the European Network on Statelessness to the Borgating Court of Appeal in Norway, in case number 17-073503ASD-BORG/01 [anonymised version – personal data omitted] (25 May 2018) 2–3 https://www.refworld .org/docid/5b361e374.html (accessed 17 April 2020). Relevant European countries include Bulgaria, France, Georgia, Hungary, Italy, Latvia, Kosovo, Moldova, Spain, Turkey, and the United Kingdom. See N Radnai 'Statelessness determination in Europe: Towards the implementation of regionally harmonised national SDP' (2017) 8 *Institute of Statelessness and Inclusion (ISI) Statelessness Working Paper Series* 6; G Gyulai Presentation on Statelessness for the Serbian Government delegation: General Framework and State Practice, held at UNHCR Regional Representation for Central Europe (4 November 2014); K Bianchini 'A comparative analysis of statelessness determination procedures in 10 EU States' (2017) 29 (1) *International Journal of Refugee Law* 43 https://doi-org.proxy.library.uu.nl/10.1093/ijrl/eex009 (accessed 17 April 2020). Countries in the Americas include Argentina, Brazil, Costa Rica, Ecuador, Mexico, Paraguay, Panama, Peru, and Uruguay. See ENS, Amicus Curiae *Op Cit.*

DOI: 10.4324/9781003278733-4

108 *Procedural Framework for Determining Statelessness*

procedures (SDP), whether of an administrative or judicial nature,[3] save for Côte d'Ivoire with its recent adoption of an SDP, the first in the African continent.[4]

This part aims to identify international norms and best practices regarding the establishment and operation of an SDP and to apply these to a future SDP in Nigeria. When proposing an SDP for Nigeria, this research strives for the most extensive protection for stateless persons, while taking the particular legal and institutional framework of Nigeria into account. Nigeria is chosen as a case study as it currently lacks a specific procedure for the protection, identification, and prevention of statelessness, although it has recently pledged to develop an SDP.[5] The development of such a procedure is urgent, as a sizable number of persons in Nigeria are at risk of statelessness,[6] mainly undocumented border populations. This includes notably the Bakassi population, which was affected by the cession of a part of Nigeria (Bakassi) to Cameroon in the wake of a judgment of the International Court of Justice.[7] It also includes the Almajiri, i.e., children sent to study Islamic education with Islamic scholars from their childhood and with no records of birth,[8] undocumented nomads who move from one place or country to another,[9] internally displaced persons, and border populations with no means of identification.[10]

For the identification of the normative framework, the study draws the relevant standards from international law, the practice of States, and practices

---

3 Many African States like Nigeria have neither conducted mapping on statelessness nor have mechanisms to identify stateless persons within their territories. Therefore, the current estimated figure of about 10 million stateless persons worldwide by the UNHCR may just be half of the actual number. No country in Africa has a statelessness determination procedure in place at the moment, but this is gradually changing with the recent initiatives by the Economic Community of West African States (ECOWAS) and the African Union (AU). At the time of writing, the AU is on the verge of finalizing a Draft Protocol to the African Charter on Human and Peoples Rights on the Specific Aspects on the Right to a Nationality and the Eradication of Statelessness in Africa. This Draft Protocol is largely influenced by the ECOWAS Abidjan Declaration of 2015, wherein State members committed 'to prevent and reduce statelessness by reforming constitutional, legislative and institutional regimes related to nationality' and 'called on the African Union to prepare and adopt a Protocol to the African Charter on Human and Peoples' Rights on the Right to Nationality.'

4 See UNHCR 'Côte d'Ivoire adopts Africa's first legal process to identify and protect stateless people' (4 September 2020) https://www.unhcr.org/news/press/2020/9/5f51f33b4/cote-divoire-adopts-africas-first-legal-process-identify-protect-stateless.html (accessed 25 November 2020).

5 See UNHCR *Results of the high-level segment on statelessness* (2019) https://www.unhcr.org/ibelong/results-of-the-high-level-segment-on-statelessness/ (accessed 17 April 2020).

6 Due to the absence of a legal framework in Nigeria, there is no official record of people who are stateless or at risk of statelessness in Nigeria.

7 *Land and Maritime Boundary between Cameroon and Nigeria (Cameroon v. Nigeria: Equatorial Guinea intervening)* Judgment, *ICJ Reports* 2002, 30.

8 B Manby *Nationality, Migration and Statelessness in West Africa: A study for UNHCR and IOM* 78.

9 *Ibid* 70.

10 UNHCR *Nigeria situation: Supplementary appeal January–December 2017* 8.

Procedural Framework for Determining Statelessness 109

recommended by the UN High Commissioner for Refugees (UNHCR). Pertinent UNHCR documents include in particular the UNHCR Global Action Plan to End Statelessness 2014–2024,[11] the resultant UNHCR Good Practice Papers on protection, identification, and prevention of statelessness,[12] and guidelines offered by the UNHCR Handbook on Protection of Stateless Persons.[13] These standards could roughly be divided into the following categories: protection, avoidance, and identification.[14]

In terms of structure, this chapter sets out to define the concept of SDP (Part 4.2), map international standards that may guide States in establishing an SDP and develop criteria through which the practices in States with existing procedures can be assessed (Part 4.3). Subsequently, these standards and criteria are applied to the situation in Nigeria (Chapter 6, Part 6.3).

4.2 Statelessness Determination Procedures: Definition and Purpose

A statelessness determination procedure (SDP) could be defined as a procedure, whether administrative or judicial, meant to determine whether or not a person or a population is considered as national of any State under the operation of its law,[15] with a view to finding durable solutions for the affected person or population. The solutions after recognition as a stateless person may range from a grant of protection status to an outright grant of nationality.[16] Mirna Adjami notes that

---

11 UNHCR *Global action plan to end statelessness 2014–2024* (November 2014).
   The ten Global Action Points agreed with State parties are: Action 1: Resolve existing major situations of statelessness. Action 2: Ensure that no child is born stateless. Action 3: Remove gender discrimination from nationality laws. Action 4: Prevent denial, loss or deprivation of nationality on discriminatory grounds. Action 5: Prevent statelessness in cases of State succession. Action 6: Grant protection status to stateless migrants and facilitate their naturalization. Action 7: Ensure birth registration for the prevention of statelessness. Action 8: Issue nationality documentation to those with entitlement to it. Action 9: Accede to the UN statelessness conventions. Action 10: Improve quantitative and qualitative data on stateless populations.

12 'In 2015 UNHCR launched a series of good practice papers, each of which corresponds to one of the 10 Actions in the Global Action Plan to end statelessness by 2024. Each paper highlights examples of how States, UNHCR and other stakeholders have addressed statelessness in a number of countries.' See web link to the already published UNHCR Statelessness Good Practice Papers https://www.refworld.org/statelessness.html (accessed 5 December 2015).

13 UNHCR *Handbook on protection of stateless persons under the 1954 Convention on Relating to the Status of Stateless Persons* (2014).

14 See K Swider and M den Heijer 'Why union law can and should protect stateless persons' (2017) 19 (2) *European Journal of Migration and Law* 106 https://doi.org/10.1163/15718166-12340004 (accessed 2 December 2019).

15 See Convention Relating to the Status of Stateless Persons 1954 Art. 1.

16 A recognition of statelessness through SDP should automatically grant protection status that would cumulate into naturalization eventually, especially for those in a migratory context. Otherwise, the SDP would not have fulfilled the obligation under Convention Relating to

110 *Procedural Framework for Determining Statelessness*

SDP 'involves first identifying all States with which an individual has ties, such as through birth, filiation, marriage, or habitual residence, and then determining whether any of those identified States considers the individual as a national, either as a matter of law or as a matter of practice.'[17] The foregoing should be done to acknowledge a person as stateless where the circumstances or findings suggest so, to subsequently grant protection, and to facilitate naturalization for stateless persons.

Article 15 of the Universal Declaration of Human Rights (UDHR) provides that 'everyone has the right to a nationality.' This reaffirms the importance of nationality for the enjoyment of human rights. By virtue of Article 15 of the UDHR, in addition to the obligations to protect, identify, and prevent statelessness, States must also ensure the eradication of statelessness by ensuring that everyone holds a nationality,[18] including from birth.[19] While the possession of nationality will lead to the enjoyment of fundamental rights, such as residency rights, health care, free movement, education, family life, and political rights, amongst others, the absence of it creates a legal impediment to the enjoyment of those rights.[20] Thus, identification of stateless persons within a territory is very important, as it would enable them to 'live in dignity until their situation can be resolved through the acquisition of a nationality.'[21] On the meaning of protection in the statelessness context, Gábor Gyulai notes that 'in its broadest sense, means that a stateless person has access to and can enjoy the rights enshrined in the 1954 Convention and in other relevant international human rights instruments.'[22] Arguably, protection in a statelessness context will encompass all

---

the Status of Stateless Persons 1954, Articles 3–32. Additionally, the *in situ* population and those with longstanding residence should be able to immediately access naturalization.

17 M Adjami *Statelessness and nationality in Côte d'Ivoire. A study for UNHCR* (December 2006) 41.

18 See UNHCR *Protecting the rights of stateless persons: The 1954 Convention relating to the Status of Stateless Persons* (2014) 2.

19 See the Convention on the Rights of the Child 1989 Art. 7, and the International Covenant on Civil and Political Rights 1966, Art. 24(3)

20 K Berényi 'An inspiring parallel between the Italian and Hungarian jurisprudence with a view to reducing statelessness' (2019) 39 (2) *DPCE Online* http://www.dpceonline.it/index .php/dpceonline/article/view/746/691 (accessed 3 December 2019).

21 UNHCR *Statelessness determination procedures, identifying and protecting stateless persons* (August 2014) 1.

22 G Gyulai 'The determination of statelessness and the establishment of a statelessness-specific protection regime' in A Edwards & L Van Waas (Eds.), *Nationality and statelessness under international law* (2014) 117 https://www-cambridge-org.proxy.library.uu.nl/core/ser-vices/aop-cambridge-core/content/view/D94BCC4432453887628F86866921D996 /9781139506007c5_p116-143_CBO.pdf/determination_of_statelessness_and_the_estab-lishment_of_a_statelessnessspecific_protection_regime.pdf (accessed 17 April 2020). This research focuses mainly on the recognition of statelessness through an SDP, as Nigeria has no SDP in place at the moment. However, Nigeria is also advised to take further steps in addition to an SDP, to ensure that recognized stateless persons enjoy a legal status that enables them to enjoy rights.

Procedural Framework for Determining Statelessness   111

activities and actions that ensure that a State identifies the existing situation of statelessness within its territory with the aim of granting legal status, preventing future occurrence, and ensuring the enjoyment of rights for stateless persons.

The absence of an SDP would often mean that stateless persons are not identified within the country. 'Without proper identification of stateless persons, it is unclear whether they are accorded appropriate treatment in line with the Member States' obligations following from international treaties.'[23] Furthermore, a determination procedure should ultimately lead to a durable solution for the stateless person, preferably the grant of nationality. States are obliged to ensure facilitated and expedited naturalization processes for stateless persons.[24] Notably, in the case of stateless persons *in situ*,[25] 'where there is a realistic prospect of acquisition of citizenship in the near future, it may be inappropriate to conduct a determination of whether they are stateless, in particular where this could delay a durable solution, i.e. the grant of nationality.'[26] Depending on the circumstances of the persons under consideration, the UNHCR may recommend that States undertake nationality campaigns or nationality verification rather than SDP.[27] In addition to an SDP, for States where the vast majority of persons do not have any form of national identification to prove their nationality, a nationality verification procedure could be added as an additional layer when an SDP is established.

Although the 1954 Convention relating to the Status of Stateless Persons[28] remains silent about how to determine who is stateless,[29] 'a few States have enacted laws establishing formal procedures to this end, including by integrating

---

23 G-R de Groot, K Swider and O Vonk 'Practice and approach in EU Member States to prevent and end statelessness' (2015) *A Study for the LIBE Committee* 53.

24 See, Convention Relating to the Status of Stateless Persons 1954 Art. 32.

25 See UNHCR *'The lost children of Côte d'Ivoire'* https://www.unhcr.org/ibelong/the-lost-children-of-cote-divoire/ (accessed 15 January 2020), which describes *in situ* statelessness as follows: '[A person who, or] population which has lived in a particular country for many generations without acquiring the nationality of that country. It could also include person or population who have been arbitrarily deprived of their previous nationality, or persons who have lived most of their lives in a country, without having any tie to any other state, even if their ancestors have not lived in the country for generations. The population basically see the country as their own country, but the authorities do not recognise their claim to such nationality, e.g., the situation of many foreigners (mainly of Burkina Faso, Mali and Guinea origin) in Ivory Coast who during colonial times and in the 1960s arrived Ivory Coast to work in Cocoa farms and did not acquire Ivorian nationality when the country gained independence.' Another example is the Rohingya population in Myanmar who for generations have been unable to acquire nationality due to the systematic discrimination of Government authorities.

26 UNHCR *Statelessness determination procedures and the status of stateless persons ('Geneva Conclusions')* (December 2010) 2–3 at para. 2.

27 UNHCR *Handbook on protection of stateless persons Op Cit* 26 at para. 58.

28 Convention Relating to the Status of Stateless Persons, 1954.

29 G Gyulai 'Statelessness determination and the protection status of stateless persons' (2013) *European Network of Statelessness (ENS)* 5.

112 Procedural Framework for Determining Statelessness

determination of statelessness into existing administrative procedures. However, many more States are confronted with situations of statelessness and are increasingly required to make determinations on nationality or statelessness regarding persons on their territory.'[30]

UNHCR advises that determination procedures should be as simple as possible and integrate existing administrative procedures as much as possible. 'Some State practice has, for instance, integrated determination of statelessness in procedures regulating residency rights.'[31] In setting up a determination procedure, States should consider their administrative structure and capacity, the size of the population who are or at risk of statelessness, and existing expertise on statelessness matters.[32]

4.3 Standards and Criteria for Good Statelessness Determination Procedures

This part lays out essential requirements for an SDP, drawing mainly from the UNHCR Statelessness Handbook,[33] Reports and Summary of conclusions of the UNHCR expert meetings on statelessness determination procedures,[34] the UNHCR Guidelines on statelessness,[35] and the two Statelessness Conventions, among other sources.

These standards pertain to the presence of a mechanism for protection, prevention, and identification of statelessness, and will be measured against the specific criteria of (a) legality and binding nature of SDP, (b) structure and location of SDP, (c) access to procedure, (d) procedural guarantees, (e) assessments of facts, (f) management of combined refugee and statelessness claims, (g) prospect for naturalisation, and (h) review and appeal of decision. The procedural guarantees and assessment of evidence will be examined in the context of the right to interview, right to an interpreter, right to legal aid, right to individual application for family members (where necessary), right to appeal and review of decision, absence of the requirement of legal residency as a basis for recognition of statelessness, length of procedure, the possibility of an *ex officio* application, and the standard and burden of proof.

---

30 UNHCR *Statelessness determination procedures and the status of stateless persons, Op Cit* 1. The note in the bracket is mine.

31 UNHCR *Commemorating the refugee and statelessness conventions* 2010–2011: *A compilation of summary conclusions from UNHCR's expert meetings* (2012) 25 at para. 3.

32 UNHCR *Handbook on protection of stateless persons, Op Cit* 27 at para. 64

33 See *Ibid.*

34 See UNHCR *Statelessness determination procedures and the status of stateless persons, Op Cit.* See also Summary Conclusions Expert meeting convened by the Office of the United Nations High Commissioner for Refugees, Tunis, Tunisia, 31 October–1 November 2013.

35 The UNHCR publishes a set of guidelines on statelessness on different thematic, especially on the ten action points in UNHCR *Global action plan to end statelessness 2014–2024* (2014).

Procedural Framework for Determining Statelessness 113

4.3.1 Legality and Binding Nature of SDP

While the 1954 Convention[36] and other relevant conventions[37] do not prescribe a particular procedure for an SDP, as a good practice standard it is recommended by the UNHCR that States ensure that a determination procedure is formalized in law, as this will ensure fairness, transparency, and efficiency of the process.[38] A state is free to design its SDP as long as it adheres to the provisions of the 1954 Convention.

Apart from the requirement of having an SDP enshrined in law, one of the very essential requirements of a good SDP, is that the decisions of the determination body be recognized and be considered as binding on other institutions in the State. An SDP should not just be an institutional policy of the agency saddled with a statelessness determination mandate; rather every institution within the State must be bound by the decision of the statelessness determination agency. For instance, institutions that render services within the State should allow recognized stateless persons to access basic services. Stateless persons should be able to access healthcare and other essential services, and the education board should allow recognized stateless persons to access education. Similarly, the immigration authority, the police, and other relevant agencies of government must recognise that stateless persons or persons undergoing a determination procedure should not be subject to deportation. In the same vein, if the agency responsible for the granting of a residence permit and naturalization is separate from the agency that grants statelessness status, the former should be bound by the decision of the latter and grant the required permit, which should, in the long run, result in naturalization.

4.3.2 Structure and Location of SDP

Where to situate an SDP institutionally is a matter of State discretion and can vary from one country to the next.[39] Current State practice is varied with respect to the location[40] of statelessness determination procedures within the national administrative

---

36 Convention Relating to the Status of Stateless Persons, 1954.
37 Notably the Hague Protocol Relating to a Certain Case of Statelessness 1930, the Universal Declaration of Human Rights 1948, the Convention Relating to the Status of Refugees 1951, the Protocol Relating to the Status of Refugees 1967, the Convention Relating to the Status of Stateless Persons 1954, the Convention on the Reduction of Statelessness 1961, the Convention on the Nationality of Married Women 1967, the Convention on the Elimination of All Forms of Discrimination Against Women 1979, the Convention on the Rights of the Child 1989, and the International Convention on the Protection of the Rights of All Migrant Workers and Members of Their Families 1990.
38 See UNHCR *Statelessness determination procedures identifying and protecting stateless persons* (2014) 5.
39 UNHCR *Good practices paper – action 6: Establishing statelessness determination procedures to protect stateless persons* (2016) 4.
40 Location in this context means the presence of an SDP either in a central authority or across various government agencies across the country.

114 *Procedural Framework for Determining Statelessness*

structures, reflecting country-specific considerations. States may choose between a centralized procedure and one that is conducted by local authorities. Centralized procedures are preferable as they are more likely to develop the necessary expertise among the officials undertaking status determination.[41] A centralized procedure could be necessary for ensuring the same standards across a country.

While a centralized system may be preferred, due consideration should be given to the need to have a certain 'balance between centralizing expertise to conduct statelessness determination within a specialized administrative or judicial unit of trained and experienced officials, and allowing individuals to lodge applications with government representatives who might be spread out across the country.'[42] This flexibility is particularly necessary in many poor countries in Africa, given the challenging context: these countries are large, and tend to have a weak national road and travel infrastructure, and poor standards of living. Allowing applications to be submitted through specialized agencies at local administrative levels spread across the country would be a preferred method.

> Government officials might encounter the question whether a person is stateless in a range of contexts, reflecting the critical role that nationality plays in everyday life. For example, consideration of nationality status is relevant when individuals apply for passports or identity documents, seek legal residence or employment in the public sector, want to exercise their voting rights, perform military service, or attempt to access government services. The issue of nationality and statelessness may also arise when an individual's right to be in a country is challenged in removal procedures.[43]

Therefore, it is important, when designing a procedure, to also make provision for the possibility of having some form of referral mechanism and pool of trained staff across relevant government agencies equipped with the knowledge to identify potential stateless persons or persons at risk of statelessness, who can help refer such persons to the central body or to the relevant government agency in the local government areas or districts. The design should also allow for officials to present an *ex officio* application on behalf of applicants when they encounter persons who are stateless or are of undetermined nationality.

4.3.3 Access to Procedure

According to UNHCR,

> for procedures to be fair and efficient, and to ensure that all stateless persons benefit from the implementation of the 1954 Convention, access to the SDP

---

41 UNHCR *Handbook on protection of stateless persons, Op Cit* 27 at para. 63.
42 IPU and UNHCR *Nationality and statelessness handbook for parliamentarians No 22* (2014) 20.
43 UNHCR *Handbook on protection of stateless persons, Op Cit* 25 at para. 57.

Procedural Framework for Determining Statelessness 115

must be guaranteed and should not be subject to time limits. Information on the procedure and counselling services must be available to potential applicants in a language they understand.[44]

Additionally, a good procedure should not impose time limits within which an application must be brought from the date of entry into the territory. In asylum systems, there is typically neither a limitation of time nor a requirement of legal entry. It would be particularly unfair if stateless persons who may, especially in the migratory context, not be aware of such a procedure to be caught by a time limit. The requirement of legal entry should not be imposed on stateless persons either.[45] 'Such a requirement is particularly inequitable given that lack of nationality denies many stateless persons the very documentation that is necessary to lawfully enter or reside in a State.'[46] In this respect, it is noteworthy that in 2015, the Hungarian Constitutional Court held that the requirement of lawful stay to qualify for statelessness status in the Law on Entry and Stay of Third-country Nationals 2007, was unconstitutional, and annulled it.[47]

4.3.4 Procedural Guarantees

To ensure fairness and efficiency, statelessness determination procedures must ensure basic due process guarantees, including the right to an effective remedy where an application is rejected.[48] For a good determination procedure in an SDP vested in either an administrative or judicial body, legal aid should also be factored in, considering the complexities faced by applicants as well as caseworkers.

As much as possible, stateless persons should not be charged administrative fees. Where it is necessary to charge an administrative fee, such fees should be reasonable and within the reach of stateless persons.[49] A proper procedure should ensure wide dissemination of information on the eligibility criteria and rights associated with the recognition of statelessness in languages spoken in and

---

44 UNHCR *Good practices paper – action 6: Establishing statelessness determination procedures to protect stateless persons* (2016) 5.
45 See the difference in approach to modes of entry in both the 1951 and 1954 Conventions as highlighted in the UNHCR *Handbook on protection of stateless persons, Op Cit* 46 at para. 127.
46 *Ibid* 28 at para. 69.
47 Hungarian Constitutional Court decision in Case III / 01664/2014. http://public.mkab .hu/dev/dontesek.nsf/0/28DDC0E14E5BC80BC1257D7100259A90?OpenDocument (accessed 27 April 2020). Pursuant to the annulment, s. 76(1) of the Act was amended to read:'The procedure for establishing statelessness shall be commenced by an application submitted by an applicant residing in the territory of Hungary to the Aliens Police Authority, which may be submitted orally or in writing by the applicant for recognition as a stateless person.'
48 UNHCR *Expert meeting statelessness determination procedures and the status of stateless persons summary conclusions* (2010) 4 at para. 10.
49 See UNHCR *Expert meeting, Ibid*. See also the Convention Relating to the Status of Stateless Persons 1954, Art. 32.

116 *Procedural Framework for Determining Statelessness*

around the country. An applicant should be attended to in a language he or she is comfortable with.[50]

Additionally, it should ensure that after an application is received, the applicant is interviewed. Where the applicant does not speak the local language or official language of that State, an interpreter should be provided.[51] An interpreter should also be provided where a written application is required, especially where the applicant is not well-versed in the official language of the State.

It is also key that a determination procedure consider the circumstances of different groups. For instance, an agency responsible for the determination of statelessness should ensure 'special protection for unaccompanied minors and those with mental disabilities requiring a legal guardian.'[52] There is also the need for gender balance amongst SDP caseworkers. This will help to ensure respect for people whose culture does not allow for a woman to be seen alone with a man who is not her husband, and ensure that women can discuss their protection concerns freely with caseworkers.

Similar to the practice in refugee status determinations, States must also ensure that applicants are not penalized on grounds of illegal entry and residence in their territory. States should also ensure that applicants are not detained pending the determination of status. A time limit from the date of application to the time for the decision must be specified, and such a time limit must be reasonable. Applicants should have a right to the *ratio decidendi*, i.e., the grounds on which a decision on their application was made; this/these ground(s) should be specified in writing. In the case of confirmation of status, the stateless person should be guided on the next steps, such as how to process the necessary documentation, residence permit, and access to naturalization.

4.3.5 *Assessment of Evidence and Establishment of Fact*

A statelessness determination procedure often requires a mixed assessment of fact and law. Therefore, to assess whether or not a person is stateless, case officers not only assess existing laws but also how the laws are implemented in practice.[53] 'It is generally up to the applicant to provide documentation from the embassy or consular offices of his/her country of origin – the country of birth or a country that issued a prior travel document – confirming that the individual is not a national.'[54] However, due to the difficulties for applicants, depending on their

---

50 UNHCR *Handbook on protection of stateless persons, Op Cit* 29.
51 The interpreter must interpret what the applicant says verbatim and not paraphrase, and the interview transcript must also record everything said by the applicant.
52 See UNHCR *Good practices paper – action 6, Ibid* 14.
53 See J George and R Elphick *Promoting citizenship and preventing statelessness in South Africa: A practitioner's guide* (2014) 47. See also UNHCR *Handbook on protection of stateless persons, Op Cit* para. 83.
54 UNHCR and IPU *Nationality and statelessness. A handbook for parliamentarians no 11* (2005) 20.

Procedural Framework for Determining Statelessness 117

circumstances, to provide sufficient facts, legislation, and documents in support of their statelessness claim, the case officers are obliged to support the applicants in their quest to present a detailed and coherent case.

Considering that an applicant cannot be reasonably expected to prove that none of world's 195 States considers him or her to be a national, case officers should also help consider States with which an applicant has a relevant link, either by birth, descent, habitual residence, or marriage.[55] To achieve this, caseworkers should 'adopt a collaborative, non-adversarial approach in investigating a person's foreign citizenship.'[56] Such government agency charged with responsibility for SDP should strive to have a collection of or access to nationality laws and rules of various countries.[57]

The UNHCR advises that the types of evidence that may be relevant can be divided into two categories: evidence relating to the applicant's circumstances, and evidence concerning the laws and other circumstances in the country in question.[58] According to the UK Home Office *Asylum Policy Instruction Statelessness and Applications for Leave to Remain*, caseworkers should be able to distinguish between applicants who show no interest in genuinely co-operating or providing necessary information or evidence, and those who may be *unable* to provide such evidence because of their particular circumstances, such as limited knowledge of the nationality law of their countries of former habitual residence, absence or loss of relevant documents, etc. In such circumstances, where the available information is lacking or inconclusive, the caseworker must assist the applicant by interviewing him, undertaking relevant research, and, if necessary, making enquiries with the relevant authorities and organizations.[59] The Home Office Guidelines further recommend that

> enquiries of the authorities of the country of former habitual residence which disclose the applicant's personal details must be done with the written

---

55 M Foster, J McAdam and D Wadley 'Part one: The protection of stateless persons in Australian law—the rationale for a statelessness determination procedure' (2017) 40 *Melbourne University Law Review* 401; UNSW Law Research Paper No. 19–27 https://ssrn.com/abstract =3368661 or http://dx.doi.org/10.2139/ssrn.3368661 (accessed 26 November 2019).

56 IPU and UNHCR *Good practices in nationality laws for the prevention and reduction of statelessness. Handbook for parliamentarians no 29* (2018) 21. See also UNHCR *Handbook on protection of stateless persons, Op Cit* paras. 89–90.

57 UNHCR and IPU *Nationality and statelessness. A handbook for parliamentarians no 11, Op Cit* 27.

58 UNHCR *Handbook on protection of stateless persons, Op Cit* 32 at para. 83. See also G Gyula *Statelessness determination procedures and the protection of stateless persons* (2013) 28–29. 'As for the first, UNHCR guidance provides a detailed list of examples, including the applicant's statements, documentary and testimonial evidence, as well as information provided by other states. As for the second, it should be up-to-date and should be obtained from a variety of reliable sources. The complexity of nationality law and practice in a particular State may justify recourse to expert evidence in some cases.'

59 See UK Home Office *Asylum policy instruction statelessness and applications for leave to remain*. Version 2.0 (2016) para. 4.2.

118 *Procedural Framework for Determining Statelessness*

consent of the applicant, but if that consent is denied without good reason (for example, it has already been established that the person's claimed fear of those authorities was not well-founded), it may be inferred that the applicant is not genuinely willing to cooperate and is failing to discharge the burden of proof, taking account of all the available information.[60]

Hereafter, who should bear the burden of proof in SDPs will be addressed, and what standard of proof applies.

4.3.5.1 *Burden of Proof*

In most jurisdictions, the legal burden of proof rests with the party bringing a claim.[61] In principle, this would mean that a stateless person bears the burden of proof. It is suggested, in line with the UNHCR's Statelessness Handbook, that, in statelessness determination procedures, the burden of proof be in principle *shared*, which means that both the applicant and examiner must cooperate to obtain evidence, to establish the facts, and ultimately clarify whether an individual comes within the scope of the 1954 Convention.[62] Stateless persons often have no documents or other evidence to prove their statelessness. Therefore, the applicants and case officers must collaborate to establish the facts. 'Authorities undertaking statelessness determination must consider all available evidence, oral or written, regarding an individual claim. This may include the analysis of nationality laws of other countries and how they are applied.'[63]

Substantiating statelessness can involve evidentiary challenges. Statelessness is rarely a well-documented situation or status, as there are per the definition no State authorities obliged to provide an individual with documentation. Therefore, establishing whether an individual 'is not considered as a national [...] under the operation of [...] law' may require considering a wide range of legal and factual evidence[64] on the part of the caseworkers. It is therefore necessary for the burden of proof to be shared between the applicant and the authorities.

The burden of proof is discharged by the applicant rendering a truthful account of facts relevant to the claim so that, based on the facts, a proper decision may be reached.[65] A proper procedure should not leave the responsibility of establishing a case solely on the applicant who more often than not is unable to solely prove their statelessness status or absence of a link to any nation.

---

60 *Ibid.*
61 See N Monaghan *Law of Evidence* (2015) 35.
62 UNHCR *Handbook on protection of stateless persons, Op Cit* 34 at para. 89.
63 UNHCR *Statelessness determination procedures – Identifying and protecting stateless persons, Op Cit* 5.
64 K Swider 'Protection and identification of stateless persons through EU law' (2014) 5 *Amsterdam Centre for European Law and Governance Working Paper Series* 5. See also UNHCR *Handbook on protection of stateless persons, Op Cit* 12–13 at paras. 23–24.
65 UNHCR *Note on burden and standard of proof in refugee claims* (1998) 2.

Procedural Framework for Determining Statelessness   119

4.3.5.2 Standard of Proof

It is well known that the standard of proof in a civil case is proof on the balance of probabilities and that this means that the party bearing the burden of proof must prove that his case is more probable than not.[66] However, as regards stateless-ness claims, it may suffice for a finding of statelessness, that it is established to a 'reasonable degree' that an individual is not considered as a national by any State under the operation of its law.[67] The standard of proof may be understood, first, as referring to the caution that must be exercised in making positive findings.[68] The adjudicator needs to decide if, based on the evidence provided, it is likely that the claim of that applicant is credible.[69]

Lord Kitchin, reiterating the points on standard of proof proffered in the UNHCR Handbook on Protection of Stateless Persons,[70] held in the UK case of *AS (Guinea) v. Secretary of State for the Home Department* as follows:

> [A]s with the burden of proof, the standard of proof or threshold of evi-dence necessary to determine statelessness must take into consideration the difficulties inherent in proving statelessness, particularly in light of the con-sequences of incorrectly rejecting an application. Requiring a high standard of proof of statelessness would undermine the object and purpose of the 1954 Convention. States are therefore advised to adopt the same standard of proof as that required in refugee status determinations, namely, a finding of statelessness would be warranted where it is established to a "reasonable degree" that an individual is not considered as a national by any State under the operation of its law.[71]

What then is a reasonable degree desired of an applicant? An applicant could be said to have proven his case to a reasonable degree even when the determinant authority is unable to find sufficient evidence of a lack of a nationality link to a particular State. A number of considerations are relevant in this context. Has the applicant made sufficient efforts to present documents supporting his or her case? Where s/he does not have sufficient documents, has the applicant demon-strated sufficiency in approach, behaviour, and cooperation with the determi-nation authorities in finding solutions for his or her predicament? Considering the requirement of a shared burden, where caseworkers are unable to find any

---

66 M Redmayne 'Standards of proof in civil litigation' (2003) 62 (2) *Modern Law Review* 167 https://doi.org/10.1111/1468-2230.00200 (accessed 16 July 2019).

67 See UNHCR *Handbook on protection of stateless persons, Op Cit* 35 at para. 91.

68 H Lai Ho 'Standard of proof' in *Philosophy of evidence law: Justice in the search for truth* (2008) 173–230.

69 UNHCR *Note on burden and standard of proof in refugee claims, Op Cit* 2.

70 See UNHCR *Handbook on protection of stateless persons, Op Cit* 34–35.

71 [2018] EWCA Civ 2234. See also UNHCR *Handbook on protection of stateless persons, Ibid* para. 91.

120 *Procedural Framework for Determining Statelessness*

information to suggest that the applicant is legally linked to any other State, it may be established to a reasonable degree that he or she is stateless.

Where an applicant does not cooperate in establishing the facts, for example by deliberately withholding information that could determine his identity, then he may fail to establish to a reasonable degree that he is stateless even if the determination authority is unable to demonstrate clear evidence of a particular nationality. The application can thus be rejected unless the evidence available nevertheless establishes statelessness to a reasonable degree. Such cases need, however, to be distinguished from instances where an applicant is unable, as opposed to unwilling, to produce supporting evidence and/or testimony about his or her personal history.[72]

4.3.6 *Management of Combined Refugee and Statelessness Claims*

'There is some overlap between UNHCR's statelessness mandate and its refugee mandate because stateless refugees are protected under the provisions of the 1951 Convention relating to the Status of Refugees. When refugee status ceases, individuals may remain stateless and therefore of concern to UNHCR.'[73] The UNHCR Statelessness Handbook advises that when an applicant raises both a refugee and a statelessness claim, it is important that each claim is assessed and that both types of status are explicitly recognized.[74] This is because protection under the 1951 Convention generally gives rise to a greater set of rights at the national level than under the 1954 Convention.[75]

Considering that sometimes there could be overlaps between refugee and statelessness claims, States may consider establishing a combined procedure for both refugee and statelessness determination. Below, the challenge of managing the confidentiality requirement in the asylum process in the case of a combined procedure,[76] as well as the challenge of setting up a combined procedure, will be discussed.

4.3.6.1 *Confidentiality*

In an SDP, contact with countries of former habitual residence may be necessary to obtain information on the nationality link of the applicant. The practice of contacting other States raises confidentiality concerns, especially in situations of mixed statelessness and refugee claims.

At all times, the confidentiality of the asylum application should be respected. In exceptional circumstances, contact with the country of origin may be justified,

---

72 UNHCR *Ibid* 35 at para. 93.
73 UNHCR *UNHCR action to address statelessness – A strategy note.* Division of International Protection (March 2010) 5.
74 See UNHCR *Handbook on protection of stateless persons, Op Cit* 31 at para. 78.
75 *Ibid.*
76 See *Ibid* 27 para. 66.

Procedural Framework for Determining Statelessness 121

but even then, the existence of the asylum application should not be disclosed,[77] unless it has been determined that the applicant does not have a 'well-founded fear,' is not a refugee or entitled to any form of protection under the Refugee Convention.[78] States must ensure that confidentiality requirements for refugees who might also be stateless are upheld in statelessness determination procedures. 'Every applicant in an SDP is to be informed at the outset of the need to raise refugee-related concerns, should they exist.'[79]

The UNHCR advises that, if there is insufficient information to conclude that an individual is stateless without contacting the authorities of a foreign State, refugee status determination shall proceed;[80] in such instances, refugee status determination will be preferred.

4.3.6.2 Setting up a Combined Determination Procedure

More often than not, it is likely to be a major challenge to set up combined refugee and SDP systems. This will especially be the case where the systems are centralized (e.g., in the capital), and the case officers who conduct refugee status determination (RSD) are the same officers who work on SDP. Having the same case officers work on both procedures may lead to a conflation of asylum criteria, procedures, and standards in statelessness procedures. To avoid a mix-up of approach, it is more beneficial to have designated officials who work on asylum procedures separate from those who work on SDP. This will also help officials develop proficiency and expertise in their respective areas of specialization.

For a combined refugee and statelessness claim, case officers from both units can come together to work on the application. Asylum case officers can work to ensure the confidentiality requirement is respected, while SDP case officers work on the nature and facts of the statelessness claim, the nationality law, and its application in the applicant's former country of habitual residence, including the applicant's link to any other State.

4.3.7 Prospect for Protection and Naturalization

Where a decision recognizing statelessness is made through an SDP, such status should immediately entitle a stateless person to a permanent residence permit, labour and social security rights, access to basic and essential services, travel

---

77 *Ibid* para. 33.
  The reason for nondisclosure of asylum information with an applicant's country of origin/habitual residence is because most times, the agent of persecution is the State. For the safety of the applicant, it is necessary for asylum information not to be disclosed to unauthorized persons.
78 UNHCR, *Handbook on protection of stateless persons, Op Cit* 36 at para. 96.
79 See *Ibid* 31 at para. 79.
80 See *Ibid* 31–32 para. 81.

documents, etc.[81] In some States with a determination procedure, a positive decision or recognition of statelessness does not necessarily lead to a legal status that permits residence and enjoyment of basic human rights, nor does it necessarily facilitate naturalization.[82] It is recalled in this respect that nationality provides people with a sense of identity and is key to full participation in society.[83] Therefore, recognition as a stateless person should not be used as a substitute for nationality, especially where such recognition of status will not guarantee any legal rights.

An SDP should lead from the acquisition of certain basic rights to a simplified naturalization process (which, as much as possible, should be without conditions). In order words, States should establish procedures that lead to a legal status that permits residence and guarantees the enjoyment of basic human rights and facilitates naturalization for stateless migrants.[84]

States have discretion as to the structure of their SDP and their method of granting nationality. After all, in the *Nottebohm Case*, the International Court of Justice held that 'it is for every sovereign State, to settle by its own legislation the rules relating to the acquisition of its nationality, and to confer that nationality by naturalisation granted by its own organs in accordance with that legislation.'[85]

However, States should ensure that applicants are immediately able, or at least in the foreseeable future, through an expedited proceeding, to acquire nationality. As provided in Article 32 of the 1954 Convention, where an administrative fee is necessary for the acquisition of nationality, as far as possible, the charges and costs of such proceedings should be reduced for stateless persons. Naturalization could be simplified by ensuring that barriers to an easy and smooth naturalization process are removed from nationality laws. This could be done through removal or reduction of naturalization application fees for stateless persons, removal of the requirement of legal residence, reduction of the number of years of residency to qualify for naturalization,[86] and removal of language requirements for stateless persons.

---

81 See Convention Relating to the Status of Stateless Persons 1954 Arts. 15, 17, 19, 21, 23, 24, and 28; UNHCR *Handbook on the protection of stateless persons, Op Cit* 49–53 at paras. 136, 137, and 150.

82 UNHCR *Global action plan to end statelessness 2014–2024, Op Cit* 16.

83 UNHCR *Preventing and reducing statelessness: The 1961 Convention on the Reduction of Statelessness* (2010) 2.

84 See UNHCR *Global action plan to end statelessness 2014–2024, Op Cit* 16.

85 *Nottebohm case (Liechtenstein v. Guatemala)* [1955] ICJ 1.
     See also the Convention on Certain Questions Relating to the Conflict of Nationality Laws, the Hague 1930, Art. 1.

86 The Republic of Brazil is a good example in this regard, reducing the number of years of residence from four to two for stateless persons. See Art. 99 of the Brazilian Decreto n° 9.199, de 20 de novembro de 2017 (Decree No. 9199 of 20 November 2017) https:// presrepublica.jusbrasil.com.br/legislacao/522434860/decreto-9199-17 (accessed 30 July 2019).

4.3.8 Review and Appeal of Decisions

A proper determination procedure should guarantee a right to appeal a first instance rejection of an application. Such status determination decisions should be subject to review in accordance with the ordinary system for the administrative and judicial review of administrative acts in that country. The lodging of appeals, whether for administrative or judicial remedies, should suspend the execution of any resolution concerning expulsion.[87]

In some States, the courts are the competent authorities for the recognition of statelessness in the first instance. An example is Belgium where the courts are the competent authority for SDP.[88] Italy has both judicial and administrative procedures.[89] In States with a judicial procedure, the applicable national court or civil procedure rules are applied for determining statelessness. For such a State, there should be another layer for review or appeal of a first instance decision to a higher court. A state may elect to have a separate administrative or judicial review process for SDP distinct from the ordinary system for administrative or judicial review. Nonetheless, it should ensure that such a review process is independent of the agency that makes first instance decisions to guarantee a free, dispassionate, and impartial review process.

The UNHCR advises that

> appeals must be possible on both points of fact and law as the possibility exists that there may have been an incorrect assessment of the evidence at first instance level. Whether an appellate body can substitute its own judgment on eligibility under the 1954 Convention or whether it can merely quash the first instance decision and send the matter back for reconsideration by the determination authority is at the discretion of the State.[90]

Though not provided in the Statelessness Conventions, nor in the UNHCR Statelessness Handbook, this research advises against a time limit within which an applicant must file an appeal or request review of a decision. In our opinion, it is advisable to leave open the time within which to appeal a negative decision, as this prevents the door from being shut on stateless persons, or other persons at risk of statelessness who should ordinarily benefit from such guarantees.

---

87 See IPU and UNHCR *Good practices in nationality laws for the prevention and reduction of statelessness. Handbook for parliamentarians no 29* (2018) 21 and 35.

88 See UNHCR *Mapping statelessness in Belgium – summary report* (2012) 48, 51. See also EMN *Ad-hoc query on recognition of stateless persons requested by LU EMN NCP* (2015) 5 https://ec.europa.eu/home-affairs/sites/homeaffairs/files/what-we-do/networks/european_migration_network/reports/docs/ad-hoc-queries/ad-hoc-queries-2015.675_lu_recognition_of_stateless_persons_wider_diss.pdf (accessed 3 December 2019) and also Judicial Code of Belgium Art. 569(1).

89 See EMN Inform *Statelessness in the EU* (2020) 7 https://emn.ie/wp-content/uploads /2020/02/2020_EMN_Inform_Statelessness.pdf (accessed 20 January 2021).

90 UNHCR *Handbook on protection of stateless persons, Op Cit* para. 77.

124 *Procedural Framework for Determining Statelessness*

4.4 Nationality Verification Procedures

4.4.1 Definition and Purpose

Nationality verification is a procedure that helps a State to confirm a person or a population's claim to its nationality. This procedure would usually be applied to *in situ* populations who have lived in a territory of a State for many generations or a person or a population with an appropriate connection[91] to the State. As noted earlier, for *in situ* populations, an SDP may not be the appropriate approach; the best approach for such population would be a nationality verification procedure.

Depending on an assessment of the population and its situation, UNHCR advises a nationality campaign or nationality verification for such a population.[92] Nationality campaigns have two aims to support nationality verification. Firstly, to sensitize a population about its statelessness status or risk of statelessness. Secondly, to demonstrate the government's political will to grant nationality where necessary.

4.4.2 Responsible Agency and Procedure

Like in SDPs, there is no one-size-fits-all approach to nationality campaigns and verifications. In Nigeria, like in many States, the relevant agency in charge of naturalization is responsible for nationality verification and campaigns. Sometimes the steps in SDPs are also required in nationality verification, except that nationality verification could be a more 'accessible, swift and straightforward process for documenting existing nationality, including the nationality of another State.'[93]

4.5 Conclusion

For many years, 'the phenomenon of statelessness has attracted particular attention, perhaps in the light of the strong connection between statelessness and irregular immigration.'[94] Yet neither of the two UN Statelessness Conventions places an explicit obligation on the Contracting States to establish a statelessness determination procedure. However, 'it is widely agreed that it is impossible to effectively implement many of the provisions of these Conventions without having a mechanism for the identification of their beneficiaries.'[95] For many decades, States have granted refugee status through refugee status determina-

---

91 The connections may include ancestry, birth on the territory, marriage habitual, or long-time residence, etc.

92 UNHCR *Handbook on protection of stateless persons, Op Cit* 26 at para. 58.

93 *Ibid* 26 at paras. 60 & 61.

94 K Konstantina 'Addressing statelessness in Greece under EU law' (2019) *LSE 9th HO PhD Symposium on Contemporary Greece and Cyprus* 6 http://www.lse.ac.uk/Hellenic-Observatory/Assets/Documents/HO-PhD-Symposia/The-9th-HO-PhD-Symposium/Symposium-Papers/Session-1/Migration-I-Security.pdf (accessed 3 December 2019).

95 K Swider and M den Heijer *Op Cit* 109.

Procedural Framework for Determining Statelessness 125

tion procedures. Now, a similar commitment is required to develop statelessness determination procedures (SDP).

This chapter puts forward several conditions which SDPs should meet. In light of these criteria, no State can be considered a single 'best practice' example. Even those States which are frequently looked to as models, exhibit persisting gaps and face challenges.[96] It remains, however, that States without SDPs, and those with weak SDPs, need to be guided by certain criteria and good practices to develop a better procedure, with due respect for their national contexts. When developing an SDP, it is key for States to give particular attention to the legality and 'bindingness' of the proposed SDP, to procedural access, and procedural guarantees. The procedure should ensure that applicants have access to an interview, an interpreter and legal aid, and have a right to appeal or a review of the decision. Also, officials should be allowed to present an *ex officio* application on behalf of stateless persons. SDPs meeting these criteria will make a significant contribution to the identification, prevention, and eradication of statelessness.

96 See G Gyulai 'Statelessness determination and the protection status of stateless persons' *Op Cit* 7.

5 Analysis of Institutional and Procedural Frameworks for Determining Statelessness in Five States

5.1 Introduction

This chapter examines statelessness determination procedure development and practice in selected States. The main aim of the chapter is to highlight some of the existing good practices in the selected States that will be relevant for Nigeria to learn from, and also discuss a bit of the shortfall observed in the procedures developed by the States with so-called good practices. The chapter provides useful guidance on what to avoid in a determination procedure. The method utilized in this chapter is both descriptive and evaluative. Most of the good legal, judicial, and administrative practices in the selected States are descriptive, while the last part of each evaluates the State practice.

5.2 Some SDP Development and Practice Examples

As noted above, only a few States operate a statelessness determination procedure that allows them to clarify someone's statelessness, or nationality for that matter. A stateless determination procedure results in a protection status for identified stateless persons, allowing access to rights under the 1954 Convention;[1] rights such as, the right to earn a living, healthcare, residency, freedom of movement, education, family life, and political rights. Some States without a procedure rely on an alternative administrative procedure for identification of statelessness, but several countries including Nigeria have no identification mechanism or stateless status at all, resulting in significant protection gaps for stateless people across the world.[2]

---

1 See Intervention by Vincent Cochetel, the UNHCR Director of the Bureau for Europe, on the occasion of the meeting of the Strategic Committee on Immigration, Frontiers and Asylum in Brussels 'Identifying stateless persons in the European Union' (25 April 2017) 5 https://www.refworld.org/pdfid/5911d8c34.pdf (accessed 20 March 2019). See also, UNHCR *Good practices paper – action* 6 2 (2016) https://www.refworld.org/docid/57836cff4.html (accessed 16 June 2022) and K Swider and M den Heijer 'Why union law can and should protect stateless persons' (2017) 19 (2) *European Journal of Migration and Law* 117.
2 See ENS online Stateless Index https://index.statelessness.eu/themes/statelessness-determination-and-status-group-1#block-views-spd-countries-block-6 (accessed 20 March 2019).

DOI: 10.4324/9781003278733-5

Analysis of Procedural Frameworks in Five States 127

For this chapter, the procedure in a few States with SDPs formalized in law, such as the UK,[3] France,[4] Moldova,[5] and Ivory Coast[6] will be analyzed, including the practice in the Netherlands[7] with no formal procedure at the moment, but with alternative means of identification which could be relevant for Nigeria as a temporary measure. Arguably, it is easier to convince Nigerian lawmakers about systems that work in Europe generally, rather than in Asia or the Americas. Therefore, for this Part, only SDPs in the European States will be highlighted for ease of reference. However, in Chapter 6 (Part 6.3.1) where the practice in Nigeria will be discussed, practices in Brazil and Paraguay in addition to the five States discussed here will be examined and applied for the purpose of a bespoke statelessness determination procedure for Nigeria.

The *European Network on Statelessness (ENS)*'s *Index*, a comparative tool that assesses European countries' law, policy, and practice on the protection, prevention, and reduction of statelessness against international norms and good practice, breaks (European) countries into four groups according to the systems in place in each country for protection, identification, and prevention of statelessness. These four groups are: 'Group 1 – countries with dedicated statelessness determination procedures (SDP) established in law, administrative guidance, or judicial procedure; Group 2 – countries with alternative administrative procedures for the identification of statelessness (APP); Group 3 – countries with stateless status without a clear identification mechanism; and Group 4 – countries with other routes to *regularization*[8] of status where there is no statelessness procedure or status.

But for this book, the countries will be broken into three groups; they are:

- **Group 1** – countries with dedicated statelessness determination procedures established in law, administrative guidance, or judicial procedure (the UK, Moldova, France, and Ivory Coast);

---

3 Nigeria is a former colony of the UK; therefore there is a shared legal culture. Nigeria and the UK both have a common law system, and their governance systems share some administrative similarities which may be relevant for developing an SDP for Nigeria.

4 France has the oldest mechanism for an SDP formalized in law; apart from that, it has lots of good examples relevant for Nigeria.

5 Moldova is a developing country like Nigeria. Therefore, in the absence of a country with an SDP in Africa, it is necessary to examine the achievement of a developing State like Moldova to see what Nigeria as a developing nation can also learn from it. Apart from being a developing State like Nigeria, the SDP in Moldova has been described by the UNHCR as one of the most advanced in Europe.

6 Ivory Coast is relevant for this research as it currently hosts the highest number of stateless persons in West Africa. Apart from being the first and only African State with an SDP formalized in law in September 2020, before that time, it had alternative routes to regularization of status (in the absence of an SDP), which is also lacking in Nigeria at the moment.

7 The Netherlands, although without an SDP, has a formal method of identifying statelessness which is relevant for Nigeria which has no mechanizing of collecting statistics at all.

8 Such as acquisition of nationality, legal residence, etc., through routes other than through an SDP.

128　*Analysis of Procedural Frameworks in Five States*

- **Group 2** – the country with alternative administrative procedures for identification of statelessness (the Netherlands);
- **Group 3** – the country with other routes to regularization (Nigeria).

The reason for the difference in Group 3 of this book with the ENS grouping system, is the thought that the ENS categorisation in Group 3, which is *countries with stateless status without a clear identification mechanism,* can be merged with the second category, i.e., *countries with alternative administrative procedures for identification of statelessness,* considering that a critical analysis of the ENS Groups 2 and 3 will reveal that some alternative administrative procedures for identification may constitute mechanisms for identification that are not very clear.

This section will examine some good practice procedures in selected States listed in Chapter 1, in the light of international law standards and criteria in the Statelessness Conventions, including UNHCR Good Practice Papers[9] on prevention of statelessness, as well as approaches prescribed in the UNHCR Handbook on Protection of Stateless Person and the 10 Actions in the Global Action Plan to End Statelessness by 2024, with a view to prescribing good practices.

5.2.1　Group 1 – States with Dedicated Statelessness Determination Procedures Established in Law, Administrative Guidance, ors Judicial Procedure

The following European countries with dedicated SDP are selected for analysis in this section; they are the United Kingdom (the UK), Moldova, and France. Ivory Coast, which recently, in September 2020, developed the first and only stateless determination procedure in the African region, is also considered for examination in this part. They have been chosen because they put in place legal and procedural frameworks. This section will start by describing the good practices in the selected States, followed by critical assessments of the practices in those states.

5.2.1.1　SDP Development and Practice in the United Kingdom

Before going into the SDP development and Practice in the UK, it is important to note that until 1 October 1960, Nigeria was a colony of the UK and as such shares many similarities in terms of judicial practices and some administrative practices, except the very obvious dissimilarities in governance structure which started with Nigeria's first military coup in 1966 and the 1979 Constitution that changed the governance structure from the parliamentary system to the present day presidential system of government.

---

9 'UNHCR is publishing a series of Good Practices Papers to help States, with the support of other stakeholders, achieve the goals of its Campaign to End Statelessness within 10 Years.'

In the UK, after ratification, international human rights laws do not automatically form part of the local laws. International law in the UK and most Commonwealth countries is not 'self-executing,' i.e., for such ratified international law to have the force of law, it must first be passed into law by the national parliament[10] (known as domestication). This means that foreign treaties do not have a direct effect in the UK unless they are domesticated.[11] This is also the practice in Nigeria.[12]

The UK is a party to most of the international human rights treaties relevant for the protection, prevention, and reduction of statelessness.[13] In addition to being one of the States that have ratified both the 1954 and 1961 Conventions,[14] it is reputed to be one of the very first states to ratify the 1961 Convention on the Reduction of Statelessness[15] which it ratified on 30 August 1961.[16] However, it has also been observed that the UK is not a party to two key regional instruments, such as the European Convention on Nationality, and the Convention on the Avoidance of Statelessness in Relation to State Succession.[17]

Although the UK has internalized most of the provisions of the 1954 and 1961 Conventions especially under Part 14 of the Immigration Rules which adopts the 1954 Stateless Convention's definition of a stateless person, the definition of a stateless person in UK law contains exclusions that exceed

---

10 United Nations Department of Economic and Social Affairs (UNESA) *Compilation of international norms and standards relating to disability Part i. National frameworks* 2/5 at 1.4 https://www.un.org/esa/socdev/enable/discom101.htm (accessed 13 August 2019).

According to UNESA, 'States follow different practices in internationalizing treaty norms that is incorporating treaties within the state's legal structure so that the provisions can be implemented by state authorities. In some countries, international (and at times regional) human rights law automatically becomes a part of national law. In other words, as soon as a state has ratified or acceded to an international agreement, that international law becomes national law. Under such systems treaties are considered to be self-executing.'

11 Immigration Law Practitioners' Association (ILPA) *Statelessness and applications for leave to remain: A best practice guide* (2016) 8 at para. A.5.b. See also A Lang *Parliament's role in ratifying treaties* Briefing Paper Number 5855 (17 February 2017) 6 at 2.1. https://www.parliament.uk/briefing-papers/sn05855.pdf (accessed 13 August 2019).

12 See s. 69 of the Constitution of the Federal Republic of Nigeria 1999. See also C Okeke and M Anushiem 'Implementation of treaties in Nigeria: Issues, challenges and the way forward' (2018) 9 (2) *Nnamdi Azikiwe University Journal of International Law and Jurisprudence* (NAUJILJ) 216.

13 ENS Statelessness Index, United Kingdom https://index.statelessness.eu/country/united-kingdom#:~:text=The%20UK%20is%20state%20party,by%20the%20EU%20Returns%20Directive (accessed 3 December 2020).

14 See United Nations *Treaty Series* vol. 360, 117 and vol. 989, 175.

15 'It is also a party to the 1930 Convention on Certain Questions relating to the Conflict of Nationality Laws, and to the Protocol Relating to a Certain Case of Statelessness (a protocol to the 1930 Convention).'

UNHCR, Asylum Aid *Mapping statelessness in the United Kingdom* (2011) 132–133.

16 See United Nations *Treaty Series* vol. 989, 175.

17 Statelessness Index. *United Kingdom – International and Regional Instrument Section* https://index.statelessness.eu/country/united-kingdom (accessed 2 February 2019).

130 *Analysis of Procedural Frameworks in Five States*

those of the 1954 Convention, in addition to its reservations to the 1954 and 1961 Statelessness Conventions which directly impact stateless people.[18] Some of these reservations relate to Article 8 with regard to exceptional measures, Article 9 on national security, Article 24 on labour legislation and social security, and Article 25 on administrative assistance.[19]

In April 2013, the UK established under Part 14 of the Immigration Rules[20] a statelessness determination procedure (SDP) to recognize stateless persons and permit them to remain lawfully in the UK. The achievement of a determination procedure in the UK was due largely to advocacy by relevant stakeholders and the 2011 report *Mapping Statelessness in the United Kingdom* by Asylum Aid and UNHCR.[21] While the adoption of an SDP was praised as a welcome development, some experts raised concerns about the difficulties in accessing the procedure. For instance, Mark Manly *et al* note that 'applications cannot be made upon arrival to the UK: the procedure can only be accessed once an individual has been admitted to the territory.'[22] The implication therefore is that only legal residents can access the procedure, stateless persons who are not legal residents in the UK cannot benefit from the procedure. There is no requirement for leave to enter for a stateless person who is not already in the territory, the requirement for leave to enter only applies to family members of a recognized stateless person in the UK.[23]

In 2017, 34,435 people were reported to have claimed asylum in the UK, ten of these people were recorded in the 'other and unknown' nationality

---

18 *Ibid.*

19 See details on the UK's reservations in the 1954 Convention in UN Treaty Collections https://treaties.un.org/pages/ViewDetailsII.aspx?src=TREATY&mtdsg_no=V-3&chapter =5&Temp=mtdsg2&clang=_en#3 (accessed 13 August 2019).

  For the reservation to the 1961 Convention, see UN Treaty Collections https://treaties .un.org/pages/ViewDetails.aspx?src=TREATY&mtdsg_no=V-4&chapter=5 and UNHCR via https://www.unhcr.org/416113864.pdf (accessed 13 August 2019) wherein '[The Government of the United Kingdom declares that], in accordance with paragraph 3 (a) of Article 8 of the Convention, notwithstanding the provisions of paragraph 1 of Article 8, the United Kingdom retains the right to deprive a naturalised person of his nationality on the following grounds, being grounds existing in United Kingdom law at the present time: that, inconsistently with his duty of loyalty to Her Britannic Majesty, the person "(i) Has, in disregard of an express prohibition of Her Britannic Majesty, rendered or continued to render services to, or received or continued to receive emoluments from, another State, or (ii) Has conducted himself in a manner seriously prejudicial to the vital interests of Her Britannic Majesty."'

20 The establishment of a determination procedure under Part 14 of the Immigration Rules was accompanied with a Stateless Guidance published on 1 April 2013 to guide case officers on operationalization of the Part 14.

21 C Orchard 'An update on statelessness determination and status in the UK – "Need for fair and timely decisions"' https://www.asylumaid.org.uk/update-statelessness-determination -status-uk-need-fair-timely-decisions/ (accessed 19 January 2019).

22 M Manly, L van Waas, Ad Berry, and L Fransman QC *Statelessness: The impact of international law and current challenges* Chatham House Royal Institute of International Affairs – International Law Programme Meeting Summary (4 November 2014) 5.

23 See Rules 411 and 413 of Part 14 of the Immigration Rules.

Analysis of Procedural Frameworks in Five States   131

category and 348 were recorded as 'stateless.'[24] With the 2013 introduction of SDP, i.e., Part 14 of Immigration Rules, the UK can be said to belong to Group 1, i.e., States with dedicated statelessness SDPs established in law, including administrative guidance.

The competent authority responsible for SDP in the UK is the Home Office – Visas and Immigration Department. The Home Office through the Department of Visas and Immigration in 2016 developed a Guidance document, the *Asylum Policy Instruction, Statelessness and applications for leave to remain* used when deciding applications by stateless people.[25] According to the Home Office, SDP in the UK is completely independent of the asylum procedure; asylum claims take priority over a statelessness application. A statelessness determination procedure will only be activated after the asylum claim has been determined or withdrawn.[26]

5.2.1.1.1 ACCESS TO PROCEDURE

An application for leave to remain as a stateless person in the UK must be made via an online application known as form FLR(S).[27] 'There is no application fee for the initial application. The applicant will be required to submit evidence in support of his/her application, including reasons why they believe that they are stateless and any evidence to show that they are not a national of their country of birth or ancestry or any other.'[28] Before the March 2019 amendment of the Immigration Rules, applicants could stay in the UK for two years and six months if permitted to stay (known as 'leave to remain'). Applicants can further apply for renewal of leave to remain upon expiration.[29] Since 7 March 2019, the provision for limited leave in Rule 405 has been amended/increased from two and a half years to five years.[30] Under the new rule, where an applicant meets the requirements for leave

---

24 Statelessness Index, United Kingdom https://index.statelessness.eu/country/united-kingdom (accessed 13 August 2019).
25 See the Home Office website https://www.gov.uk/government/publications/stateless-guidance (accessed 1 March 2019).
26 EMN INFORM *Statelessness in the EU* (11 November 2016) 7.
27 Such applications can only be made once admitted in the territory or for a person who is already legally in the territory. 'Applicants can get help completing an online immigration form if they do not feel confident using a computer or do not have access to one. Applicant can get help with: accessing a computer or the internet, finding the right information on GOV.UK. However, this service cannot be used to get advice on: whether one is eligible to apply, what information to put in an application, an application already made.' See GOV.UK https://www.gov.uk/government/publications/application-to-extend-stay-in-uk-as-stateless-person-form-flrs (accessed 2 February 2019).
28 Immigration Law Practitioners' Association (ILPA) *Statelessness, Op Cit* 2.
29 See, UK Home Office website https://www.gov.uk/stay-in-uk-stateless (accessed 20 February 2019).
30 Explanatory Memorandum to the Statement of Changes in Immigration Rules Presented to Parliament on 7 March 2019 (HC 1919) 13 at para. 7.56 https://assets.publishing.service.gov.uk/government/uploads/system/uploads/attachment_data/file/784060/CCS207_CCS0319710302-002_HC_1919_Immigration_Rules__EXPLANATORY_MEMO_

132   *Analysis of Procedural Frameworks in Five States*

to remain in the UK, they may be granted limited leave to remain in the United Kingdom for a period not exceeding five years.[31]

According to the Home Office, the applicant is expected to provide the following documents: current passports and other travel documents, such as visas, official letters confirming immigration status, birth certificates, marriage certificates, etc. The applicant is expected to provide as many documents as possible to prove statelessness. The principal applicant is also expected to provide documents for their dependants if they are equally stateless; identity, immigration and travel documents, documents that prove residence or domicile before coming to the UK. For example school certificates, medical records, or sworn statements from neighbours, documents from applications for citizenship, or requests for proof of nationality in other countries.[32] On interviews, the Home Office guidelines further provide:

> An interview will normally be arranged to assist the applicant to fully set out their case for being considered stateless and to submit any other relevant evidence. In other instances, questions about evidence submitted as part of the application may be resolved through additional written communications. Where the applicant does not complete all relevant sections of the application form, caseworkers may request the missing information by writing to the applicant or their legal representative if they have one.[33]

The Home Office would usually not conduct a personal interview 'if there is sufficient evidence of statelessness, including previous findings of fact established during the asylum claim and the individual is eligible for leave to remain on this basis.'[34] The applicant is provided with interpreter during the interview if required.[35] On burden of proof, the Home Office Guidance provides specially that 'in all cases, the burden of proof rests with the applicant.' An applicant is thus expected to provide information to prove his/her statelessness, working with caseworkers to establish that 'no country to which they can be removed'

PRINT.pdf (accessed 13 August 2019); see also Rule 405 of Immigration Rules: Part 14, March 2019 amendment.

31 See Rules 405 of Part 14 of the Immigration Rules.

32 See UK Home Office website https://www.gov.uk/stay-in-uk-stateless.

33 'An interview will not be arranged, and the application may be refused, where recent and reliable information including the applicant's previous evidence or findings of fact made by an immigration judge, have already established that the applicant is not stateless or is clearly admissible to another country for purposes of permanent residence and where no evidence to the contrary has been provided.'

 UK Home Office *Asylum policy instruction statelessness and applications for leave to remain*. Version 2.0 (18 February 2016) 9–10.

34 *Applications for leave to remain as a stateless person* (1 May 2013) 5.

35 G Gyulai 'Stateless determination and the protection status of stateless persons' (2013) *ENS* 21.

Analysis of Procedural Frameworks in Five States   133

or considers him/her a national. Additionally, the Guidelines provide that the standard of proof for applicants is the balance of probabilities.[36]

There is no legal requirement for initiation of statelessness determination *ex officio* in the UK, neither are officials prohibited from initiating an *ex officio* procedure. In practice, officials refer persons they deem should go through the statelessness procedure. ENS notes that 'for children, an obligation might be inferred deriving from the obligation to consider children's best interests in any immigration decision.'[37] This is also in line with Article 3 of the CRC, which provides, that 'in all actions concerning children, whether undertaken by public or private social welfare institutions, courts of law, administrative authorities or legislative bodies, the best interests of the child shall be a primary consideration.'

5.2.1.1.2 GRANT OF LEAVE TO REMAIN IN THE UK

Stateless persons in the UK are granted either a limed leave to remain as a stateless person or an indefinite leave to remain as a stateless person. Rule 405 of the Immigration Rule provides that 'where an applicant meets the requirements of paragraph 403, they may be granted limited leave to remain in the United Kingdom for a period not exceeding five years.'[38]

Where an applicant does not meet the requirement in paragraph 403, the application to remain in the UK as a stateless person will be refused. Additionally, an

> application will be refused if there are reasonable grounds for considering that an applicant is a danger to the security of the United Kingdom, a danger to the public order of the United Kingdom, or the application would fall to be refused under any of the grounds set out in Part 9 of these Rules.[39]

---

36 UK Home Office *Asylum policy instruction statelessness and applications for leave to remain, Op Cit* 11.
37 ENS Statelessness Index: United Kingdom *Op Cit* 16. See also, s. 55 of the Borders Citizenship and Immigration Act 2009 and s. 11 of the Children's Act 2004 (Local Authorities in England and Wales).
38 The following are requirements referred to in para. 403, they are: submission of a valid application to the Secretary of State for limited leave to remain as a stateless person; recognition as a stateless person by the Secretary of State in accordance with the Immigration Rules; prove that applicant has taken reasonable steps to facilitate admission to their country of former habitual residence or any other country but has been unable to secure the right of admission; prove that applicant has sought and failed to obtain or re-establish their nationality with the appropriate authorities of the relevant country; provision of reasonable evidence to enable the Secretary of State to determine whether they are stateless or whether they are admissible to another country. In the case of a child born in the UK, has provided evidence that they have attempted to register their birth with the relevant authorities but have been refused.
39 Immigration Rules Part 14: stateless persons, para. 404.
    The grounds under the *Immigration Rules Part 9: grounds for refusal* mentioned in para. 404 of Part 14 include exclusion or deportation order grounds; exclusion from asylum or humanitarian protection grounds; involvement in a sham marriage or sham civil partnership

134 *Analysis of Procedural Frameworks in Five States*

A stateless person with lawful leave to remain in the UK for a continuous period of five years may be granted indefinite leave to remain as a stateless person in the UK, or even become eligible for naturalization upon application to the Secretary of State.[40] Dependents already accepted as such who are accompanying the applicant in the UK should, irrespective of their national status, be included in the application form submitted in support of a claim. Rules 410–411 set out the requirements for limited leave, Rule 412 for refusal or curtailment, and Rules 415–416 for the grant or refusal of indefinite leave to remain, respectively. Where an individual is granted leave to remain as a stateless person, family members will be granted leave to enter or remain in line[41] with Rules 410 and 411 of the Immigration Rules.

For leave to enter and remain in the UK as the family member of a stateless person, Rule 410 specifies in detail those who qualify as family members of a stateless person as follows: spouse, civil partner, unmarried partner with whom a stateless person has lived together in a subsisting relationship akin to marriage or a civil partnership for two years or more, a dependent child below the age of 18 years who is not married, not in a civil partnership, or has an unmarried partner with whom they have lived together in a subsisting relationship akin to marriage, or a civil partnership and has not formed an independent family unit.

5.2.1.1.3 REFUSAL OF LEAVE TO REMAIN IN THE UK

The Home Office Guidelines provide that 'there is no statutory right of appeal against the decision to refuse to grant leave as a stateless person in the UK, but unsuccessful applicants can apply for an administrative review, in accordance with paragraph AR2.3 of Appendix AR of the Immigration Rules.' The Guidelines further provide that applicants must be advised in the decision letter that they have a right to apply for administrative review using the Home Office online form for administrative review.[42]

Applicants must submit their application for administrative review within 14 calendar days from the date the decision notice or biometric residence permit (BRP) is received, or seven calendar days if detained.[43] 'Where administrative

---

    grounds; false representations; previous breach of immigration laws; and failure to provide required information, amongst others.

40 See Rule 407 of the Immigration Rules.

41 *Applications for leave to remain as a stateless person, Op Cit* 16.

42 Home Office *Asylum policy instruction statelessness and applications for leave to remain, Op Cit* 23.

    'The eligible decision will be reviewed to establish whether there is a case working error, either as identified in the application for administrative review, or identified by the Reviewer in the course of conducting the administrative review.'

    Immigration Rules Appendix AR: administrative review, AR2.3.

43 Home Office *Administrative review* Version 8.0 (6 April 2017) 5 https://assets.publishing.service.gov.uk/government/uploads/system/uploads/attachment_data/file/618626/admin_review_guidance_v8_0.pdf (accessed 2 March 2019).

Analysis of Procedural Frameworks in Five States   135

review is pending, the Home Office will not seek to remove the applicant from the United Kingdom.'[44] Another option available to applicants is judicial review. Judicial review in the UK system is a type of 'court proceeding in which a judge reviews the lawfulness of a decision or action made by a public body.' Judicial review is more focused on compliance with procedure than with whether the decision was rightly made. 'The court will not substitute what it thinks is the 'correct' decision. This may mean that the public body will be able to make the same decision again, so long as it does so in a lawful way.'[45] According to the Home Office *Administrative Review Guidelines* on how to apply for judicial review.

> If a person wishes to seek judicial review of the decision on their application, they must apply to the Upper Tribunal or High Court for permission as soon as possible and normally no longer than 3 months from the date of the decision [...] judicial review can only be sought where there is no alternative remedy available. Therefore, if a decision is eligible for administrative review, the person must first apply for administrative review and be served with notice of the outcome before they can seek judicial review.[46]

Though there is generally no appeal right in the UK SDP, a UK guidance document on applications for leave to remain as a stateless person in the UK suggests that in some circumstances, such as that 'an applicant has leave to enter or remain at the time that he made his statelessness application, but this has expired by the time that the decision to refuse leave is made' and 'the applicant is served with a decision to remove at the same time as his application for leave is refused.' In these cases, an applicant may be able to appeal under the Nationality, Immigration and Asylum Act 2002. The guidance document further advised that an 'appropriate appeal papers should be issued with the decision to refuse leave' in these situations.[47]

5.2.1.1.4 IDENTIFIED GAPS IN THE UK SYSTEM

Despite the achievement of the UK with regard to the establishment of a statelessness determination procedure and the 2019 review of Part 14 of its Immigration Rules, there continue to be gaps in the UK system. As noted earlier, the UK is one of the countries with reservations to the 1954 and 1961 Conventions, it is not a party to some international and regional instruments, such as the European Convention on Nationality, the Convention on the Avoidance of Statelessness in

---

44 AR2.8 Immigration Rules – Appendix AR: Administrative Review.
45 UK Courts and Tribunal Judiciary 'Judicial review' https://www.judiciary.uk/you-and-the
    -judiciary/judicial-review/ (accessed 14 August 2019).
46 Home Office *Administrative review* Version 10.0 73. https://assets.publishing.service.gov
    .uk/government/uploads/system/uploads/attachment_data/file/806921/Admin-review
    -guidance-v10.0-ext.pdf (accessed 14 August 2019).
47 Home Office *Applications for leave to remain as a stateless person, Op Cit* 16.

136 Analysis of Procedural Frameworks in Five States

Relation to State Succession, and the International Convention on the Protection of the Rights of all Migrant Workers and Members of their Families, nor is it bound by the EU Returns Directive.

Part 14 of the UK Immigration Rules provides the basis and procedures for protection of stateless persons in the UK. Rule 401[48] of the Immigrations Rules defines who a stateless person is, referencing Article 1(1) of the 1954 Convention; it, however, went beyond and contrary to the intent and purpose of the definition of a stateless person in the 1954 Convention by adding the requirement of 'being in the UK' to the definition.

Under Part 14 of the Immigration Rules, a person must be in the UK to apply for statelessness status. The Immigration Law Practitioners' Association (ILPA) notes that even port applicants (i.e., applicants applying at a port of entry) are excluded. An applicant will generally benefit from Part 14 of the Immigration Rules if the applicant meets the definition of a stateless person in the 1954 Convention and is not excluded. The ILPA further notes that though 'the reasons for exclusion are based on the 1954 Convention, but the way in which they are dealt with in the immigration rules are not precisely reflective of the Convention.'[49]

The UK's Immigration Rules, Part 14's definition of statelessness deviates from the intention and principle in the definition in Article 1 of the 1954 Convention which provides that a 'stateless person means a person who is not considered as a national by any State under the operation of its law.'[50] This is particularly so with

48 For the purposes of this Part a stateless person is a person who:

(a) satisfies the requirements of Article 1(1) of the 1954 United Nations Convention relating to the Status of Stateless Persons, as a person who is not considered as a national by any State under the operation of its law;

(b) is in the United Kingdom; and

(c) is not excluded from recognition as a Stateless person under paragraph 402.

49 Immigration Law Practitioners' Association (ILPA) *Statelessness, Op Cit* 1 www.ilpa.org.uk/data/resources/17840/13-05-13-Statelessness.pdf (accessed 2 February 2019).

See Art. 402 of the UK Immigration Rules, which provides thus:

'A person is excluded from recognition as a stateless person if there are serious reasons for considering that they:

(a) are at present receiving from organs or agencies of the United Nations, other than the United Nations High Commissioner for Refugees, protection or assistance, so long as they are receiving such protection or assistance;

(b) are recognised by the competent authorities of the country of their former habitual residence as having the rights and obligations which are attached to the possession of the nationality of that country;

(c) have committed a crime against peace, a war crime, or a crime against humanity, as defined in the international instruments drawn up to make provisions in respect of such crimes;

(d) have committed a serious non-political crime outside the UK prior to their arrival in the UK;

(e) have been guilty of acts contrary to the purposes and principles of the United Nations.'

50 This definition is unconditional.

Analysis of Procedural Frameworks in Five States   137

the use of the words 'for the purposes of this part' in paragraph 401 of the Rules which connotes that a different approach may be applied in another section,[51] and also the inclusion of a UK residence and exclusion clauses as part of the definition.[52]

With regard to childhood statelessness, some gaps in the UK's nationality law allow for some categories of children born in the UK or to British citizens living abroad to be stateless.

> For example, a child born in the UK to stateless parents who do not yet have permanent residence in the UK will be stateless at birth. The child will be able to register as a British citizen after five years, or upon one of their parents being granted permanent residence or naturalising as a British citizen, but there is a £1,012 application fee.[53]

The requirement for acquisition of nationality after five years of birth is not explicitly a violation of international law,[54] but an excessive application fee of £1,012 goes against the UK's international law obligation in Article 32 of the 1954 Convention which provides that 'contracting States shall as far as possible facilitate the assimilation and naturalization of stateless persons. They shall in particular make every effort to expedite naturalization proceedings and to reduce as far as possible the charges and costs of such proceedings.'

The application of the naturalization requirement of 'Good Character'[55] in the British Nationality Act (BNA) is a bit problematic.[56] Although the BNA does not define what amounts to good character, the Home Office's *Nationality: Good Character Requirement* guidance 'sets out the types of conduct which must be taken into account when assessing whether a person has satisfied the requirement of good character.' The Home Office's Guidance on Good Character provides that in considering good character:

> Consideration must be given to all aspects of a person's character, including both negative factors, for example criminality, immigration law breaches and deception, and positive factors, for example contributions a person has made to society. The list of factors is not exhaustive.[57]

---

51 Migrants Resource Centre, University of Liverpool Law Clinic, European Network on Statelessness, and Institute on Statelessness and Inclusion, *Joint submission to the Human Rights Council at the 27th session of the Universal Periodic Review United Kingdom* (22 September 2016) 7 at para. 16.

52 See Part 14 of the UK Immigration Rules, Rule 401 particularly sub-rules (b) and (c).

53 See Statelessness Index *Country Briefing – United Kingdom* (March 2019) 2 https://index .statelessness.eu/sites/statelessindex.eu/files/ENS-Index_Country-Briefing_UK_0.pdf (accessed 29 August 2019).

54 See Arts. 1 & 2 of the 1961 Convention.

55 See Schedule 1 of the British Nationality Act 1981.

56 According to the Home Office's *Nationality: Good character requirement*, 'the good character requirement applies to a person who is aged 10 or over at the date of application.'

57 See *Ibid* 9 https://assets.publishing.service.gov.uk/government/uploads/system/uploads /attachment_data/file/770960/good-character-guidance.pdf (accessed 30 August 2019).

138 Analysis of Procedural Frameworks in Five States

Stateless persons will be more often than not in breach of immigration rules, by way of illegal entry, overstay, evasion of immigration control, etc., considering that they are often in a precarious situation. The implication of inclusion of immigration breaches as part of the list of infringements in the Home Office's *Nationality: Good Character Requirement* to warrant a bad character tag for denial of naturalization without any exceptions for stateless persons is that a stateless person who illegally enters the UK within the preceding ten years of application for citizenship will be denied. The only exceptions for illegal entry mentioned in the Home Office Guide are concerning refugees in certain situations. The same denial of naturalization is applicable for stateless persons who overstay or work in the UK without a permit.

The same defence advanced for refugees charged with certain breaches provided in the 1999 Immigration and Asylum Act should be made to apply to stateless persons in the same circumstance. For instance, section 31(1) of the above-mentioned Act provides that:

> It is a defence for a refugee charged with an offence to which this section applies to show that, having come to the United Kingdom directly from a country where his life or freedom was threatened (within the meaning of the Refugee Convention), he—
>
> (a)   presented himself to the authorities in the United Kingdom without delay;
> (b)   showed good cause for his illegal entry or presence; and
> (c)   made a claim for asylum as soon as was reasonably practicable after his arrival in the United Kingdom.

The naturalization process for a stateless person should not be delayed or denied on the ground of illegal entry as long as there is a good cause (statelessness) for the illegal entry. There is also the requirement of contribution to society, though what actions or activities amount to contribution to society is not defined, whether the requirement applies to stateless persons is not specified in the Guidance, but the fact that there is no *proviso* in the Guidance suggests that it applies to everyone. It is expedient that stateless persons should be exempted from this requirement.

> The UK does not treat statelessness as a protection status equivalent to refugee status or humanitarian protection. In practice, this means that there are deficiencies in the process and the rights associated with the grant of leave.' For instance, a person applying to be recognized as a stateless person in the UK does not get legal aid or right of appeal, nor is a recognized stateless person entitled to 'home student fees and access to student finance in order to attend University, and entitlement to social housing and other benefits.[58]

---

58 J Bezzano and J Carter *Statelessness in practice: Implementation of the UK Statelessness Application Procedure* (2018) 7.

Analysis of Procedural Frameworks in Five States 139

The aforementioned is contrary to the UK's obligation under the 1954 Convention which provides for equal treatment of stateless persons lawfully staying in the territory with nationals. For instance, stateless persons should be accorded the same treatment concerning rationing as nationals,[59] the same access to public housing,[60] the same access to education,[61] the same treatment with respect to public relief and assistance,[62] and the same treatment with regard to labour legislation and social security.[63]

Also, an applicant who is the subject of a deportation order, or a decision to make a deportation order, including an exclusion order, will not be granted leave to remain in the UK.[64] Johanna Bezzano and Judith Carter note that many applicants in such situations 'without a legal representative will not appreciate that they should make a revocation application,' emphasizing that 'where there is a decision to deport or a deportation order, a statelessness application should, ideally, be accompanied by a request to revoke the deportation order.'[65] The grounds for revocation of a deportation order in Rule 390[66] appear to be very elusive and somewhat vague; stateless person would not readily be able to benefit from such revocation grounds. In accordance with relevant human rights instruments, the UK implements administrative detention.[67] An example of such instruments is the European Convention on Human Rights which permits the detention of a person to whom a deportation order is made or to prevent unauthorized entry into the territory of a State,[68] provided such person detained would have access to court to speedily determine the lawfulness or otherwise of the detention. And where such detention is found to be unlawful, the person is immediately released.[69]

Despite the protections against arbitrary detention and some remedies to challenge detention established in law and policy in the UK, 'there is no maximum time limit on detention, and access to remedies is limited in practice for some detainees.'[70] It is moreover noted that 'data on number of stateless

---

59 The 1954 Convention Relating to the Status of Stateless Persons, Art. 20.
60 *Ibid* Art. 21.
61 *Ibid* Art. 22.
62 *Ibid* Art. 23.
63 *Ibid* Art. 24.
64 Immigration Rules Part 9: grounds for refusal, 9.2.1.
65 J Bezzano and J Carter *Op Cit* 15. See also S Woodhouse and J Carter, ILPA *Statelessness and applications for leave to remain: A best practice guide*, *Op Cit* 45.
66 An application for revocation of a deportation order will be considered in the light of all the circumstances including the following: (i) the grounds on which the order was made; (ii) any representations made in support of revocation; (iii) the interests of the community, including the maintenance of an effective immigration control; (iv) the interests of the applicant, including any compassionate circumstances.
67 ENS *Protecting stateless persons from arbitrary detention in the United Kingdom* (2016) 12 https://www.statelessness.eu/sites/www.statelessness.eu/files/ENS_Detention_Reports _UK.pdf (accessed 12 September 2019).
68 ECHR Art. 5(1)(f).
69 ECHR Art. 5(4).
70 See Statelessness Index *Country briefing – United Kingdom*, *Op Cit* 2.

140 *Analysis of Procedural Frameworks in Five States*

persons in detention in the UK is flawed and incomplete. The stateless are often wrongly attributed a nationality or categorised as "persons with unknown nationality", so the real numbers are likely to be higher than the published figures.[71]

The is no indication in the Home Office *Guidance on Asylum and Statelessness Procedures* that establishing a statelessness claim is shared between the applicant and the caseworker, neither is there mention of a shared burden in the Guidance. The Guidance specifically provides that, 'in all cases, the burden of proof rests with the applicant, who is expected to cooperate with the caseworker to provide information to demonstrate they are stateless and that there is no country to which they can be removed.' This means leaving the entire burden on the applicant alone. The Guidance also does not provide for a specific length of procedure, meaning cases could be unresolved for an excessive period.

Cynthia Orchard, emphasizing the changes in the Immigration Rules, asserts that under the old Rules, 'a person granted leave to remain in some other category, such as a student, say for 3 years, and was later granted leave to remain as a stateless person, after a total of 5 years with leave to remain, they could apply for indefinite leave to remain.' But under the new Rules, such a person will still be required to complete five years leave to remain *as a stateless person.* It would be more beneficial if stateless persons could acquire nationality at the earliest possible time,[72] as envisaged in the 1954 Convention, Article 32 which obliges States to expedite naturalization proceedings.

5.2.1.2 *SDP Development and Practice in Moldova*

The Republic of Moldova acceded to the 1954 Convention relating to the Status of Stateless Persons and the 1961 Convention on the Reduction of Statelessness on 19 April 2012.[73] The country is also a party to other relevant human rights instruments, such as the European Convention on Nationality and the Council of Europe Convention on the Avoidance of Statelessness in relation to State Succession.[74]

---

71 ENS *Protecting stateless persons from arbitrary detention: An agenda for change* (2016) 9 https://www.statelessness.eu/sites/www.statelessness.eu/files/attachments/resources/ ENS_LockeInLimbo_Detention_Agenda_online.pdf (accessed 12 September 2019).

72 C Orchard *UK Home Office changes to immigration rules on statelessness: A mixed bag* European Network on Statelessness https://www.statelessness.eu/blog/uk-home-office -changes-immigration-rules-statelessness-mixed-bag (accessed 29 August 2019).

73 See UN Treaty Collections https://treaties.un.org/pages/ViewDetailsII.aspx?src=TREATY &mtdsg_no=V-3&chapter=5&Temp=mtdsg2&clang=_en (accessed 2 March 2019). Also see https://treaties.un.org/Pages/ViewDetails.aspx?src=IND&mtdsg_no=V-4&chapter=5 &clang=_en (accessed 2 March 2019).

74 UNHCR *Legal aid to stateless persons. Call for expression of interest No. 2* (7 October 2015) www.un.md/media/tender_supportdoc/2015/.../CFP%20Statelessness%202015.doc (accessed 2 March 2019).

Analysis of Procedural Frameworks in Five States 141

Since 2011,[75] the Republic of Moldova established a dedicated statelessness determination procedure under Law No. 200 of 16 July 2010 on *Foreigners in the Republic of Moldova* which entered in force on 10 February 2012.[76] In the same year, 'Moldova became the fifth state in the world alongside France, Hungary, Italy and Spain, to prepare a functional procedure of defining statelessness.'[77] The definitions of statelessness in the Law on Foreigners in the Republic of Moldova and the Law on Citizenship of the Republic of Moldova are compliant with the definition of the term in the 1954 Convention.[78]

Between 2012 and 2013, 'UNHCR assisted the Government in conducting a citizenship campaign, including in selected Roma communities. A total of 213,041 individuals were prevented from becoming stateless since 2013 within an effort which became one of the largest campaigns to address statelessness in Europe.'[79] Victoria Cojocariu noted that in 2016, there were over 9,000 stateless people in the Republic of Moldova; she further highlighted thus:

> Over 7000 of them were born on the current territory of the Republic of Moldova, and about 2,000 were of undetermined citizenship. Most of them come from the former Soviet space and failed to obtain the citizenship of the Republic of Moldova or of the former Soviet countries of origin. However, some of them went through the involuntary loss of citizenship due to: legislative contradictions; fluctuant borders; law on marriage; absence of birth registration or due to the failure to re-enter the country during a certain period of time.[80]

---

75 ENS *Statelessness Index – Moldova*. Updated March 2021 <https://index.statelessness.eu/country/moldova> (accessed 14 June 2022).

76 O Cotoman, M Vremis, and I Popov *Analytical report regarding stateless persons in the Republic of Moldova* 35 http://www.cda.md/files/Analytical_Report_Mapping_en_final_rev_26.11.2017.pdf (accessed 5 February 2019). See also Law No. 284 of 28 December 2011 for amending and supplementing certain legislative acts.

77 V Cojocariu 'Statelessness in the Republic of Moldova: A story of success' *Laboratory Initiative for Development* https://www.lidmoldova.org/en/news/statelessness-republic-moldova (accessed 14 September 2019).

78 See the Law on Foreigners in the Republic of Moldova, Art. 3 and the Law on Citizenship of the Republic of Moldova, Art. 1.

79 UNHCR *Legal aid to stateless persons, Op Cit.*
    The risk of statelessness in Moldova is mainly due to the collapse of the USSR, as many people became at risk of statelessness across different countries that made up the Soviet Union.
    'The distribution by country of birth of the persons in regards of whom decisions on the applications for the recognition of the statelessness status during 2012–2016 were, place on the first rank the Russian Federation Federația Rusă (43%), on the second one – Ukraine (24%), on the third one – Kazakhstan (11%), followed by Uzbekistan and Armenia (~ 4%), other states constituting 3% and less for each.'
    O Cotoman, M Vremis and I Popov *Op Cit* 26.

80 V Cojocariu *Op Cit.*

142 *Analysis of Procedural Frameworks in Five States*

Moldova's record on treaty accession has been described as generally good; it is moreover one of the few States with an SDP established in law.[81] Moldova used to be 'the only European country that has an unconditional rule of *ius soli* citizenship,'[82] until the law changed in 2017. In line with its obligations under the Convention on the Rights of the Child, the country grants nationality to children born in its territory, 'whose parents are stateless persons, born on the territory of Moldova, whose parents possess the citizenship of another state, or one of them is stateless and the other one is a foreign citizen, if that state does not grant citizenship to the child.'[83]

The Law on Foreigners in the Republic of Moldova mandates the Bureau for Migration and Asylum, which is within the Ministry of Internal Affairs, as the competent authority for foreigners in Moldova.[84] The law allows the procedure for recognizing stateless status to be initiated *ex officio* by the competent authority for foreigners, or upon request by the person who claims that he/she is stateless.[85]

5.2.1.2.1 ACCESS TO PROCEDURE

The Law on Foreigners in the Republic of Moldova permits a written or oral application to be made by an applicant applying to be recognized as a stateless person to the competent authority for foreigners. However, such application whether oral or written must contain 'clear and detailed description of the facts, information and proofs necessary to substantiate the applicant's claim and, in particular indicate the place of birth, affinity, and country of habitual residence, final decision by the competent authority made based on the available evidence.' Where an application is made in writing, it must be signed by the applicant. For an illiterate applicant who makes a verbal application, it must be recorded in the report. The law further guarantees applicants a right to legal representation and a right to an interpreter for applicants who do not speak the official language of the State.[86]

The law requires the competent authority to interview an applicant within 15 working days following the submission of an application.[87] The interview

---

81 ENS Stateless Index – Moldova https://index.statelessness.eu/country/moldova (accessed 8 February 2019).
82 C Dumbrava 'Comparative report: Citizenship in Central and Eastern Europe' (April 2017) 2–3 https://cadmus.eui.eu/bitstream/handle/1814/46112/RSCAS_GLOBALCIT _Comp_2017_02.pdf?sequence=1 (accessed 21 September 2019).
83 Citizenship of the Republic of Moldova. LAW No. 1024-XIV (Amendments as of September 2014), Art. 11.
84 Law No. 200 of 16 July 2010 on the Regime of Foreigners in the Republic of Moldova, Art. 3.
85 *Ibid*, Art. 87(1).
86 Law No. 200 of 16 July 2010 on the Regime of Foreigners in the Republic of Moldova, Art. 87(2)–(6). See also the Law Regarding the Legal Assistance Guaranteed by The State No. 198 of 26 July 2007, Arts. 6 and 7 http://lex.justice.md/viewdoc.php?action=view&view =doc&id=325350&lang=1.
87 Law No. 200 of 16.07.2010 on the Regime of Foreigners in the Republic of Moldova, Art. 87(1).

must be recorded in writing in an interview note which would include the applicant's biodata, the type of evidence submitted, data regarding any submitted documents, such as document type and number, validity period, date and place of issuance, name of the issuing authority, employment, and place of residence in the Republic of Moldova.[88] During the interview, the applicant is obliged to state the reasons for submitting the application and any additional information which was not previously presented, in order to substantiate his/her claim.[89]

The Bureau for Migration and Asylum examines applications within six months from the date of the registration of the application. Depending on the complexity of a case, the law allows for a subsequent extension of examination of cases term for one month each, but which must not exceed a total of six months.[90] In the case of recognition of status, the applicant must be informed about the decision by direct communication, within three working days from the date of the decision and issued identity documents such as a residence permit, identity card for stateless persons, and, upon request, travel documents and other necessary documents.[91] The same three days' notice in writing is required in the case of rejection of an application.[92] The Law on Foreigners in the Republic of Moldova does not establish a standard of proof for the SDP. In practice 'the standard of proof is the same as in asylum procedures, and cross-referral between asylum and statelessness procedures.' The burden of proof is shared between the applicants and the authorities.[93] For instance, the applicant has an obligation to present facts, information, and evidence necessary to support his or her claim;[94] however, during the examination procedure, the competent authority is obliged to take appropriate steps to collect information from the applicant's place of birth, of his or her place of residence or last domicile, as well as to request information from the State whose citizenship the applicant's family members and parents possess or have ties to.[95]

5.2.1.2.2 GRANT AND REFUSAL OF STATUS

Considering the special situation of unaccompanied minors and persons with a mental disorder or limited capacity, the Law on Foreigners in the Republic of

---

88 *Ibid* Art. 87(2); UNHCR *Good practices paper – action 6, Op Cit* 14–15.
89 *Ibid* Art. 87(3).
90 *Ibid* Art. 87(1).
91 *Ibid* Art. 87[7](1)–(3), Art. 72(1)(c).
92 *Ibid* Art. 87(2).
93 ENS Statelessness Index Country Briefing – Moldova (January 2019) https://index .statelessness.eu/sites/statelessindex.eu/files/Country%20Briefing%20Moldova%202018 %20EN_FINAL_1.pdf and ENS Statelessness Survey – Moldova https://index.stateless- ness.eu/sites/statelessindex.eu/files/ENS_Statelessness_Index_Survey-Moldova-2018.pdf (accessed 24 September 2019).
94 Law No. 200 of 16 July 2010 on the Regime of Foreigners in the Republic of Moldova, Art. 87(5).
95 *Ibid* Art. 87(2).

144 Analysis of Procedural Frameworks in Five States

Moldova 'gives consideration and special protection to unaccompanied minors and persons with mental disabilities both of whom are to be represented via a legal guardian.'[96] After an interview, in the case of an unaccompanied minor the interview note must be signed by the appointed representative of the minor, while in the case of a person with a mental disorder or with limited capacity, it must be signed by his/her guardian.[97]

Foreigner minors who enter and remain unaccompanied in Moldova are provided with protection and care by the state, including accommodation in special protection centres of minors, under the same conditions as children with Moldovan citizenship.[98] 'People recognised as stateless in Moldova are granted rights in line with nationals. Although there is an accelerated route to naturalisation, reduced from ten years.'[99] A recognized stateless person or refugee in Moldova must have resided lawfully and habitually in the territory of the Republic of Moldova for at least eight years to acquire Moldovan nationality.[100]

It is imperative to note that by law, Moldova 'cooperates with other States and international organizations with a view to finding solutions to statelessness issues.' Particularly, it allows the Office of United Nations High Commissioner for Refugees upon request, 'access to information regarding applications, access to monitor or observe procedure and issued decisions, subject to the consent of the applicants.'[101] The Law on Citizenship of the Republic of Moldova gives an applicant the right to stay on the territory of the Republic of Moldova during the examination of the statelessness application. An applicant may only be removed from the territory for reasons of national security and public order. Applicants are issued with a 'confirmation certificate' confirming their status for the whole period of the examination of their application. It is interesting to note that an applicant making an application orally or in writing may use his/her mother tongue or any other language which s/he speaks and not necessarily the official language of the State.[102]

---

96 UNHCR *Good practices paper – action 6, Op Cit* 15; Law No. 200 of 16 July 2010 on the Regime of Foreigners in the Republic of Moldova 87(4), 87(5), and 87(4).

97 *Ibid* 87(6).

98 Law No. 200 of 2010 on Foreigners [Republic of Moldova], 16 July 2010, Art. 85.

99 ENS Statelessness Index – Moldova *Op Cit.*

100 The Law on Citizenship of the Republic of Moldova, Art. 17(c).

101 Law No. 200 of 16 July 2010 on the Regime of Foreigners in the Republic of Moldova, Art. 87(1)–(2).

102 *Ibid* Art. 87(1)–(3). This section citing national security as a reason to deny a person or applicant the enjoyment of the benefit of an SDP, however right it may appear, does not make provision as to which State a person 'removed' on grounds of national security will be deported, especially where the Republic of Moldova is the 'place of habitual residence' of the applicant. The *Law on Foreigners in the Republic of Moldova* also did not define or give an interpretation of what would amount to a breach of "public order" with regard to an applicant. The danger of leaving the interpretation of such terms at the discretion of the Bureau for Migration and Asylum is that it may be given many meanings or object abuse.

Analysis of Procedural Frameworks in Five States 145

In Moldova, an applicant whose application for statelessness recognition has been rejected or cancelled can appeal the decision in a regular court of law.[103] According to the Administrative Litigation of Law of the Republic of Moldova, appeals or request for the annulment of an administrative act must be filed within 30 days,[104] unless the law being applied provides otherwise. This same rule applies to statelessness recognition appeals, which also go to the national court.

It has been observed that 'law, policy and practice on the protection of stateless people and prevention and reduction of statelessness is generally positive in Moldova.'[105]

5.2.1.2.3 IDENTIFIED GAPS IN THE MOLDOVA SYSTEM

According to the UNHCR, the Republic of Moldova has one of the most detailed SDPs established through legislation and is a good example for other States to follow.[106] Despite a good example, a few shortfalls have been observed in the law and policy especially with its application in practice. For instance, Thomas Huddleston notes in a study for the Organization for Security and Co-operation in Europe (OSCE) and the Office for Democratic Institutions and Human Rights (ODIHR):

> the process to become a Moldovan citizen is one of the longest, most discretionary and most cumbersome. Ordinary foreigners must wait 10 years (8 for stateless people and beneficiaries of international protection) and pass vague good character and income requirements as well as pass/fail tests on the state language and Constitution without a clear link to the state-sponsored language courses.[107]

In December 2017, Moldova amended its Citizenship Law which came into force in April 2018. Contrary to the old law which provided that all children who would otherwise be stateless born on the territory were automatically citizens in line with international law, the new law limited such safeguards to children born on the territory of Moldova with at least one parent with a right of residence or benefits from international protection or recognized as a stateless person.[108] The

---

103 *Ibid* Art. 87(2) and 87(3).
104 The Administrative Litigation of the **Republic of Moldova. Law** No. 793 of 10 February 2000, Art. 17(1) http://lex.justice.md/index.php?action=view&view=doc&lang=1&id =350170 (accessed 2 March 2019). Also see, O Cotoman, M Vremis, and I Popov *Op Cit* 45.
105 ENS Stateless Index – Moldova *Op Cit.*
106 UNHCR *Good practices paper – action 6, Op Cit* 2.
107 T Huddleston 'Republic of Moldova: A migrant integration policy index assessment' (2015) *OSCE & ODIHR, Migration Policy Group* 9 https://www.osce.org/odihr/201021 ?download=true (accessed 17 September 2019); Law on Citizenship of the Republic of Moldova, Art. 17(c)–(f).
108 Republic of Moldova LAW No. 132 of 21 December 2017 for amending and supplementing the Law on citizenship of the Republic of Moldova no. 1024/2000, Art. I(c). http://

146 *Analysis of Procedural Frameworks in Five States*

new law also has an impediment to universal birth registration in Moldova, as it prevents undocumented parents from registering new births.

In a 2016 submission on the Republic of Moldova by the Office of the UNHCR for the OHCHR's Universal Periodic Review, it was stated that though Moldova has a statelessness identification mechanism, the exact number of stateless persons in the country remains unclear. It was also noted that 'majority of the registered stateless persons reside in the breakaway Transnistrian region of the country, where central authorities do not have access to relevant archives and are thus unable to facilitate the naturalization process.'[109] To effectively protect stateless persons, authorities have to know the numbers, composition, and profile of stateless persons or persons at risk of statelessness in their territory.

Legal aid for applicants for statelessness procedures is provided for under the Law Regarding the Legal Assistance Guaranteed by The State;[110] despite the legal requirement for legal aid for SDP applicants in Moldova, in practice, the state-funded legal aid is not provided by the State but is provided by NGOs who are not legally mandated.[111] Moreover, despite the provision of some safeguards for applicants for statelessness status, they do not however cover fully all basic needs, especially medical care and social assistance during the SDP. Another challenge for applicants is the length of the procedure. Normally, SDP in Moldova should be concluded in six months (with the possibility to extend up to 12 months), but often applicants have to wait the entire 12 months. During the examination of an application, the Bureau for Migration and Asylum takes necessary measures to collect information on the place of birth of the applicant, place of residence or last residence, and information on the nationality held by members of the applicant's family and parents. Getting information from foreign authorities can be very complicated; in some cases no information is found. As a result, the time frame for examining an application is extended to the maximum.[112]

---

lex.justice.md/md/373813%20/ (accessed 21 September 2019); ENS Statelessness Index Survey: Moldova *Op Cit* 41.

109 Submission by the United Nations High Commissioner for Refugees for the Office of the High Commissioner for Human Rights's Compilation Report Universal Periodic Review: 2nd Cycle, 26th Session on Republic of Moldova 9.

Transnistria is a 'disputed sliver of land between Ukraine and Moldova [that] is called the Pridnestrovian Moldavian Republic. But to visitors to Transnistria, a breakaway region that declared its independence in the 1990s but which most of the world considers part of Moldova, it looks more like a Soviet state frozen in time.' See JTA online newspaper http://www.jta.org/2019/09/20/global/transnistria-is-a-poor-breakaway-state-in-eastern-europe-the-few-jews-left-there-eye-an-escape (accessed 21 September 2019).

110 The Law Regarding the Legal Assistance Guaranteed by The State No. 198 of 26 July 2007, Arts. 6 and 7.

111 See ENS Stateless Index, Country Briefing – Moldova *Op Cit* 2 https://index.statelessness.eu/sites/statelessindex.eu/files/Country%20Briefing%20Moldova%202018%20EN_FINAL_1.pdf (accessed 21 September 2019).

112 Email interview with an official of the Moldovan Bureau for Migration and Asylum 17 August 2019.

Analysis of Procedural Frameworks in Five States   147

On gaps relating to detention law and practice in Moldova, the ENS notes that despite the presence of some protections against the arbitrary detention of stateless persons in Moldova, the law gives the authorities powers to detain applicants. It also emphasized that 'in practice, it is unclear how these principles are implemented and no alternatives to immigration detention are established in law or practice. [...] The provision of information to detainees on their rights is not set in law and provided by UNHCR's NGO partners at the discretion of the government.'[113]

5.2.1.3 SDP Development and Practice in France

As far back as 1952, France had established a statelessness determination procedure established in law and under the authority of the French Office for the Protection of Refugees and Stateless Persons (OFPRA) and became the first State with a procedure in place;[114] therefore France is in Group 1 as a country with an existing SDP. France signed and ratified the 1954 Convention in 1955 and 1960 respectively,[115] but is not a party to three very relevant statelessness instruments such as the 1961 Convention, which it signed on 31 May 1962 but has yet to ratify,[116] the European Convention on Nationality, and the Convention on the Avoidance of Statelessness in Relation to State Succession. The ENS notes that although France is a party to most other relevant instruments, it retains reservations, especially reservations which impact stateless persons in France.[117]

The UNHCR reports that since 2010, France has received an average of 200 applications for stateless status each year.[118] Further to the forgoing, the ENS reported that:

> In 2018, 420 new claims were lodged (23% increase on 2017); and 327 decisions were issued – 71 positive (22% recognition rate). Data is disaggregated by country of birth and gender but does not include accompanying minors. The largest group of applicants (31%) were Saharawi, followed by people from the former Soviet Union (13%), and Kuwaiti bidoon (11%).
>
> As of 31 December 2018, 1493 stateless people were protected by OFPRA (34% women). In 2018, OFPRA recognised 122 'stateless-refugees' (slightly more than in 2017 (114) and 2016 (91).[119]

---

113 'Detention should be a last resort and a country of removal must be set prior to detaining'; see ICCPR, Art. 7.
    ENS Stateless Index, Country Briefing – Moldova *Op Cit* 2.
114 C Queval, 'A new tool to raise awareness on gaps in French law, policy and practice' *ENS. #StatelessnessINDEX.* https://www.statelessness.eu/blog/statelessnessindex-new-tool -raise-awareness-gaps-french-law-policy-and-practice (accessed 2 March 2019).
115 United Nations *Treaty Series* vol. 360, 117.
116 United Nations, Treaty Ratification table as at 21 December 2020.
117 ENS Statelessness Index – France https://index.statelessness.eu/country/france (accessed 2 March 2019).
118 UNHCR *Good practices paper – action 6, Op Cit* 3.
119 ENS Statelessness Index – France *Op Cit.*

148   *Analysis of Procedural Frameworks in Five States*

The Code for Entry and Residence of Foreign Persons and the Right of Asylum (hereinafter CESEDA) retains the definition of statelessness as provided in the 1954 Convention relating to the status of stateless persons without limiting and broadening the scope of the definition.[120] The competent authority in France for SDP is the French Office for the Protection of Refugees and Stateless Persons (hereinafter referred to as OFPRA) which is under the authority of the administrative court, and the supervision of the Ministry of Interior.[121] The OFPRA exercises legal and administrative protection for and on behalf of stateless persons; it is empowered to issue to stateless persons all necessary documents to enable them to stay in France.[122]

5.2.1.3.1 ACCESS TO PROCEDURE

According to the OFPRA Procedure Guide, applications for stateless status are made directly to the OFPRA requesting the statelessness application form. The request must be written in French, and include the name and address of the applicant. Additionally, the application form must be enclosed with two passport photographs, a travel document (if available), civil status documents, and a copy of a valid residence permit. Upon submission of the application, the OFPRA registers and issues a registration certificate or attestation document to the applicant.[123] Though not mandatory, the OFPRA may invite the applicant for a personal interview. The applicant is free to express himself/herself in a language s/he is comfortable in, and where necessary be assisted with a translator and with legal representation.[124]

The burden of proving one's statelessness though lies with the applicant; this burden is shared with OFPRA.[125] The OFPRA assist applicants with contacting relevant authorities in other countries,[126] exploring 'to which States the applicant

---

120 CESEDA, Art. L. 812-1.
121 CESEDA, Art. L. 812-2. See also, French Ministry of the Interior – General Directorate for Foreign Nationals in France, *Guide for asylum seekers in France (gAS)* (November 2015) 4 https://ofpra.gouv.fr/sites/default/files/atoms/files/guide-da-france_anglais .pdf (accessed 12 February 2019). Also see the OFPRA website https://www.ofpra.gouv .fr/fr/l-ofpra/presentation-generale (accessed 12 February 2019).
122 CESEDA, Art. L. 812-4.
123 OFPRA, *Procedures* https://www.ofpra.gouv.fr/fr/apatridie/procedure (accessed 12 February 2019). See also, OFPRA *Guide of the procedures to OFPRA* 44 https://www.ofpra .gouv.fr/sites/default/files/atoms/files/guide_de_procedure-ext_web_10-11-2015_vd .pdf (accessed 12 February 2019). See also, EMN INFORM *Statelessness in the EU* Version 4 *Op Cit* 5. Note that the 'certificate of registration' in this case is not the same thing as a resident permit.
124 EMN INFORM *Statelessness in the EU, Op. Cit.*
125 ENS Statelessness Index Survey: France *Op Cit* 19 and 20.
126 'The guide of procedures never refers to the applicant's obligation to "prove" their statelessness; it rather talks about the authority's methodology to establish the facts. OFPRA requires the applicant to demonstrate they have taken the necessary steps to obtain the nationality they would be entitled to according to the relevant legal provisions (if there is

Analysis of Procedural Frameworks in Five States 149

may have ties and whether he or she would be considered a national of any of them.' During an interview, where necessary, OFPRA provides an interpreter free of charge.[127] Where the OFPRA has established that an applicant has no fear of persecution, it will request that the applicant signs a declaration allowing it to contact relevant State authorities.[128] The OFPRA documents all material elements during the processing of the statelessness application, to ascertain which of the countries the applicant is affiliated or linked to; these include the country of origin of the applicant's parents, the applicant's country of birth, and the applicant's country of habitual residence. The essence of the forgoing, as noted above, is to determine amongst the States contacted, in which State(s) the applicant can acquire a nationality.[129]

The *Guide for Asylum Seekers in France* provides that during an interview (unlike for the asylum process), an applicant would not be provided with any representation. However, such an interview is conducted in the language the applicant understands and the outcome is communicated to the applicant through 'registered post with recorded delivery.'[130]

5.2.1.3.2 GRANT AND REFUSAL OF APPLICATION

Applicants whose statelessness status is recognised are placed under the legal and administrative protection of the OFPRA, which includes the right to a residency permit, travel documents, healthcare, and the right to private and family life.[131] 'Recognized stateless persons are issued a temporary residence permit which indicates in it, 'private and family life' (*Vie privée et familiale*) authorizing them to work. After three years of lawful residence in France, a stateless person may be granted a ten-year residence permit.'[132] On the status of spouses and children of recognized stateless persons, the Guide further provides thus:

> The same kind of residence permit is also be issued to spouses of a recognized stateless person (if the marriage took place prior to obtaining stateless person status, or, if this is not the case, if the marriage took place at least one year previously) and to children who were underage when the applicant's status was granted – as soon as they reach the age of 18 years (or 16 years, if they wish to work). The permit is renewable and gives a recognized stateless

---

      such a country). A genuine attachment to the country in question is not a requirement in this assessment.'
        Ibid 5 & 21.

127 UNHCR *Good practices paper – action 6, Op Cit* 10.
128 ENS Statelessness Index Survey: France *Op Cit* 19.
129 OFPRA *Procedures, Op Cit.*
130 French Ministry of the Interior – Directorate General for Foreign Nationals in France, *Guide for asylum seekers in France (gAS), Op Cit* 5.
131 *Ibid.*
132 OFPRA *Procedures, Op Cit.* CESEDA. See also Art. L. 314-11 9°.

150 *Analysis of Procedural Frameworks in Five States*

person the right to work. A recognized stateless person who wishes to travel outside of France may approach the Prefecture to obtain a stateless person's travel document.[133]

On access to nationality, foreigners, including recognized stateless persons who have legally resided in France for at least five years, qualify for naturalization;[134] this requirement is reduced to two years for foreigners (including stateless persons) who complete two years of university education with a diploma conferred by a French university or establishment of higher education.[135] Unlike in the asylum procedure, applicants for stateless status are not entitled to a temporary residence permit while their application is processed.[136] The French Civil Code further allows a child born to stateless parents on French territory to acquire French nationality automatically at birth; it also grants nationality to foundlings.[137]

Where an application has been rejected, the applicant must be informed of his right to appeal directly to the Administrative Court, provided such appeal is made within two months from the notification date of the decision of the OFPRA.[138] The judgment of the Administrative Court may be appealed to the Administrative Court of Appeal. It is important to note that an appeal to the Administrative Tribunal for a review of the decision of the OFPRA does not suspend the effect of the decision of OFPRA. In other words, a deportation order could be implemented without having to wait for the outcome of the applicant's appeal to the Administrative Court challenging the decision of the OFPRA.[139]

5.2.1.3.3 IDENTIFIED GAPS IN THE FRENCH SYSTEM

In addition to not being party to some relevant statelessness instruments,[140] some of the shortfalls in the French procedure, like in many other countries

---

133 OFPRA *Ibid*. The above is a translated version from the original French version.

134 The French Civil Code, Art. 21-17 and Art. 21-18.

135 *Ibid* Art. 21-18.

136 French Ministry of Interior – General Directorate for Foreign Nationals in France *Guide for asylum seekers in France (gAS), Op Cit* 5.

137 The Civil Code, Arts. 19-1 and 58. As envisaged by Art. 19-1, for a stateless child born in France, there is no age limit, but Art. 58 makes reference only to a newborn child.

138 The Code of Administrative Justice, R. 312-6; CESEDA, Art. L. 812-3.

139 See OFPRA 'Statelessness – remedies' https://www.ofpra.gouv.fr/fr/apatridie/les-voies-de -recours (accessed 12 February 2019). Also see, French Ministry of the Interior 'Immigration, asylum, reception and accompaniment of foreigners in France' https://www .immigration.interieur.gouv.fr/Asile/Le-droit-d-asile/Le-statut-d-apatride (accessed 12 February 2019). See also, French Ministry of the Interior – General Directorate for Foreign Nationals in France, *Guide for asylum seekers*. Information and Orientation 2013, 22 https://www.immigration.interieur.gouv.fr/content/download/69983/510865/file/ Guidedemandeurasile_2013Anglais.pdf (accessed 14 February 2019).

140 'France has signed and ratified the 1954 Convention Relating to the Status of Stateless Persons but is not party to three of the core statelessness instruments: the 1961 Convention on the Reduction of Statelessness (has signed but not acceded, with reservations), the

Analysis of Procedural Frameworks in Five States 151

with an SDP, include the non-issuance of a provisional residence permit pending the determination of the application,[141] meaning an applicant can be removed from France even while his application is still before the authorities. Although an applicant whose stateless application is rejected has a right of appeal to the Administrative Court, such appeal has no suspensive effect. This is particularly so for an applicant in respect of whom a deportation order has been made; the *Prefecture* may still carry out the deportation even when the administrative court is yet to rule on the appeal.[142] On data collection, the ENS notes 'that France collects and publishes disaggregated data on the statelessness determination procedure, stateless refugees, and limited data on stateless people's acquisition of nationality and residence permits.' It also emphasizes that France does not have a system to capture or select anything other than a nationality (other responses are captured as 'non-answers') in its national census system, thereby making it impossible to take a record of stateless persons in its national census.[143]

There is no possibility to initiate a statelessness procedure *ex officio* in France. If a person files both asylum and statelessness applications, the asylum procedure takes priority. Should the asylum procedure fail, the OFPRA does not refer it to the statelessness procedure, officials simply inform the applicant about the statelessness procedure.[144] Applicants are not provided with legal representation for the statelessness procedure. Neither the CESEDA nor the OFPRA guidelines provide for the length of procedure for statelessness applications; the implication of this vacuum is a tendency for applications to be pending before the OFPRA for a prolonged period.

According to the OFPRA *Procedures Guide*, all the elements of a statelessness claim must be established sufficiently and with clear evidence.[145] This is higher

---

European Convention on Nationality (has signed but not acceded, no reservation), and the Convention on the Avoidance of Statelessness in Relation to State Succession (neither signed nor acceded), which protects the right to a nationality and obliges the State to prevent statelessness in cases of State succession.'

ENS Country Briefing – France *Op Cit* 1 https://index.statelessness.eu/sites/statelessindex.eu/files/Country%20Briefing%20France%20ENG_FINAL_1.pdf (accessed 12 October, 2019).

141 See French Ministry of Interior – General Directorate for Foreign Nationals in France *Guide for asylum seekers in France (gAS)*, *Op Cit* 5.
142 French Office for the Protection of Refugees and Stateless Persons (OFPRA) https://www.ofpra.gouv.fr/fr/apatridie/les-voies-de-recours (accessed 9 October 2019).
143 ENS Country Briefing – France *Op Cit* 2.
144 EU Commission & ENS *Ad-Hoc Query on recognition of stateless persons Requested by LU EMN NCP on 26th February 2015 Compilation of 4th May 2015* 13 https://ec.europa.eu/home-affairs/sites/homeaffairs/files/what-we-do/networks/european_migration_network/reports/docs/ad-hoc-queries/ad-hoc-queries-2015.675_lu_recognition_of_stateless_persons_wider_diss.pdf (accessed 12 October 2019), ENS Statelessness Index Survey 2019: France *Op Cit* 18 & 25.
145 OFPRA *Procedures Guide*, *Op Cit* para. 9.2 (accessed 23 October 2019; translated from French).

152 *Analysis of Procedural Frameworks in Five States*

than what is ordinarily required in civil cases (i.e., the balance of probabilities) and guidance provided in the UNHCR Statelessness Handbook.

5.2.1.4 SDP and Practice in Côte d'Ivoire (Ivory Coast)

Ivory Coast acceded to the two international statelessness conventions in 2013. The country played host to the Ministerial Conference on Statelessness for the Member States of the Economic Community of West African States (ECOWAS) from 23 to 25 February 2015.[146] Ivory Coast developed a National Action Plan to end statelessness which it adopted on 8 January 2020 at the minister's council, thereby becoming the ninth of the 15 ECOWAS member States to do so.[147]

Moreover, the country appointed a statelessness focal point within the Ministry of Justice, and conducted a study on statelessness.[148] And in September 2020, Ivory Coast became the first African country to adopt a law for the determination of statelessness status.[149] On 2 September 2021, it adopted two laws on statelessness determination procedures. The first is Law No. 836 on the Creation, Organization and Functioning of the National Eligibility Commission on Statelessness Status (this law creates a Commission that determines statelessness otherwise known as *Commission Nationale d'Eligibilite* or CNESA).[150] The second is Law No. 837 on Creation, Organization and Functioning of The National Appeal Commission on Stateless Status (otherwise known as *la Commission Nationale de Recours* or CNRSA).

With a stateless population of about 700,000 persons, Ivory Coast has one of the highest numbers of stateless persons in the world.[151] The two main groups most affected in Ivory Coast are 'historic migrants and their descendants, who have lost ties to their country of origin over the generations as well as foundlings, or children of unknown parentage.' The main causes of statelessness in Ivory Coast have been identified to include lack of safeguards in nationality laws, low level of birth registration, and migrations,[152] which resulted mainly due to

---

146 M Adjami *Statelessness and nationality in Côte d'Ivoire. A study for UNHCR* (2006) 5.
147 UNHCR Côte d'Ivoire Factsheet (January 2020) 3 https://reliefweb.int/sites/reliefweb .int/files/resources/UNHCR%20C%C3%B4te%20d%27Ivoire%20Factsheet%20-%20Jan- uary%202020.pdf (accessed 29 September 2020).
148 Institute on Statelessness and Inclusion (ISI) & La Coalition De La Société Civile De Lutte Contre L'Apatridie Joint Submission to the Human Rights Council at the 33rd Session of the Universal Periodic Review Côte d'Ivoire para. 15.
149 UNHCR 'Côte d'Ivoire adopts Africa's first legal process to identify and protect stateless people' (4 September 2020) https://www.unhcr.org/news/press/2020/9/5f51f33b4/ cote-divoire-adopts-africas-first-legal-process-identify-protect-stateless.html (accessed 29 December 2020).
150 CNESA Law Art. 1.
151 Submission by the United Nations High Commissioner for Refugees for the Office of the High Commissioner for Human Rights's Compilation Report Universal Periodic Review: 3rd Cycle, 33rd Session for Côte d'Ivoire 1.
152 L Farias and C Arnaud 'UNHCR launch mapping of statelessness in Côte d'Ivoire' UNHCR Blog (3 September 2018) https://www.unhcr.org/blogs/mapping-statelessness -cote-divoire/ (accessed 7 March 2019).

Analysis of Procedural Frameworks in Five States 153

the official policy of the Ivorian State between 1960 and 1993 under the then President Felix Houphouët-Boigny, who right after the country's independence in 1960 welcomed and encouraged immigration.[153]

The policy was made because the country had many cocoa and coffee plantations and was in dire need of labourers at the time.[154] By virtue of the policy, which was based on the key principle of 'Land belongs to those who cultivate it,' foreign farmers and labourers trooped in and settled in Ivory Coast in large numbers,[155] with many later generations disconnected from their ancestral places of origin.

5.2.1.4.1 ACCESS TO PROCEDURE

The *Commission Nationale d'Eligibilite* (CNESA), which is under the Ministry of Foreign Affairs, is mandated to handle all statelessness matters by virtue of Article 3 of Law No. 836 on the creation of the CNESA.[156] In the absence of implementation guidelines for the new statelessness determination procedure laws, not much is known or can be projected on the effectiveness or otherwise of the law, or even how the provisions of the law would be implemented. On access to procedure, Law No. 836 on creation of the CNESA provides that an applicant for statelessness status must submit an application in writing to the Secretariat which will examine the file and refer it to the CNESA.[157]

5.2.1.4.2 GRANT AND REFUSAL OF APPLICATION

In the case of a negative decision, applicants have 15 days from the date of notification of the decision of the *Commission Nationale d'Eligibilite* to appeal at the National Appeal Commission.[158]

---

153 BBC World Service 'Article 15: Right to nationality' http://www.bbc.co.uk/worldservice /people/features/ihavearightto/four_b/casestudy_art15.shtml (accessed 7 March 2019).
154 'During this relatively peaceful period, foreign residents were even allowed to own land and vote.' *Ibid.*
155 European Asylum Support Office (EASO) *Côte d'Ivoire country focus: Country of origin information report* (June 2019) 20; see also, A Babo 'The crisis of public policies in Côte d'Ivoire: Land law and the nationality trap in Tabou's rural communities' (2013) 83 (1) *Journal of International African Institute (IAI) (Land Politics in Africa: Constituent Authority, Property and Persons)* 107 https://www.academia.edu/7401231/THE_CRI-SIS_OF_PUBLIC_POLICIES_IN_C%C3%94TE_DIVOIRE_LAND_LAW_AND_THE _NATIONALITY_TRAP_IN_TABOUS_RURAL_COMMUNITIES (accessed 12 February 2019).
156 Law No. 836 on creation of the CNESA, Arts. 2 & 3.
157 *Ibid* Art. 8. The Directorate of Aid and Assistance to Refugees and Stateless Persons (otherwise known as DAARA) is the Secretariat of the National Eligibility Commission by virtue of Art. 7.
158 *Ibid* Art. 12.

154 *Analysis of Procedural Frameworks in Five States*

5.2.1.4.3 IDENTIFIED GAPS IN THE IVORIAN SYSTEM

The new statelessness determination regulations adopted in 2020 are yet to be tested in practice. Therefore, it is not immediately possible to ascertain whether it will lead to a significant increase in facilitated naturalization. This is in consideration of the fact that, like in many African countries, only a few foreigners have successfully acquired Ivorian nationality through naturalization.

Mirna Adjami notes that the official Ivorian Government's record of individuals that acquired Ivorian nationality through naturalization between 1962 and 2012 indicates that 32,819 individuals acquired Ivorian nationality through naturalization, out of which there were 7,121 signed decrees in the Official Journal. Even with the publication of these figures, there are still some concerns as to the accuracy of the numbers.[159]

Specifically, with regard to the new statelessness determination regulations, there is a need for more clarity on its implementation. This can be made possible through the development of implementation guidelines; in the absence of implementation guidelines, there are several gaps in the current legal framework. These gaps relate to the absence of clarity on the method of initiating an application for statelessness status, whether in writing or otherwise; it is also not clear whether officials can initiate application *ex officio*. The regulations fail to address the question relating to the length of the procedure. The regulations are moreover not clear on whether applicants are entitled to an interview by officials of the *Commission Nationale d'Eligibilite*, and whether they get access to legal aid and an interpreter during interviews. More importantly, the standard and burden of proof for SDP are not specified in the regulations.

5.2.2 Group 2 – Country with Alternative Administrative Procedures for Identification of Statelessness

In this section, the Netherlands will be assessed. Although the Netherlands does not have a statelessness determination procedure in place nor does it grant legal rights to stateless persons, the Netherlands has alternative administrative procedures for identification of statelessness which many countries including Nigeria do not have at the moment. This section will assess the alternative procedures with a view to suggesting possible temporary alternative procedures for Nigeria.

5.2.2.1 SDP Development and Practice in the Netherlands

The Dutch Government reports that more than 12,000 people are registered as stateless in the Personal Records Database system in the Netherlands. The number it says, 'make[s] up only a small percentage of the 40,000 individuals

---

159 M Adjami *Op Cit* 24.

Analysis of Procedural Frameworks in Five States 155

with the designation 'unknown nationality'.[160] The Netherlands is a State party to the 1954 Convention relating to the Status of Stateless Persons and the 1961 Convention on the Reduction of Statelessness. It ratified both Conventions on 12 April 1962 and 13 May 1985 respectively.[161]

The 'legal system in the Netherlands grants a number of specific rights to stateless persons,' but lacks a proper mechanism for the identification of stateless persons who should be beneficiaries of those rights[162] as it is in countries in Group 1 that have dedicated statelessness determination procedures. The Netherlands, therefore, falls under Group 2, i.e., countries with alternative administrative procedures for identification of statelessness, which give less protection.

The State Secretary of Security, in 2016, presented a legislative proposal for a statelessness determination procedure in the Netherlands.[163] The move for the procedure was greatly influenced by the recommendations of the 2011 UNHCR mapping of statelessness in the Netherlands and the Advisory Committee on Migration Affairs' advice to the Dutch government to establish an SDP 'backed by guarantees and a new residence ground for the purpose of statelessness in the Aliens Act.'[164] Uliana Ermolaeva *et al* note that the Dutch government, while acknowledging the need for a statelessness determination procedure, suggests that it complies with its international treaty obligations and provides protection to stateless persons in the Netherlands.[165]

The legislative proposal, which has been pending since 2016, is yet to be passed by the Parliament. Arguably, with the absence of a determination procedure that is essential for the identification and protection of stateless persons, the position of the Dutch government suggesting that it complies with its international law obligation towards stateless persons is not accurate. This is in consideration of the fact that stateless persons and persons without residence permit who have the tag 'nationality unknown' indicated in the Basic Registration of Persons (BRP) in the municipalities do not enjoy the legal protection of the State or have access to basic services.

The competent authority in the Netherlands for residency and naturalization is the *Immigratie en Naturalisatie Dienst* (IND), otherwise known as the Immigration and Naturalization Service. It is an administrative body within the

---

160 See the Government of the Netherlands's website https://www.government.nl/topics/dutch-nationality/statelessness (accessed 24 December 2020).

161 United Nations *Treaty Series* vol. 360, 117; United Nations *Treaty Series* vol. 989, 175.

162 K Swider 'Statelessness determination in the Netherlands' (2014) 4 *Amsterdam Centre for European Law and Governance Working Paper Series* 3 & 9.

163 The Public Interest Litigation Project (PILP) *Statelessness* https://pilpnjcm.nl/en/dossiers/statelessness/ (accessed 20 February 2019).

164 Statelessness in Holland https://staatloosinnederland.wordpress.com/2015/02/22/what-happens-when-a-stateless-person-arrives-or-wants-to-stay-in-holland/ (accessed 21 February 2019).

165 U Ermolaeva, E Faltinat, and D Tentere 'The concept of "stateless persons" in European Union law. Final report' (August 2017) 8 euromedmonitor.org/uploads/reports/Stateless-EN.pdf (accessed 20 February 2019).

156 *Analysis of Procedural Frameworks in Five States*

Dutch Ministry of Security and Justice that implements foreign nationals' policy in the Netherlands. The IND is responsible for the issuance of residence permits and handles applications for naturalization in the Netherlands.[166] It registers information of all foreigners who reside in the Netherlands, including their nationality and their statelessness status in the *Basisvoorziening Vreemdelingen* (BVV), otherwise known as the Database on Foreigners.

5.2.2.1.1 ACCESS TO PROCEDURE (ALTERNATIVE ADMINISTRATIVE PROCEDURES)

As noted earlier, the Netherlands does not have an adequate mechanism for determining statelessness. After many years, the proposed SDP is still under consideration. For example, how to manage issues regarding access to procedure, issues regarding the burden and standard of proof, and identification of an appropriate authority for statelessness determination is still being discussed.[167] In a joint submission of the Institute on Statelessness and Inclusion, ASKV Refugee Support, and the European Network on Statelessness and Defence for Children Human Rights Council at the 27th Session of the Universal Periodic Review for the Netherlands, it was submitted that until the proposed SDP is introduced, the Netherlands identifies stateless persons and those at risk of statelessness in two ways; they are (1) through registration in the Personal Records Database or Basic Registration of Persons Database *Basisregistratie Personen* (BRP) of the municipality of residence of the applicant, and (2) regularization of residence in the 'no-fault' procedure.[168]

Stateless persons without legal residence do not get the right to residence in the Netherlands. The Dutch Government website specifically states that 'statelessness in itself is no reason for a residence permit in the Netherlands.' Therefore, stateless persons, like other foreign nationals, obtain a residence permit if they meet the conditions for a residence permit set by the Immigration and Naturalization Service. The consideration, according to the Dutch Government, will be an assessment of whether or not there is a country the applicant can return to. If it is established that there is no country to which the stateless applicant can return to or that wants the applicant back, then that person can get a special residence permit (no-fault permit),[169] which shall be examined later in this book.

---

166 The Netherlands's Immigration and Naturalisation (IND) website https://ind.nl/en/about-ind/Pages/What-does-the-IND-do.aspx (accessed 20 February 2019).

167 G-R de Groot, K Swider, and O Vonk 'Practices and approaches in EU Member States to prevent and end statelessness' (2015) 51 https://policycommons.net/artifacts/2057505/practices-and-approaches-in-eu-member-states-to-prevent-and-end-statelessness/2810596/ (accessed 16 June 2022).

168 Institute on Statelessness and Inclusion (ISI) *ASKV Refugee Support, European Network on Statelessness and Defence for Children – The Netherlands.* Joint Submission to the Human Rights Council at the 27th Session of the Universal Periodic Review the Netherlands 22 September 2016 paras. 25 & 27.

169 The Netherlands Ministry of Justice and Security website https://www.rijksoverheid.nl/onderwerpen/nederlandse-nationaliteit/staatloosheid (accessed 20 February 2019).

Analysis of Procedural Frameworks in Five States 157

The Netherlands Nationality Act[170] defines a stateless person as 'a person who is not considered citizen by any state by virtue of its legislation.' The above definition is a little bit narrower than the definition in the 1954 Convention which uses the words 'under the operation of its law.' Arguably, applying the Dutch definition of statelessness may narrow the concept to only *de jure* statelessness, considering that the operation of the laws of certain States may exclude some of its nationals from enjoying effective access to the benefits and protection of the State.

The Netherlands Nationality Act allows acquisition of Dutch nationality by option (option procedure[171]) for a person born in the territory of the Netherlands who would be otherwise stateless, provided that the person's habitual residence is in the Netherlands, Aruba, Curaçao, Sint Maarten, or public bodies Bonaire, Sint Eustatius, and Saba (Territories of the Netherlands), is stateless since birth, and has lived in the territory of the Netherlands for an uninterrupted period of at least three years.[172] It also allows the acquisition of Dutch nationality for 'identified' stateless or foreign persons after three years of legal residence,[173] including Dutch nationality for foundlings.[174]

5.2.2.1.1.1 The Personal Records Database or Basic Registration of Persons Database Basisregistratie Personen (BRP) Procedure

The BRP procedure is a procedure whereby the municipalities record the personal data of all residents in its database called the BRP. 'The BRP contains the personal data of people who live in the Netherlands (residents) and of people who live abroad (non-residents). People who live in the Netherlands for less than 4 months – to work or study, for example – can also be registered with the BRP.' These data include marital status, the birth of a child, and address. The data are transmitted to any municipality that the holder moves to.[175] The 2003 Manual on Dutch Nationality Act indicates that to determine if a person is stateless in the Netherlands, the registration in BRP is considered for an apparently stateless person with legal residence in the Netherlands. For such an individual, the BRP status is indicated as 'stateless',

---

170 The Netherlands Nationality Act 2010 (as amended in 2017) in force since 1 March 2017.
171 The option procedure is available to persons who can establish special links to the Netherlands. It is a much easier and an accelerated way of acquiring Dutch nationality than the naturalization process.
172 See the Netherlands Nationality Act, Art. 6(1)(b). The procedure is not automatic; a written declaration must be made to that effect as provided in Art. 6(1). There is no age restriction on such application in the Nationality Act. However, a stateless child or any or both parents must have a resident permit in order for the child to be entitled to the grant of Dutch nationality.
173 See Arts. 6(1)(b) & 8(4) of the Netherlands Nationality Act.
    'Recognized' used here does not connote that the applicant has been recognized through an SDP, but that the applicant has proved his or her statelessness to the Dutch authorities who also agree that the applicant cannot be accepted by another State.
174 Art. 3(2).
175 Government of the Netherlands *Personal Records Database (BRP)* https://www.government.nl/topics/personal-data/personal-records-database-brp (accessed 25 January 2019).

158   *Analysis of Procedural Frameworks in Five States*

while for a person whose nationality cannot be determined, the default status, i.e., 'unknown' is indicated.[176] Concerning 'unknown' nationality, the Dutch Government clarifies thus:

> The designation 'unknown nationality' in the Personal Records Database is not the same as statelessness. Most migrants with this designation do actually have a nationality, but do not have any documents to prove it. Most do hold a residence permit.[177]

The designation 'nationality unknown' does not guarantee any form of protection safeguards that are applicable for stateless persons. In Communication No. 2918/2016 of December 2020,[178] concerning Mr. Denny Zhao, born in the Netherlands on 18 February 2010 to a Chinese woman who herself could not establish her Chinese nationality due to non-registration in the civil record in China. Following from his mother's apparent statelessness, Mr. Zhao had no recognised nationality and could not acquire Dutch nationality because of his mother's status as an 'illegal alien' in the Netherlands. Due to the forgoing reason, he was registered under the 'nationality unknown' category. In his communication to the Human Rights Committee, he alleged that the Dutch authorities registering him under the 'nationality unknown' category since his birth, and leaving him with no prospect of acquiring a nationality, has violated his rights under the International Covenant on Civil and Political Rights (ICCPR), Article 24,[179] read alone and in conjunction with Articles 2(2)[180] and 2(3).[181] The Human Rights

---

176 *Handleiding Rijkswet op het Nederlanderschap 2003* (Manual on Dutch Nationality Act 2003). 1-1 f. Explanation on Article 1, first paragraph, opening words and under f. https://wetten.overheid.nl/BWBW33099/2017-04-01 (accessed 20 February 2019).
    Unfortunately, stateless children born in the Netherlands with no legal residence or whose parents do not have legal residence cannot acquire Dutch nationality.

177 The Netherlands Government website https://www.government.nl/topics/dutch-nationality/statelessness (accessed 20 February 2019).

178 CCPR/C/130/D/2918/2016 https://tbinternet.ohchr.org/_layouts/15/treatybody-external/Download.aspx?symbolno=CCPR/C/130/D/2918/2016&Lang=en (accessed 15 February 2021).

179 ICCPR Art. 24 provides that:
    '(1). Every child shall have, without any discrimination as to race, colour, sex, language, religion, national or social origin, property or birth, the right to such measures of protection as are required by his status as a minor, on the part of his family, society and the State. (2). Every child shall be registered immediately after birth and shall have a name. 3. Every child has the right to acquire a nationality.'

180 *Ibid* Art. 2(2):
    'Where not already provided for by existing legislative or other measures, each State Party to the present Covenant undertakes to take the necessary steps, in accordance with its constitutional processes and with the provisions of the present Covenant, to adopt such laws or other measures as may be necessary to give effect to the rights recognized in the present Covenant.'

181 *Ibid* Art. 2(3):
    'Each State Party to the present Covenant undertakes: (a) To ensure that any person whose rights or freedoms as herein recognized are violated shall have an effective remedy,

Analysis of Procedural Frameworks in Five States 159

Committee, considering the facts before it and acting under the guidance of the provision of Article 5(4),[182] of the Optional Protocol to the ICCPR, was of the view that the Netherlands violated Mr. Zhao's rights under Article 24(3), read alone and in conjunction with Article 2(3) of the ICCPR.

The BRP is centrally managed by the National Office for Identity Data under the supervision of the Ministry of the Interior and Kingdom Relations, and it contains the personal data of all legal residents in the Netherlands. The data collected includes the name of the applicant, date, place and country of birth, address, nationality (and right of residence, if applicable), marriage and registered partnership, children, travel document, and ID card, etc.[183] It is important to note that registration in the BRP is not possible except where the applicant first applies for a residence permit in the IND system.[184] As stated earlier, the IND is responsible for the issuance of residence permits and handles applications for naturalization in the Netherlands[185] in its *Basisvoorziening Vreemdelingen* (BVV), also known as the Database on Foreigners. In other words, only a person with a residence permit can register in the BRP. The foregoing requirement, therefore, excludes stateless persons who do not have a residence permit from registering in the municipalities.

For non-legal residents, the 2018 ENS Survey for the Netherlands indicates that the 'IND also has a procedure to identify statelessness after which registration can take place in the Basisvoorziening Vreemdelingen (BVV), which, unlike the BRP, allows for identification of a stateless person who is not legally residing in the Netherlands,' the registration does not grant any legal rights. The ENS moreover states that 'there is no independent assessment of statelessness within the asylum procedure,' emphasizing that the 'BRP registration is the only administrative procedure with significant legal implications for a stateless person.'[186] The burden of proving statelessness lies on the applicant due, perhaps, to the

---

notwithstanding that the violation has been committed by persons acting in an official capacity; (b) To ensure that any person claiming such a remedy shall have his right thereto determined by competent judicial, administrative or legislative authorities, or by any other competent authority provided for by the legal system of the State, and to develop the possibilities of judicial remedy; (c) To ensure that the competent authorities shall enforce such remedies when granted.'

182 The Optional Protocol of ICCPR, Art. 5(4) provides that 'the Committee shall forward its views to the State Party concerned and to the individual.'

183 The National Office for Identity Data of the Dutch Ministry of Interior and Kingdom Relations *The Dutch BRP Register: Registration of Personal Details for the Government and for You* https://www.government.nl/binaries/government/documents/leaflets/2017/01/19/brochure-brp-engelstalig/Brochure+BRP+-+Engelstalig+-+def+versie+voor+publicatie+lowres.pdf (accessed 24 February 2019). See also https://www.rvig.nl/about-rvig (accessed 24 February 2019).

184 The Netherlands Ministry of Interior and Kingdom Relations https://www.government.nl/topics/personal-data/question-and-answer/when-should-i-register-with-the-personal-records-database-as-a-resident (accessed 24 February 2019).

185 The Netherlands's Immigration and Naturalisation (IND) website https://ind.nl/en/about-ind/Pages/What-does-the-IND-do.aspx (accessed 20 February 2019).

186 ENS Statelessness Index Survey: The Netherlands 18.

160   *Analysis of Procedural Frameworks in Five States*

absence of a procedure. Uliana Ermolaeva *et al* note that despite the option to register as 'stateless' in the BRP:

> Official guidelines for municipal authorities do not specify on which basis this entry should be made and even affirm that statelessness 'rarely ever occurs.' In this manner, the 'unknown nationality' category becomes prone to misuse.[187]

The forgoing will deny applicants so designated of the benefits in Articles 6(1) (b) and 8(4) of the Dutch Nationality Act which allows a stateless person to be naturalized after three years instead of the usual five years provided for in other cases.[188] The IND may offer legal protection to asylum seekers or stateless refugees not legally resident through its asylum system, leaving stateless persons who are not legal residents and who are not refugees with little or no protection. In addition to the requirement of a residence permit, Uliana Ermolaeva *et al* note that to be registered as stateless in the BRP:

> Aliens need to be in possession of documents that prove no country recognises them as its citizens, such as a declaration from the authorities or an endorsement in their alien's passport indicating that they are stateless.[189]

Registration in the BRP is therefore not SDP in the proper sense, considering that only persons who can already prove their statelessness status and are legal residents in the Netherlands are allowed to register in the BRP. This could be said to be noncompliance with the requirement of the 1954 Statelessness Convention.

5.2.2.1.1.2 *The 'No-Fault' Procedure*

Under this procedure, the applicant is issued with the no-fault permit – *buitenschuldvergunning*. The no-fault permit grants legal residence to applicants who through no fault of theirs cannot leave the territory of the Netherlands. To be eligible for the no-fault permit through the no-fault procedure conducted by the IND, the statelessness status of the applicant is not relevant; therefore it is not probed in the no-fault procedure.[190]

---

187 U Ermolaeva, E Faltinat, and D Tentere *Op Cit* 9.

188 The Advisory Committee on Migration Affairs (ACVZ) *No country of one's own*. An Advisory Report on Treaty Protection for Stateless Persons in the Netherlands. The Hague (September 2014) 41.

189 U Ermolaeva, E Faltinat, and D Tentere *Op Cit* 8–9.

190 The no-fault procedure 'cannot be regarded as identifying statelessness as it is implicitly required under the 1954 Convention relating to the Status of Stateless Persons.'
Statelessness in Holland *Op Cit.*

5.2.2.1.2 IDENTIFIED GAPS IN THE DUTCH SYSTEM

Although the Netherlands is a contracting State to both the 1954 Convention Relating to the Status of Stateless Persons and the 1961 Convention on the Reduction of Statelessness, and other relevant human rights instruments, the country is yet to develop a legal framework for the determination of statelessness.[191] Additionally, the Netherlands retains reservations to the 1954 Convention and other relevant Conventions which have serious implication for statelessness or persons at risk of statelessness. Specifically, on these reservations, the 2019 ENS Country Briefing on the Netherlands reports that:

> The Netherlands continues to retain reservations to Articles 8 (exceptional measures) and 26 (freedom of movement) of the 1954 Convention. It has reservations to Article 7 (Loss of nationality *ex lege*) of the European Convention on Nationality, which impacts on childhood statelessness as it allows for the loss of the Dutch nationality by a child whose parents renounce Dutch nationality. Additionally, its reservations to the Convention on the Rights of the Child, including in relation to the right to legal representation, age of majority, and access to social security, do not directly affect statelessness but may affect stateless children in The Netherlands.[192]

As noted earlier, stateless persons without legal residence in the Netherlands do not get a right of residence because they are stateless. They can apply for a residence permit like every other person if they meet the conditions set in the Dutch Nationality Act; otherwise, they enjoy no legal protection by the State. Moreover, the requirement for a residence permit is not reduced for stateless persons.

With no legal protection attached, statelessness has been described to be 'merely an administrative category in Dutch law, not an immigration status or protection status.' Only persons with legal residence in the Netherlands are allowed to register in the BRP procedure.[193] There is moreover no administrative or judicial review of decisions; this is expected considering that there is no dedicated SDP in the Netherlands.

Contrary to the position in the Europe Convention on the Avoidance of Statelessness in Relation to State Succession, the Handbook on implementation of the law on BRP suggests that people who are affected by state dissolution and

---

191 The country has a legislative proposal for an SDP by the State Secretary of Security pending before parliament since 2016 with little or no progress on the Bill since then.

192 Country Briefing – Netherlands (2019) 1 https://index.statelessness.eu/sites/statelessindex.eu/files/INDEX-Country_Briefing_Netherlands_ENG_update%20July%202019.pdf (accessed 19 October 2019).

193 ENS Statelessness Index Survey: The Netherlands *Op Cit* 24.

162 Analysis of Procedural Frameworks in Five States

who are unable to acquire new nationality are not stateless.[194] Furthermore, due to a lack of clarity in the Handbook on the type of evidence needed to register as a stateless person, more persons who should ordinarily be registered as stateless in the BRP database are registered under the 'unknown' nationality category.[195] The implication for 'nationality unknown' registration, as Katja Swider notes, is that 'an individual's nationality can in principle be registered as 'unknown' forever and be passed on from generation to generation.' This will only change if the affected individual acquires nationality, or the offspring of such an individual acquire nationality through some other means.[196]

As stated above, stateless persons in the Netherlands without legal residence can register in the IND's Database on Foreigners – *Basisvoorziening Vreemdelingen* (BVV), but persons identifying as stateless in the BVV are not granted any legal protection.[197] The Public Interest Litigation Project (PILP) notes that 'of the 14 European countries that ratified the conventions on statelessness, the Netherlands is the only country that does not provide a residence permit for those with stateless status.'[198] Contrary to international law, statelessness is not a ground for a residence permit in the Netherlands.[199] There is also the requirement for foreigners, including identified stateless persons, to have a birth certificate before they can apply for naturalization, and the legal residence requirement for stateless children born in the Netherlands who wish to acquire Dutch nationality by option,[200] contrary to the Netherland's obligations in Article 32 (facilitated naturalization) of the 1954 Convention and Article 7 (right to nationality) of the CRC.

Due to several factors, including the absence of a standard procedure for identification and recording of statelessness, the data on statelessness in the Netherlands may not be reliable as many stateless persons may not be captured;

---

194 K Swider *Op Cit* 17.
195 B Safradin *The 'Legal Limbo' of Stateless Syrian Refugees in Exile: A comparative legal and empirical analysis at the national, international and European level on addressing refugee statelessness in the EU.* Master Thesis LLM Legal Research – Faculty of Law, Economics and Governance – Utrecht University (2017) 56.
196 K Swider *Op Cit* 18. See also L Evers and G-R de Groot 'Staatloos of van onbekende nationaliteit of nationaliteit in onderzoek?' ('Stateless, or of unknown nationality, or nationality under investigation') (2011, unpublished).
197 See ENS Statelessness Index Survey: The Netherlands *Op Cit* 18.
198 The Public Interest Litigation Project (PILP) *Statelessness* https://pilpnjcm.nl/en/dossiers/statelessness/ (accessed 19 October 2019).
199 See the Netherlands Ministry of Justice and Security website https://www.rijksoverheid.nl/onderwerpen/nederlandse-nationaliteit/staatloosheid (accessed 20 February 2019).
200 European Network on Statelessness (ENS) *Protecting stateless persons from arbitrary detention in the Netherlands* (2015) 9 https://www.statelessness.eu/sites/www.statelessness.eu/files/ENS_Detention_Reports_Netherlands.pdf (accessed 22 October 2019).

Analysis of Procedural Frameworks in Five States 163

the closest they may come is registration in the 'unknown' category.[201] It was noted in a 2016 submission for the Netherlands at the 27th Session of the Universal Periodic Review that there is a conflict between the data from the government and the estimate by the UNHCR. The report also suggests that there are more than 80,000 individuals who are registered under the nationality 'unknown' category in the Netherlands.[202]

The Netherlands currently has a legislative proposal[203] for a procedure to determine statelessness before the parliament. Scholars have argued that though the draft is a welcome development, it would require further tweaking to ensure sufficient legal protections for stateless people.[204] By virtue of the proposed bill, the burden of proving one's statelessness rests on the applicant who must demonstrate that no State considers him/her a national; it moreover does not establish the standard of proof required,[205] which is contrary to the guidance provided in UNHCR's Statelessness Handbook and the practice in asylum matters where the burden of proof is to be shared. Notable in the proposal is the fact that submission of an application or even the eventual recognition of statelessness status will not lead to the grant of a residence permit.[206] Moreover, an applicant can be deported while his/her application is being processed, and there is no clear path for a recognized stateless person without a prior right of residence. Although the legislative proposal for a procedure to determine statelessness in the Netherlands by the State Secretary of Security was proposed in 2016, as at the time of writing, not much has been achieved with regard to the legislative proposal.

---

201 This is apparent as there is no SDP to determine statelessness in the Netherlands at the moment.

202 Institute on Statelessness and Inclusion, ASKV Refugee Support, European Network on Statelessness and Defence for Children – The Netherlands Joint Submission to the Human Rights Council at the 27th Session of the Universal Periodic Review (22 September 2016) para. 11 https://files.institutesi.org/NetherlandsUPR2016.pdf (accessed 19 October 2019).

203 See the draft legislative proposal https://www.internetconsultatie.nl/staatloosheid/details (accessed 25 January 2020).

204 See K Swider and C Vlieks 'Proposal for legislation on statelessness in the Netherlands: A bittersweet victory' *ENS Blog* (12 October 2016) https://www.statelessness.eu/updates/blog/proposal-legislation-statelessness-netherlands-bittersweet-victory (accessed 29 December 2020); the Public Interest Litigation Project (PILP) *Statelessness, Op Cit.* J Venkov 'In the state but not of the state – stateless or nationality unknown in the Netherlands' *The Torn Identity* (16 September 2018) https://www.thetornidentity.org/2018/09/16/stateless-or-nationality-unknown/ (accessed 29 December 2020); Institute on Statelessness and Inclusion Comments on Draft Law introducing a statelessness determination procedure in the Netherlands 28 November 2016 para. IV.

205 The Public Interest Litigation Project (PILP) *Statelessness, Op Cit.*

206 See the proposed Statelessness Determination Procedure (Rijkswet vaststellingsprocedure staatloosheid), Arts. 2 and 4.

5.3 Comparative Table of Procedures in the Selected States

Table 5.1 Comparative Table of Procedures in the Selected States

State practice (Groups)/ rights	Group 1				Group 2	N/A
States	*UK*	*Moldova*	*France*	*Ivory Coast*	*Netherlands*	*Nigeria*
Ratification of Statelessness Conventions	Yes	Yes[a]	Party to only the 1954 Convention	Yes	Yes	Yes (not domesticated yet)[b]
SDP established in Law	Yes[c]	Yes[d]	Yes[e]	Yes[f]	No – alternative identification	NA
Centralized SDP Body	Yes – Home Office	Yes – Bureau for Asylum and Migration	Yes – OFPRA	Yes – National Eligibility Commission on Statelessness Status	No – several alternative routes to identification	NA
Combined statelessness and asylum procedures	No – separate procedure	No – separate procedure	No – separate procedure	Not specified	No determination procedure	NA
Written application	No – online application	Yes – could also be made orally	Yes	Yes	NA	NA
Ex officio initiation of application	Not provided in the immigration rules	Yes	No	Not specified	NA	NA
Interview	Yes	Yes – within 15 days	Not compulsory	Not specified	NA	NA
Access to interpreter	Yes	Yes	Yes	Not specified	NA	NA
Legal representation	Not provided in law	Yes[g]	No	Not specified		NA
Standard of proof	Balance of probabilities[h]	Balance of proof	Slightly higher than in asylum applications[i]	Not specified	NA	NA
Burden of proof	On the applicant[j]	Shared	Shared	Not specified	NA	NA

Length of procedure	Not specified	Within six months[k]	Not specified	Not specified	NA	NA
Residence permit	Yes – i.e., leave to remain in the UK[l]	Yes[m]	Yes, if status is granted (*Vie privée et familiale*)[n]	Not specified	No[o]	No
Access to basic services	Yes	Yes	Yes	Not specified	Only when legally resident	No
Access to travel document	Yes	Yes	Yes	Not specified	NA	No
Access to naturalization	Yes – after five years of lawful stay[p]	Yes – after eight years	Yes – after five years of legal residence	Yes[q]	Only when legally resident	No[r]
Access to administrative/ judicial review	Not in all cases[s]	Yes – in a regular court	Yes – in an administrative court/tribunal	Yes – to the National Appeal Commission on Stateless Status	NA	NA

[a]In April 2012.
[b]Like in the UK, foreign treaties do not have direct application in Nigeria until they are domesticated by parliament.
[c]Part 14 of the Immigration Rules.
[d]Regime of Foreigners in the Republic of Moldova.
[e]In the OFPRA.
[f]Law No. 836 on the Creation, Organization and Functioning of the National Eligibility Commission on Statelessness Status; and Law No. 837 on Creation, Organization and Functioning of The National Appeal Commission on Stateless Status.
[g]Arts. 6 and 7 of the Moldovan Law Regarding the Legal Assistance Guaranteed by The State No. 198 of 26 July 2007.
[h]See, UK Home Office *Asylum policy instruction statelessness and application for leave to remain, Op Cit* 11.
[i]See ENS Index Survey – France *Op Cit* 20.
[j]ENS Index UK.
[k]Depending on the complexity of the case, the term may be extended by one month each but not exceeding a total of six months.
[l]It could be limited leave (for five years/renewable) or indefinite leave.
[m]A 'Confirmation Certificate' is issued to an applicant to allow him or her to remain in Moldova pending the determination of the application.
[n]After three years of lawful residence, a stateless person may be granted a ten-year residence permit, including to their spouse and children when they reach 18 years or 16 if they wish to get work. However, unlike asylum applications, no residence permit is granted pending determination of a statelessness application. See more in the French Ministry of Interior, *Guide for asylum seekers in France (gAS), Op Cit* 5.
[o]Stateless persons who are not legally resident in the Netherlands do not get a residence permit, as statelessness in itself is not a ground for a residence permit in the Netherlands.
[p]See Rule 407 of the UK Immigration Rules.
[q]Foreigners may naturalize after five years of habitual residence in Ivory Coast Subject to the conditions in Arts. 25–33 of the Ivory Coast Nationality Code of 1972 and because they are stateless.
[r]Foreign nationals may apply for naturalization in Nigeria if they have resided in Nigeria for a continuous period of 15 years in addition to other requirements in s. 27 of the Constitution.
[s]See AR2.3 Immigration Rules – Appendix AR: Administrative Review.

166 *Analysis of Procedural Frameworks in Five States*

5.4 Conclusion

It has been observed that 'there is a growing interest among States in establishing SDPs.'[207] This is indeed a welcome development for the protection, identification, prevention, and eradication of statelessness globally. This chapter has examined the legal, administrative, as well as judicial practices with regard to SDPs in the selected States. It also examined the shortfalls in the existing State practice with the aim of highlighting the grey areas that Nigeria and any State in the process of developing its statelessness determination procedure would have to focus on to avoid the flaws in the existing State practice.[208]

For ease of reference of the SDP practices in the selected States, the chapter concludes with a comparative table of procedures of the three groups of States selected for analyses. These State practices together with the rights itemized in Table 5.1, and the standards and criteria analysed in Chapter 5 will form the basis of the arguments and recommendations of an SDP for Nigeria in Chapter 6 below.

---

207 UNHCR *Good Practices Paper – Action 6, Op Cit* 2.
208 The practice in the State discussed in this chapter will be applied in Chapter 6, particularly at Part 6.3.1 which discusses Nigeria.

6 Adapting (Legal Transplantation) Some of the Existing Best Practices on Statelessness Determination Procedure in the Nigeria Context

6.1 Introduction

In this chapter, the book examines how Nigeria can replicate some of the good practice procedures in the States listed and examined in Chapter 5, taking into account the legal, cultural, and where appropriate, political differences between these States and Nigeria. In doing so, due analysis of existing administrative structures within Nigeria to possibly situate a determination procedure or alternative route to regularization of status will be discussed.

The first part of this chapter will focus on principles of legal transplant and types of transplant. It will also examine whether legal transplant is possible or not, and reference examples of previous legal and administrative transplants in Nigeria. The other part of this chapter will examine and apply the options available to Nigeria with regard to borrowing of legal and/or administrative statelessness determination procedure from a wide range of State practices. A flowchart for a determination procedure for Nigeria will be proposed, taking into consideration the practice in the States analyzed in this research.

It is important to note that due to the general nature of international norms, at the edges of the *standards and criteria*[1] discussed in Chapter 5 (which would be applied to the current situation in Nigeria in Part 6.3 below), some legal transplanting would occur. Therefore, this chapter moreover examines the theory of legal transplant with the aim of applying it to a possible borrowing of a statelessness protection, identification, and prevention system for Nigeria.

6.2 The Legal Transplant Option

For structure, this part starts by examining legal transplant options as a method of legal and administrative borrowing, probing whether these options are possible

---

1 The standards pertain to the presence of a mechanism for protection, prevention, and identification of statelessness, and the criteria refer to the: (a) legality and binding nature of SDP, (b) structure and location of SDP, (c) access to procedure, (d) procedural guarantees, (e) assessments of facts, (f) management of combined refugee and stateliness claims, (g) prospect for naturalization, and (h) review and appeal of decision.

DOI: 10.4324/9781003278733-6

168   *Legal Transplantation*

and why they are necessary (Part 6.2.1). It examines the different types of legal transplants and why they occur, citing examples of the previous transplant of laws and administrative systems in Nigeria (Parts 6.2.3 and 6.2.4), with the aim of highlighting that the same can be done to protect stateless persons or persons at risk of statelessness in Nigeria. This part moreover examines the factors that could militate against legal transplant (Part 6.2.5), how to ensure that due attention is paid to legal, administrative, and cultural differences of States, and also how to take advantage of certain commonalities when considering a State's legal or administrative structure (Parts 6.2.6 and 6.2.7).

Legal transplant is a form of legal borrowing. Out of the many types of 'legal borrowing,' this book will focus on legal transplant, which perhaps is 'the most common method of borrowing of legal ideas, in whole or in parts from one context to another.'[2] Legal transplant moreover has been described as 'the process whereby a national legal system implements the rules of another legal system in its own legal order'[3] and 'a species of a more general genus known as "policy transfer" or "lesson-drawing".'[4] On the close relationship between legal transplant and comparative law study, Shen Zongling stated that one of the important tasks of a comparative lawyer is to compare different laws of different countries and be ready to recommend their application 'if after an objective and critical examination, they are found to be preferable to his own, provided, of course, such laws are carefully woven into the fabric, style and language of one's legal system.'[5]

It has been observed that the legal order of many countries was derived from Europe, especially during the 19th and the early 20th centuries.[6] Borrowing

---

2 See N Tebbe and R Tsai 'Constitutional borrowing' (2010) 108 (4) *Michigan Law Review* 471–472. 'Several common types of borrowing: (a) transplantation; (b) hedging; (c) displacement; and (d) corruption. These do not comprise the complete universe of types, but they capture much of the action.'

3 M Amos 'Transplanting human rights norms: The case of the United Kingdom's Human Rights Act' (2013) 35 (2) *Human Rights Quarterly* 386. See also O Khan-Freund 'On uses and misuses of comparative law' (1974) 37 *Mod. L. Rev.* 1; A Watson *Legal transplants* (2nd ed. 1993); W Ewald 'Comparative jurisprudence (II): The logic of legal transplants' (1995) 43 (4) *The American Journal of Comparative Law* 489–510.

4 M de Jong and S Stoter 'Institutional transplantation and the rule of law: How this interdisciplinary method can enhance the legitimacy of international organisations' (2009) 2 (3) *Erasmus Law Review* 316.

J Miller notes that: 'The movement of laws and legal institutions between states, have become central to the study of comparative and international law.'

J Miller 'A typology of legal transplants: Using sociology, legal history and Argentine examples to explain the transplant process' (2003) 51 (4) *The American Journal of Comparative Law* 839. See also A Watson *Op Cit* 22–24.

5 S Zongling 'Legal transplant and comparative law' (1999) 51 (4) *Revue Internationale de Droit Comparé* 853.

6 'Earlier legal transplants are well known, including the reception of Roman law in Europe, the enactment of the Chinese codes in other parts of Asia, or the transfer of Spanish and Portuguese law to Latin America. Indeed, as Watson argues, legal transplants are as old as the law is.'

Legal Transplantation   169

has also been observed to be the most fruitful source of legal change in many jurisdictions. Watson notes that 'borrowing may be from within the system, by analogy – from negligence in torts to negligence in contract, for instance – or from another legal system.'[7]

In line with the above assertion of borrowing within the same system, this research would also propose the transplant of the existing Nigerian system in the development of an SDP. In this regard, in addition to examining the State practice, the relevant practice in the current refugee status determination procedure (RSD) in Nigeria, a system closest to SDP, will also be examined.

6.2.1 Is Legal Transplant Possible?

According to Mindy Chen-Wishart, 'the stark bipolarity of a "yes" or "no" answer attracted by such a question is much less interesting and revealing than the question: what shapes the life of legal transplants? The answer to the latter question is contingent on a wide range of variables triggered by the particular transplant; the result can occupy any point along the spectrum from faithful replication to outright rejection.'[8] Arguably, there is a middle ground, wherein not every legal and administrative order is borrowed. This middle ground tickles the creative thinking of researchers, as well as lawmakers, who should take into account their individual legal, administrative, and socio-cultural context.[9] In the absence of a mechanism in Nigeria for determining statelessness, the middle ground approach could be used in approaching the so-called good practice examples in coining a procedure to suit the Nigerian context.

6.2.2 Why Is Legal Transplant Necessary?

On the necessity of legal borrowing, Nelson Tebbe noted in his article, *Constitutional Borrowing*,[10] that the

> common reasons include an intention to achieve a durable synthesis of areas of law whose connections have been neglected; to take advantage of accumulated wisdom; to blur doctrinal boundaries and unsettle existing categories

---

  D Berkowitz *et al.* 'The transplant effect' (2003) 51 (1) *The American Journal of Comparative Law* 172.

7 A Watson 'Aspects of reception of law' (1996) 44 (2) *The American Journal of Comparative Law* 335.

8 M Chen-Wishart 'Legal transplant and undue influence: Lost in translation or a working misunderstanding?' (2013) 62 (1) *The International and Comparative Law Quarterly* 1.

9 In domestication of the Convention of the Right of the Child, Nigeria used the middle-ground approach, ensuring wide consultations amongst the different regions, cultures, and religions.

10 N Tebbe and R Tsai *Op Cit* 459–522.

170 Legal Transplantation

deliberately; or to perceived strategic advantage in debate more generally. In fact, a borrower's reasons for acting ordinarily consist of some combination of private and public intentions.[11]

For a legal transplant to occur, it sometimes, if not often, involves comparing laws of different jurisdictions. On the necessity to compare the operation of laws in different jurisdictions, Henry Walter Ehrmann in *Comparative Legal Cultures*[12] postulates that it is necessary to compare other legal cultures *inter alia*:

> only the analysis of a variety of legal cultures will recognise what is accidental rather than necessary, what is permanent rather than changeable in legal norms and legal agencies, and what characterises the beliefs underlying both. The law of a single culture will take for granted the ethical theory on which it is grounded.[13]

Be that as it may, this book will propose an SDP for Nigeria based on practices in States assessed in Chapter 5, with a view to proposing a 'hybrid' SDP for Nigeria. Due attention will be paid to existing legal, administrative, and institutional structures in Nigeria.[14] This book will not toe the line of 'rigid perception of legal change suggested by the theorisation of legal transplants.' Instead, to find solutions for the absence of statelessness protection, identification, and preventive norms in Nigeria, the approach in this research will be towards a proposal of a 'hybrid' determination procedure. 'Hybridisation recognises the complexities of cross-cultural exchange and gives meaning to the consequences of borrowing.'[15]

6.2.3 Types of Transplant

Different scholars have postulated various theories on why legal transplantations occur. According to Irma Johanna Mosquera Valderrama, legal transplantation takes place due to the following reasons: authority; prestige and imposition; chance and necessity; expected efficacy of the law; and political, economic, and reputational incentives from the countries and third parties.[16] For Jonathan M.

---

11 *Ibid* 467.
12 H Ehrmann *Comparative legal cultures* (1976).
13 *Ibid*.
14 For existing Nigerian law, the National Commission for Refugees Act is assessed to see what can be borrowed. For administrative procedure, administrative procedure in management of refugee status determination procedure by the Refugee Commission will also be given a close look for possible good practice. For assessment of institutions with a view to locating a more suitable location to place an SDP, institutions such as the National Refugee Commission and the Ministry of Interior will be assessed.
15 See M Solinas 'Hybridisation and legal reception' in *Legal Evolution and Hybridisation* (2014) 35.
16 I Johanna Mosquera Valderrama 'Legal transplants and comparative law' (2004) *International Law Journal* 265.

Miller, the following are the types of legal transplants that occur: the cost-saving; the externally dictate; the entrepreneurial transplant; and the legitimacy-generating transplant.[17] For this book, legitimacy and prestige, necessity and context, obligation and need to conform, and efficacy of an existing system will be discussed as types of legal transplants.

As noted in paragraph 6.2 above, there is a close relationship between legal transplant and comparative law. To transplant a law, reference must be made to the laws of another jurisdiction; by so doing, a comparative aspect of the procedure occurs. There are several types of comparative law theories. According to Peter de Cruz in *Comparative Law in a Changing World*:[18]

> Various factors cohered to produce the comparative line of study, two distinct roots of modern comparative law may be identified: (a) legislative comparative law; and (b) scholarly comparative law.

While scholarly comparative law could be described as the study of law whereby the researcher basically compares laws, perhaps just as an academic exercise, Peter de Cruz described legislative comparative law as the process whereby foreign laws are invoked in order to draft new national laws.[19] One of the main 'objectives of comparative law has traditionally been the systematic study of foreign laws with the view to deriving models that would assist the formulation and implementation of the legislative policies of States.'[20] In this book, the scholarly comparative law approach will be employed with the aim of inspiring legislative changes to nationality law in Nigeria.

6.2.3.1 Transplant Due to Legitimacy and Prestige

With regard to the legitimacy and prestige attached to the donor model, Jonathan M. Miller postulated that transplants often occur and even succeed because of the prestige of the foreign model. He emphasized that, while the basis for the prestige varies, 'sometimes the prestige will be of a particular legal institution, sometimes of an entire legal system.'[21] It has also been observed that in some cases, transplant occurs solely based on the prestige of the model and the drivers of the model.[22] Based on the foregoing, Kacper Van Wallendael stated that legal transplant 'is not just embodiments of mostly nasty dependency, but also examples of reverence for well-developed legal solutions that are worthy of being

---

17 J Miller *Op Cit* 843–897.
18 P de Cruz *Comparative Law in a Changing World* (1995) 13.
19 *Ibid.*
20 G Mousourakis 'Legal transplants and legal development: A jurisprudential and comparative law approach' (2013) 54 (3) *Acta Juridica Hungarica* 227.
21 J Miller *Op Cit* 854.
22 G Ajani 'By chance and prestige: Legal transplants in Russia and Eastern Europe' (1995) 43 (1) *The American Journal of Comparative Law* 110.

172 Legal Transplantation

introduced in another country.'[23] The attraction in a prestigious system could be in a specific area of interest, institution, or an entire legal system.[24] In this regard, Mathias Siems notes thus:

> More subjective are transplants that reflect the internal preferences and interests of the transplant country. For example, as law makers cannot evaluate the potential benefits of all countries of the world, they will choose a foreign model that the general public perceives to be the most legitimate one. It is also likely that interest groups of the transplant country will shape the choice of the model that is most favourable to them.[25]

Therefore, a system may be chosen generally because of the admiration the borrowing State has for the donor system.[26]

It has been observed that 'the need to "look good before global public opinion" and concern for "international legitimacy" is an important factor that motivates a country to adopt outside influences.'[27] This need to look good could sometimes lead to mimicry, also known as emulation. Emulation, in most contexts, according to David Marsh and J.C. Sharman is 'the process of copying foreign models in terms of symbolic or normative factors, rather than a technical or rational concern with functional efficiency,' describing it as a ploy by States to acquire legitimacy.[28]

Legal transplant can also occur as a result of the prestige attached to a legal system; an example is the case of the received English Common Law system in many of its former colonies.[29] The reception and adoption of English Common

---

23 K Van Wallendael *Legal Transplants: Profitable Borrowing or Harmful Dependency? The Use of the Legal Transplant Framework for the Adoption of EU Law: The Case of Croatia* 76 https://www.academia.edu/10797415/Legal_transplants_profitable_borrowing_or_harmful_dependency_Use_of_legal_transplant_framework_for_adoption_of_EU_law_case_study_of_Croatia (accessed 20 January 2021).

24 S Mancuso 'Legal transplants and economic development: Civil law vs. common law?' in J Oliveira, P Cardinal (Eds.) *One country, two systems, three legal orders – Perspectives of evolution* (2009) 77.

25 M Siems 'Malicious legal transplants' (2018) 38 (1) *Legal Studies* 108.

26 A Watson *Society and legal change* (2nd ed. 2001) 98.

27 A Darr 'The role of institutions in generating successful legal transplants: A comparative analysis of the adoption of competition laws in India and Pakistan' (2019) 14 (1) *Asian Journal of Comparative Law* 5. See also, K Gerhard Weyland *Bounded rationality and policy diffusion: Social sector reform in Latin America* (2006) 39–42; D Marsh and J Sharman 'Policy diffusion and policy transfer' (2009) 30 *Policy Studies* 269, 272; F Giraldi 'Transnational diffusion: Norms, ideas and policies' in W Carlsnaes, T Risse-Kappen, and B Simmons (Eds.) *Handbook of International Relations* (2012) 23.

28 See D Marsh and S Jason 'Policy diffusion and policy transfer' (2009) 30 (3) *Policy Studies* 272.

29 Even after independence many former British colonies retained the Common Law system. A few countries in Africa such as Liberia and Sudan who are not former British colonies even adopted the system after independence as shall be discussed below.

Legal Transplantation 173

Law was generally a result of British 'colonization' and the 'political dominance' on its former colonies during the colonial eras and was never voluntarily adopted in the real sense by States practising it today. Its reception in many States was as a result of the 'principle of English law that, in a settled colony, the colonists would bring with them and follow the laws of their home country.'[30] While this position may be correct to a large extent, in Africa, there are a few States which have voluntarily adopted the English Common law; countries such as Liberia and Sudan,[31] perhaps for the prestige attached to the system.

6.2.3.2 Necessity and Context

On necessity generating transplant, George Mousourakis stated that

> foreign rules or doctrines are usually 'borrowed' [...] because they fill a gap or meet a particular need in the importing country [...] Legal rules emanate as a response to social needs (according to the socio-functional view of law), the emergence of a global society will almost inevitably lead to a degree of convergence between different legal systems.[32]

Richard Small argues that although culture may shape the form of a particular law, it is the context that determines the necessity for a law in the first place, and that context is transferable in certain situations.[33] In some circumstances, 'the borrowing takes place not as a matter of choice but as a matter of chance or necessity.' An example is the type of transplant that occurs in Eastern European countries in order to qualify to join the European Union.[34]

---

30 G Mousourakis 'The development and function of equity in the English Common Law tradition' in *Comparative Law and Legal Traditions* (2019) 251; J Ogbonnaya and V Iteshi Chioma 'The jurisprudential issues arising from legal transplant: An appraisal' (2016) 50 *Journal of Law, Policy and Globalization* 6.
31 J Ogbonnaya and V Iteshi Chioma *Ibid* 6. See more on voluntary adoption of Common Law system by Liberia and Sudan at 8–9. On the position of Common Law not voluntarily adopted by States, A Goodhart 'What is common law?' (1960) 76 *The Law Quarterly Review* 45 *Ibid*.
32 G Mousourakis 'Legal transplants and legal development' *Op Cit* 227 and 234. See also M King 'Comparing legal cultures in the quest for law's identity' in D Nelken (Ed.) *Comparing legal cultures* (1997) 119.
33 R Small 'Towards a theory of contextual transplants' (2005) 19 (3) *Emory International Law Review* 1431. Small further argued at 1437–1438 that 'the term "culture" must [...] be distinguished from the word "context." [...] the term "culture" refers to a society's entire background, one that might shape the form that the rules will take, whereas "context" refers to those circumstances that specifically drive the development of a particular rule. While culture might dictate what shape a rule takes and in certain cases might serve to reject a law that is transplanted without being revised to match the culture, context more specifically dictates whether such a rule is necessary in the first place.'
34 I Johanna Mosquera Valderrama *Op Cit* 266. See also, E Örücü 'Family trees for legal systems: Towards a contemporary approach', paper presented at the Conference of Epistemol-

174   *Legal Transplantation*

6.2.3.3 *Obligation and Need to Conform*

On obligation and the need to conform as a basis for legal transplant, Sally Engle Merry highlighted thus, 'participation in the global economy and society is important for many countries and conforming to the expectations of transnational human rights institutions is one cost of that participation. At domestic level, NGO leaders and their rights-conscious clientele promote institutions that respond to rights claims, such as human rights Commissions.'[35] On the perception of these institutions at the domestic level, Karen Knop notes that although these institutions promote best practices, they are met with suspicion of promoting imperialism, especially as those who will implement them were mostly not part of their formulation and therefore do not see their peculiarities reflected in the laws.[36] To compare States to conform in this regard, the international community often results in mounting pressure on non-conforming States using the instruments of 'naming and shaming,' sanctions, restriction and reduction of aid, amongst others. Considering the indirect nature of these pressures, Sally Engle notes further that using socio-legal studies of law as a basis for how States would react, compliance of States due to such pressures 'depends largely on individual consciousness and commitment, not policing and force.'[37]

6.2.3.4 *Efficacy of an Existing System*

Despite varying legal, institutional, and administrative systems, the need to move towards efficiency has been noted as the driving force for modern legal systems. Due to the foregoing, Ugo Mattei postulated that some intersections between efficient and prestigious models could be observed in legal transplants. He further noted that 'efficiency may be used to evaluate legal transplants.'[38] Further to the above, George Mousourakis recommends the following two key approaches. First, that the legislator should first review how efficient a proposed foreign rule is in its State of origin with regard to the specific problem for which the borrowing State is borrowing the rule. Second, whether the proposed rule will produce the desired or same result in the borrowing State. To my mind, the reason for these two key approaches could be retrieved in his submission where he noted that 'in a market of a legal culture, where rule suppliers are concerned with satisfying demand, ultimately the most efficient rule will be the winner.'[39]

---

ogy and Methodology of Comparative Law in the Light of European Integration, Brussels, 24–26 October 2002 9.

35 S Engle Merry 'New legal realism and the ethnography of transnational law' (2006) 31 (4) *Law & Social Inquiry* 989.

36 K Knop 'Here and there: International law in domestic courts (2000) 32 (2) *New York University Journal of International Law and Politics* 504.

37 S Engle Merry *Op Cit* 979.

38 U Mattei 'Transplants: An essay in comparative law and economics' (1994) 14 *International Review of Law and Economics* 8.

39 G Mousourakis 'Legal transplants and legal development' *Op Cit* 220 and 227.

Legal Transplantation 175

On the effectiveness of law and the relationship with the society, Jan Torpman and Fredrik Jörgensen Stockholm stated thus:[40]

> In legal sociology the effectiveness of law is defined with an explicit purpose of explaining how law can be used as a regulatory device for governmental control. A law and society tradition has emerged, which attempts to explain not only the development and meaning of formal legal doctrine or the behavioural aspects of judicial decision-making, but the broader question of the effects of law on society at large.[41]

On the point of effectiveness and relevance of law to society, Denis Galligan in his book, *Law in Modern Society*,[42] further postulates as follows:

> the focus is on the interaction between law and other social formations where the law itself is taken as a fairly unproblematic constant, so that the kinds of issues arising are: how do people regard law, what happens when they come into contact with it, how they use it, and what happens when they get embroiled in its processes.[43]

The usefulness of existing law to the society it is borrowed from can be argued as a determining factor that the law is efficient, and the same result will be achieved in the borrowing State. This book does not suggest that an efficient law in one society will necessarily be efficient in the borrowing State. Rather, the point being made here is that the efficiency or usefulness of an existing law in a particular society is a good indicator that there is a strong possibility that it will be useful and efficient in the borrowing State, especially where due attention is paid to institutional and administrative differences as this research will try to do later in the applied part of this book in Part 6.3 below.

The following part highlights some examples of legal and administrative transplant that have occurred in Nigeria since colonial times.

6.2.4 Legal Transplant Examples in Nigeria

Nigeria, like any other State in the world, has had to borrow laws and administrative structures from other jurisdictions for various reasons. These reasons include necessity and local context; obligation and need to conform; legitimacy and prestige; and need to have the same level of efficacy and efficiency as the 'donor State', amongst others.

---

40 J Torpman and F Jörgensen 'Legal effectiveness: Theoretical developments on legal transplants' (2005) 91 (4) *Arsp: Archiv Für Rechts- Und Sozialphilosophie/Archives for Philosophy of Law and Social Philosophy* 522.
41 *Ibid.*
42 D Galligan *Law in Modern Society* (2006).
43 *Ibid* 29.

176 *Legal Transplantation*

To examine legal *transplant in Nigeria due to legitimacy and prestige*, it is necessary to highlight that the legal system and culture in Nigeria are based on the English Common Law received in Nigeria through colonization by the British. Although the Common Law was adopted mainly due to colonial influence, even after independence, a lot more English rules were received into the Nigerian legal culture through legal transplant, perhaps due to the prestige attached to the system.[44] Therefore, English law has remained a veritable source of law in Nigeria to date.[45] English laws made before 1 October 1960, and extending to Nigeria which are not yet repealed, laws made by the local colonial legislature are treated as part of Nigerian legislation.[46] In this regard, the Nigerian Interpretation Act[47] provides as follows:

> Subject to the provisions of this section and except in so far as other provision is made by any Federal law, the common law of England and the doctrines of equity, together with the statutes of general application that were in force in England on the 1st day of January, 1900, shall, in so far as they relate to any matter within the legislative competence of the Federal legislature, be in force in Nigeria.[48]

The section further provides that, 'such imperial laws shall be in force so far as the limits of the Nigerian legal system and local circumstances permit and subject to any Federal law in Nigeria.'[49] Similarly, in the Nigerian case of *Ibidapo v. Lufthansa Airlines*[50] the Nigerian Supreme court held, *inter alia*:

> from 1960 to date, all the received English Laws, multilateral and bilateral agreements concluded and extended to Nigeria, unless expressly repealed or declared invalid by a court of law or tribunal established by law, remain in force subject to the provisions of Section 274(1) of the 1979 Constitution.[51]

The implication of the foregoing is that certain English legislation could be applied in Nigeria. However, despite the strong influence of British law on the

---

44 J Lokulo-Sodipe, O Akintola, and C Adebamowo 'Introduction to the legal system of Nigeria. Training and resources in research ethics evaluation' https://elearning.trree.org/mod/page/view.php?id=142 (accessed 3 February 2019).

45 B Karumi 'Nigerian legal system and the protection of the right against torture under emergency situation: The Boko Haram insurgency experience' (2017) 2 (2) *Journal of Law and Global Policy* 5.

46 Y Dina, J Akintayo, and F Ekundayo 'Guide to Nigerian legal information' *Globalex. Global Law and Justice* https://www.nyulawglobal.org/globalex/Nigeria1.html (accessed 8 April 2020).

47 Interpretation Act Cap 192 Laws of the Federation of Nigeria 1990.

48 *Ibid* s. 32(1).

49 See *Ibid* s. 31(2)

50 (SC 238/1994) [1997] 5 (4 April 1997). Nigeria Legal Information Institute https://nigerialii.org/ng/judgment/supreme-court/1997/5 (accessed 8 April 2020).

51 *Ibid*.

Legal Transplantation 177

Nigerian legal system, local rules in both old and novel areas have been made by Nigerian authorities to handle specific local contexts.[52]

With regard to the example of transplant in *Nigeria due to necessity and local context*, it is important to highlight the example of the presidential system of government borrowed from the United States of America. In 1979, during the first military to civilian rule transition, Nigeria adopted the American presidential system in the 1979 Constitution to mitigate societal divisions. The circumstance leading to the adoption of the American model was described by Donald L. Horowitz thus:

> Under the parliamentary system inherited at independence, a cluster of ethnic groups from the North had managed to secure a majority of seats and shut all other groups out of power. This game of total inclusion and exclusion characterised Nigerian politics after 1960, precipitating the military coups of 1966 and the war of Biafran secession from 1967 to 1970. By choosing a separation of powers, the Nigerians aimed to prevent any group from controlling the country by controlling parliament.[53]

The same 1979 Constitution also adopted the American government model with a separate legislature from the executive to ensure checks and balances, as well as to ensure oversight. This was necessitated by the prolonged military rule with its resultant abuse of power.[54]

Nigeria has transplanted a few laws, administrative structures, and practices from international and regional laws, municipal laws and practices due to its *obligation and need to conform*. For instance, to comply with Nigeria's obligation in line with Resolution 48/134 of the United Nations General Assembly[55] which enjoins all member States to establish independent national institutions for the promotion, protection, and enforcement of human rights, the National Human Rights Commission of Nigeria (NHRC) was established in 1995.[56] To implement Nigeria's obligation with regard to Resolution 48/134 of the United Nations General Assembly, some legal transplant occurred with the establishment of the NHRC with a mandate and powers in line with the model law,

---

52 E Ojomo *Sources of law: The application of English law in Nigeria.* (2014) 5 https://www.academia.edu/32105425/SOURCES_OF_LAW_THE_APPLICATION_OF_ENGLISH_LAW_IN_NIGERIA (accessed 8 April 2020).

53 D Horowitz 'Presidents vs. parliaments: Comparing democratic systems' (1990) 1 (4) *Journal of Democracy* 74. Published by Johns Hopkins University Press https://doi.org/10.1353/jod.1990.0056 (accessed 12 February 2020).

54 See J Yinka Fashagba 'Legislative oversight under the Nigerian presidential system' (2009) 15 (4) *The Journal of Legislative Studies* 439–440.

55 See Principles Relating to the Status of National Institutions (The Paris Principles). Adopted by General Assembly Resolution 48/134 of 20 December 1993.

56 See the National Human Rights Commission (NHRC) website https://www.nigeriarights.gov.ng/about/overview.html (accessed 29 May 2020). The Commission's Act was amended through the National Human Rights Commission (Amendment) Act 2010.

178   *Legal Transplantation*

i.e., *principles relating to the status of national institutions* in the Annex to the Resolution.[57]

Obligation and necessity can sometimes be intertwined. Apart from the obligation of States to enact certain legislation or set up certain institutions, there would be a need for enactment of particular legislation or establishment of an institution to meet domestic needs.[58] For example, in the late 1990s, to manage the influx of refugees from the Liberian civil war, the Federal Government of Nigeria established the National Commission for Refugees (NCFR).[59] The same commitment is required to tackle the growing number of persons at risk of statelessness in Nigeria.[60]

Having discussed the types of legal transplants, it is important to discuss factors that could prevent a successful plant.

6.2.5 Factors that Could Militate Against Legal Transplant

Various factors could mitigate the smooth adoption and operationalization of foreign laws and administrative structures of another State; their effectiveness or otherwise may depend on the transplant process.[61] Therefore, 'in examining how laws and legal institutions move across jurisdictions, comparative law scholars have employed the metaphor of a legal transplant to conceptualize both the hazards and benefits of taking in another legal system's rules.'[62] Nelson Tebbe and Robert L. Tsai opined that 'it is not always easy to tell when borrowing happens, so it helps to know what to look for. Questions of legitimacy surround all exercises in [...] borrowing because they involve exchanges between potentially incompatible domains of legal knowledge.'[63] According to Helen Xanthaki, due to a lack of attention to established theories of comparative law with regard to the legitimacy of the laws to be transplanted, transplanted laws are often met

---

57 See Principles Relating to the Status of National Institutions (The Paris Principles). Adopted by General Assembly Resolution 48/134 of 20 December 1993. Particularly 3–6. The NHRC moreover maintains some administrative similarities with the Office of the United Nations High Commissioner for Human Rights (OHCHR).

58 The difference between obligation and necessity could sometimes be far-fetched.

59 A Afon *et al.* 'Linkages between responses to the available amenities and expressed environment-related health needs in international refugee camp, Oru-Ijebu, Nigeria' (2010) 142 *WIT Transactions on Ecology and the Environment* 70 https://www.scopus.com/record/display.uri?eid=2-s2.0-84865560379&doi=10.2495%2fSW100071&origin=inward&txGid=bcfcae607ba345557abc10cb7db4291a&featureToggles=FEATURE_NEW_DOC_DETAILS_EXPORT:1 (accessed 26 April 2020).

60 As noted earlier, with regard to Nigeria, this research uses 'risk of statelessness' especially because Nigeria has not yet conducted any mapping of statelessness and does not have a procedure to determine who is stateless at the moment. Therefore, no one can confirm the number of stateless persons or persons at risk of statelessness in Nigeria.

61 See P Yu 'Customizing fair use transplants' (2018) 7 (1) *Laws* 3 https://doi-org.proxy.library.uu.nl/10.3390/laws7010009 (accessed 4 June 2020).

62 T Goldbach 'Why legal transplants?' (2019) *Annual Review of Law and Social Science* 583.

63 N Tebbe and R Tsai *Op Cit* 465.

with inapplicability issues compounded by the limited options available to the legislative drafters.[64] The need for a quick and efficient law to solve domestic problems could lead to 'blind copying' of legal norms and/or institutions which may not work well for the receiving State.

The existence of the necessary institutional infrastructure is key to the success of legal transplants. Without institutional infrastructures, such as executive institutions that would implement the rule and a functional and effective court system that would provide judicial safeguards and interpretation of laws, transplanted laws are very likely to fail.[65] Despite the beauty of the legitimacy-generating transplant, Jonathan M. Miller asserts it

> will suffer in the face of a sharp decline in the prestige of the transplant donor, since the transplant will lose its purpose. Regardless of their advantages or disadvantages, Soviet models have lost sway in developing countries in part because they lack prestige after the fall of the Soviet Union. Likewise, the rise of alternative sources of authority may cause a legitimacy-generating transplant to lose ground.[66]

A small aspect of this research touches on the transplantation of institutions or the realignment of institutional mandates for efficient management of a statelessness determination procedure, targeting existing relevant institutions in Nigeria (Part 6.3.1.2). On the idea of institutional transplants and the required attention for their functionality, Martin de Jong and Suzan Stoter postulated thus:

> In general, institutional transfer processes target formal legal institutions. Installing legal safeguards to ensure that international law and legal bodies introduce and sanction the rule of law can be seen as an example of this aim. This can be regarded as the promotion of having the legality principle in place around the world and ensuring political and civil rights in all countries. However, if the informal institutions are not transformed or if no new body of informal practices develops around a new legal transplant, such transplants will merely be a dead letter and will not enjoy any acceptance or functionality.[67]

It is important to pay attention to existing institutions, which are usually the recipient of transplanted norms, to avoid a situation whereby (proposed) recipient institutions are not able to function as effectively as the systems they draw from. For instance, Nigeria signed and ratified the African Union Convention for

---

64 H Xanthaki 'Legal transplants in legislation: Defusing the trap' (2008) 57 (3) *The International and Comparative Law Quarterly* 659.
65 A Alshorbagy 'On the failure of a legal transplant: The case of Egyptian takeover law' (2012) 22 (2) *Indiana International & Comparative Law Review* 249.
66 J Miller *Op Cit* 869.
67 M de Jong and S Stoter *Op Cit* 318.

180 *Legal Transplantation*

the Protection and Assistance of Internally Displaced Persons (also known as the Kampala Convention)[68] in 2009 and 2012 respectively.[69] As of the time of writing, Nigeria has not domesticated the Kampala Convention to give it the force of law in Nigeria.[70] The main reasons for the non-domestication of the Convention is the confusion as to which agency in Nigeria is better equipped to coordinate the management of displacement interventions on one hand, and the interagency rivalry between the National Commission for Refugees, Migrants and Internally Displaced Persons (NCFRMI) and the National Emergency Management Commission (NEMA)[71] on the other hand, which has led to a division within the executive and legislative arms of government on which agency to situate the coordination mandate for internal displacement interventions. This lack of clarity arguably has prevented lawmakers from agreeing on how best to domesticate the Kampala Convention since its signing in 2009; this is particularly so because domesticating the Convention will require identifying a focal agency for coordination of the activities in the legislation.

Legal transplantation is possible if due attention is paid to how and when it is done, including taking into perspective existing institutions. However, at the extreme, some scholars believe that legal transplant is impossible; one such scholar who believes in the impossibility of legal transplantation is Pierre Legrand.[72] According to him:

> At best, what can be displaced from one jurisdiction to another is, literally, a meaningless form of words. To claim more is to claim too much. In any meaningful sense of the term, 'legal transplants', therefore, cannot happen. No rule in the borrowing jurisdiction can have any significance as regards the rule in the jurisdiction from which it is borrowed. This is because, as it crosses boundaries, the original rule necessarily undergoes a change that affects it qua rule.[73]

---

68 Adopted by the Special Submit of the African Union held in Kampala, Uganda on 23 October 2009.

69 African Union 'List of countries which have signed, ratified/acceded to the African Union Convention for the Protection and Assistance of Internally Displaced Persons in Africa' https://au.int/sites/default/files/treaties/36846-sl-AFRICAN%20UNION%20CONVENTION%20FOR%20THE%20PROTECTION%20AND%20ASSISTANCE%20OF%20INTERNALLY%20DISPLACED%20PERSONS%20IN%20AFRICA%20%28KAMPALA%20CONVENTION%29.pdf (accessed 7 June 2020).

70 Nigeria being a dualist State, there is a requirement that foreign treaties or international laws must first be received through an Act of the National Assembly before they can become binding in Nigeria.

71 See A Jibril *The management of internally displaced persons and enhanced human security in North East Nigeria* (2019) 18 https://bdex.eb.mil.br/jspui/bitstream/123456789/4934/1/MO%200031.pdf (accessed 7 June 2020).

72 See P Legrand 'The impossibility of legal transplants' (1997) 4 (2) *Maastricht Journal of European and Comparative Law* 111–124.

73 *Ibid* 20.

Legal Transplantation   181

In this book, I will align with the scholars who believe that legal transplant is possible, especially those who approach legal transplantation from a mixed or hybrid point of view. One such scholar is Matteo Solinas, who believes that:

> the idea of pure transferable forms and transparent knowledge is largely an illusion. It is only by considering the process of hybridisation where an area of mediation peculiar to each specific contact situation is created (a hybrid paradigm) that an appropriate meaning can be given to legal borrowing and to the mechanism of reception.[74]

As noted earlier, in searching for a legal and administrative structure for Nigeria to aid the protection, identification, and prevention of statelessness, different jurisdictions with varying legal and administrative systems for SDP will be tested against existing Nigerian institutional structures. It is necessary that when shopping for a system to borrow from, the difference in legal, administrative, and cultural differences between the borrowing and donor State is examined to achieve a more or less perfect transplant.

6.2.6 Paying Attention to Legal, Administrative, and Cultural Differences

In adopting a particular legal or administrative system, lawyers and policymakers must pay attention to their individual legal, administrative, and cultural dynamics. This is because, as David Nelken rightly observed, 'studies of law in relation to culture can cover a large range of topics including the role of culture in law to the part played by law as culture, seen as a way of making meaning.'[75] Today, States are governed by a set of rules established by various institutions of government, known as the 'formal legal order.' Despite these formal rules and institutions, States are still guided by lots of informal norms.[76] To establish a functional legal order compatible with the way and approach of the colonialist during the colonial era in African, George Mousourakis in his book *Comparative Law and*

---

74 M Solinas *Op Cit* 41.
75 'Those interested in the relationship between law and culture might wish to study law as a cultural artifact, examine the way it becomes present in everyday life and experience, or through the media, or consider the role of law in accommodating cultural defenses or protecting cultural treasures.'

D Nelken 'Comparative legal cultures' in G Bruinsma and D Weisburd (Eds.) *Encyclopedia of criminology and criminal justice* (2014) 459.
76 'Virtually all countries today have a set of rules embodied in codes or court cases that were established by designated State organs, and State institutions in charge of enforcing these rules. We call this set of rules the formal legal order. Although it is quite important in many countries today, the formal legal order is but one element of the governance structure of society.'

D Berkowitz, K Pistor, and J-F Richard 'The transplant effect' (2003) 51 (1) *The American Journal of Comparative Law* 170.

182 *Legal Transplantation*

Legal Traditions: Historical and Contemporary Perspectives[77] stated that the colonialist took the following actions:

> For this purpose, colonial agents forged new institutions whereby African societies could be both governed and "civilised": chiefs, tribes and customary courts are "invented traditions", which "became in themselves realities through which a good deal of colonial encounter was expressed. Modernisation was also achieved by backing official customary law, the development of which required the "unification" of native customary law, that is, the progressive amalgamation of its local variations. Its unification was achieved by fostering either "codification" or "restatement".[78]

While Montesquieu in his book, *The Spirit of the Law,*[79] made the assertion of tailor-made law thus:

> Law in general is human reason, in as much as it governs all the inhabitants of the earth: the political and civil laws of each nation ought to be only the particular cases in which human reason is applied. They should be adapted in such a manner to the people for whom they are framed that it should be a great chance if those of one nation suit another.[80]

In the English case of *Nyali Ltd v. Attorney General*, Lord Denning making a similar assertion noted thus:

> just as with an English oak, so with the English common law. You cannot transplant it to the African continent and expect it to retain the tough character which it has in England. It will flourish indeed but it needs careful tending.[81]

The difference between Montesquieu's sentiments on legal transplant and those of Lord Denning is that while Montesquieu believed that laws are crafted in such a way that they can only be functional in a particular society, Lord Denning believed that transplanting laws may be difficult and may even be watered down in the recipient State, but with careful attention, crafting, and time, they will eventually flourish.[82] It is important to note that in many cases, because of the dif-

---

77 G Mousourakis *Comparative law and legal traditions: Historical and contemporary perspectives* (2019) 284–285.
78 *Ibid* 284–285.
79 Baron de Montesquieu *The spirit of the law* (1748) 23. Translated by T Nugent 1752 https://socialsciences.mcmaster.ca/econ/ugcm/3ll3/montesquieu/spiritoflaws.pdf (accessed 11 May 2020).
80 *Ibid.*
81 *Nyali Ltd. v. Attorney-General* [1956] 1 QB 16.
82 It is important to note that the approach of the British colonialist in Africa was the indirect rule system, wherein they did not dismantle the existing traditional rulership system or cus-

Legal Transplantation 183

ference in legal systems and cultures, it may be difficult to strictly adopt a foreign rule without necessary alterations.[83]

Therefore, 'ensuring that controversial political, legal, ideological, cultural and/or religious symbols attached to the transplant are avoided and that positive connotations are emphasized is extremely important for increasing its chances of acceptance.'[84] While paying attention to legal and administrative differences, due attention must also be paid to certain commonalities between the receiving and donor States; these commonalities improve the chances for a successful transplant.

6.2.7 Paying Attention to Commonalities

On the concept of shared legal tradition as a basis for transplant, Alan Watson[85] puts it thus:

> The main causes of this transplant bias are, I think obvious: [...] a shared legal tradition of the donor and borrower; and the accessibility-for instance, in writing or in a code of the law to be borrowed [...] the legal tradition itself plays an important role in shaping legal change in a number of ways. For example, borrowing from other systems, the form taken by most legal change, is by no means always the result of a systematic search for the best solution. A bias tends to favor some particular system, and this bias is rooted to some extent in the legal tradition.[86]

As already noted, the Nigerian legal system is an adaptation of the English system of law; as a result, it is usually easy for Nigerian scholars to quickly acquaint themselves with the English system. In addition to Customary and Islamic legal traditions, Nigeria shares to a large extent some Western legal traditions introduced to it by the United Kingdom.

Moreover, it has been observed that when legislators draft or adopt a new law, they often draw from States with similar legal traditions, languages, and systems.[87] This is because, 'within the realm of comparative study in the legislative process, when drafting legislation, the policy maker and the drafting team utilize foreign experiences as a means of falsifying or verifying the relationship between the policy choice under consideration and the results of the application of that policy choice elsewhere.'[88] In some instances, the legal, administrative, and socio-

---

tomary method of dispute resolution, but complemented such existing systems by colonizing the territories through the traditional rulers.

83 G Mousourakis 'Legal transplants and legal development' *Op Cit* 220.

84 M de Jong and S Stoter *Op Cit* 322.

85 A Watson 'Legal change: Sources of law and legal culture' (1983) 131 (5) *University of Pennsylvania Law Review* 1121–1157.

86 *Ibid* 1147 and 1152.

87 H Xanthaki *Op Cit* 660.

88 *Ibid* 659.

184 *Legal Transplantation*

cultural difference between the donor and receiving State may not affect the success or otherwise of legal transplant; it is however important to examine how desirable and compatible the rules to be transplanted are with existing legal, judicial, and administrative structures with the receiving State before adoption.[89]

This book will approach the issue of legal borrowing with the aim of trying to localize the approaches in the donor or selected States. Umar Alkali *et al.* note:

> Nigeria is a pluralized state due to its diverse multi-cultural, ethnic and religious diversity. That has substantially influenced the nature and sources of the Nigerian legal system. The nature of the Nigerian legal System is a microcosm of Africa at large. Many factors have played significant role in shaping the present-day Nigerian Legal System. Islamic law [especially in the north], local customs and traditions, English law, local legislations, court decisions and foreign laws are key players whenever discussion is to be made on the nature of the Nigerian legal system.[90] (Bracket mine.)

Be that as it may, it is for Nigeria and indeed any State that wishes to transplant a foreign norm to pay due attention to common factors between it and the donor State. However, there may be some minor legal, cultural, administrative approach by the various States[91] which is not to be considered significant enough to affect transposing the practices into the Nigerian system, as long as due care is given to context, culture, as well as existing institutional and administrative structures in Nigeria, as I will try to do in the applied part of this research below.

6.3 Bespoke Statelessness Determination Procedure for Nigeria[92]

Having examined the different types of legal transplants and why they occur, including examples of previously transplanted laws and administrative systems in Nigeria,[93] this part will use the standards and criteria analyzed in Chapter 5 above to propose useful guidance for Nigeria to develop its SDP. Inspiration will also

---

89 G Mousourakis 'Legal transplants and legal development' *Op Cit* 229.

90 U Alkali, A Jimeta, A Ilyas Magashi, and T Musa Buba 'Nature and sources of Nigerian legal system: An exorcism of a wrong notion' (2014) 5 (4) *International Journal of Business, Economics and Law* 4.

91 Such as the number of years of legal residence required to naturalize varies from country to country; some countries prefer a separate or the same agency for nationality and refugee status to be combined, etc.

92 Part 6.3 draws mainly from my joint article published by *The Statelessness and Citizenship Review* (SCR) in June 2020 – S Oseghale Momoh, H van Eijken, and C Ryngaert 'Statelessness determination procedures: Towards a bespoke procedure for Nigeria' (2020) 2 (1) *The Statelessness and Citizenship Review* 86–111.

93 As noted earlier, the aspects on legal transplant have been discussed with the aim of highlighting that the same can be done to protect stateless persons or persons at risk of statelessness in Nigeria.

Legal Transplantation   185

be drawn from countries such as Brazil, France, Ivory Coast, Moldova, Paraguay, and the UK,[94] which have a more or less appropriate legal framework in place for the protection, identification, and prevention of statelessness. It will moreover propose areas for possible legal and administrative transplants from these countries to Nigeria. The discussion in this part is largely based on the structure used in Chapter 4, particularly Part 4.3.

6.3.1 Road-Testing Existing Best Practices in Nigeria

The current National Action Plan (NAP)[95] on statelessness, which was approved by the Federal Executive Council[96] on 25 November 2020,[97] makes provision for a determination procedure. The NAP provides for synergies amongst different government agencies; it named the National Commission for Refugee as the focal agency to draft Standard Operating Procedures (SOPs) for the stateless person determination procedure with the support of the Ministry of Communication, the Ministry of Information and Culture, and the National Orientation Agency and technical support from the UNHCR, but failed to include the Nigerian

---

94 These States have been selected because of their compliance with the criteria listed in Chapter 5: criteria such as legality and binding nature of their SDP, structure and location of SDP, access to procedure, procedural guarantees, method of assessments of facts, management of combined refugee and statelessness claims, prospect for naturalization, and review and appeal of decision. The UK SDP system is criticized by scholars especially with regard to its limitations on access to protection, which is arguably not in line with the 1954 Convention, as well as its extremely low recognition rates as compared to other countries with a functioning SDP – see J Bezzano and J Carter 'Statelessness in practice: Implementation of the UK Statelessness Application Procedure' (July 2018) *University of Liverpool Law Clinic* 14, 20, 24, 30 and 42. See also Asylum Aid 'The UK's approach to statelessness: Need for fair and timely decisions' *Policy Briefing* (September 2016). Nevertheless, the UK is included in this research because of the fact that Nigerian lawmakers, lawyers, and scholars easily connect with the UK system. Nigeria and the UK both have a common law system, and their governance systems share some administrative similarities, which may be relevant for developing an SDP for Nigeria. It is easier to convince Nigerian lawmakers about systems that work in the UK (and in Europe generally) rather than in Asia or the Americas. This explains why mostly European States have been included in this research, especially in the descriptive part in Chapter 5.

95 *National Action Plan to End Statelessness—Nigeria* (unpublished, 2018). The plan of action was first drafted in 2016 and updated in 2018. A copy of the updated plan was obtained and discussed in the course of the research with an official of the Civil Society Legislative Advocacy Centre (CISLAC) in June 2019.

96 As stated earlier, the Federal Executive Council, sometimes referred to as the cabinet or simply referred to by its acronym, 'FEC,' is the Executive arm of Government, made of the President, the Vice-President, the Secretary of the Government of the Federation, the Head of Service, and the Federal Ministers. The Federal Executive Council advises and makes decision at the federal executive level. See the Government of Nigeria website https://nigeria.gov.ng/members-of-thefederal-executive-council/ (accessed 10 February 2020).

97 Information on the approval of the NAP can be obtained from the Ministry of Information website https://fmic.gov.ng/fec-approves-action-plan-to-end-statelessness/ (accessed 10 February 2021).

186 *Legal Transplantation*

agency with the mandate on nationality, i.e., the Ministry of Interior. The NAP also did not include the Nigeria Immigration Service (NIS), which is the Ministry of Interior's agency responsible for immigration services amongst the agencies to draft the statelessness SOP. Below, this research will try to provide guidance on how an SDP's administrative structure should look like using examples from other States.

6.3.1.1 Current Legal Framework

Nigeria acceded to the 1954 Convention Relating to Status of Stateless Persons and the 1961 Convention in 2011.[98] Despite being the first country to ratify these conventions in the ECOWAS region, Nigeria has not domesticated them to give them the force of law amongst the laws of the Federation of the Nigerian State. Accordingly, Nigeria currently does not have a legal framework for the determination of statelessness. Instead, when confronted with cases of statelessness, it relies on its refugee status determination procedure set out in the National Commission for Refugees, Migrants and Internally Displaced Persons Act (hereinafter the NCFRMI Act).[99] This leads to incorrect decisions, due to the confusion between refugee status determination criteria and standards for determining statelessness.

Realizing that the NCFRMI Act is not tailored towards protection, identification, and prevention of statelessness, the Government of Nigeria, as a result of repeated advocacy and the technical support of the UNHCR, has taken some steps towards developing a framework on statelessness. In this regard, in 2018, the Government of Nigeria, with the support of the UNHCR and other key stakeholders, drafted a National Action Plan (NAP) on statelessness. The NAP is a step in the right direction for Nigeria, especially as it makes provision for the establishment of a determination procedure for Nigeria.[100] In October 2019, at the UNHCR High-Level Segment on Statelessness held in Geneva, Nigeria pledged to develop an SDP to identify stateless persons, grant protection status, and facilitate appropriate solutions.[101]

In 2015, an application for a refugee status case involving a 'Georgian' woman was presented before the Refugee Eligibility Committee in Nigeria. The woman, now in her late 50s, had come to Nigeria in the 1980s, before the collapse of the Soviet Union. At the time she came to Nigeria, the Republic of Georgia was

---

98 UNHCR *Submission by the United Nations High Commissioner for Refugees (UNHCR) For the Office of the High Commissioner for Human Rights' Compilation Report – Universal Periodic Review: NIGERIA* 1 https://uprdoc.ohchr.org/uprweb/downloadfile.aspx?filename=639&file=EnglishTranslation (accessed 3 February 2020).

99 Decree 52 of 1989 now Cap. N21, Laws of the Federation of Nigeria 2004 (NCFRMI Act).

100 Action 5 of the unpublished draft NAP provides for the establishment of a determination procedure for Nigeria.

101 See UNHCR *Results of the high-level segment on statelessness* https://www.unhcr.org/ibelong/results-of-the-high-level-segment-on-statelessness/ (accessed 17 April 2020).

Legal Transplantation 187

part of the Soviet Union (USSR), and all her national documents were Soviet documents. With no SDP in place, her application was brought under the Refugee Status Determination (RSD) procedure. Thereafter, she was granted refugee status by the RSD Eligibility Committee on the grounds that she had no home country to return to, as the USSR no longer existed, a reason which did not meet the requirements prescribed in the 1951 Refugee Convention. The Eligibility Committee also considered, arguably wrongly, that she was unable to prove her Georgian nationality, and therefore did not recognize her as Georgian.[102] The outcome of this case would have been different if Nigeria had an SDP in place. Instead of being recognized as a refugee, the woman would have gone through an SDP and been granted statelessness status, which in turn would have facilitated her naturalization.

Another example is the case of a 35-year-old male deportee from Switzerland to Nigeria in 2012.[103] The deportee was arrested in 2012 in Switzerland for a drug-related offence, he was subsequently deported to Nigeria on the ground that a nationality assessment conducted on the deportee by the Swiss authorities revealed that he was a Nigerian. On arrival in Nigeria, a further nationality assessment on the deportee by the NIS revealed that the deportee was wrongly identified as a Nigerian by the Swiss authority, a fact which the deportee also alluded to, stating that he is from South Sudan and not Nigeria. The NIS made contact with the South Sudanese authorities who rejected the deportee's claim to South Sudanese nationality. The deportee thereafter requested that a 'Nigerian passport' (nationality) be issued to him. The request was turned down by the Nigerian government, as the deportee did not meet the requirements for Nigerian nationality provided in Chapter III of the 1999 Constitution. The *ex officio* asylum application presented by the NIS on his behalf was also rejected by the RSD Eligibility Committee and Appeal Board, respectively. Arguably, apart from his criminal record, which may have influenced the rejection of his applications, his situation to some extent is similar to that of the woman from the USSR cited above, but the outcomes were different due to the absence of procedure.

As at the time of writing, due to the confusion as to how to proceed with the deportee's situation, he is still being held at the holding centre of the NIS Headquarters in Abuja. The approach and outcome would have been different if Nigeria had legislation that provides for an SDP and protection of stateless persons. In line with international standards, it is recommended that Nigeria take further steps to domesticate the 1954 Convention Relating to Status of

---

102 This example was cited in an interview with a Refugee Status Determination (RSD) Official at the National Commission for Refugees, Migrants and Internally Displaced Persons (NCFRMI) during the course of this research. I contacted the Official with the aim of finding out if there had been any known statelessness case brought before the Refugee Eligibility Committee in Nigeria.
103 This example was cited in an interview with a Senior Official at the Nigeria Immigration Service (NIS) during the course of this research. I contacted the Official with the aim of finding out if the NIS has been faced with a situation of statelessness.

188 *Legal Transplantation*

Stateless Persons and the 1961 Convention on the Reduction of Statelessness. In particular, it should develop a determination procedure formalized in law, similar to what it has done with the 1951 Refugee Convention,[104] as this will ensure fairness, transparency, and efficiency of the process[105] as argued in Chapter 4, Part 4.3 at paragraph 4.3.1. Below, this research outlines how an SDP for Nigeria could look.

6.3.1.2 *Proposed Structure and Location of SDP*

When proposing a structure and location of an SDP for Nigeria, it is important to draw from practices in States with fairly good SDPs in place. States that could guide Nigeria in this regard are the UK and Brazil. In the UK, the competent authority for the determination of statelessness is the Home Office Department of Visas and Immigration. The Home Office's Department of Visas and Immigration is responsible for considering applications for British citizenship from foreign nationals as well as the determination of statelessness.[106] Similarly, in Brazil, the National Secretariat of Justice of the Ministry of Justice and Public Security is responsible for matters related to nationality, naturalization, recognition of refugee status, statelessness, and residence permits.[107]

In Nigeria, somewhat similarly, the Ministry of Interior is currently responsible, amongst others, for granting Nigerian Citizenship and for immigration services. The MOI has a Department known as the Directorate of Citizenship and Business (C&B), which is responsible, *inter alia*, for expatriate quota administration and matters relating to the grant of Nigerian citizenship.[108] It also has the responsibility for administering and enforcing the provisions of the Immigration Act, evaluating applications for citizenship by naturalization, confirmation, or registration, granting of Special Immigration Status, granting of a Temporary Residence Permit, and granting of Renunciation of Nigerian Citizenship, etc.[109] The Nigeria Immigration Service (NIS) is a Department under the Ministry of Interior, just like the Department of Visa and Immigration of the UK Home Office.

---

104 Nigeria domesticated the 1951 Convention and its 1967 Protocol through the NCFRMI Act, wherein the two Conventions were added as annexes.

105 See UNHCR *Statelessness determination procedures identifying and protecting stateless persons* (2014) 5.

106 See Home Office website https://www.gov.uk/apply-citizenship-stateless (accessed 20 April 2020).

107 National Secretariat of Justice of Brazil's website https://legado.justica.gov.br/seus-direitos/migracoes (accessed 20 April 2020). The National Secretariat of Justice has a Department of Migration and the National Committee for Refugees (CONARE).

108 See the Nigeria Ministry of Interior website http://interior.gov.ng/index.php/resources/citizenship-and-business (accessed 3 February 2020).

109 Nigeria Immigration Services website 'Expatriate quota revised guideline(s) on business permit and quota' https://portal.immigration.gov.ng/pages/about (accessed 3 February 2020). Also, the Ministry of Interior Department of Citizenship and Business eCitiBiz website https://www.ecitibiz.interior.gov.ng/home/about (accessed 3 February 2020).

Legal Transplantation 189

Unlike the National Secretariat of Justice of Brazil and the UK Department of Visas and Immigration, both of which are responsible for both citizenship, asylum, and statelessness matters,[110] the competent agency for *asylum matters* in Nigeria is the National Commission for Refugees, Migrants and Internally Displaced Persons (NCFRMI).[111] The NCFRMI, through its Refugee Determination Procedures (RSD), determines refugee status in Nigeria, but it is not mandated to handle or grant Nigerian citizenship. This is the preserve of the Ministry of Interior's Directorate of Citizenship and Business.

It is proposed here to place the relevant statelessness determination/verification body within this Directorate, i.e., the department responsible for citizenship and naturalization. This department is the most appropriate body, especially for individuals who may have been in Nigeria for generations, such as an *in situ* population.[112] Admittedly, 'best practice' States like France, Moldova, and Paraguay may have agencies for statelessness determination that are separate from those that grant nationality,[113] but this is by no means required. In fact, according to the UNHCR, a State is at liberty to locate an SDP within its immigration authorities, or within the body responsible for nationality issues (e.g., naturalization applications or verification of nationality requests).[114] The UNHCR has advised that locating an SDP within the latter type of body is particularly appropriate where the individuals concerned are likely to be longstanding residents of the State.[115]

---

110 In Brazil, the Department of Migration, which grants access to nationality, is separate from CONARE, but they are both within the National Secretariat of Justice.

111 NCFRMI is under the Ministry of Humanitarian Affairs, while the Citizenship and Business Department that grants access to nationality in Nigeria is under the Ministry of Interior.

112 See Nigeria Ministry of Interior Affairs website for more details https://ecitibiz.interior .gov.ng/citizenship/overview (accessed 22 February 2019). In general, this department is responsible for any person who may be entitled to Nigerian nationality by confirmation, naturalization, or registration, or who may be entitled to a residence permit.

113 In France, the French Office for the Protection of Refugees and Stateless Persons (OFPRA) is responsible for refugee and statelessness matters, while the local Préfectures (Towns) are responsible for the granting of French nationality and residence permits. The OFPRA and the Préfectures are both departments of the French Ministry of Interior. For more information, see the Ministry websites https://www.ofpra.gouv.fr/ and https://www.interieur .gouv.fr/Le-ministere/Prefectures respectively (accessed 22 February 2019). In Moldova, the Bureau for Migration and Asylum within the Ministry of Internal Affairs is responsible for statelessness and refugee matters, see http://bma.gov.md/en (accessed 22 February 2020) while the agency responsible for Moldovan nationality and residence permits is the Public Services Agency. See more information via http://www.asp.gov.md/node/1376. In Paraguay, 'the National Constitution explicitly recognised the Judicial Power as the institution responsible for citizenship, considering the legal conditions for its acquisition and loss, together with the content of rights for citizens (article 154).' See E Brey, Report on Citizenship Law: Paraguay (March 2016) *EUDO Citizenship Observatory* 9. The National Refugee Commission for Stateless Persons and Refugees (CONARE) is responsible for statelessness and asylum issues in Paraguay. See Law No. 6, 149 on Protection and Facilities for the Naturalization of Stateless Persons 2018, Arts. 31 & 32.

114 UNHCR *Handbook on protection of stateless persons under the 1954 Convention Relating to The Status of Stateless Persons* (2014) 27 at para. 65.

115 *Ibid* 26–27 at paras. 59, 65.

190   *Legal Transplantation*

With regard to the precise location of the SDP within the Ministry of Interior, Nigeria may choose a central SDP within the Ministry, or decentralize SDP as appropriate. One should bear in mind, however, that Nigeria is a Federal State with 36 component States and 774 Local Governments Areas (LGAs), in addition to its many Federal and State Ministries, Departments, and Agencies (MDAs). Therefore, as recommended above, Nigeria may want to ensure that its SDP allows for referrals of cases from the Component States, LGAs, and MDAs to the central body for the determination of statelessness. The SDP should also allow for cross-referrals between refugee determination procedures and statelessness determination procedures: the NCFRMI can refer potential statelessness cases from its refugee procedure to the statelessness procedure, and *vice versa*.

6.3.1.3 Proposed Access to Procedure

As noted in the previous section, Nigeria has an existing citizenship acquisition procedure through a Directorate at the Ministry of Interior, which would be the appropriate department to locate an SDP. The Ministry of Interior has launched an online platform to apply for Nigerian nationality, called eCitiBiz. The eCitiBiz platform is a highly customizable and industry standard organizational operations system designed to electronically capture and pivot all aspects of the operations and workflow of the Directorate of Citizenship and Business.[116] Similar to the UK's FLR(s) online form to apply for leave to remain as a stateless person in the UK through a UK Government website,[117] this eCitiBiz could become a tool for individuals to apply for a determination as a stateless person, for nationality verification, or a residence permit. When a determination procedure is finally adopted, the adjustment that needs to be made to the existing eCitiBiz is to create a provision for application for leave or a permit to remain in Nigeria as a stateless person and removal of the requirement of paying an application fee for stateless persons.

Additionally, the proposed SDP framework should allow for Nigerian officials to initiate *ex officio* SDP for stateless persons, as it is done for instance in Moldova;[118] this would allow for people who would otherwise not be aware of such a procedure, or indigent and uneducated applicants, to be assisted by the State. As argued above, access to the SDP should not be subject to time limits. Also, like in the current refugee status determination procedure,[119] information on the procedure and counselling services should be available to applicants.[120]

---

116 See Ministry of Interior Department of Citizenship and Business website. *Op Cit.*

117 *Application to extend stay in UK as stateless person: form FLR (S)* https://www.gov.uk/government/publications/application-to-extend-stay-in-uk-as-stateless-person-form-flrs (accessed 3 February 2020).

118 See Law No. 200 of 16 July 2010 on the Regime of Foreigners in the Republic of Moldova, Article 87(1). See also the suggestions in Chapter 4, particularly at Part 4.1.

119 NCFRMI Act, Part V.

120 See UNHCR *Good practices paper – action 6: Establishing statelessness determination procedures to protect stateless persons* (2016) 5, and the suggestion in Chapter 4, particularly at Part 4.3.4.

Legal Transplantation 191

Also, considering the history of gender discrimination with regard to access to nationality in Nigeria,[121] it is important for an SDP for Nigeria to spell out that women shall have access to the procedure and be able to transmit their status where necessary on an equal footing with men.

6.3.1.4 Proposed Procedural Guarantees

To understand the procedural guarantees for a possible SDP in Nigeria, in the current absence of an SDP it is important to examine the refugee status determination (RSD) procedure, i.e., the asylum procedure. Examining the current asylum procedure is relevant because, by virtue of Action 5 of the National Action Plan,[122] the NCFRMI, the Government's refugee agency, is inadvertently tipped to be the lead agency for SDP in Nigeria. The agency is also in the process of drafting Standard Operation Procedures (SOPs) for an SDP in Nigeria. The NCFRMI will likely rely on the existing asylum procedure when developing an SDP for Nigeria.[123] After all, Refugee Status Determination (RSD) is the procedure that is closest to an SDP.

According to section 8 of the NCFRMI Act, an application for the grant of refugee status could be made on behalf of an applicant by a competent officer or through the office of the UNHCR. The NCFRMI Act does not specify that the applicant must be interviewed, nor does it guarantee the right to an interpreter and legal aid.[124] In any event, following what was earlier suggested in Chapter 4, Part 4.3.4, this research recommends that when drafting an SDP for Nigeria, drawing on the asylum procedure, the following rights be specified in the SDP framework: the right to interview,[125] the right to free interpretation in the

---

121 Nigerian women are unable to transmit their nationality to their foreign husbands as Nigerian men would to their foreign wives. Men married to Nigerian women must wait for 15 years before they qualify to apply for naturalization as opposed to women married to Nigerian men who are almost immediately able to register as Nigerian citizens. See the Constitution of Nigeria 1999, ss. 26(2)(a) and 27.

122 In activity 3 of Action 5 of the N, the NCFRMI was made the focal agency to 'review the existing national framework in order to mandate a State agency responsible for the determination of stateless persons and the protection of stateless persons.'

123 In addition to part V of the NCFRMI Act on the steps to apply for refugee status in Nigeria, the NCFRMI has an unpublished supplementary Standard Operating Procedures (SOPs) on RSD jointly developed by NCFRMI and UNHCR. A hard copy of the SOPs was retrieved and discussed with the official of NCFRMI.

124 In practice, the UNHCR sponsors legal aid for refugees, as the government has no provision for it. However, the NCFRMI supplementary Standard Operating Procedures (SOPs) (unpublished) do guarantee the right to an interpreter and legal aid in its paras. 2.1(xii), 3.4(iii), and 6.1.

125 Interview is compulsory in Moldova, see Law No. 200 of 16 July 2010 on the Regime of Foreigners in the Republic of Moldova, Art. 87. Interview is also compulsory in Paraguay, see Law No. 6,149 on Protection and Facilities for the Naturalization of Stateless Persons 2018, Art. 33(e) and 36 http://www.bacn.gov.py/leyes-paraguayas/8669/ley-n -6149-proteccion-y-facilidades-para-la-naturalizacion-de-las-personas-apatridas (accessed

192 *Legal Transplantation*

language of the applicant,[126] and the right to legal aid.[127] Legal aid should start at the beginning of an SDP application and not commence only at the appeals stage, i.e., like the current asylum procedure in Nigeria. It should be clearly stated that no administrative fee will be charged for SDP.[128] Regarding the timeframe within which a decision must be made, it is recommended that Nigeria set a (reasonable) time frame from the date of application to the time for statelessness status decisions. A best practice in this regard is Moldova, where decisions are normally made within six months, and exceptionally within 12 months.[129]

It is also important for Nigeria to transpose the practice of non-penalization of applicants on the grounds of illegal entry and residence in its asylum procedure to the proposed SDP (see 4.3.4 above). This would ensure that applicants are not detained pending the determination of status.

6.3.1.5 *Proposed Method for Assessment of Evidence and Establishment of Facts*

In the current asylum procedure, in keeping with the UNHCR Handbook on Procedures and Criteria for Determining Refugee Status and Guidelines on

---

20 April 2020). However, it is optional in France and the UK. For France, see the Code for Entry and Residence of Foreign Persons and the Right of Asylum (CESEDA), Art. R. 812-2, and OFPRA, *Guide of The Procedures to OFPRA* (2018) 44 https://www.ofpra.gouv.fr/sites/default/files/atoms/files/guide_des_procedures_a_lofpra_-_2019.pdf (accessed 22 February 2020). For the UK, see Home Office *Applications for leave to remain as a stateless person* (1st May 2013) 5 https://webarchive.nationalarchives.gov.uk/20131002094719/http://www.ukba.homeoffice.gov.uk/sitecontent/documents/policyandlaw/stateless-guide/stateless-guide.pdf?view=Binary (accessed 2 February 2019).

126 Applicants in Moldova, the UK, Paraguay, and France get free interpretation. For Moldova, see Law No. 200 of 16.07.2010 on the Regime of Foreigners in the Republic of Moldova, Art. 87. For the UK, see Home Office, *Asylum policy instruction statelessness and applications for leave to remain* Version 2.0 (2016) 12. For France, see CESEDA, Art. R.812-2. For Paraguay, see Law Protection and Facilities for the Naturalization of Stateless Persons 2018, Art. 33(e).

127 Legal aid is guaranteed by law in Moldova; see Law Regarding the Legal Assistance Guaranteed by The State No. 198 of 26 July 2007, Arts. 6 and 7. For Paraguay, legal aid only guaranteed for applicants without financial means; see Law on Protection and Facilities for the Naturalization of Stateless Persons 2018, Art. 38. In the UK and France, there is no such provision. For the UK, see J Bezzano and J Carter *Op Cit* 7. Meanwhile for France, legal aid is only available to French nationals and nationals of the member States of the European Union. Foreign nationals habitually and regularly residing in France are also eligible for legal aid. However, legal aid may exceptionally be granted to persons (including stateless persons) who do not fulfil the conditions set out in the Law on Legal Aid, when their situation appears particularly worthy of interest. See Legal Aid, Law No. 91-647 1991, Art 3 https://www.legifrance.gouv.fr/affichTexteArticle.do?cidTexte=JORFTEXT000000537611&idArticle=LEGIARTI000030022902&dateTexte=&categorieLien=id (accessed 22 February 2019).

128 Although no administrative fee is charged in RSD practice in Nigeria, the NCFRMI Act and its SOPs are silent on it.

129 See UNHCR *Handbook on protection of stateless persons, Op Cit* para. 75. See also the Regime of Foreigners in the Republic of Moldova, Art. 87(1).

International Protection,[130] the burden of proof is shared between the applicant and the case officer, even if the NCFRMI Act and the refugee procedure Standard Operation Procedures (SOPs) do not explicitly provide for a shared burden. This burden-sharing system should be retained in the proposed SDP framework. As argued in Chapter 4, Part 4.3.5, Nigeria could draw inspiration in this respect from the SDP systems in France, Moldova, and Paraguay, where case officers can collect information from the applicant's place of birth and place of residence, including from State authorities in the last place of habitual residence of the applicant. [131]

The standard of proof that is used in RSD in Nigeria is the balance of probabilities. For SDP, this book proposes a somewhat lower standard, i.e., proof to a reasonable degree, as recommended by the UNHCR,[132] and in this research in Chapter 4, Part 4.3.5.

6.3.1.6 Management of Combined Refugee and Statelessness Claims

As noted earlier, the UNHCR advises that when an applicant raises both a refugee and a statelessness claim, it is important that each claim is assessed and that both types of status are explicitly recognized.[133] The UNHCR acknowledges that sometimes there could be overlaps between refugee and statelessness claims, and on that ground advises States to consider establishing a combined procedure for both refugee and statelessness determination. Although this book recommends *separate* determination procedures as well as different agencies for SDP and asylum procedures (see Chapter 4, Part 4.3.6, if procedures were to be combined in Nigeria, it is imperative that Nigeria examine how to manage confidentiality concerns, especially in situations of mixed statelessness and refugee claims, considering the extreme confidentiality required in asylum procedures.[134] An example is the UK, where for confidentiality reasons, the SDP is entirely independent of the asylum procedure.[135] The UK system allows for the asylum claim to be considered first, and the statelessness claim to be considered only after the asylum claim has been determined or withdrawn.

---

130 UNHCR *Handbook on procedures and criteria for determining refugee status and guidelines on international protection under the 1951 Convention and the 1967 Protocol Relating to the Status of Refugees* (April 2019) 43.

131 See OFPRA, Guide of the Procedures to OFPRA para 9.2, EMN Inform Statelessness in the EU. Version 4 – 11th November 2016 5. Law No. 200 of 16.07.2010 on the Regime of Foreigners in the Republic of Moldova, Article 87(2). Paraguay Law on Protection and Facilities for the Naturalization of Stateless Persons 2018, Art. 44.

132 See UNHCR *Handbook on protection of stateless persons, Op Cit* 34, para. 91.

133 *Ibid* 31 at para. 78.

134 As recommended by UNHCR, unless extremely necessary, contact with State authorities should not be made. Where such contacts are made, the existence of an asylum application should not be disclosed.

135 EMN INFORM *Statelessness in the EU* (2016) 7 https://ec.europa.eu/home-affairs/sites/homeaffairs/files/00_inform_statelessness_final_en.pdf (accessed 22 February 2020).

194 *Legal Transplantation*

6.3.1.7 *Prospect of Protection and Naturalization*

As discussed earlier, an SDP should lead from the acquisition of certain basic rights to a simplified naturalization process.[136] This is not the practice in Nigeria at the moment based on its asylum procedure, even if section 17 of the NCFRMI Act in principle allows for refugees to naturalize. The Nigerian Constitution requires that the applicant has resided in Nigeria for at least 15 years before qualifying to apply for naturalization.[137] It also imposes other conditions such as that the person must be of 'good character,'[138] must make a 'useful contribution'[139] to the advancement, progress, and well-being of Nigeria, and must be 'acceptable' and 'assimilated into a local community.'[140] The Nigerian Constitution does not define character and useful contribution, leaving their definition to the discretion of the authorities charged with applying or interpreting these terms, usually the Governors of the states, the Ministry of Interior and the Advisory Committee on Nigerian Citizenship (ACNC).

These requirements do not as such violate international law. However, for stateless persons, it is recommended for them to immediately have access to nationality as a more durable solution for their plight. Arguably, as advised in Chapter 4, Part 4.3.7, an SDP should lead to immediate access to a facilitated or simplified naturalization process. This is similar to the system in Brazil, where a recognized stateless person has access to naturalization within 30 days of the decision recognizing statelessness.[141] If Nigeria is not disposed to granting access to naturalization to stateless persons immediately after recognition like it is done in Brazil, as regards temporal conditions for naturalization, the practice in France is recommended. In France, a recognized stateless person obtains access to naturalization after five years, reduced to two years for foreigners, including stateless persons who complete two years of university education with a diploma conferred by a French university or establishment of higher education.[142] Recognized stateless persons should, however, be immediately entitled to a permanent residence permit, labour and social security rights, access to basic and essential services, travel documents, etc., as argued in Chapter 4, Part 4.3.7.[143]

---

136 See UNHCR *Global action plan to end statelessness 2014–2024* (2014) 16.
137 See Constitution of the Federal Republic of Nigeria 1999 (as amended), s 27(2)(i)–(ii).
138 See *Ibid* ss. 26(1)(a), 27(1)(b).
139 See *Ibid* s. 27(1)(e).
140 See *Ibid* s. 72(2)d).
141 Stateless persons have immediate access to permanent residency. See Migration Act Law No. 13,445 of 24 May 2017, Art. 26(7)(8) http://www.planalto.gov.br/ccivil_03/_ato2015-2018/2017/lei/L13445.htm (accessed 20 April 2020).
142 See French Civil Code, Art. 21-17 and Art. 21-18. Translated by Georges Rouhette and Anne Rouhette-Berton, updated 4 April 2006 https://www.legifrance.gouv.fr/content/download/1950/13681/version/3/file/Code_22.pdf (accessed 25 February 2019).
143 See Convention Relating to the Status of Stateless Persons 1954, Arts. 15, 17, 19, 21, 23, 24, and 28; UNHCR, *Handbook on protection of stateless persons, Op Cit* paras. 136, 137, and 150; Brazil's Migration Act Law No. 13,445 of 24 May 2017 Art. 26. For France, see

Legal Transplantation 195

In terms of responsible agencies, Brazil and the UK are recommended as best practices. In these countries, the same agency is responsible for both SDP and naturalization.[144] An SDP embedded in the Directorate of Citizenship and Business of the Nigerian Ministry of Interior may thus create a pathway from a determination of statelessness status to acquisition of nationality.

6.3.1.8 Proposed Review and Appeal of Decisions

Section 8 of the NCFRMI Act guarantees the right to an effective remedy where an application for a grant of refugee status is rejected, by providing that the applicant may appeal against the decision of the Eligibility Committee to the Refugee Appeal Board. This is a good practice that should be retained when an SDP is developed in Nigeria. Still, there are some doubts regarding the requirement in the NCFRMI Act that the applicant should appeal within 30 days of being notified of the refusal. While such a time limit does not as such violate international law,[145] as argued in Chapter 4, Part 4.3.8, it is advised to leave open the time within which to appeal a negative decision.

As far as an administrative review is concerned, it is of note that Nigeria has an Advisory Committee on Nigerian Citizenship (ACNC),[146] which reviews applications and decisions of the Ministry of Interior and makes recommendations

---

Code for Entry and Residence of Foreign Persons and the Right of Asylum (CESEDA), Arts. L. 313-1, L. 313-26, L. 812-7, L. 380-1 and French Civil Code, Art. 21-17. For Moldova, see Law No. 200 of 16 July 2010 on the Regime of Foreigners in the Republic of Moldova, Arts. 4, 87(3). For Paraguay, see Law on Protection and Facilities for the Naturalization of Stateless Persons 2018, Arts. 23–28. For the UK, see Immigration Act 1971, s. 3(1)(c), Housing Act 1996 Parts 6 & 7, Immigration Rules, Part 14, Rules 405, 410–416. Note that, in the UK, permanent residency is only granted to a person who has had leave to remain as a stateless person for at least five years. In France, the resident permit issued is not a permanent residence permit (renewable). However, stateless persons have access to naturalization after five years of legal residence.

144 See Brazil's National Secretariat of Justice website https://legado.justica.gov.br/seus-direitos/migracoes; Home Office *Statelessness leave. Version 3* (2019) https://assets.publishing .service.gov.uk/government/uploads/system/uploads/attachment_data/file/843704/ stateless-leave-guidance-v3.0ext.pdf; Home Office *Guide AN naturalisation booklet – the requirements* (2019) https://assets.publishing.service.gov.uk/government/uploads/ system/uploads/attachment_data/file/794168/Guide_AN__Naturalisation_Booklet .pdf; and Home Office website https://www.gov.uk/browse/citizenship/citizenship (all accessed 22 February 2020.)

145 See NCFRMI Act, Art. 8(7) and Administrative Litigation of Law of the Republic of Moldova, Art. 17(1) both of which provide for a 30-day appeal period, while for France it is within two months; see OFPRA website for more information, https://www.ofpra.gouv.fr /fr/apatridie/les-voies-de-recours. The international law instruments such as 1951 Refugee Convention, Art. 31(2) on appeal; the 1954 Statelessness Convention, and UNHCR *Handbook on protection of stateless persons, Op Cit* 19 at para. 47 on appeal/review did impose a specific time frame for submission of appeal applications.

146 See, the Ministry of Interior C&B website http://www.interior.gov.ng/index.php/84 -press-release?start=60 (accessed 13 March 2019). See also, E I Nwogugu 'Recent changes

196 *Legal Transplantation*

for the grant or refusal of Nigerian nationality. What is not clear, however, is the extent to which the ACNC reviews the decisions of the Ministry. If the ACNC actually reviews the decisions of the Ministry, then this could be adapted when a determination procedure is finally established. Like in the UK,[147] applications for administrative review of negative decisions regarding statelessness determinations could be sent to the ACNC. The problems with such a system, however, are that administrative review committees, such as the ACNC, usually only look into the procedural correctness of a decision, and do not reverse decisions: they only make recommendations to the responsible agency. Appeals, however, usually lead to a reversal of earlier decisions if the procedures were not properly applied.[148]

The system in Moldova where SDP appeals go to regular courts[149] is therefore recommended. In the case of Nigeria, the Federal High Court, as the court with constitutional power to entertain matters concerning citizenship and naturalization,[150] is specifically recommended, or alternatively, the establishment of a special Administrative Court, as France has done,[151] or a special Appeals Commission on statelessness status (*la Commission Nationale de Recours*) in the case of Ivory Coast.[152] However, the French Administrative Court's decision has no suspensive effect, which means that, if a deportation order is issued on the applicant, the authorities can carry it out, even if the Administrative Court has not yet decided on the appeal.[153] Whatever approach Nigeria decides to take, administrative review or judicial appeal, as argued in Chapter 4, Part 4.3.8, the

---

in Nigerian nationality and citizenship law' (1976) 25 *International and Comparative Law Quarterly* 434.

147 See para. AR2.3 of Appendix AR of the UK Immigration Rules.

148 Note that in both the review and appeal procedure, the applicant has to challenge the earlier decision. That being said, it would also be appropriate for an SDP system to allow self-auditing of decisions.

149 See Law No. 200 of 16th July 2010 on the Regime of Foreigners in the Republic of Moldova, Art. 87(2) and 87(3).

150 The Constitution of the Federal Republic of Nigeria 1999, s 251(1)(i) provides *inter alia* that 'the Federal High Court shall have and exercise jurisdiction to the exclusion of any other court in civil causes and matters" relating to "citizenship, naturalisation and aliens, deportation of persons who are not citizens of Nigeria, extradition, immigration into and emigration from Nigeria, passports and visas.' The Federal High Court is the only competent court in Nigeria to entertain issues of citizenship, naturalization, and other immigration matters in Nigeria. The court is a central court but with divisions in each of the 36 states of Nigeria.

151 'ENS Statelessness Index Survey: France' 23 https://index.statelessness.eu/sites/statelessindex .eu/files/ENS_Statelessness_Index_Survey-France-2018.pdf (accessed 25 February 2020). See also the French Public Administration website on appeals to an administrative judge https:// www.service-public.fr/particuliers/vosdroits/F15402 (accessed 25 February 2020).

152 See CNESA Law, Art. 12.

153 See more information on OFPRA website https://www.ofpra.gouv.fr/fr/apatridie/les -voies-de-recours (accessed 25 February 2020).

initiation of the relevant procedure should suspend the order of expulsion pending the outcome of the review or appeal.

6.4 Proposed Flowchart for a Determination Procedure for Nigeria

Drawing inspiration from the determination procedures in the selected States and recommendations from the European Migration Network (EMN) study,[154] the below flowchart is recommended for a determination procedure in Nigeria.

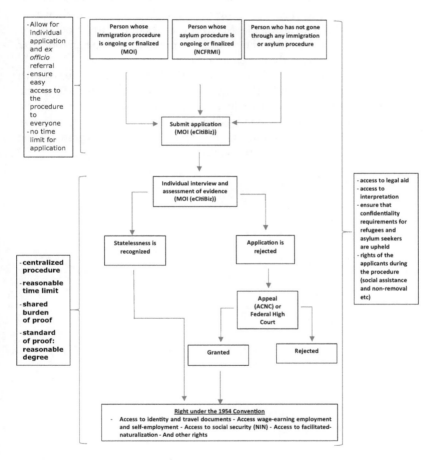

Figure 6.1 Proposed SDP Flowchart[155]

154 EMN Inform – *Statelessness in the EU, Op Cit* 17.
155 *Ibid.*

198   *Legal Transplantation*

6.5 Conclusion

As George Mousourakis puts it, 'the starting-point of comparative law is often the appearance of common social problems in different legal orders.'[156] This chapter examined the place of legal borrowing and comparative law in resolving common legal and societal issues in borrowing States, linking it to developing a statelessness determination procedure for Nigeria.

This chapter applied the standards and criteria discussed in Chapter 5 to Nigeria which is in the process of developing a statelessness determination procedure. As discussed earlier, Nigeria and any State which has or does not yet have an SDP, may want to give particular attention to standards relating to legality and 'bindingness' of the proposed SDP, to procedural access, and procedural guarantees. However, it remains that bespoke SDP procedures ought to be developed for individual States, as the effectiveness of such procedures depends on their embeddedness in, and relationship to existing institutions.

Whether Nigeria chooses to locate the SDP at the Ministry of Interior or with the Refugee Commission, including having a fused system, it is advised that the country needs to ensure that the procedure is formalized in law, rather than just an agency policy or proclamation, considering how easy a policy or an executive order can be revised by a new administration. This chapter has suggested some tailor-made solutions for Nigeria in this respect.

---

156 G Mousourakis *Comparative law and legal traditions, Op Cit* 284–285.

7 Conclusion

Statelessness and the Right to Nationality – Summary of Key Discussions and Findings

7.1 Introduction

This chapter, which is the concluding chapter, begins with a summary of the approach used to achieve the aim of this book, followed by a recap of key observations and conclusions. This chapter highlights both the societal and scientific relevance of the book, especially as the aim of the book is to contribute to the research on statelessness generally and to make recommendations for Nigeria and any State in the process of developing its SDP using a comparative lens. The chapter then concludes with recommendations on how the book can be used by national, local, and international stakeholders (Part 7.3).

This book, like previous research on the right to nationality in Nigeria, emphasizes the need for legislative reforms, especially on the right and access to nationality (see Chapter 6, particularly Parts 6.1–6.2). However, a review of existing literature in this regard, especially regarding Nigeria, reveals that there are no previous studies on the risk of statelessness in Nigeria. Therefore, in addition to examining the peculiarity of the risk of statelessness in Nigeria, this book focused on the need for identification, prevention, and a protection regime for stateless persons. It further proposed an SDP established by legislation to provide comprehensive protection for stateless persons in the migratory context and a nationality verification process for the *in situ* population to prevent the risk of statelessness in Nigeria.

The book identified some good State practices, international norms,[1] as well as 'standards and criteria' regarding the establishment and operation of an SDP to guide States globally in developing a determination procedure, and to apply these to a future SDP in Nigeria. With regard to the proposed SDP for Nigeria, the approach in this book was for the most extensive protection for stateless persons,

---

1 Such as protection, identification, prevention, and reduction norms. See UNHCR *Conclusion on Identification, Prevention and Reduction of Statelessness and Protection of Stateless Persons No. 106 (LVII) – 2006, Executive Committee 56th session.* Contained in United Nations General Assembly Document A/AC.96/1035 https://www.unhcr.org/afr/excom/exconc/453497302/conclusion-identification-prevention-reduction-statelessness-protection.html (accessed 3 July 2020).

DOI: 10.4324/9781003278733-7

200   *Conclusion*

i.e., from a human rights perspective, while taking the particular legal and institutional framework of Nigeria, and the possibility for flexibility, into account.

7.2 Summary of Approach

This part summarizes the approach used in this book and the key observations and discussions (summarized in Part 7.2.1).

Before giving a summary of the approach and discussions, it is important to start with a recap of the method used to achieve its results. This book, which is a descriptive and evaluative study, examined the phenomenon and nature of the risk of statelessness, nationality challenges in Nigeria, and proposed concrete solutions. The book referenced and compared nationality and statelessness protection, identification, and preventive measures in jurisdictions in Europe, the Americas, and Africa. For methods, the book relied heavily on primary and secondary sources of law. For primary sources, it particularly relied on statutes, treaties, and conventions such as the 1999 Constitution of Nigeria; the 1954 and 1961 Statelessness Conventions; and case law, among others. For secondary sources, it relied on reported and unreported cases, journals, textbooks, and publications in national dailies; interviews of Government and NGO officials; UNHCR reports and publications; and reports of the Economic Community of West African States (ECOWAS) and other relevant bodies.

As stated in Chapter 1, the main focus of this book is on statelessness and the right to nationality in Nigeria. The book highlighted the nature and scope of the risk of statelessness in Nigeria, as well as the proposed method for identification, prevention, as well as protection of stateless persons. The first part of the book (Chapters 1 to 3) examined the nature and conceptual ideas of statelessness with particular reference to Nigeria, reviewing some of the relevant conventions, treaties, and legislation. It discussed some of the population exposed to statelessness in Nigeria, such as children born to foreign parents, including offspring of naturalized Nigerians within the territory of Nigeria who would otherwise be stateless, foundlings and children adopted in Nigeria whose nationality is unknown or unclear, foreign men married to Nigerian women, persons in the territory of Nigeria who hold no nationality or citizenship of another country, border populations including the people of Bakassi affected by the 2002 ICJ judgment ceding Bakassi to Cameroon, Almajiris, nomads, and displaced populations with no form of identity document, etc.[2]

The second part of the book (Chapters 4 to 7) examined the practices in other jurisdictions selected for this book, together with the *standards and criteria*[3]

---

2 These groups were explained thoroughly in Chapter 2.
3 Standards relate to the presence of a mechanism for protection, prevention, and identification of statelessness, and will be measured against the specific criteria of: (a) legality and binding nature of SDP; (b) structure and location of SDP; (c) access to procedure; (d) procedural guarantees; (e) assessment of facts; (f) management of combined refugee and statelessness claims; (g) prospect for naturalization; and (h) review and appeal of decision.

Conclusion 201

discussed in Chapter 4 to make useful recommendations for Nigeria on how to improve and develop its legal and policy framework to protect, identify, and prevent statelessness.

7.2.1 Findings and Discussions

This part succinctly surveys and summarizes the book's findings and key discussions, starting with the emphasis on how important it is to discuss challenges associated with statelessness and the right to a nationality. The book attempts to propose a definition for statelessness determination procedure, followed by a discussion on why States should adopt a procedure for determining statelessness if they are to prevent it in their territories. The need for a comparative approach to tackling the issue of statelessness and the right to nationality was moreover re-emphasized here. The major gaps in existing international and regional instruments for statelessness and the right to nationality were discussed, concluding with a thought on the novelty of the topic of statelessness in Nigeria and why close attention should be paid to the topic.

7.2.1.1 The 'Right to have Rights'

It has been stated in *Trop v. Dulles*[4] that nationality is the 'right to have rights,' reaffirming that the right to nationality is a fundamental human right that everyone is entitled to.[5] As stated earlier, without the possession of nationality, a person could be said to be in a situation of legal nonexistence and unable to enforce certain rights. For many years, 'the phenomenon of statelessness has attracted particular attention, perhaps in the light of the strong connection between statelessness and irregular immigration.'[6] In Chapter 2, this book examined the general phenomenon, scale, and nature of statelessness or risk of statelessness. The sociological effect of statelessness and how it affects society were discussed, with a particular emphasis on the peculiarity of the risk in Nigeria.

Moreover, the book examined the notions of *de jure* and *de facto* statelessness against the backdrop of the question, what is statelessness? The arguments in this book were more aligned with the opinions of scholars who 'believe that the 1954 Convention's definition of statelessness is too narrow and limiting because it excludes those persons whose citizenship is practically useless or who cannot prove or verify their nationality.'[7] This line of thought is in consideration of the similarities of deprivations of both categories of statelessness.

---

4 See *Trop v. Dulles*, 356 U.S. 86 (1958) 102.
5 UDHR Art. 15.
6 K Konstantina 'Addressing statelessness in Greece under EU law' LSE 9th HO PhD Symposium on Contemporary Greece and Cyprus (2019) 6 http://www.lse.ac.uk/Hellenic -Observatory/Assets/Documents/HO-PhD-Symposia/The-9th-HO-PhD-Symposium/ Symposium-Papers/Session-1/Migration-I-Security.pdf (accessed 3 December 2019).
7 D Weissbrodt and C Collins 'The human rights of stateless persons' (2006) 28 *Hum. Rts. Q.* 251. See also A de Chickera 'Critiquing the categorisation of the stateless' (July 2010) *The*

202 *Conclusion*

Unlike in the other States examined in this book, there is neither an official record nor an estimated number of stateless persons in Nigeria. The reason is not farfetched; Nigeria does not have an SDP at the moment to help identify stateless persons, and no official State mapping has been conducted on the risk of statelessness in Nigeria. Arguably, the reason for the absence of a statelessness study or an SDP for Nigeria is because of the lack of understanding of the phenomenon and risk of statelessness in Nigeria by government officials. To stem the tide, this book examined the factors that expose a large part of the Nigerian population to the risk of statelessness. The need for a statelessness determination procedure, as well as a procedure to verify the nationality of the very many *in situ* populations without any means of identification, was also discussed (See Part 6.3.1.2 above).

Neither of the two UN Statelessness Conventions places an explicit obligation on the Contracting States to establish a statelessness determination procedure. However, 'there is a growing interest among States in establishing SDPs.'[8] This could be attributed to increased awareness-raising and campaigns by the UNHCR[9] and NGOs working in the field of statelessness and the right to nationality.[10] Therefore, this book (Chapter 5) examined the procedures for determining statelessness in *seven*[11] states from across Africa, Europe, and the Americas, highlighting the shortfalls in the existing State practice to propose a bespoke procedure for Nigeria and indeed any State in the process of developing an SDP. 'It is widely agreed that it is impossible to effectively implement many of the provisions of these Conventions without having a mechanism for the identification of their beneficiaries.'[12]

7.2.1.2 Why a Procedure for Determining Statelessness?

This book discussed elaborately the peculiarity of the risk of statelessness in Nigeria and its implications for society. It moreover proposed how to prevent the risk and fill the administrative and legal gaps using examples from other States with fairly good State practice, and how Nigeria can develop its SDP and nationality

---

Equal Rights Trust 53 & 54 https://www.equalrightstrust.org/ertdocumentbank/chapter%202.pdf (accessed 20 November 2020).

8 UNHCR *Good practices paper – action 6: Establishing statelessness determination procedures to protect stateless persons* (2016) 2.

9 In 2014, UNHCR launched the #IBELONG campaign, which is a ten-year global campaign (2014–2024) to end statelessness across the world.

10 Some of the well-known NGOs include the Institute of Statelessness and Inclusion (ISI), the Global Citizenship Observatory (GLOBALCIT), and the European Network on Statelessness (ENS).

11 While five States were more specifically and thoroughly examined in Chapter 5 for reasons first above mentioned. The other two countries, Brazil and Paraguay, were used as part of the analysis of good practice in Chapter 6 (6.3), specifically for their laudable good practice and for the purpose of proposing a bespoke statelessness determination procedure for Nigeria.

12 K Swider and M den Heijer 'Why union law can and should protect stateless persons' (2017) 19 (2) *European Journal of Migration and Law* 109.

Conclusion 203

verification system to ensure protection, identification, prevention, and eradication of the phenomenon in Nigeria. An SDP is necessary to identify stateless persons to enable them to enjoy State protection and access basic services until they can acquire a nationality.[13] The development of an SDP is urgent, as a sizable number of persons in Nigeria are at risk of statelessness.[14] Without an SDP, people could live in a perpetual state of nonexistence and be unable to access basic services.

One of the major reasons for the absence of data on statelessness in Nigeria could be linked to the absence of a procedure to determine statelessness. Given the absence of statelessness legislation in Nigeria, one can say that there is no agency of the government officially charged with a mandate for statelessness.[15] Consequently, no government agency is assessing the risk of statelessness or collecting and/or recording data of stateless persons or persons at risk of statelessness in Nigeria.

This absence of a statelessness mandate and absence of data, together with the lack of strict implementation of the use of the National Identity Number (NIN) of the National Identity Management Commission (NIMC) for access to basic services could be said to be responsible for the very little knowledge about statelessness in Nigeria, even amongst legal practitioners, academia, and civil society organizations in the country.

7.2.1.3 Absence of a Definition of Statelessness Determination Procedure

There is no explicit provision for States to develop an SDP in the Statelessness Conventions, neither is there a definition of SDP in current international and regional instruments. A review of the existing literature on statelessness and the right to nationality also revealed a gap concerning the definition of SDP. A definition of SDP is supposed to highlight the meaning of SDP to readers before they are introduced to the methods and application of an SDP. What is found in statelessness literature is arguably a collection of practices of what makes up an SDP without first giving the reader a concrete clue as to what SDP is about. Arguably, a definition of SDP, whether generally accepted or not, would play a role in introducing readers to what an SDP does, how it is done, and what is expected of a good SDP without being expected to read up an entire section or a chapter to get the meaning and its essence. Further to the absence of the definition of SDP in the Statelessness Conventions,[16] the UNHCR handbook on the

---

13 UNHCR *Statelessness determination procedures: Identifying and protecting stateless persons* (2014) 1.

14 As noted earlier, due to the absence of a legal framework in Nigeria, there is no official record of people who are stateless or at risk of statelessness in Nigeria.

15 Though Nigeria has ratified both the 1954 and 1961 Statelessness Conventions, it is yet to domesticate the conventions and designate an official focal agency.

16 'Whilst the 1954 Convention establishes the international legal definition of "stateless person" and the standards of treatment to which such individuals are entitled, it does not prescribe any mechanism to identify stateless persons as such.'

UNHCR *Handbook on protection of stateless persons. Op Cit* 6 at para. 8.

204 *Conclusion*

protection of stateless persons, and various UNHCR guidelines on statelessness proffer no definition of SDP either.

Part 2 of the UNHCR Handbook on the protection of stateless persons which focuses on SDPs offers no clear definition of an SDP either. Therefore, this book sought to bridge that gap to enable a smooth landing for readers and future studies in the field. For a definition of SDP in this book, the definition of stateless person in Article 1 of the 1954 Convention Relating to the Status of Stateless Persons was used: this provision describes a stateless person as 'a person who is not considered as a national by any State under the operation of its law.' Thus, this book proposed that an SDP is 'a procedure, whether administrative or judicial, meant to determine whether or not a person or a population is considered as national of any state under the operation of its law, to find durable solutions for the affected person or population. The solutions after recognition as a stateless person may range from a grant of protection status to an outright grant of nationality.'[17] See Part 4.2 above.

7.2.1.4 Why a Comparative Approach to Tackling the Issue of Statelessness and the Right to Nationality?

One of the main 'objectives of comparative law has traditionally been the systematic study of foreign laws with the view to deriving models that would assist the formulation and implementation of the legislative policies of States.' As noted earlier, a scholarly comparative law approach was employed in this book to inspire legislative changes to nationality law in Nigeria and in any State in the process of developing its SDP. To evaluate the existence of effective statelessness determination procedures, the book developed assessment criteria based on international standards and an assessment of best practices identified in other jurisdictions in Africa, Europe, and the Americas, especially States with effective Statelessness Determination Procedures (SDPs). These standards pertain to identification and prevention/reduction norms. The specific criteria formulated include: (a) legality and binding nature of SDP; (b) structure and location of SDP; (c) access to procedure; (d) procedural guarantees; (e) assessments of facts; (f) management of combined refugee and statelessness claims; (g) prospect for naturalization; and (h) review and appeal of decisions (see Chapter 4).

It is of note that no State can be considered a single 'best practice' example. Even those States which are frequently looked to as a model exhibit persisting gaps and face challenges.[18] Therefore, States without SDPs, and those with weak SDPs, need to be guided by certain criteria and good practices to develop a better procedure, with due respect for their national contexts. Using the theory of legal transplant, the book examined how legal, administrative, and institutional norms for the protection, prevention, and identification of statelessness

---

17 See Chapter 4, specifically Part 4.2 for more on SDPs.
18 See G Gyulai *Stateless determination and the protection status of stateless persons* ENS (2013) 7.

Conclusion   205

can be transplanted or adapted by existing institutions in the country, bearing in mind differences in legal cultures and factors that could facilitate or obstruct the transplant of SDP norms. This is bearing in mind the presence of 'common social problems in different legal orders,'[19] which in this case are the issue of statelessness and the right to nationality. Therefore, the book examined the place of legal borrowing and comparative law in resolving common legal and societal issues in borrowing States, linking it to developing a statelessness determination procedure for Nigeria. See Chapter 6 (particularly Part 6.3).

The selected reference States include Brazil, France, Ivory Coast, Moldova, Paraguay, and the United Kingdom, all known to have a statelessness determination procedure, as well as the Netherlands, known for its alternative procedure. While the Dutch alternative measure does not translate into protection of statelessness persons in the Netherlands, the Netherlands was referenced to determine the extent to which an alternative method of identifying stateless persons and keeping a record of stateless persons may provide a useful reference point for Nigeria, given the absence of a formal SDP. For ease of reference, a comparative Table of SDPs was developed (see Chapter 5, particularly Part 5.3).

7.2.1.5 Gaps in the Existing International and Regional Instruments

The issue of statelessness and the right to nationality have been a major issue of global significance since the beginning of the United Nations,[20] especially as no region of the world is free of the problem of statelessness. Therefore, there have been some international and regional instruments to tackle the issue. In this book, several international legal and policy frameworks on the right to nationality and prevention of statelessness were discussed in Chapter 3, emphasizing how sufficient or otherwise these frameworks are. Some of the major gaps identified in that chapter include, first, the gap relating to lack of provision allowing people access to the territory to apply for statelessness status. The second is absence of a specific approach to the issue of naturalization for stateless persons. And the third, on the absence of provisions against *refoulement*.

7.2.1.6 The Novelty of the Research Topic – Statelessness (Risk) in Nigeria

There have been many scholarly studies on citizenship law in Nigeria,[21] with only a few having sentences or a paragraph or two on statelessness. For instance,

---

19 G Mousourakis *Comparative law and legal traditions: Historical and contemporary perspectives* (2019) 284–285.
20 N Ahmad 'The right to nationality and the reduction of statelessness – the responses of the international migration law framework' (2017) 5 (1) *Groningen Journal of International Law* 2. See also L Van Waas 'The UN statelessness conventions' in A Edwards & L Van Waas (Eds.) *Nationality and statelessness under international law* (2014) 64.
21 See E Nwogugu 'Recent changes in Nigerian nationality and citizenship law' (1976) *International and Comparative Law Quarterly*, G Okeke and C Okeke 'The acquisition

206 Conclusion

Chidi Odinkalu's *Statelessness in Bakassi: How a Changed Border Left Inhabitants Adrift*[22] focuses only on the risk of statelessness of the Bakassi people affected by the ICJ judgment ceding Bakassi to Cameroon in 2002, while Bronwen Manby and Solomon Momoh's *Report on Citizenship Law: Nigeria*[23] focuses on citizenship law in Nigeria with only a few paragraphs describing the risk of statelessness in Nigeria. There have been no previous scholarly studies on Nigeria which focus (elaborately) on statelessness. To bridge this scholarly gap on the dangerous statelessness 'time bomb' in Nigeria, this book focused on 'statelessness,' while also examining the legislative and policy gaps on access to nationality in Nigeria, and proposed reforms and methods of ensuring protection, identification, and prevention of statelessness in Nigeria.

The novelty of a 'statelessness' focused research on Nigeria in itself could arguably be said to be a contribution to knowledge, especially against the background that there has been no previous significant literature on statelessness in the Nigerian context.

7.3 Conclusion

This book elaborates the peculiarity of the risk of statelessness in Nigeria and its implications for the society, proposes how to possibly bridge those gaps using examples from other States with fairly good state practice, and discusses how Nigeria can develop its statelessness determination procedure and nationality verification system to ensure protection, identification, prevention, and eradication of the phenomenon in Nigeria. As has been discussed, an SDP is necessary to identify stateless persons to enable them to enjoy State protection and access basic services until they can acquire a nationality.[24]

It is expected that this book will support researchers interested in broadening the scope of statelessness study in Nigeria with information, and serve as advocacy material for the UN, international and local organizations, and civil society groups working to ensure citizenship reforms in Nigeria. As Nigeria prepares to domesticate the 1954 and 1961 Statelessness Conventions and develop a statelessness determination procedure, it is further expected that this book feeds into good reference material for lawmakers in this regard.

---

of Nigerian citizenship by naturalization: An analytical approach' (2013) 8 (2) *Journal of Humanities and Social Science* (IOSR-JHSS); K Okoli, 'Nigerian citizenship law: A current perspective' (1990) *Journal of African Law*.

22 C Odinkalu 'Statelessness in Bakassi: How a changed border left inhabitants adrift' *Open Society Foundation* (2 April 2012).

23 B Manby and S Oseghale Momoh 'Report on citizenship law: Nigeria' Global Governance Programme (Global Citizenship Observatory (GLOBALCIT)) Country Reports, 2020/12, [Global Citizenship].

24 UNHCR *Statelessness determination procedures: Identifying and protecting stateless persons* (2014) 1.

Bibliography

Books and Chapters

M Adjami 'Statelessness and nationality in Côte d'Ivoire' (2016) https://www.refworld.org/docid/58594d114.html.

M Adjami & J Harrington 'The scope and content of article 15 of the universal declaration of human rights' (2008) 27 (3) *Refugee Survey Quarterly* 93–109.

JAH Baba 'The management of internally displaced persons and enhanced human security in North East Nigeria' (2019) https://bdex.eb.mil.br/jspui/bitstream/123456789/4934/1/MO%200031.pdf.

C Batchelor 'The 1954 convention relating to the status of stateless persons: Implementation within the European Union Member States and recommendations for harmonisation' UNHCR Department of International Protection UNHCR (2003).

F Benoît-Rohmer & H Klebes *Council of Europe Law: Towards a Pan-European legal area* (2005).

BK Blitz & M Lynch, eds *Statelessness and the benefits of citizenship: A comparative study* (2009).

J Brandvoll 'Deprivation of nationality: Limitations on rendering persons stateless under international law' in Alice Edwards and Laura van Waas *Nationality and statelessness under international law* (2014) 194–216.

A Byrnes & M Freeman 'The impact of the CEDAW convention: Paths to equality' *UNSW Law Research Paper* (2012), 2012–7.

M Chen-Wishart 'Legal transplant and undue influence: Lost in translation or a working misunderstanding' (2013) 62 *International & Comparative Law Quarterly* 1.

A Conte & R Burchill *Defining civil and political rights: The jurisprudence of the United Nations Human Rights Committee* (2016).

P de Cruz *Comparative law in a changing world* (1995).

GR de Groot 'Children, their right to a nationality and child statelessness' in A Edwards & L Van Waas *Nationality and statelessness under international law* (2014) 64–87.

GR de Groot, K Swider & O Vonk *Practice and approach in EU member states to prevent and end statelessness* (2015).

KM de Vries 'Right to respect for private and family life (Article 8)' in P. Van Dijk, F. Van Hoof, A. Van Rijn, & L. Zwaak *Theory and practice of the European Convention on Human Rights* (5th ed.) (2018) 667–733.

208 Bibliography

A Edwards 'The meaning of nationality in international law in an era of human rights' in A Edwards & L Van Waas *Nationality and statelessness under international law* (2014) 11–43.

HW Ehrmann *Comparative legal cultures* (1976).

W Ewald 'Comparative jurisprudence (II): The logic of legal transplants' (1995) 43(4) *The American Journal of Comparative Law* 489–510.

N Flowers *Human rights here and now: Celebrating the universal declaration of human rights* (1998).

MA Freeman, B Rudolf, C Chinkin, S Kroworsch & A Sherrier, eds *The UN convention on the elimination of all forms of discrimination against women: A commentary* (2012).

G Gábor *Statelessness determination procedures and the protection of stateless persons* (2013).

G Gábor 'The determination of statelessness and the establishment of a statelessness-specific protection regime' in A Edwards & L Van Waas *Nationality and statelessness under international law* (2014) 116–143 at 117.

G Gaja 'European community and union law and domestic (municipal) law' in R Wolfrum *The Max Planck encyclopedia of public international law* (2014) 822–827.

D Galligan *Law in modern society*. Clarendon Law Series (2006).

F Gilardi 'Transnational diffusion: Norms, ideas and policies' in Walter Carlsnaes, Thomas Risse-Kappen & Beth A Simmons *Handbook of international relations* (2012) 453–477.

R Govil & A Edwards 'Women, nationality and statelessness: The problem of unequal rights' in A Edwards & L Van Waas *Nationality and statelessness under international law* (2014) 169–193.

HL Ho *A philosophy of evidence law: Justice in the search for truth* (2008).

F Horn 'Conception and principles of citizenship in modern western democracies' (1998) 21 *Science and Technique of Democracy* 39–80.

Human Rights Watch 'They do not own this place: Government discrimination against 'Non-Indigenes' in Nigeria' 18(3(a)) (2006) *Human Rights Watch* 1–64.

Institute on Statelessness and Inclusion *The world's stateless*. Edited by Laura van Waas & Amal de Chickera (2014).

Institute on Statelessness and Inclusion *The world's stateless: Children*. Edited by Laura van Waas & Amal de Chickera (2017).

T Jan & F Jörgensen 'Legal effectiveness: Theoretical developments concerning legal transplants' (2005) 91(4) *ARSP. Archiv Für Rechts- Und Sozialphilosophie / Archives for Philosophy of Law and Social Philosophy* 515–534.

O Kahn-Freund 'On uses and misuses of comparative law' (1974) 37(1) *The Modern Law Review* 1–27.

M King 'Comparing legal cultures in the quest for law's identity' in D Nelken *Comparing legal cultures* (1997) 107–122.

K Krūma *EU citizenship, nationality and migrant status: An ongoing challenge* (2014).

Lawyers for Human Rights *Promoting citizenship and preventing statelessness in South Africa: A practitioner's guide* (2014).

TL Lee *Statelessness, human rights and gender: Irregular migrant workers from Burma in Thailand* (2005).

CA Malischewsk 'Where the exception is the norm: The production of statelessness in India' (2014) 2(8) *International Human Rights Internship Working Paper Series*.

B Manby *Citizenship law in Africa: A comparative study*. 3rd ed. (2016).

Bibliography 209

B Manby 'Nationality, migration and statelessness in West Africa: A study for UNHCR and IOM' (2015).

B Manby *Struggles for citizenship in Africa* (2009).

S Mancuso 'Legal transplants and economic development: Civil law Vs. common law?' in JC Oliveira & P Cardinal *One country, two systems, three legal orders – Perspectives of evolution* (2009) 75–90 https://link.springer.com/content/pdf/bfm%3A978-3-540-68572-2%2F1.pdf.

M Manly 'UNHCR's mandate and activities to address statelessness' in A Edwards & L van Waas *Nationality and statelessness under international law* (2014) 88–115.

H Massey *UNHCR and 'de Facto' statelessness* (2010).

U Mattei 'Efficiency in legal transplants: An essay in comparative law and economics' (1994) 14(1) *International Review of Law and Economics* 3–19.

N Monaghan *Law of evidence* (2015).

C de S Montesquieu, DW Carrithers & T Nugent. *The spirit of the law.* 1748. Translated by Thomas Nugent 1752 (2001) https://socialsciences.mcmaster.ca/econ/ugcm/3ll3/montesquieu/spiritoflaws.pdf.

J Morsink *The universal declaration of human rights: Origins, drafting, and intent* (2000).

G Mousourakis *Comparative law and legal traditions: Historical and contemporary perspectives* (2019).

D Nelken 'Comparative legal cultures' in G Bruinsma & D Weisburd *Encyclopedia of criminology and criminal justice* (2014) https://link.springer.com/referenceworkentry/10.1007/978-1-4614-5690-2_35.

BO Nwabueze *A constitutional history of Nigeria* (1982).

C Odinkalu 'Stateless in Bakassi: How a changed border left inhabitants adrift' (2012) https://www.opensocietyfoundations.org/voices/stateless-bakassi-how-changed-border-left-inhabitants-adrift.

KK Oyeyemi & LA La-Kadri *Realizing the rights of child under the Nigerian Child's Rights Act, 2003: An exploratory critique* https://docplayer.net/95392260-Realizing-the-rights-of-child-under-the-nigerian-child-s-rights-act-2003-an-exploratory-critique-by-kolawole-kazeem-oyeyemi.html.

M Redmayne 'Standards of proof in civil litigation' (1999) 62 *Modern Law Review* 167.

M Rürup 'Lives in Limbo: Statelessness after two world wars' (2011) 49 *Bulletin of German Historic Institute (GHI)* 113–134.

CMJ Ryngaert 'Whither territoriality? The European Union's use of territoriality to set norms with universal effects' *The European Union's Use of Territoriality to Set Norms with Universal Effects (November 11, 2014)* (2014).

W Schabas 'Introductory essay: The drafting and significance of the universal declaration of human rights' in W. Schaba *The universal declaration of human rights: The travaux préparatoires* (2013).

MN Shaw *International law.* 5th ed. (2003).

IA Shearer & BR Opeskin 'Nationality and statelessness' in B Opeskin, R Perruchoud & J Redpath-Cross *Foundations of international migration law* (2012) 93–122.

Z Shen 'Legal transplant and comparative law' (1999) 51(4) *Revue internationale de droit comparé* 853–857.

VN Sherry & Human Rights Watch/Middle East 'Syria: The silenced Kurds' (Ser. [publications]) (1996) 8(4(e)) *Human Rights Watch/Middle East.*

DL Sloss 'Domestic application of treaties' in Duncan Hollis *The Oxford guide to treaties* (2011). Santa Clara Univ. Legal Studies Research Paper No. 08-11.

210   Bibliography

M Solinas *Legal evolution and hybridisation: The law of shares transfer in England* (2014) https://intersentia.com/en/legal-evolution-and-hybridisation.html.

HJ Steiner, P Alston & R Goodman *International human rights in context: Law, politics, morals, text and materials.* 3rd ed. (2008).

K Swider 'Protection and identification of stateless persons through EU law' *Amsterdam Law School legal Studies Research Paper* 2014-38 (2014).

J Tucker 'The indefinite statelessness of refugees in Denmark and Sweden: Comparing the impacts of the temporary asylum laws' (2017) https://mau.diva-portal.org/smash/get/diva2:1409996/FULLTEXT01.pdf.

EI Utuk 'Britain's colonial administrations and developments, 1861–1960: An analysis of Britain's colonial administrations and developments in Nigeria' (1975) Dissertations and Theses. Paper 2525.

H Van Eijken *EU citizenship & the constitutionalisation of the European Union* (2015).

H Van Eijken & P Phoa 'Exploring obstacles in exercising core EU citizenship rights' (2016) 7 *bEUcitizen Project Deliverable* 1–220.

L Van Waas 'Nationality matters: Statelessness under international law' A thesis to obtain the degree of Doctor at the University of Tilburg (2008). Published in School of Human Rights Research Series, Volume 29.

L Van Waas 'The UN statelessness conventions' in A Edwards & L Van Waas *Nationality and statelessness under international law* (2014) 64–87.

K Van Wallendael *Legal transplants: Profitable borrowing or harmful dependency? The use of the legal transplant framework for the adoption of EU law: The case of Croatia* (2014).

M Vremis & I Popov 'Analytical report regarding stateless persons in the Republic of Moldova' (2017) https://cda.md/files/Analytical_Report_Mapping_en_final_rev_26.11.2017.pdf.

A Watson *Legal transplants: An approach to comparative law* (1993).

A Watson *Society and legal change*, 2nd ed. (2010).

JH Weiler 'European citizenship and human rights' in A Winter Jan, M Curtin Deider, E Kellermann Alfred & De Witte Bruno *Reforming the treaty on European Union. The legal debate* (1996) 57–68.

K Weyland *Bounded rationality and policy diffusion: Social sector reform in Latin America* (2009).

Journals

IM Abbass 'No retreat no surrender: Conflict for survival between Fulani pastoralists and farmers in Northern Nigeria' (2012) 8(1) *European Scientific Journal* 331–346.

AG Adebayo 'Contemporary dimensions of migration among historically migrant Nigerians' (1997) 32(1–2) *Journal of Asian and African Studies* 93–109.

A Adepoju, A Boulton & M Levin 'Promoting integration through mobility: Free movement under ECOWAS' (2010) 29(3) *Refugee Survey Quarterly* 120–144.

AO Afon, MA Asani, SA Adeyinka, MS Hasan, AZ Jimah, TU Ilogho, TG Faborode, GB Faniran & KO Popoola 'Linkages between responses to the available amenities and expressed environment-related health needs in international refugee camp, Oru-Ijebu, Nigeria' (2010) 142 *WIT Transactions on Ecology and the Environment* 69–78.

Bibliography 211

AT Aghemelo & S Ibhasebhor 'Colonialism as a source of boundary dispute and conflict among African States: The world court judgement on the Bakassi Pennisula and its implications for Nigeria' (2006) 13(3) *Journal of Social Sciences* 177–181.

N Ahmad 'The right to nationality and the reduction of statelessness – The responses of the international migration law framework' (2017) 5(1) *Groningen Journal of International Law* 1–22.

G Ajani 'By chance and prestige: Legal transplants in Russia and Eastern Europe' (1995) 43(1) *The American Journal of Comparative Law* 93–117.

OS Akinwumi 'Legal impediments on the practical implementation of the Child Right Act 2003' (2010) 37(3) *International Journal of Legal Information* 10.

CI Alarima & FE Obikwelu 'Assessment of utilization of primary health care services among settled Fulani agro-pastoralists in Ogun State, Nigeria' (2018) 17(1) *Agro-Science* 27–34.

AU Alkali, UA Jimeta, AI Magashi & TM Buba 'Nature and sources of Nigerian legal system: An exorcism of a wrong notion' (2014) 5(4) *International Journal of Business, Economics and Law* 1–10.

AA Alshorbagy 'On the failure of a legal transplant: The case of Egyptian takeover law' (2012) 22 *Indiana International & Comparative Law Review* 237.

M Amos 'Transplanting human rights norms: The case of the United Kingdom's Human Rights Act' (2013) 35 *Human Rights Quarterly* 386.

RA Atuguba, FXD Tuokuu & V Gbang 'Statelessness in West Africa: An assessment of stateless populations and legal, policy, and administrative frameworks in Ghana' (2020) 8(1) *Journal on Migration and Human Security* 14–31.

EO Babatunde 'Rethinking the 1999 constitution within recent dynamics of Nigeria's National Security: Indigene-settler crisis in jos, plateau, state in focus' (2017) 62 *Journal of Law and Pol'y & Globalization* 45.

A Babo 'The crisis of public policies in Côted'ivoire: Land law and the nationality trap in Tabou's rural communities' (2013) 83(Special Issue 1) *Journal of International African Institute (IAI)* (Land Politics in Africa: Constituent Authority, Property and Persons).

JR Bassey 'An assessment of impact of neglect of history on political stability in African countries: The case of Cote d'Ivoire' (2014) 6(9) *African Journal of History and Culture* 149–163.

CA Batchelor 'Statelessness and the problem of resolving nationality status' (1998) 10(1–2) *International Journal of Refugee Law* 156–182.

CA Batchelor 'Transforming international legal principles into national law: The right to a nationality and the avoidance of statelessness' (2006) 25(3) *Refugee Survey Quarterly* 8–25.

F Baye 'Implications of the Bakassi conflict resolution for Cameroon' (2010) 10(1) *African Journal on Conflict Resolution* 9–34.

D Berkowitz, K Pistor & JF Richard 'The transplant effect' (2003) 51 *American Journal of Comparative Law* 163.

K Bianchini 'A comparative analysis of statelessness determination procedures in 10 EU states' (2017) 29(1) *International Journal of Refugee Law* 42–83.

K Bianchini 'Protecting stateless persons: The implementation of the convention relating to the status of stateless persons across EU states' (2018) 11 *International Refugee Law Series* 1–371.

212 *Bibliography*

Đ Bolanča Kekez 'The relevance of the universal declaration of human rights' in *International workshop on law and politics-proceedings booklet* (2013) 333–344.

JC Carter & J Bezzano 'Statelessness in practice: Implementation of the UK statelessness application procedure' University of Liverpool Law Clinic (July 2018).

RJ Cook 'Enforcing women's rights through law' (1995) 3(2) *Gender & Development* 8–15.

RJ Cook 'Reservations to the convention on the elimination of all forms of discrimination against women' (1989) 30 *Virginia Journal of International Law* 643.

A Darr 'The role of institutions in generating successful legal transplants: A comparative analysis of the adoption of competition laws in India and Pakistan' (2019) 14(1) *Asian Journal of Comparative Law* 65–89.

R de Groot *Survey on rules on loss of nationality in international treaties and case law* (2013).

M de Jong & S Stoter 'Institutional transplantation and the rule of law: How this interdisciplinary method can enhance the legitimacy of international organisations' (2009) 2 *Erasmus Law Review* 311.

RM D'Sa 'The African charter on human and peoples' rights: Problems and prospects for regional action' (1981) 10 *Australian Yearbook of International Law* 101.

C Dumbrava *Comparative report: Citizenship in central and eastern Europe* (2017) European University Institute (EUI) and GLOBALCIT. Comparative Report 2017.

A Eckert 'Universality by consensus: The evolution of universality in the drafting of the UDHR' (2001) 1(2) *Human Rights & Human Welfare* 5.

FH Eid 'Citizenship, community and national identity: Young people perceptions in a Bahraini context' (2015) 7 *Journal of Case Studies in Education* 1–32.

E Fabusoro & A Oyegbami 'Key issues in livelihoods security of migrant Fulani pastoralists: Empirical evidence from Southwest Nigeria' (2009) 4(2) *Journal of Humanities Social Sciences and Creative Arts* 1–20.

M Foster & H Lambert 'Statelessness as a human rights issue: A concept whose time has come' (2016) 28(4) *International Journal of Refugee Law* 564–584.

M Foster, J McAdam & D Wadley 'Part one: The protection of stateless persons in Australian law-the rationale for a statelessness determination procedure' (2016) 40 *Melbourne University Law Review* 401.

M Fullerton 'The intersection of statelessness and refugee protection in US asylum policy' (2014) 2(3) *Journal on Migration and Human Security* 144–164.

M Fullerton 'Without protection: Refugees and statelessness-A commentary and challenge' (2013) *Brooklyn Law School, Legal Studies Paper* 351.

R Gittleman 'The African charter on human and peoples' rights: A legal analysis' (1981) 22 *Virginia Journal of International Law* 67.

TS Goldbach 'Why legal transplants?' (2019) 15 *Annual Review of Law and Social Science* 583–601.

I Goris, J Harrington & S Köhn 'Statelessness: What it is and why it matters' (2009) 32 *Forced Migration Review* 4.

L Gregg, C Nash & N Oakeshott 'Mapping statelessness in The United Kingdom' (2011) *UNHCR report* 1–164.

G Gyulai 'Statelessness in the EU framework for international protection' (2012) 14(3) *European Journal of Migration and Law* 279–295.

Bibliography 213

H Hannum 'The status of the universal declaration of human rights in national and international law' (1995) 25 *Georgia Journal of International and Comparative Law* 287.

A Harvey 'Statelessness: The 'de facto' Statelessness Debate' (2010) 24 *Journal of IANL* 257.

L Hodson 'Women's rights and the periphery: CEDAW's optional protocol' (2014) 25(2) *European Journal of International Law* 561–578.

DL Horowitz 'Presidents vs. parliaments: Comparing democratic systems' (1990) 1(4) *Journal of Democracy* 73–79.

B Karumi 'Nigerian legal system and the protection of the right against torture under emergency situation: The Boko Haram insurgency experience' (2017) 2(2) *Journal of Law and Global Policy* 1–12.

T Kerikmae 'European convention on nationality and states' competence: The issue of human rights' (1997) 2 *Juridica International* 25.

K Knop 'Here and there: International law in domestic courts' (1999) 32 *New York University Journal of International Law and Politics* 501.

L Krappmann 'The weight of the child's view (Article 12 of the Convention on the Rights of the Child)' (2010) 18(4) *The International Journal of Children's Rights* 501–513.

P Legrand 'The impossibility of "legal transplants"' (1997) 4(2) *Maastricht Journal of European and Comparative Law* 111–124.

HM Liesl *Legal identity for all – Ending statelessness in SADC. Goal 16 of the sustainable development goals* (2016) Southern Africa Litigation Centre.

RB Lillich 'The growing importance of customary international human rights law' (1995) 25 *Georgia Journal of International and Comparative Law* 1.

M Lynch 'Lives on hold: The human cost of statelessness' (2005) *Refugees International* 1–52.

M Lynch & P Ali *Buried alive: Stateless Kurds in Syria* (2006).

M Lynch & T Cook 'Left behind: Stateless Russians search for equality in Estonia' (2004) *Refugee International* 1–2.

B Manby 'People without a country: The state of statelessness' (2016) 17 *Insights on Law and Society* 14–19.

B Manby 'Who belongs? Statelessness and nationality in West Africa' *The Online Journal of Migration Policy Institute* https://www.migrationpolicy.org/article/who-belongs-statelessness-and-nationality-west-africa.

B Manby & SO Momoh 'Report on citizenship law: Nigeria' (2020) *Global citizenship observatory* (GLOBALCIT) RSCAS/GLOBALCIT-CR 2020, 12 July 2020.

M Manly, L Van Waas, A Berry & L Fransman *Statelessness: The impact of international law and current challenges* (2014) Chatham House Royal Institute of International Affairs – International Law Programme Meeting Summary, 4 November 2014.

D Marsh & JC Sharman 'Policy diffusion and policy transfer' (2009) 30(3) *Policy Studies* 269–288.

SE Merry 'New legal realism and the ethnography of transnational law' (2006) 31(4) *Law & Social Inquiry* 975–995.

JM Miller 'A typology of legal transplants: Using sociology, legal history and argentine examples to explain the transplant process' (2003) 51(4) *The American Journal of Comparative Law* 839–886.

214 *Bibliography*

T Molnár 'Remembering the forgotten: International legal regime protecting the stateless persons-stocktaking and new tendencies' (2014) 11 *US-China Law Review* 822.

T Molnár 'Stateless persons under international law and EU law: A comparative analysis concerning their legal status, with particular attention to the added value of the EU legal order' (2010) 51(4) *Acta Juridica Hungarica* 293–304.

SO Momoh, H van Eijken & C Ryngaert 'Statelessness determination procedures: Towards a bespoke procedure for Nigeria' (2020) 2 *Statelessness & Citizenship Review* 86.

LG Morra & AC Friedlander *Case study evaluations* (1999).

IJ Mosquera Valderrama 'Legal transplants and comparative law' (2004) *International Law Journal* 261–276.

G Mousourakis 'Legal transplants and legal development: A jurisprudential and comparative law approach' (2013) 54(3) *Acta Juridica Hungarica* 219–236.

G Mousourakis 'The development and function of equity in the English common law tradition' in *Comparative law and legal traditions* (2019) 251–280.

G Ngbea 'Poverty in northern Nigeria' (2014) 2(2) *Asian Journal of Humanities and Social Studies*.

ES Nwauche 'Enforcing ECOWAS law in West African national courts' (2011) *Journal of African Law* 181–202.

EI Nwogugu 'Recent changes in Nigerian nationality and citizenship law' (1976) 25 *ICLQ* 432–439.

FD Nzarga 'Impediments to the domestication of Nigeria Child Rights Act by the states' (2016) 6(9) *Research on Humanities and Social Sciences* 123–130.

GO Obiechina 'Violation of child's rights in Nigeria: Implications for child health' (2014) 5(1) *Academic Research International* 151.

JO Ogbonnaya & CV Iteshi 'The jurisprudential issues arising from legal transplant: An appraisal' (2016) 50 *Journal of Law, Policy & Globalization* 1.

CE Okeke & MI Anushiem 'Implementation of treaties in Nigeria: Issues, challenges and the way forward' (2018) 9(2) *Nnamdi Azikiwe University Journal of International Law and Jurisprudence* 216–229.

GN Okeke & CE Okeke 'The acquisition of Nigerian citizenship by naturalization: An analytical approach' (2013) 8(2) *IOSR Journal of Humanities and Social Science (IOSR-JHSS)* 58–63.

KC Okoli 'Nigerian citizenship law: A current perspective' (1990) 34 *Journal of African Law* 27.

MP Okom & JA Dada 'ECOWAS citizenship: A critical review' (2012) 2(3) *American Journal of Social Issues & Humanities* 100–116.

F Omotoso 'Indigeneity and problems of citizenship in Nigeria' (2010) 7(2) *Pakistan Journal of Social Sciences* 146–150.

D Owen 'On the right to have nationality rights: Statelessness, citizenship and human rights' (2018) 65(3) *Netherlands International Law Review* 299–317.

D Phillips & Y Berman 'Social quality and community citizenship' (2001) 4(1) *European Journal of Social Work* 17–28.

L Pilgram 'European Convention on Nationality (ECN) 1997 and European nationality laws' (2011) *Research for the European Union Democracy Observatory (EUDO) citizenship observatory policy briefs* (EUDO Policy Brief No. 4).

L Pilgram 'International law and European nationality laws' (2011) *Research for the EUDO citizenship observatory comparative reports* CITMODES 2011.

Bibliography 215

N Radnai 'Statelessness determination in Europe: Towards the implementation of regionally harmonised national SDPs' (2017) Institute on Statelessness and Inclusion.

M Siems 'Malicious legal transplants' (2018) 38(1) *Legal Studies* 103–119.

RG Small 'Towards a theory of contextual transplants' (2005) 19 *Emory International Law Review* 1431.

C Sokoloff & R Lewis 'Denial of citizenship: A challenge to human security' (2005) *Report prepared for the Advisory Board on Human Security with the support of the Ford Foundation.*

M Stiller 'Statelessness in international law: A historic overview' (2012) 37 *DAJV Newsletter* 94.

P Sun 'Drafting process of the UDHR with non-western influence' in P. Sun *Historic achievement of a common standard* (2018) 137–179.

K Swider 'Protection and identification of stateless persons through EU law' (2014) *Amsterdam Law School legal studies research paper* 2014-38.

K Swider & M den Heijer 'Why union law can and should protect stateless persons' (2017) 19(2) *European Journal of Migration and Law* 101–135.

FJ Taiwo 'Transforming the Almajiri education for the benefit of the Nigerian society' (2013) 3(9) *Journal of Educational and Social Research* 67.

N Tebbe & RL Tsai 'Constitutional borrowing' (2010) 108(4) *Michigan Law Review* 459–522.

LA Thio 'Reading rights rightly: The UDHR and its creeping influence on the development of Singapore public law' (2008) *Singapore Journal of Legal Studies* 264.

J Tucker 'Questioning de facto statelessness: By looking at de facto citizenship' (2014) 19(1–2) *Tilburg Law Review* 276–284.

DC Turack 'The African charter on human and peoples' rights: Some preliminary thoughts' (1983) 17 *Akron Law Review* 365.

NJ Udombana 'Toward the African Court on human and peoples' rights: Better late than never' (2000) 3 *Yale Human Rights & Development Law Journal* 45.

H Van Eijken 'European citizenship and the competence of member states to grant and to withdraw the nationality of their nationals' (2011) 27 *Merkourios-Utrecht Journal of International and European Law* 65.

D Vitkauskaite-Meurice 'The Arab charter on human rights: The naissance of new regional human rights system or a challenge to the universality of human rights?' (2010) 1(119) *Jurisprudencija* 165–180.

O Vonk, MP Vink & GR de Groot *Protection against statelessness: Trends and regulations in Europe* (2013).

S Waltz 'Reclaiming and rebuilding the history of the universal declaration of human rights' (2002) 23(3) *Third World Quarterly* 437–448.

A Watson 'Aspects of reception of law' (1996) 44(2) *The American Journal of Comparative Law* 335–351.

A Watson 'Legal change: Sources of law and legal culture' (1983) 131(5) *University of Pennsylvania Law Review* 1121–1157.

P Weis 'The United Nations Convention on the reduction of statelessness, 1961' (1962) 11(4) *International & Comparative Law Quarterly* 1073–1096.

D Weissbrodt & C Collins 'The human rights of stateless persons' (2006) 28 *Human Rights Quarterly* 245–276.

H Xanthaki 'Legal transplants in legislation: Defusing the trap' (2008) 57 *International and Comparative Law Quarterly* 659.

216 *Bibliography*

J Yinka Fashagba 'Legislative oversight under the Nigerian presidential system' (2009) 15(4) *The Journal of Legislative Studies* 439–459.

L Yoshikawa & M Teff 'Bangladesh: The silent crisis' (2011) *Refugees international field report* (19 April 2011).

PK Yu 'Customizing fair use transplants' (2018) 7(1) *Laws* 9.

MA Yusha'u, AK Tsafe, SI Babangida & NI Lawal 'Problems and prospects of integrated almajiri education in northern Nigeria' (2013) 2(3) *Scientific Journal of Pure and Applied Sciences* 125–134.

A Zimmermann 'Council of Europe: European convention on nationality' (1998) 37(1) *International Legal Materials* 44–55.

Presented Papers

IA Abdulqadir 'The Almajiri system of education in Nigeria today' (2003) A paper presented at the *21st Convocation Ceremony of Bayero University Kano.*

DC Bach 'Nigeria: Towards a country without a state' (2004) In paper delivered at the conference on *Nigeria: Maximizing Pro-Poor Growth: Regenerating the Socio-Economic Database*, organized by Overseas Development Institute in collaboration with Nigeria Economic Summit Group, London, 16–17.

SE Edeko 'Statelessness: The implication of the deprivation of nationality in Africa' (2017) *Public lecture at Baze University, Abuja to Mark UNHCR Nigeria 3rd anniversary of the #ibelong campaign*, November 2017.

E Örücü 'Family trees for legal systems: Towards a contemporary approach' (2002) In paper presented at the *Conference of Epistemology and Methodology of Comparative Law in the Light of European Integration*, Brussels, 24–26 October 2002.

Reports and Guidelines from International/Regional Bodies

Z Albarazi *Stateless: A global issue.* Amnesty International workshop on Arbitrary Deprivation of Citizenship (October 2016).

EEO Alemika, I Chukwuma, D Lafratta, D Messerli & J Souckova 'Rights of the child in Nigeria: Report on the implementation of the convention on the rights of the child by Nigeria' Geneva: World Organisation Against Torture/Organization Mondiale Contre la Torture (OMCT)/Cleen Foundation (2005).

Annual Report of the United Nations High Commissioner for Human Rights and Reports of the Office of the High Commissioner and the Secretary-General *Human rights and arbitrary deprivation of nationality*, A/HRC/25/28 (19 December 2013).

CA Batchelor, P Leclerc & M Achiron *Nationality and statelessness: A handbook for Parliamentarians* (2005).

Centre for Reproductive Health *The protocol on the rights of women in Africa: An instrument for advancing reproductive and sexual rights* Briefing Paper (February 2006).

V Cojocariu *Statelessness in the Republic of Moldova: A story of success.* Laboratory Initiative for Development (2019).

Commission on Human Security 'Human security now: Protecting and empowering people' New York (2003).

Bibliography 217

Committee on the Rights of the Child 'Concluding observations of the Committee on the Rights of the Child, Nigeria' U.N. Doc. CRC/C/15/Add.61 (1996).

Council of Europe 'European Court of human rights, deprivation of citizenship' January 2018 http://www.refworld.org/docid/5a5f7ce94.html.

Council of Europe: Parliamentary Assembly 'Access to nationality and the effective implementation of the European convention on nationality' (23 January 2014).

A de Chickera 'Stateless persons in detention' *Legal working paper: The protection of stateless persons in detention under international law.* The Equal Rights Trust (January 2009).

A de Chickera 'The protection of stateless persons in detention under international law' *Legal working paper: Project 'stateless persons in detention'* prepared for The Equal Rights Trust (ERT) (2009).

Department of Political Affairs African Union Commission 'Statelessness impact on Africa's development and the need for its eradication, The African Union approach to the right to nationality in Africa' http://www.achpr.org/files/news/2016/07/d249/presentation_approach_on_statelessness_in_africa_dpa_auc.pdf.

Y Dina, J Akintayo & F Ekundayo 'Guide to Nigerian legal information' *Globalex. Global Law and Justice* (2020) https://www.nyulawglobal.org/globalex/Nigeria1.html.

Economic Community of West African States (ECOWAS) *Joint statement of the ECOWAS ministers responsible for nationality matters on the ministerial meeting for the validation and adoption of the banjul plan of action to eradicate statelessness in the ECOWAS region* (9 May 2017) https://www.refworld.org/docid/5915c7004.html.

ECOWAS *Strategy on the adoption of the draft protocol to the African charter on human and peoples' rights on the right to nationality and the eradication of statelessness in Africa* (2017).

ECOWAS Commission *ECOWAS members adopt a declaration on eradication of statelessness in West Africa* (2015). Joint UNHCR/ECOWAS press release http://www.ecowas.int/ecowas-members-adopt-a-declaration-on-eradication-of-statelessness-in-west-africa/.

Global Campaign for Equal Nationality Rights, UNHCR and UNICEF 'Gender discrimination and childhood statelessness' (2019) https://www.unhcr.org/ibelong/wp-content/uploads/Gender-discrimination-childhood-statelessness-web.pdf.

L Gregg, C Nash & N Oakeshott 'Mapping statelessness in the United Kingdom' (2011) *UNHCR Report* 1–164.

Home Office *Administrative review* Version 8.0 (6 April 2017) https://assets.publishing.service.gov.uk/government/uploads/system/uploads/attachment_data/file/618626/admin_review_guidance_v8_0.pdf.

Home Office *Administrative review* Version 20.0 (2021) https://assets.publishing.service.gov.uk/government/uploads/system/uploads/attachment_data/file/806921/Admin-review-guidance-v10.0-ext.pdf.

Home Office *Asylum policy instruction statelessness and applications for leave to remain* Version 2.0 (2016).

Home Office *Nationality: Good character requirement* Version 2.0 (2020) https://assets.publishing.service.gov.uk/government/uploads/system/uploads/attachment_data/file/770960/good-character-guidance.pdf.

218 *Bibliography*

House of Commons Library 'The Treaty of Lisbon: Amendments to the Treaty establishing the European Community' *Research Paper* 07/86 (6 December 2007). Introductory page researchbriefings.files.parliament.uk/documents/RP07 -86/RP07-86.pdf.

MO Hutson *Report on nationality, including statelessness.* International Law Commission (1952) https://legal.un.org/ilc/documentation/english/a_cn4_50.pdf.

W Iliyasu 'A critical assessment on the exploitation of Almajirai (beggars) labour in Northern Nigeria' (2019) https://www.researchgate.net/publication /330135447_A_Critical_Assessment_on_the_Exploitation_of_Almajirai_beggars _Labour_in_Northern_Nigeria.

International Law Commission, 'Yearbook of The International Law Commission 1953 Volume II' *Nationality, Including Statelessness.* Document A/CN.4/64, *Report on the elimination or reduction of statelessness* (30 March 1953).

IPU and UNHCR *Nationality and statelessness handbook for parliamentarians N° 22.* (2014).

ISI *ASKV refugee support, European network on statelessness and defence for children – The Netherlands.* Joint Submission to the Human Rights Council at the 27th Session of the Universal Periodic Review the Netherlands (22 September 2016).

ISI & La Coalition De La Société Civile De Lutte Contre L'Apatridie Joint Submission to the Human Rights Council at the 33rd session of the universal periodic review Côte d'Ivoire (2019).

U Kilkelly *The right to respect for private and family life: A guide to the implementation of Article 8 of the European convention on Human Rights* (August 2003). *Human rights handbooks*, No. 1.

Meeting of AU Member States on the Draft Protocol on the Right to a Nationality in Africa 'A press release' (7 May 2018). Kenya Human Rights Commission https:// www.khrc.or.ke/images/docs/AbidjanMeetingonNationalityStatelessnessPro tocolMay72018.pdf.

Meeting of the Committee on Trade, Customs, Immigration Customs, Immigration, Accra (25–27 September 2007).

Migrants Resource Centre, University of Liverpool Law Clinic, European Network on Statelessness, and Institute on Statelessness and Inclusion *Joint submission to the Human Rights Council at the 27th session of the universal periodic review,* United Kingdom (22 September 2016) https://www.statelessness.eu/sites/www .statelessness.eu/files/attachments/resources/ISI-MRC-LLC-ENS-UK-UPR -Submission-Session-27-2016.pdf.

Nwankwo, Oby 'Briefing on the domestication of the convention on the elimination of all forms of discrimination against women (CEDAW)' (n.d.) Civil Resource Development and Documentation Centre (CIRDDOC), Nigeria.

OHCHR *CCPR general comment no. 17: Article 24 (rights of the child).* Adopted at the Thirty-fifth session of the Human Rights Committee (7 April 1989).

OHCHR 'The United Nations Human Rights Treaty System Fact Sheet No. 30/ Rev.1' Geneva (2012) https://www.ohchr.org/Documents/Publications/ FactSheet30Rev1.pdf.

Open Society Justice Initiative 'African court on human and peoples' rights' *Fact Sheet* (June 2013).

Open Society Justice Initiative 'Human rights and legal identity: Approaches to combating statelessness and arbitrary deprivation of nationality' In *Thematic conference paper* (May 2006).

Bibliography 219

OSCE and UNHCR (2017) *Handbook on statelessness in the OSCE area: International standards and good practices.*

Principles Relating to the Status of National Institutions (The Paris Principles). Adopted by General Assembly resolution 48/134 (20 December 1993).

Submission by the United Nations High Commissioner for Refugees for the Office of the High Commissioner for Human Rights' Compilation Report Universal Periodic Review: 2nd Cycle, 26th Session on Republic of Moldova (2016).

Submission by the United Nations High Commissioner for Refugees for the Office of the High Commissioner for Human Rights' Compilation Report Universal Periodic Review: 3rd Cycle, 33rd Session for COTE D'IVOIRE (2018).

Summary Conclusions Expert meeting convened by the Office of the United Nations High Commissioner for Refugees, Tunis, Tunisia (31 October–1 November 2013) https://www.refworld.org/pdfid/533a754b4.pdf.

The Advisory Committee on Migration Affairs (ACVZ) *No country of one's own.* An Advisory Report on Treaty Protection for Stateless Persons in the Netherlands. The Hague (September 2014).

The ECOWAS Vanguard *Sovereignty, supra-nationality and trade: The case of ECOWAS laws.* NANTS Regional Trade Advocacy Series. Volume 2 Issue 4 (February 2013).

The Home Office *United Kingdom: Applications for leave to remain as a stateless* (1 May 2013).

The UN *Yearbook of the International Law Commission 1961.* Summary records of the thirteenth session (1 May – 7 July 1961).

Thomas Huddleston 'Republic of Moldova: A migrant integration policy index assessment' *OSCE & ODIHR, Migration Policy Group* (September 2015) https://www.osce.org/odihr/201021?download=true.

UK Home Office *Asylum policy instruction statelessness and applications for leave to remain.* Version 2.0 (2016).

Uliana Ermolaeva, Elisabeth Faltinat & Dārta Tentere *The concept of 'stateless persons' in European Union Law.* Final Report, Amsterdam International Law Clinic (August 2017) euromedmonitor.org/uploads/reports/Stateless-EN.pdf.

UN *History of the document: Universal declaration of human rights* http://www.un .org/en/sections/universal-declaration/history-document/index.html.

UN *The foundation of international human rights law* http://www.un.org/en/ sections/universal-declaration/foundation-international-human-rights-law/index .html.

UN Audio Visual Library of International Law 'Convention on the rights of the child' New York (20 November 1989) http://legal.un.org/avl/ha/crc/crc.html.

UN General Assembly *Annual report of the United Nations High Commissioner for Human Rights and reports of the Office of the High Commissioner and the Secretary-General'* A/HRC/25/28 (19 December 2013).

UNHCR '50th anniversary of the 1954 convention relating to the status of stateless persons' Panel Discussion (6 October 2004) (1500–1630) Conference Room XIX, Palais des Nations, Geneva https://www.refworld.org/pdfid/415ae0f94.pdf.

UNHCR *A compilation of summary conclusions from UNHCR's expert meetings* (2012).

UNHCR *Acceding to the UN statelessness conventions.* Ending Statelessness within 10 Years – Good Practices Paper Action 9 (2015).

220   *Bibliography*

UNHCR *Action to address statelessness—A strategy note.* Report, UNHCR (March 2010).

UNHCR *Background note on gender equality, nationality laws and statelessness,* 8 March 2018.

UNHCR *Background note on gender equality, nationality laws and statelessness.* Geneva (2020).

UNHCR *Commemorating the refugee and statelessness conventions.* 2010–2011 A Compilation of Summary Conclusions from UNHCR's Expert Meetings (2012).

UNHCR *Conclusion on identification, prevention and reduction of statelessness and protection of stateless persons No. 106 (LVII)* (2006). Executive Committee 56th session. Contained in United Nations General Assembly Document A/AC.96/1035.

UNHCR *Côte d'Ivoire adopts Africa's first legal process to identify and protect stateless people* (4 September 2020) https://www.unhcr.org/news/press/2020/9/5f51f33b4/cote-divoire-adopts-africas-first-legal-process-identify-protect-stateless.html.

UNHCR 'Côte d'Ivoire factsheet' (January 2020) https://reliefweb.int/sites/reliefweb.int/files/resources/UNHCR%20C%C3%B4te%20d%27Ivoire%20Factsheet%20-%20January%202020.pdf.

UNHCR *Draft protocol to the African charter on human and peoples' rights on the specific aspects of the right to a nationality and the eradication of statelessness in Africa UNHCR's observations* (2018).

UNHCR *Ending statelessness in South Eastern Europe: #IBelong Campaign* (2018).

UNHCR *Ending statelessness within 10 years.* A special report (4 Nov 2014).

UNHCR *Expert meeting statelessness determination procedures and the status of stateless persons summary conclusions* (2010).

UNHCR *First anniversary of the Abidjan Declaration on the eradication of statelessness* (25 February 2016) http://www.unhcr.org/news/press/2016/2/56ceda796/first-anniversary-abidjan-declaration-eradication-statelessness.html#.

UNHCR *Global action plan to end 2014–24 statelessness* (November 2014).

UNHCR *Good practices in nationality laws for the prevention and reduction of statelessness.* Handbook for Parliamentarians No. 29 (2018).

UNHCR *Good practices paper – action 6: Establishing statelessness determination procedures to protect stateless persons* (2016).

UNHCR *Handbook on protection of stateless persons under the 1954 convention on relating to the status of stateless persons.* Geneva (2014).

UNHCR *I am here, I belong: The urgent need to end childhood statelessness* (2015).

UNHCR *Information and accession package: The 1954 convention relating to the status of stateless persons and the 1961 convention on the reduction of statelessness.* First published in June 1996; revised (January 1999) https://www.refworld.org/pdfid/3ae6b3350.pdf.

UNHCR *Mapping statelessness in Belgium - Summary report* (2012).

UNHCR *Mobilizing governments and civil society* #ibelong Campaign (2017) http://www.refworld.org/pdfid/59661b4e4.pdf.

UNHCR *Nigeria situation: Supplementary appeal January–December 2017* (2017) https://www.unhcr.org/597704b87.pdf.

UNHCR *Nigeria vulnerability screening report* (November 2017).

UNHCR *Note on burden and standard of proof in refugee claims* (1998) https://www.refworld.org/pdfid/3ae6b3338.pdf.

Bibliography 221

UNHCR *Preventing and reducing statelessness: The 1961 convention on the reduction of statelessness* (2010).

UNHCR *Protecting the rights of stateless persons: The 1954 convention relating to the status of stateless persons* (January 2014).

UNHCR *Protecting the rights of stateless persons: The 1954 convention relating to the status of stateless persons* (March 2014) http://www.refworld.org/docid/4cad88292.html.

UNHCR *Results of the high-level segment on statelessness* (2019) https://www.unhcr.org/ibelong/results-of-the-high-level-segment-on-statelessness/.

UNHCR *Self-study module on statelessness* (2012).

UNHCR *Statelessness determination procedures and the status of stateless persons ('Geneva Conclusions')* (December 2010).

UNHCR *Statelessness determination procedures, identifying and protecting stateless persons* (August 2014).

UNHCR *Statelessness in West Africa: Turning your world upside down* (2014) https://data2.unhcr.org/ar/documents/download/53820.

UNHCR *Submission by the United Nations High Commissioner for Refugees (UNHCR) for the office of the high commissioner for human rights' compilation report – Universal periodic review: NIGERIA* (2013) https://uprdoc.ohchr.org/uprweb/downloadfile.aspx?filename=639&file=EnglishTranslation.

UNHCR 'The concept of stateless persons under international law' Expert Meeting Prato, Italy (27–28 May 2010).

UNHCR *The lost children of Côte d'Ivoire.* https://www.unhcr.org/ibelong/the-lost-children-of-cote-divoire/.

UNHCR 'The state of the world's refugees: A humanitarian agenda' (January 1997).

UNHCR *UNHCR action to address statelessness- A strategy note.* Division of International Protection (March 2010).

UNHCR *Vulnerability screening on-going operational screening in Borno, Yobe and Adamawa States* (November 2017).

UNHCR *What is statelessness? #IBELONG The campaign to end statelessness by 2024* (2014).

UNHCR & IPU *Nationality and statelessness. A handbook for parliamentarians.* No. 11 (2005).

UNHCR and Open Society Justice Initiative Report *Citizen of nowhere: Solution for the stateless in the US* (December 2012).

UNHCR and Plan International. *Under the radar and under protected: The urgent need to address stateless children's rights* (June 2012).

UNHCR & UNICEF 'Convention on the rights of the child: Quick reference guide statelessness and human rights treaties' (2017) http://www.unhcr.org/ibelong/wp-content/uploads/UNHCR-CRC-02-UNHCR-UNICEF.pdf.

UNICEF 'Children adjust to life outside Nigeria's Almajiri system' (17 September 2020) https://www.unicef.org/nigeria/stories/children-adjust-life-outside-nigerias-almajiri-system.

UNICEF 'Despite significant increase in birth registration, 17 million of Nigeria's children remain "invisible"' (11 December 2019) https://www.unicef.org/nigeria/press-releases/despite-significant-increase-birth-registration-17-million-nigerias-children-remain.

222   Bibliography

United Nations Department of Economic and Social Affairs (UNESA) *Compilation of international norms and standards relating to disability part i. National frameworks* (2003) https://www.un.org/esa/socdev/enable/discom101.htm.

V van Hüllen 'Just leave us alone: The Arab League and human rights' in T. Börzel, V. Van Hüllen, & M. Lohaus *Governance transfer by regional organizations* (2015) 125–140.

C Vlieks 'Strategic litigation: An obligation for statelessness determination under the European convention on human rights?' *Discussion paper 09/14 on strategic litigation. A commissioned research by the European Network on Statelessness (ENS) with Support from Oak Foundation* (2014).

Miscellaneous/Online Sources

African Union *African Commission on Human and Peoples' Rights, the right to nationality in Africa.* African Commission on Human and Peoples' Rights (ACHPR) (2015).

All Africa *Cote d'Ivoire: Row over mass naturalizations in Côte D'ivoire.* Online Newspaper (22 March 2013) https://allafrica.com/stories/201303221074.html.

E Allen 'What is the treaty of Rome?' *The Telegraph* (24 March 2017). https://www.telegraph.co.uk/news/0/treaty-rome/.

Associated Press (AP) *A look at the Kurds, a stateless nation in a restive region* (25 September 2017) https://apnews.com/a5f111ce84bd4e41a27f0ff2289efa1c/A-look-at-the-Kurds,-a-stateless-nation-in-a-restive-region#:~:text=The%20Kurds%20are%20among%20the,Most%20are%20Sunni%20Muslims.

Asylum Aid 'Gender equality, displacement and statelessness: Putting CEDAW to work'. *Women and Asylum News (WAN)*, Issue 89 (January/February 2010). https://www.asylumaid.org.uk/wp-content/uploads/2013/02/WAN_JanFeb_2010_issue_89.pdf.

BBC World Service *Article 15: Right to nationality* http://www.bbc.co.uk/worldservice/people/features/ihavearightto/four_b/casestudy_art15.shtml.

K Berényi 'Addressing the anomaly of statelessness in Europe: An EU law and human rights perspective' A doctoral (PhD) thesis submitted to the National Public Service University (2018) https://akk.uni-nke.hu/document/akk-uni-nke-hu/Statelessness_PhD%20dissertation_Katalin%20Berenyi_20180312.pdf.

K Berényi 'An inspiring parallel between the Italian and Hungarian jurisprudence with a view to reducing statelessness' *DPCE Online*, 39(2) (2019) http://www.dpceonline.it/index.php/dpceonline/article/view/746/691.

JC Carter & S Woodhouse 'Statelessness and applications for leave to remain: A best practice guide' (2016) 1–91.

Center for Women, Peace and Security 'American convention on human rights'. http://blogs.lse.ac.uk/vaw/regional/the-americas/american-convention/.

Amal de Chickera 'Chapter 2: Critiquing the categorisation of the stateless' *The Equal Rights Trust* (July 2010) https://www.equalrightstrust.org/ertdocumentbank/chapter%202.pdf.

Citizenship Rights in Africa (CRA) Blog/Nigeria http://citizenshiprightsafrica.org/region/nigeria/

CoE 'Council of Europe activities in the field of nationality/citizenship' OSCE Human Dimension Implementation Meeting Warsaw (2–13 October 2006). Working Session 10 'Democratic Institutions' Citizenship and Political Rights Contribution of the Council of Europe https://www.osce.org/odihr/21396?download=true.

Bibliography 223

DW 'West Africa: Fulani conflict getting worse' (7 August 2018) https://www.dw
.com/en/west-africa-fulani-conflict-getting-worse/a-43679371.

G Edwards *How effective is the United Nations in dealing with statelessness?* (2018)
https://gareviewnyu.com/2018/03/13/how-effective-is-the-united-nations-in
-dealing-with-statelessness/.

Emily Allen 'What is the Treaty of Rome?' *The Telegraph* (24 March 2017) https://
www.telegraph.co.uk/news/0/treaty-rome/.

EMN *Ad-Hoc Query on recognition of stateless persons Requested by LU EMN NCP*
(2015)

ENS 'Amicus Curiae by Gábor Gyulai, submitted by the European Network on
Statelessness to the Borgating Court of Appeal in Norway', in case number
17-073503ASD-BORG/01 [anonymised version – personal data omitted] (25
May 2018) https://www.refworld.org/docid/5b361e374.html.

ENS 'Country briefing' (January 2019) France https://index.statelessness.eu/sites
/statelessindex.eu/files/Country%20Briefing%20France%20ENG_FINAL_1.pdf

ENS *Statelessness Index Survey: The Netherlands* (2019).

ENS *Statelessness Index Survey: United Kingdom* (2019).

ENS *Stateless Index country briefing – Moldova* (January 2019) https://index
.statelessness.eu/sites/statelessindex.eu/files/Country%20Briefing%20Moldova
%202018%20EN_FINAL_1.pdf.

ENS *Ensuring gender equal nationality laws is key to ending statelessness* https://
www.statelessness.eu/blog/ensuring-gender-equal-nationality-laws-key-ending
-statelessness (2016).

ENS *Issues: What is statelessness* https://www.statelessness.eu/issues#:~:text=The
%20dissolution%20of%20the%20Soviet,undetermined%20nationality%20in
%20Eastern%20Europe.

EU Commission & ENS *Ad-hoc query on recognition of stateless persons.* Requested
by LU EMN NCP on 26th February 2015 compilation of 4th May 2015 (2015)
https://ec.europa.eu/home-affairs/sites/homeaffairs/files/what-we-do/
networks/european_migration_network/reports/docs/ad-hoc-queries/ad-hoc
-queries-2015.675_lu_recognition_of_stateless_persons_wider_diss.pdf.

EUR-Lex 'Treaty on the Function of the European Union' (2017) https://eur-lex
.europa.eu/legal-content/EN/TXT/?uri=LEGISSUM%3A4301854.

European Asylum Support Office (EASO) *Côte d'Ivoire country focus: Country of
origin information report* (June 2019).

European Commission 'Lisbon treaty' (2017) https://ec.europa.eu/home-affairs
/what-we-do/networks/european_migration_network/glossary_search/lisbon
-treaty_en (accessed 30 September 2020).

European Economic Community *A handbook on the European Economic Community.*
Edited by Gordon L. Weil 1965.

European Parliament 'Treaty of Lisbon' (2022). https://www.europarl.europa.eu/
factsheets/en/sheet/5/the-treaty-of-lisbon.

L Farias & C Arnaud 'UNHCR launch mapping of statelessness in Côte d'Ivoire'
UNHCR Blog (3 September 2018). https://www.unhcr.org/blogs/mapping
-statelessness-cote-divoire/.

French Ministry of the Interior – General Directorate for Foreign Nationals in France
Guide for Asylum seekers. Information and orientation (2013) https://www
.immigration.interieur.gouv.fr/content/download/69983/510865/file/Guide
_demandeur_asile_2013_Anglais.pdf.

224 *Bibliography*

G Gábor *Presentation on statelessness for the Serbian Government delegation: General framework and state practice* Held at UNHCR Regional Representation for Central Europe (4 November 2014).

AS Gonzalez '"We have a state": Confronting the statelessness of the Rohingya people' *Refugee International Blogpost* https://www.refugeesinternational.org /reports/2019/6/3/wenbsphave-anbspstate-confronting-the-statelessness-of -the-rohingya-peoplenbsp#:~:text=The%20Myanmar%20government's%20refusa l%20to,in%20Myanmar%20to%20this%20day.

GS Goodwin-Gill 'Convention on the reduction of statelessness', *United Nations Audiovisual Library of International Law* (2011) http://legal.un.org/avl/pdf/ ha/crs/crs_e.pdf.

Humanium 'The beginnings of the convention on the rights of the child' https:// www.humanium.org/en/convention/beginnings/.

J Ibrahim 'Democratic governance and the citizenship question: All Nigerians are settlers' *Dawodu. com* (2006) https://www.dawodu.com/jibo1.htm.

ICRC *Internal displacement in northeast of Nigeria: Operationalising the Kampala convention in Borno, Adamawa and Yobe States* (2016).

International Justice Resources Centre *Citizenship & nationality* https://ijrcenter .org/thematic-research-guides/nationality-citizenship/.

ISI *Cause of statelessness* http://www.institutesi.org/world/causes.php.

ISI *Comments on draft law introducing a statelessness determination procedure in the Netherlands* (28 November 2016).

ISI *Every mother's right* http://www.institutesi.org/gender_factsheet.pdf.

ISI *Gender equality, nationality and statelessness* http://www.institutesi.org/ourwork /equality.php.

ISI *Statelessness and human rights* (2017) http://www.statelessnessandhumanrights .org/other-human-rights-frameworks/the-international-covenant-on-civil-and -political-rights-iccpr.

ISI *World's stateless children* (January 2017) https://emnbelgium.be/sites/default/ files/publications/worldsstateless17.pdf.

JTA Online Newspaper http://www.jta.org/2019/09/20/global/transnistria-is-a -poor-breakaway-state-in-eastern-europe-the-few-jews-left-there-eye-an-escape.

K Keramitsi 'Addressing statelessness in Greece under EU law' LSE 9th HO PhD Symposium on Contemporary Greece and Cyprus (2019) http://www.lse.ac.uk /Hellenic-Observatory/Assets/Documents/HO-PhD-Symposia/The-9th-HO -PhD-Symposium/Symposium-Papers/Session-1/Migration-I-Security.pdf.

A Lang *Parliament's role in ratifying treaties.* Briefing Paper No. 5855 (17 February 2017). House of Commons Library https://www.parliament.uk/briefing-papers /sn05855.pdf.

JO Lokulo-Sodipe, O Akintola & C Adebamowo *Introduction to the legal system of Nigeria.* Training and Resources in Research Ethics Evaluation https://elearning .trree.org/mod/page/view.php?id=142.

M MacGregor 'Living in limbo: Europe's stateless refugees' *Info Migrants* (2018) https://www.infomigrants.net/en/post/11941/living-in-limbo-europe-s -stateless-refugees.

Naijainfoman *History of Almajiri Education in Nigeria* (2012) https://naijainfoman .wordpress.com/2012/06/07/history-of-almajiri-educational-system/.

Bibliography 225

NEMA & IOM *Northeast Nigeria: Displacement report* 32 (June 2020).

(Non)Citizens of the World *Statelessness versus legal invisibility under international law*. Online blog (May 2011) http://noncitizensoftheworld.blogspot.com.ng /2011/05/statelessness-versus-legal-invisibility.html.

OFPRA *Guide of the procedures to OFPRA* (2015) https://www.ofpra.gouv.fr/sites /default/files/atoms/files/guide_de_procedure-ext_web_10-11-2015_vd.pdf.

OHCHR *About the universal declaration of human rights translation project*. https:// www.ohchr.org/en/udhr/pages/introduction.aspx (accessed 20 June 2018).

E Ojomo *Sources of law: The application of English law in Nigeria* (2014) https:// www.academia.edu/32105425/SOURCES_OF_LAW_THE_APPLICATION _OF_ENGLISH_LAW_IN_NIGERIA.

C Orchard 'An update on statelessness determination and status in the UK – Need for fair and timely decisions' *Asylum Aid* (2016) https://www.asylumaid.org.uk/ update-statelessness-determination-status-uk-need-fair-timely-decisions/.

C Orchard 'UK home office changes to immigration rules on statelessness: A mixed bag' *European Network on Statelessness* (2019) https://www.statelessness.eu/blog /uk-home-office-changes-immigration-rules-statelessness-mixed-bag.

A Pazzynski 'How statelessness affects global poverty' *The Borgen Project Blog* (24 July 2016) https://borgenproject.org/statelessness-global-poverty/.

Premium Times Newspaper 'A street perspective of the citizen-indigene debate' *Nigeria Research Network* (10 February 2014) https://www.premiumtimesng .com/opinion/154905-street-perspective-citizen-indigene-debate-nrn.html (accessed 06 April 2019).

C Queval 'A new tool to raise awareness on gaps in French law, policy and practice' *ENS. #StatelessnessINDEX* https://www.statelessness.eu/blog/statelessnessindex -new-tool-raise-awareness-gaps-french-law-policy-and-practice.

Ratification Table of the African Commission on Human and Peoples' Rights *African charter on the rights and welfare of the child* (2019) https://au.int/sites/default/ files/treaties/36804-sl-AFRICAN%20CHARTER%20ON%20THE%20RIGHTS %20AND%20WELFARE%20OF%20THE%20CHILD.pdf.

B Safradin *The 'Legal Limbo' of stateless Syrian refugees in exile a comparative legal and empirical analysis at the national, international and European level on addressing refugee statelessness in the EU*. Master Thesis LLM Legal Research (20th of August 2017). Faculty of Law, Economics and Governance – Utrecht University.

Statelessness in Holland https://staatloosinnederland.wordpress.com/2015/02/22 /what-happens-when-a-stateless-person-arrives-or-wants-to-stay-in-holland/.

K Swider & C Caia Vlieks 'Proposal for legislation on statelessness in the Netherlands: A bittersweet victory' *ENS Blog* (12 October 2016) https://www.statelessness .eu/updates/blog/proposal-legislation-statelessness-netherlands-bittersweet -victory.

Syrianationality.org *The link between refugees and statelessness* http://www .syrianationality.org/pdf/link-between-refugees-statelessness.pdf.

The Economist *Côte d'Ivoire reforms citizenship and land ownership laws* (29 August 2013) http://country.eiu.com/article.aspx?articleid=30905187&Country=C %C3%B4te%20d%27Ivoire&topic=Polit_3.

The Public Interest Litigation Project (PILP) *Statelessness* (2015) https://pilpnjcm.nl /en/dossiers/statelessness/.

226 *Bibliography*

UNHCR. Intervention by Vincent Cochetel, the UNHCR Director of the Bureau for Europe, on the occasion of the meeting of the Strategic Committee on Immigration, Frontiers and Asylum in Brussels, 25 April 2017 https://www.refworld.org/pdfid/5911d8c34.pdf.

J Venkov 'In the state but not of the state – Stateless or nationality unknown in the Netherlands' *The Torn Identity* (16 September 2018) https://www.thetornidentity.org/2018/09/16/stateless-or-nationality-unknown/.

Index

Note: Page numbers in *italics* indicate figures, and page numbers in **bold** indicate tables.

Abidjan Declaration of Ministers of ECOWAS on the Eradication of Statelessness 101–3
accession 36, 102, 104, 141–2
Adjami, M. 79, 109–10, 154
administrative review 81, 123; France 150; Moldova 145; Nigeria 195–7; United Kingdom 134–5
Advisory Committee on Nigerian Citizenship (ACNC) 194–196
Advisory Opinion 85
Africa: African Union 88–100; colonisation, as causes statelessness in 23–4; economic community of west African states 100–4; prevention of statelessness in 88–100; right to nationality in 88–100; *see also* Ivory Coast; Kenya; Nigeria; South Africa; West Africa
African Charter on Human and Peoples' Right (ACHPR) 88, 89–91
African Charter on the Rights and Welfare of the Child (ACRWC) 89, 97–8
African Commission on Human and Peoples' Rights 4, 91–3
African Committee of Experts on the Rights and Welfare of the Child 98–9
African Union (AU) 5, 88–100
African Union Commission on International Law (AUCIL) 93
Aghemelo, A.T. 23–4
Ahmad, N. 48
Alice, E. 54
Alkali, U. 184
Almajiri system of education 5, 39; in northern part of Nigeria 40–1; in pre-colonial time 40

alternative administrative procedures: access to 156–60; identification of gaps in 161–3; for identification of statelessness 154–63; in Netherlands 154–63
American Convention on Freedom of Movement and Residence 86
American Convention on Human Rights 84
American government model, adoption of 177
appropriate connection 83, 95–6, 124
Arab Charter on Human Rights (ArCHR) 86–7
Arab League 86–8
Arab World: Arab League 86–8; prevention of statelessness in 86–8; right to nationality 86–8
Argentina 70
asylum: combined refugee and statelessness claims in 121; confidentiality of application 120–1; in France 150–1; in Moldova 143; in Netherlands 159–60; in Nigeria 191–2; in United Kingdom 130–1, 140
Austria 36, 71–2

Babangida, S.I. 39
Bakassi Peninsula 29–30, 44–5
Bakassi returnees 5, 44–5
Baluarte, D. C. 52
Banda, W. S. 92
Banjul Charter *see* African Charter on Human and Peoples' Right (ACHPR)
Banjul Plan of Action *see* ECOWAS Plan of Action on Eradication of Statelessness

228   Index

Basic Registration of Persons (BRP) 155, 156–60
Basisvoorziening Vreemdelingen (BVV) 156, 159, 162
Batchelor, C. 7
Baye, F.M. 24
Bayerischer Verwaltungsgerichtshof 36, 72
Berényi, K. 78
Berry, A. 130
Bezzano, J. 139
biometric residence permit (BRP) 134
birth certificates 6, 39, 42–3; in Netherlands 162; in United Kingdom 132
birth on territory 20, 63, 79–80, 92, 95–8; of Moldova 141–2, 145; of Netherlands 157; of Nigeria 26, 27, 56; *see also jus soli*
birth registration 56, 98–9, 145–6, 152
Blitz, B. K. 30
Boko Haram insurgents 44
Botswana National Front 91
Brazil 188–9, 194–5
British Nationality Act (BNA) 137
Bundesverwaltungsgericht 36
burden of proof 118; France 148; Moldova 143; Netherlands 156, 159, 163; Nigeria 193; United Kingdom 132–3
Bureau for Migration and Asylum 143, 146
Burmese citizenship 30–1

Cameroon 29–30, 44–5
Carter, J. 139
Chen-Wishart, M. 169
Child Rights Act 43
Chinula, J. L. 92
citizenship: defined 14; of European Union 69–70; nationality and 19; in national law 18–19; pre-Union citizenship case 70–1; *see also* nationality
Civil Society Organizations (CSOs) 38
Code for Entry and Residence of Foreign Persons and the Right of Asylum (CESEDA) (France) 148
Cojocariu, V. 141
colonisation, as causes of statelessness 23–5
Commission Nationale d'Eligibilite (CNESA) 152–4
community law 73–5

confidentiality of asylum application 120–1
conflict of laws, as causes of statelessness 26–8
Constitution of the Federal Republic of Nigeria (1999) 2, 7
Convention on the Elimination of All Forms of Discrimination against Women (CEDAW) 33, 34, 35, 36, 49, 53–4
Convention on the Elimination of All Forms of Racial Discrimination (CERD) (1965) 64
Convention on the Nationality of Married Women (CNMW) (1957) 36, 63–4
Convention on the Reduction of Statelessness (1961) 35–6, 61–2
Convention on the Rights of Persons with Disabilities (CRPD) (1996) 64
Convention on the Rights of the Child (CRC) (1990) 49, 54–6
Convention Relating to the Status of Refugees (1951) 20, 21–2, 58–60, 97, 120, 187–8
Convention Relating to the Status of Stateless Persons (1954) 16, 58–61, 111–12
Cook, R. 53
Cook, T. 28
Córdova, R. 57
Côte d'Ivoire *see* Ivory Coast
Council of Europe (CoE) law 65–6, 75; nationality, rules on 75–81; statelessness, rules on 81–4
Court of Justice of the European Union (CJEU) 37

Database on Foreigners *see Basisvoorziening Vreemdelingen* (BVV)
de Cruz, P. 171
de facto (by fact) 16–18
de Groot, G.R. 80
de Jong, M. 179
de jure (by law) 16–18
democracy 65, 66
Denmark 77
deprivation 17–18, 23; arbitrary 61–2, 88; discriminatory 30; of nationality under 35–8
Directorate of Citizenship and Business (C&B) 188
discretion 35–7, 61, 122

Index 229

discrimination: ethnic 7, 30–3; gender 7, 33–5; racial 30–3
displaced population: Bakassi returnees 30, 44–5; internally displaced persons 43–4
draft Protocol on nationality 93–7
Dutch *see* Netherlands
Dutch Ministry of Security and Justice 156

eCitiBiz online application form 190
Economic and Social Council (ECOSOC) 57
Economic Community of West African States (ECOWAS) 5, 38, 94, 100–4
ECOWAS Plan of Action on Eradication of Statelessness 103–4
EEC Treaty *see* Treaty Establishing the European Community (TEC)
Ehrmann, H. W. 170
Ermolaeva, U. 155, 160
Estonia 28–30
ethnic discrimination 7; as causes of statelessness 30–3
EU Court of Justice (ECJ) 70–1
Europe 65–6; Council of Europe law 75–84; EU Law 66–7; statelessness in 5; Treaty of Lisbon 67–75; *see also* France; Moldova; Netherlands; United Kingdom (UK)
European Convention on Human Rights (ECHR) (1950) 75–6
European Convention on Nationality (ECN) (1997) 75, 78–81
European Convention on the Avoidance of Statelessness in Relation to State Succession 75, 81–4
European Court of Human Rights (ECtHR) 76
European Economic Community (EEC) 68
European Migration Network (EMN) 197
European Network on Statelessness (ENS) 5, 127–8
European Union (EU) law 65–7
ex officio application 144; France 151; Ivory Coast 154; Moldova 142; United Kingdom 133

Fabusoro, E. 41
Faltinat, E. 155, 160
France 11, 68; access to procedure in 148–9; *ex officio* application 151;

grant and refusal of application in 149–50; identification of gaps in 150–2; refused to register births of children 78; right to appeal and review of decision 150; right to individual application for family members 149; right to interpreter 149; right to interview 148–9; statelessness determination procedure in 147–52, **164–5**
Fransman, L. 130
French Civil Code 150
French Office for the Protection of Refugees and Stateless Persons (OFPRA) 147–52
Fulani ethnic group 41–2, 44

Galligan, D. 175
gender discrimination 7; as causes of statelessness 33–5
gender equality 34, 87, 100
Georgia 186–7
Germany 27, 65, 68, 71–2
Goodwin-Gill, G. S. 60–1
Goris, I. 52
Govil, R. 54
Greentree Agreement (GTA) 29, 45
Gregg, L. 8
Guide for Asylum Seekers in France (gAS) 149
Gyulai, G. 110

habitual residence 17, 20, 22, 69–70, 81, 96, 117, 120, 193; of France 149; of Moldova 142; of the Netherlands 157
Harrington, J. 52, 79
Hausa ethnic group 39, 42, 44
Home Office (UK): Administrative Review Guidelines 135; Guidance on Asylum and Statelessness Procedures 140; Guidance on Good Character 137; Guidelines 117–18; Visas and Immigration Department 131, 188–9
Horowitz, D. L. 177
Houphouët-Boigny, F. 153
Huddleston, T. 145
Hudson, M. O. 57
Hungary 141

Ibhasebhor, S. 23–4
identification of statelessness *see* statelessness determination procedure (SDP)

230 *Index*

Immigratie en Naturalisatie Dienst
  (IND) 155–6
Immigration and Naturalisation Service
  see Immigratie en Naturalisatie Dienst
  (IND)
Immigration Law Practitioners'
  Association (ILPA) 136
Immigration Rules of UK 129–30;
  Appendix AR of 134; gaps in system
  135–6; stateless person, defined in
  136–7
Independent National Electoral
  Commission (INEC) 6
in situ populations 3, 17, 46, 111, 124,
  189, 199
Institute of Statelessness and Inclusion
  (ISI) 62–3, 100, 102
Inter-American Court of Human
  Rights' Advisory Opinion 85
internally displaced persons (IDPs) 38,
  43–4
International Court of Justice (ICJ) 29
International Covenant on Civil and
  Political Rights (ICCPR) 26, 35,
  62–3, 158–9
International Covenant on Economic,
  Social and Cultural Rights
  (ICESCR) 62
International Law Commission
  (ILC) 57, 61
International Refugee Organisation 58
Italy 65, 68, 123, 141
Ivory Coast 11; access to procedure
  in 153; causes of statelessness in
  152–3; *ex officio* application 154;
  grant and refusal of application in
  153; identification of gaps in 154;
  right to appeal and review of decision
  153; right to interpreter 154; right to
  interview 154; right to legal aid 154;
  statelessness determination procedure
  in 152–4, **164–5**

judicial review 81, 123; France 150;
  Moldova 145; Nigeria 195–7; United
  Kingdom 135
jus sanguinis 20, 27, 34
jus soli 20, 27,142

Kampala Convention 179–80
Kanem-Borno Empire 40
Kenya 30–1
Kerikmäe, K. 19
Klebes, H. 65

Knop, K. 174
Köhn, S. 52

la Commission Nationale de Recoursor
  (CNRSA) 152
Lawal, N.I. 39
Law on Foreigners in the Republic of
  Moldova 141–4
leave to remain in United Kingdom:
  application for 131; form FLR(S)
  131; grant of 133–4; refusal of 134–5
legal borrowing 168; *see also* legal
  transplant
legal transplant 167–9, 175–8,
  181–3; commonalities for 183–4;
  and comparative law 168, 171;
  context of 173; defined 168; due
  to legitimacy and prestige 171–3;
  efficacy of existing system 174–5;
  factors militating against 178–81;
  institutional infrastructures for 179;
  necessity of 169–70, 173; obligation
  and need to conform for 174; types
  of 170–5
Legrand, P. 180
Liberia 31–2
Local Government Areas (LGAs) 6,
  29, 114
Luxembourg 68
Lynch, M. 28

Maastricht Treaty *see* Treaty on
  European Union (TEU)
Malischewsk, C.-A. 37
Maltese Citizenship Act 77
Manby, B. 18
Manly, M. 130
Maputo Protocol *see* Protocol to the
  African Charter on Human and
  Peoples' Rights on the Rights of
  Women in Africa
marriage 91, 95, 134, 149, 159;
  dissolution of 64, 79; to foreign man
  100; registration of 26
Marsh, D. 172
Massey, H. 17
Mattar, M. Y. 87
Mattei, U. 174
Merry, S. E. 174
Miller, J. M. 170–1, 179
Ministry of Interior (MOI) 188,
  190, 194
Moldova 11; access to procedure 142–3;
  ex officio application 142; grant and

Index   231

refusal of status 143–5; identification of gaps 145–7; right to appeal and review of decision 145; right to individual application for family members 149; right to interpreter 142; right to interview 142–3; right to legal aid 146; statelessness determination procedure in 140–7, **164–5**

Montenegro 5

Montesquieu 182

Mosquera Valderrama, I. J. 170

Mousourakis, G. 173, 174, 181–2

Myanmar, ethnic and racial discrimination in 30–1

Nash, C. 8

National Action Plan (NAP): of Ivory Coast 152; of Nigeria 185, 186

National Commission for Refugees (NCFR) 178, 185

National Commission for Refugees, Migrants and Internally Displaced Persons Act (NCFRMI Act) 180, 186, 189, 191

National Council for the Welfare of Destitute (NCWD) 40

National Emergency Management Commission (NEMA) 180

National Human Rights Commission of Nigeria (NHRC) 177

National Identity Management Commission (NIMC) 6, 38–9, 44

National Identity Number (NIN) 6

National Office for Identity Data (Netherlands) 159

National Population Commission (NPC) 39

National Secretariat of Justice of the Ministry of Justice and Public Security (Brazil) 188–9

naturalisation 2, 25–6; in France 150; in Ivory Coast 154; lack of approaches to issue of 105; in Nigeria 194–5; through statelessness determination procedure 121–2; in United Kingdom 137–8; withdrawal of 71–3

Nelken, D. 181

Netherlands 11, 68; access to procedure 156–60; alternative administrative procedures in 154–63, **164–5**; competent authority for residency and naturalisation in 155; gaps in 161–3; identification of statelessness

in 154–63; ratification of Statelessness Convention by 155; statelessness and asylum 159–60

Netherlands Nationality Act 157

NGOs 146, 147, 174

Nigeria: access to procedure in 190–1; administrative review 195–7; Almajiri education system in 39–41; appeal of decisions 195–7; assessment of evidence 192–3; Bakassi returnees in 44–5; CEDAW, ratifying Optional Protocol to 54; children born to foreign parents in 42–3; colonisation, as causes statelessness in 24–5; combined refugee and statelessness claims in 193; conflict of laws, as causes statelessness in 27–8; domestication in 129; establishment of fact 192–3; ethnic and racial discrimination, as causes statelessness in 32–3; Fulani ethnic group in 41–2; gaps in legislation and administrative procedures, as causes statelessness in 25–6; gender discrimination, as causes statelessness in 35; indigenous community in 3; internally displaced persons in 43–4; judicial review 195–7; legal framework in 186–8; legal transplant in 175–8; legitimacy and prestige, legal transplant due to 176–7; loss or deprivation of nationality, as causes statelessness in 38; nationality campaigns and verifications in 124; nationality to stateless children in 56; necessity and local context, legal transplant due to 177; nomads in 41–2; obligation and need to conform, legal transplant due to 177–8; pastoralists in 41–2; procedural guarantees in 191–2; right to nationality of children in 7; risk of statelessness in 38–9; SDP in, protection and naturalisation through 194–5; SDP in, structure and location of 188–90; statelessness determination procedure for 108, **164–5**; statelessness in 5–6; transfer of territory, as causes statelessness in 29–30

Nigeria Immigration Service (NIS) 25, 186, 188

no-fault procedure 156, 160

nomads 41–2

non-penalisation 21, 192

232 *Index*

non-refoulement principles 21, 60, 69, 86
Nubian Children's case 98–9

Oakeshott, N. 8
Office for Democratic Institutions and
  Human Rights (ODIHR) 145
Office of United Nations High
  Commissioner for Refugees
  (UNHCR) 57, 60, 144
Orchard, C. 140
Organization for Security and
  Co-operation in Europe (OSCE)
  82, 145
Organization of American States (OAS)
  84–6
Oyegbami, A. 41

Pact of San José *see* American
  Convention on Human Rights
Paraguay 127, 193
pastoralists 41–2
Personal Records Database in
  Netherlands 154, 156–60
Pilgram, L. 81
Poland 54
prevention of statelessness: Africa
  88–100; America 84–6; Arab World
  86–8; Europe 81–4; international law
  on 56–64
Protocol on Specific Aspects of the
  Right to a Nationality and the
  Eradication of Statelessness in Africa
  89, 93–7
Protocol to the African Charter on
  Human and Peoples' Rights on the
  Rights of Women in Africa 26, 35,
  89, 99–100
Public Interest Litigation Project
  (PILP) 162

racial discrimination 30–3
Reform Treaty *see* Treaty on the
  Functioning of the European Union
  (TFEU)
refoulement 60, 105–6
refugee: defence for 138; defined 20;
  statelessness and 20–2; stateless
  persons as 86; status determinations
  of 116
refugee status determination
  (RSD) 186–7, 191; statelessness
  determination procedure and 120–1
Regional Economic Communities
  (RECs) 47, 101

registration: acquisition of citizenship
  by 2, 25–6; of birth 56, 98–9, 145–6,
  152; of marriage 26
residence permit: in France 149–51;
  in Moldova 143; in Netherlands
  155–63; *see also* leave to remain in
  United Kingdom
right to respect for private and family life
  76, 78, 110, 126, 149
Rohingya, in Myanmar 30–1
Rohmer, F. B. 65

Senegal 92
shared legal tradition, concept of 183
Sharman, J. C. 172
Siems, M. 172
Small, R. 173
Solinas, M. 181
South Africa 91
Southern African Development
  Community (SADC) 93
Soviet Union 5, 28, 52, 58, 186–7
Spain 70, 141
Staatsbürgerschaftsgesetz (StbG) 36, 71
standard of proof 119–20; Moldova
  143; Nigeria 193; United
  Kingdom 133
Standard Operating Procedures
  (SOPs) 185
statelessness: alternative administrative
  procedures for 154–63; categories
  of 16–18; colonisation, as causes of
  23–5; conflict of laws, as causes of
  26–8; *de facto* 16–18; defined 16–18;
  de jure 16–18; description of 4–7;
  ethnic and racial discrimination, as
  causes of 30–3; gaps in legislation and
  administrative procedures, as causes of
  25–6; gender discrimination, as causes
  of 33–5; impact on society 15; loss or
  deprivation of nationality, as causes of
  35–8; protection and naturalisation
  of 121–2; and refugees 20–2; risk of
  38–9; sociological effect of 14–15;
  transfer of territory, as causes of 28–
  30; *see also* prevention of statelessness;
  statelessness determination procedure
  (SDP); stateless persons
statelessness determination procedure
  (SDP): absence of 111; access to
  114–15; administrative review 123;
  appeal of decisions 123; assessment
  of evidence 116–20; burden of
  proof in 118; combined refugee and

Index 233

statelessness claims 120–1; criteria for 112–23; dedicated 128–54; defined 109–10; establishment of fact 116–20; fairness and efficiency of 115–16; flowchart for 197, *197*; in France 147–52, **164–5**; good practice for 112–23; hybrid, for Nigeria 170, 184–97; in Ivory Coast 152–4, **164–5**; judicial review 123; legality and binding nature of 113; location of 113–14; in Moldova 140–7, **164–5**; procedural guarantees 115–16; protection and naturalisation through 121–2; purpose of 109–11; requirements for 112; standard of proof in 119–20; standards for 112–23; structure of 113–14; in United Kingdom 128–40, **164–5**
State succession 28, 79–83, 96
Stiller, M. 27
Stockholm, F., J. 175
Stoter, S. 179
Swider, K. 66, 80, 162
Syria 30–1

Tebbe, N. 169–70, 178
Tentere, D. 155, 160
Torpman, J. 175
traditional birth attendant (TBA) 39
transfer of territory 28–30
Treaty Establishing the European Community (TEC) 68
Treaty of Lisbon 67–75
Treaty on European Union (TEU) 68, 69–70
Treaty on the Functioning of the European Union (TFEU) 68–9
Tsafe, A.K. 39
Tsai, R. L. 178
Tucker, J. 21

United Arab Republic 90
United Kingdom (UK) 11, 194–5; access to procedure 131–3; *ex officio* application 133; grant of leave to remain 133–4; identification of gaps 135–40; refusal of leave to remain 134–5; right to appeal and review of decision 134–5; right to individual application for family members 134; right to interpreter 132; right

to interview 132; statelessness determination procedure in 128–40, **164–5**
United Nations High Commissioner for Human Rights 35
United Nations High Commissioner for Refugees (UNHCR) 5, 15, 28, 38, 57, 60, 108–9, 123, 193; evidence, types of 117; Good Practice Papers 128; Handbook on Protection of Stateless Persons 119, 128; nationality verification by 124; statelessness determination procedure, access to 114–15; Statelessness Handbook 112, 118, 120, 152, 163
United Nations International Children's Fund (UNICEF) 40, 55, 56
United States of America: birth of child to U.S.-American parents in Germany 27; Organization of American States 84–6; presidential system of 177; prevention of statelessness in 84–6; right to nationality in 84–6
Universal Declaration of Human Rights (UDHR) 49, 50–3, 62, 110
unknown nationality registration 158, 160, 162–3

Van Waas, L. 30, 47–8, 130
Van Wallendael, K. 171–2
Vitkauskaite-Meurice, D. 87
Vlieks, C. 76
Vonk, O. 80

Watson, A. 169, 183
West Africa 2, 101–2; estimated stateless people in 4–5; plan of action to end statelessness 103–4; *see also* Ivory Coast; Nigeria; Senegal
women: rights in Arab Charter on Human Rights 87–8; right to nationality of 53–4; *see also* gender equality

Xanthaki, H. 178

Yugoslavia 5, 28, 75
Yusha'u, M.A. 39

Zongling, S. 168

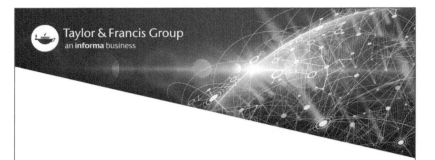